CHANGING TRANSATLANTIC
SECURITY RELATIONS

This book uses the concept of a strategic triangle as an organizing principle for the study of the security relationship between the United States, the EU and Russia and provides a fresh look at the development of transatlantic security relations after September 11. To understand these relations the contributors have explored each of the three actors in the triangle. The volume first analyses the actor capability of the EU in the transatlantic context and explains how the Union can maintain such a capability, despite the controversy surrounding the proposed EU Constitution. Secondly, as Russia is now able to play a role in this strategic relationship, this book demonstrates how Russia needs to develop its democratic system and modernise its economy more if it is to become fully integrated into the new strategic triangle. Finally, this volume provides a qualified assessment of the role of the new strategic triangle in the broader scheme of US grand strategy and strives to answer the question: under what US grand strategy, if any, might the strategic triangle be an important way of characterizing the security relationship among the United States, Russia and the EU?

This book will be of interest to students and researchers in security and strategic studies and international relations.

Jan Hallenberg is professor of political science at the Swedish National Defence College. He specializes in US foreign policy and transatlantic security relations.
Håkan Karlsson is a specialist on US strategy and nuclear weapons. His publications include *Bureaucratic Politics and Weapons Acquisition: The Case of the MX ICBM Program* (two volumes, 2002).

Both editors work in the Department of Security and Strategic Studies at the Swedish National Defence College and have recently published *The Iraq War: European perspectives on politics, strategy and operations* (Routledge, 2005).

CONTEMPORARY SECURITY STUDIES

THEORETICAL ROOTS OF US FOREIGN POLICY
Machiavelli and American unilateralism
Thomas M. Kane

CORPORATE SOLDIERS AND INTERNATIONAL SECURITY
The rise of private military companies
Christopher Kinsey

TRANSFORMING EUROPEAN MILITARIES
Coalition operations and the technology gap
Gordon Adams and Guy Ben-Ari

GLOBALIZATION AND CONFLICT
National security in a 'new' strategic era
Robert G. Patman (ed.)

THE POLITICAL ROAD TO WAR WITH IRAQ
Bush, 9/11 and the drive to overthrow Saddam
Nick Ritchie and Paul Rogers

BOSNIAN SECURITY AFTER DAYTON
New perspectives
Michael A. Innes (ed.)

KENNEDY, JOHNSON AND NATO
Britain, America and the dynamics of alliance
Andrew Priest

CHANGING TRANSATLANTIC SECURITY RELATIONS

Do the US, the EU and Russia form
a new strategic triangle?

*Edited by Jan Hallenberg
and Håkan Karlsson*

LONDON AND NEW YORK

First published 2006
by Routledge
2 Park Square, Milton Park, Abingdon, Oxon OX14 4RN

Simultaneously published in the USA and Canada
by Routledge
270 Madison Ave, New York, NY 10016

Routledge is an imprint of the Taylor & Francis Group, an informa business

Typeset in Times New Roman by
Keystroke, Jacaranda Lodge, Wolverhampton
Printed and bound in Great Britain by
Antony Rowe Ltd, Chippenham, Wiltshire

British Library Cataloguing in Publication Data
A catalogue record for this book is available from the British Library

Library of Congress Cataloging in Publication Data
Changing transatlantic security relations : do the U.S., EU, and Russia form a
new strategic triangle? / edited by Jan Hallenberg and Håkan Karlsson.–1st ed.
p. cm. – (Contemporary security studies)
Includes bibliographical references and index.
1. United States–Foreign relations–European Union countries.
2. European Union countries–Foreign relations–United States.
3. United States–Foreign relations–Russia (Federation) 4. Russia
(Federation)–Foreign relations–United States. 5. European Union
countries–Foreign relations–Russia (Federation). 6. Russia (Federation)–Foreign
relations–European Union countries. 7. Security, International. I. Hallenberg, Jan.
II. Karlsson, Håkan. III. Series: Cass contemporary security studies series.
JZ1480.A5 /E883 2006
355'.03300511–dc22
2005029259

ISBN 10: 0–415–39116–4
ISBN 13: 978–0–415–39116–0

CONTENTS

CONTRIBUTORS

Fredrik Bynander is Assistant Professor of Political Science at the Swedish National Defence College.

Peter Dombrowski is Professor of Strategic Studies in the Strategic Research Department of the Naval War College's Center for Naval Warfare Studies.

Magnus Ekengren is Assistant Professor of Political Science at the Swedish National Defence College.

Kjell Engelbrekt is Assistant Professor of Political Science at the Swedish National Defence College and at the Department of Political Science, Stockholm University.

Arita Eriksson is Ph.D. candidate in Political Science, Stockholm University and is employed at the Swedish National Defence College.

Jan Hallenberg is Professor of Political Science at the Swedish National Defence College and adjunct Professor at the Department of Political Science, Stockholm University.

Adrian Hyde-Price is Professor of Politics and Head of Department at the Department of Politics, Leicester University.

Håkan Karlsson is Ph.D. in political science and a research associate at the Swedish National Defence College.

Bertil Nygren is Associate Professor of Political Science at the Department of Political Science, Stockholm University and at the Swedish National Defence College.

Andrew L. Ross is Director of the Office of Policy, Security, and Technology and Professor of Political Science at the University of New Mexico.

Charlotte Wagnsson is Assistant Professor of Politics at the Swedish National Defence College.

PREFACE

This volume is the result of cooperation among a group of scholars at the Department of Security and Strategic Studies at the Swedish National Defence College. Our group has been fortunate to interact with three scholars from outside Sweden, two from the United States and one from the United Kingdom. We are very grateful to Professor Andrew L. Ross, now Director of the Office of Policy, Security, and Technology and Professor of Political Science at the University of New Mexico and his colleague Peter Dombrowski, Professor of Strategic Studies in the Strategic Research Department of the Naval War College's Center for Naval Warfare Studies for writing a chapter together for this volume. Likewise, we wish to thank our colleague Adrian Hyde-Price, Professor of Political Science and Head of Department at the Department of Politics, Leicester University for contributing a chapter to our book.

As editor, I also wish to thank my co-editor Dr Håkan Karlsson for his work on this volume.

During the last few months of work on this book, we have also been fortunate enough to be very ably assisted by Ms Nina Matzén in the work on this volume. We wish to thank her for the great work that she has done.

Finally, as always, I wish to thank my wife Ulrika Mörth for her love and support during my work on this volume.

Jan Hallenberg
Stockholm/Järlåsa
July 2005

ABBREVIATIONS

ABM = Anti-Ballistic Missile
APEC = Asia–Pacific Economic Cooperation
CAP = Common Agricultural Policy
CDM = Capabilities Development Mechanism
CEE = Central and East European States
CFSP = Common Foreign and Security Policy
CIS = Commonwealth Of Independent States
CMEA = Council Of Mutual Economic Assistance
DPG = Defense Planning Guidance
DRC = Democratic Republic Of Congo
DSACEUR = Deputy Supreme Allied Commander, Europe
EBRD = European Bank For Reconstruction And Development
EC = European Community
ECAP = European Capacity Action Plan
EFTA = European Free Trade Agreement
EMU = Economic And Monetary Union
ESDP = European Security And Defence Policy
EU = European Union
EUMC = European Union Military Committee
EUMS = European Union Military Staff
EUPM = European Union Police Mission
FDI = Foreign Direct Investment
FSB = Federal'naya Sluzhba Bezopasnosti (Federal Security Service)
FYROM = Former Yugoslav Republic Of Macedonia
GUUAM = Georgia, Ukraine, Uzbekistan, Azerbaijan, Moldova (Eurasian
    Economic Community)
HHG = Helsinki Headline Goals
HTF = Headline Task Force
IEMF = Interim Emergency National Force
IGO = Inter-Governmental Organization
IMF = International Monetary Fund

ISTAR= Intelligence, Surveillance, Target Acquisition And Reconnaissance Equipment
JHA = Justice And Home Affairs
MNC = Multinational Company
MONUC = United Nations Mission In The Congo
NAFTA = North American Free Trade Agreement
NATO = North Atlantic Treaty Organization
NGO = Non-Governmental Organization
NMD = National Missile Defence
OECD = Organization For Economic Cooperation And Development
OSCE = Organization For Security And Economic Cooperation In Europe
PARP = Planning And Review Process
PCC = Prague Capabilities Commitment
PFP = Partnership For Peace
PG = Project Groups (In Ecap)
PSC = Political And Security Committee
SES = Single Economic Space
SLOC = Sea Lines Of Communication
SORT= Strategic Offensive Reductions Treaty
START = Strategic Arms Reduction Treaty
UAV = Unmanned Aerial Vehicle
UN = United Nations
UNDP = United Nations Development Program
WEU = West European Union
WMD = Weapons Of Mass Destruction
WTO = World Trade Organization

1

A NEW STRATEGIC TRIANGLE

Defining changing transatlantic security relations

Jan Hallenberg and Håkan Karlsson

Introduction

As the 1970s turned into the 1980s, global politics were often characterized in terms of a strategic triangle. This metaphor provided a way to conceptualize the security relations between the United States, the Soviet Union and China. In the words of the former Secretary of State Henry Kissinger:

> Triangular diplomacy, to be effective, must rely on the natural incentives and propensities of the players. It must avoid the impression that one is 'using' either of the contenders against the other; otherwise one becomes vulnerable to retaliation or blackmail. The hostility between China and the Soviet Union served our purposes best if we maintained closer relations with each side than they did with each other. The rest could be left to the dynamic of events.
>
> (Kissinger 1979: 712[1])

Although global politics look very different today from what they did 30 years ago, we believe that the metaphor of a strategic triangle can once again be fruitfully applied to the study of international security relations. In this book, we set out to use it as an organizing principle for studying transatlantic security relations involving three international actors: the United States, Russia and the European Union (EU). These three actors form a constellation that we call 'a new strategic triangle' by interacting in what we here term the 'greater transatlantic region'.[2] Like the previous strategic triangle, this new one is about power[3] relations among important international actors. There are several reasons why we have chosen to study transatlantic security relations in the modern world. First, we believe that this aspect of world politics has during the last decade – and particularly after 11 September – been understudied. Given the fact that the United States has embarked upon a global campaign to try to eradicate terrorism, this has spawned a large literature on US global strategy generally, and its strategies regarding terrorism and the Middle East in particular.[4] We feel, however, that in this literature the broad scope of transatlantic security relations is often forgotten. We attempt in this book to cover broader aspects of these relations than what recent literature has commonly done, even if we do not forget the struggle against terrorism. Our primary motivation for using the strategic triangle as an organizing principle to analyse security relations among three important actors in the greater transatlantic region is that we wish to take a fresh look at these relations from a new angle and believe that the triangle concept enables us to better comprehend the current dynamics of the changing relations and that it will also help us lay a better foundation for understanding the future of transatlantic security relations.

The criterion for the existence of a strategic triangle is essentially a very simple one: do all three actors, in formulating their policies in a given issue area, take each other into consideration or not. If they do, a triangle exists, if they do not, there is no triangle. According to this criterion, formalized contacts are not sufficient to create a triangle. Formally, of course, each actor in the new strategic triangle always considers the other two actors. In addition to the traditional meetings between the US and Russian presidents, there are now regular US–EU and EU–Russian summits. Long-term partnership has been mutually declared in each dyad. However, we base our recognition of a triangular structure in the greater transatlantic region on the practical substance of policy-making.

In addition to our analysis of relations among the three actors, our book has a special focus on what we call the 'actorness' of the EU.[5] Under what circumstances can the EU act as one actor in a given policy area – does it have internal legitimacy – and is the EU accepted as an actor by other actors in this policy area – does it have external legitimacy? In our conception of the triangle, the actorness of the Union is absolutely vital to the existence of a relationship among all three actors.

Our conception of security policy is a fairly broad one. It includes the traditional issues of defence policy, military alliances and the threat of conventional conflicts. It also includes the ties created by economic relations of various kinds, and the links between economic issues and the traditional issues of security.

The limited geographical coverage of our new strategic triangle virtually settles the question about its appropriate composition. Arguably, the United States, Russia and the EU are the three most important actors in the greater transatlantic region. While this premise may be easy to accept for this volume's European editors, it is far from obvious from a US perspective. It is, however, in our opinion obvious why the United States, the world's only superpower, must be included. This assertive giant dominates world politics and consequently plays a dominant role in the greater transatlantic region as well. One can even go so far as to say that the United States, being by far the strongest of the three actors, to a very large extent determines under what circumstances, and on what issues, any strategic triangle really exists in the region. The inclusion of Russia and the EU may appear somewhat less self-evident. We do recognize that Russia is much less important in global politics than the Soviet Union was before its collapse but we believe that Russia is still a major regional power whose role has tended to be downplayed in research and policy analysis of transatlantic security issues and that the triangle framework covering the greater transatlantic region therefore should encompass Russia. Likewise, we believe that the EU is such an important emerging international actor that it should be included in our framework. There is a tendency, especially in the United States, to emphasize the economic aspects of European integration and to dismiss the geopolitical significance of the EU because it is still very weak militarily. It is our belief, however, that a united Europe should be taken seriously as a new political entity in the transatlantic security environment.[6]

Although the book is about transatlantic security relationships, the North Atlantic Treaty Organization (NATO) is not treated in depth. This does not mean that we fail to appreciate the importance of the Atlantic alliance, but it reflects our assumption that NATO, while possibly remaining the key organization in transatlantic security, will play a less important role over time in this context than it has for the past half century. One reason why we believe that NATO will become less important is that over the years there has been an explicit link between the existence of NATO and the growth of the European Union. The military strength that characterized the former to a large extent made possible the construction of the latter as a civilian power. Since 1999, the EU, drawing on its substantial economic resources, has also been in the process of building at least some military capacity. The main argument supporting our belief that NATO will lose importance is thus that its role will be overtaken by the EU, at least to some extent. In addition, we feel that it is fruitful to analyse the future of transatlantic security without highlighting NATO, as has been done in so many studies. At the very least, such an approach opens up our thinking and indicates that different constellations, unimaginable while NATO still reigned supreme as the pivot of European security, may be realized. In this book, NATO is an arena for interaction among the three actors in the strategic triangle, rather than an actor in its own right.

As a theoretical framework, our triangle construct is, generally speaking, modelled on the original strategic triangle, consisting of the United States, the Soviet Union and China, but there are several differences between the triangles. One obvious difference is that the old triangle was intended to cover tripartite relations on a global level, whereas, in our conception, the new strategic triangle covers such relations in a subsection of world politics, albeit a large and important one. Incidentally, we believe that an attempt to create a model that has the same purpose as the old strategic triangle, covering virtually all of world politics, is not worthwhile in today's global arena. World politics are today too multi-faceted to characterize by way of a single analytic model.

A second difference between the two triangles is that in the old one, there was no question about what constitutes an 'actor', or that all three actors in the triangle recognized each other. In the new triangle, however, the concept 'actor' is more problematic, particularly when it comes to the European Union. It is fundamentally unclear whether the Union may be regarded as an 'actor' in the same sense as the other two in the triangle are. We believe that the EU's ability to act internationally depends largely on the issue at hand, a question on which we elaborate later in this chapter. Another aspect of this 'actor problem' is whether or not each actor in the triangle even accepts the premise that the other two are actors of such importance to itself that they need to be considered when policies are formulated in the relevant realm. It is obvious that this issue is most pertinent to policy-making in the United States.

A third difference between the two triangles is that the power base that largely determined great power status and hence membership in the original strategic triangle was the possession of vast amounts of weapons, particularly nuclear arms. In the new strategic triangle, military strength is still important, but it is less crucial than it was in the old one. The importance of economic power and diplomatic skills has increased. We feel that the crucial role that economic ties, particularly trade relations, play for modern security relations today need to be studied to a greater extent than has been typically the case in modern literature on transatlantic security relations.

In the original triangle, diplomatic skills were important, as the quote from Kissinger indicates. They played a role as the three actors manoeuvred to create alliances. However, the only power base that really counted in great power diplomacy was military strength. In the new triangle, other strengths weigh heavily in the diplomatic games played. Moreover, the diplomatic arena itself has gained in significance. The new triangle is situated in a global environment, where diplomatic processes, typically undertaken within International Governmental Organizations (IGOs), are more significant than they were three decades ago. Even if this is sometimes forgotten, following, for instance, the transatlantic quarrels in connection with the conflict in Iraq, IGOs are active in more areas, and also have a larger capacity to influence the outcomes of global politics than they did three decades ago.[7] In addition, in some policy areas, Non-Governmental Organizations (NGOs) have also been active after the end of the Cold War to an extent that was not the case before that time. Taken together this means that diplomatic skills, as well as the basic approach to diplomacy, are thus more crucial for the actors in the new triangle than they were for the actors in the old one. To state that diplomatic skills are more important now than they were 30 years ago is not to say that diplomacy in this day and age can be conducted without any link to other aspects of policy such as trade or military matters. For instance, what many have termed the 'unilateralist policies' of the United States under the first George W. Bush administration would not have been possible to conduct effectively without the overwhelming military superiority that the United States has had ever since the end of the Cold War.

The assertion that military power is less important in the new strategic triangle content than it was in the old also needs some qualification by way of differentiating between military means. In the old triangle, the strategic nuclear dimension of military power was by far the most important, but, in the new context, this aspect is clearly less crucial, whereas capabilities associated with concepts such as 'strategic coercion' and 'crisis management' play a greater role.

A fourth difference between the old triangle and the new one has already been suggested. The new triangle is *asymmetrical*, to a larger extent than was the case with the original triangle, due to the enormous military *and* economic strength of the United States. Consequently, the interests of the EU and Russia in the alignments of the United States are much greater than are the interests of the United States in the triangular behaviour of the two other parties.[8] In the opinion of the authors in this volume, the asymmetry with regard to the critical dimensions of power does not invalidate the notion of the strategic triangle, even if it makes the three players approach the game in distinctive ways. This is because the new triangle in important respects is similar to the old one. The fundamental similarity is that the three actors, for all their differences, tend to take the policies and relations of the other two actors into account when formulating their own policies, at least in the part of the world that we focus upon here. Although the United States is clearly dominant, it is hard, even for the superpower, to completely ignore the others in the delimited part of global politics that is studied in this book. It is this basic characteristic of almost unavoidable relationships between the three actors of the new strategic triangle that forms the idea upon which our book is based.

The new strategic triangle also contains other asymmetries. Only two of the actors in the triangle are European actors, the EU and Russia. The United States has since the end of the Second World War been a European power, but this is by choice, not because it is by necessity a European actor. Washington is the only one of the three that has such a choice – whether or not it wants to remain a European actor. Only two are large and important global economic actors, the United States and the EU. Only two are military great powers in the sense that they control arsenals of strategic nuclear weapons, Russia and the United States. Two of the actors in the triangle – the United States and Russia – also have a choice as to how they approach the third, the European Union. Washington and Moscow can choose either to approach Brussels or the national capitals. This means that the dyadic relationships between the three parties, at the very least, vary. It also means that the three actors within the new triangle necessarily play different roles.

This book examines the central aspects of the relations among these three actors as they attempt to find their way in a world that has been fundamentally changed through several events and processes during the last 15 years. In promoting or adjusting to the fundamental changes, all three actors have had reason to redefine their geopolitical roles and ambitions. Their search for new security identities is a major theme in this book. The book focuses on the strategic outlook and approaches of the three actors and the resulting interrelationships. In so doing, it also covers aspects of a domestic character within each actor, but primarily to the extent that such aspects impinge on the relations among the three.

The profound changes during the last 15 years started with the demise of the Soviet Union and the concomitant fall of the Soviet empire in Central and Eastern Europe. This momentous upheaval was followed by the deepening and enlargement of the co-operation between the states of Western Europe, in what was the European Communities and became the EU in 1993. Next came the process leading to the enlargement of NATO. Then, there was NATO's reluctant intervention in the Balkans, spurring the development of the EU's military capacity. After that, terrorists carried out their unprecedented attacks against the United States on

11 September 2001, an event unleashing awesome displays of American military power. Finally, the United States, with the support of the United Kingdom and some other countries, but without the authorization of the United Nations Security Council, invaded Iraq to topple the Saddam Hussein regime.

The preceding paragraph is merely an extremely brief overview of some crucial events and processes that have profoundly affected the security policies pursued by the three actors in the greater transatlantic region and hence also the development of transatlantic security relations, and that thus need to be kept in mind if we are to try to understand the state of current affairs in this sphere, and to lay a foundation for trying to grasp what may happen in the future.

Employing the notion of the strategic triangle

It should be clear from the outset, first, that our use of the strategic triangle as an organizing principle for this volume does not mean that the triangle serves as a straitjacket imposing rigid discipline on each author or authors to subscribe to exactly the same view on the importance of the triangle and of what ought to be studied in their respective chapters. Instead, the editors have done their best to see to it that each chapter makes at least some contribution towards a better under-standing of the relationships among the three actors, even if the emphasis in some of the chapters is strongly on one or two of the three actors.

Second, the use of the triangle might be construed to mean that all three actors in the triangle must be treated to exactly the same extent in a book that purports to cover the development of their security relations. We do not believe that this is necessary. The most important reason why we do not cover all three actors equally is that one of the actors, the European Union, is very different from the other two, the United States and Russia. The latter two are nation-states, that is, actors for the analysis of which there is an immense literature with different strands of well-established theorizing. When it comes to the EU, however, things are very different. The EU is more difficult to understand because it is an amorphous entity that defies standard analytical categories. Moreover, it is contested in the academic literature, as well as in practical politics, whether or not the Union is indeed an international actor of any importance in its own right, outside the trade sphere where its role is readily acknowledged.

For all these reasons, this book contains more chapters on the European Union than it does on either the United States or Russia. We devote several chapters to analysing EU actorness, that is, the ability of the Union to be an international actor. A central subject here is the construction of EU actorness, or, to put it differently, the internal building of the EU's actor capacity in the area of security and defence policy. The argument in this book is not that the EU is a fully fledged actor in this area. We recognize that it is very much an international actor in development; at the same time, we believe that the development of the Union's actorness is absolutely vital for future relations within the greater transatlantic region. To the extent that the Union is coming closer to being an actor more like Russia or the

United States than it is at the time of writing in 2005, our notion of a strategic triangle in all likelihood becomes more applicable to additional policy areas and to ever more issues. Thus, there is an urgent need to study the characteristics of this new entity and to attempt to determine what might become of it in the future.

Third, the notion of the strategic triangle has very different analytical usefulness depending on the type of policy area or even on the individual issue. This is true in several senses. One way in which it is true concerns the role of the European Union, whether it is regarded by other actors in the triangle as a unified actor, or whether it is, instead, the national capitals that are the interlocutors for Washington and Moscow. In the case of the Iraq War in 2003, the Union was unable to act as a unified actor, and it was, instead, the capitals that each pursued its own policy regarding the issue and the United States, the prime mover behind the invasion. The EU fared much better in dealing with the political turmoil surrounding the presidential elections in the Ukraine in the winter of 2004. To quote Robert Kagan's poignant phrase: 'In the unfolding drama of Ukraine, the Bush administration and the European Union have committed a flagrant act of transatlantic cooperation'.[9] Regarding the Ukrainian presidential election, then, the United States and the EU clearly co-operated with each other in a way that implied that Washington in this case recognized the EU as a legitimate actor, with which it should interact on an issue with clear ramifications for transatlantic security relations. Another way in which the type of issue may play differently in the triangle is where one of the corners in the relationship may serve as a link between the other two, such as the question of the destruction of Russian nuclear weapons that Russia seems unable to handle on its own, which unites the EU and the United States in common concern.

Finally, in a non-exhaustive survey of the significance of policy areas and issues for the applicability of the notion of the strategic triangle, there are issues where two of the actors in the triangle are very strongly linked to each other, whereas the third actor plays virtually no role. A case in point is international trade, where the United States and the EU are the two most important actors in the global arena, which means that they interact to a very large degree in this issue area, whereas Russia is very peripheral. As we write this, in mid-2005, Russia is not even a member of the World Trade Organization (WTO).

It should also be recognized that the notion of a new strategic triangle has been developed by European scholars. When it comes to studying the role and relations of the United States in the triangular context, it remains to be seen if the new strategic triangle is a notion that may catch on. In our section on the United States, the third section of this book, we address the question of whether or not, or perhaps rather under what circumstances, the new strategic triangle – when seen from the vantage point of Washington – may be fruitfully applied to studying the relationships between Washington, Brussels and Moscow.

Three related actors undergoing change

As indicated earlier, we regard the European Union as the most problematic and, at the same time, in many ways the most intriguing actor of the three we have chosen to study from our perspective of a transatlantic strategic triangle. It is an emerging international actor, now containing 25 member states, which is undergoing important changes, not least in the sphere of foreign, security and defence policy. This actor has an immense potential strength if all the assets that the 25 states bring to the table can be utilized in international affairs.

The new emerging actor, the European Union, exemplifies, to a large extent, the new conception of security in the twenty-first century. The general character of EU foreign and security policy is expressed in this way in the Treaty Establishing a Constitution for the European Union: 'The European Union shall conduct a common foreign and security policy, based on the development of mutual political solidarity among Member States, the identification of questions of general interest and the achievement of an ever-increasing degree of convergence of Member States' actions'.[10] In the next article, I-41, the Constitutional Treaty spells out the essence of the defence aspects of the European Union:

> The common security and defence policy shall be an integral part of the common foreign and security policy. It shall provide the Union with an operational capacity drawing on civil and military assets. The Union may use them on missions outside the Union for peace-keeping, conflict prevention and strengthening international security in accordance with the principles of the United Nations Charter. The performance of these tasks shall be undertaken using capabilities provided by the Member States.
>
> (EC Treaty Establishing a Constitution for Europe, Article I-41)

At the time of writing in mid-2005, the Constitutional Treaty has been rejected in referenda in both France and the Netherlands. Despite the fact that the future of the Constitutional Treaty looks very uncertain, we still believe that this is the most formal expression of the projected role of the Union in foreign, security and defence policy in Europe in the near future. The brief quotes printed above provide a clear indication of the fact that the EU is a particular kind of international actor. It views security differently than traditional nation-states do, and its policies are defined in a complex interaction with and among member states.

We are aware of the fact that the European Union and the role that the organization is playing and ought to play in the greater transatlantic region is a matter of contention among practitioners as well as scholars. British Prime Minister Tony Blair has clearly expressed one notion of the EU and the role it ought to play in international affairs, while simultaneously outlining the role he sees for Great Britain in this context. In November 2004, Prime Minister Blair stated his conception of the relationship between Europe (read the European Union) and the United States:

'So my contention is simple: Britain should be proud of its alliance with America; clear in its role in Europe; and a tireless advocate of a strong bond between the two'.[11] Although Blair, in a major policy reversal, agreed in 1998 that the EU should develop a military capacity outside of NATO, the British conception of the EU thus envisages a union in an intimate alliance relationship with the United States.

The French Government has consistently provided the alternative conception of an EU that is an actor with a more independent role in relation to the United States. President Jacques Chirac expressed this second vision of the European Union in a speech given during a visit to London in November 2004:

> Europe has created a model: after totalitarianism, two World Wars, the Holocaust and nearly 50 years of Cold War, it decided to break free of the power games. Its peoples have established an area of peace, democracy, solidarity and prosperity founded on the freely conferred sharing of sovereignty. This has made the European Union an original and exemplary international player.
>
> (Chirac 2004[12])

The assessment of the actual and potential role of the EU in the strategic triangle in this book is closer to the French conception of European independence from the United States than it is to the British notion of transatlantic intimacy. We argue that the EU is seeking to define its identity, at least in part, by aspiring to greater self-reliance in matters of international security, especially in the event that the United States is reluctant to become involved via NATO, thereby asserting more European autonomy vis-à-vis the United States. Whether the EU will counterbalance the United States on the world stage is a different question lacking immediate relevance.

Although supportive of the EU's security and defence policy, Germany, a third European state of great importance for the future development of the EU as an actor in international affairs, is apparently loath to join France in pressing the Union to form one united counterweight to the United States. Helga Haftendorn and Michael Kolkmann provide this perceptive analysis and contrast of the views of Berlin and Paris on these issues during the first years of the twenty-first century:

> Paris wants to develop the European Union into a counterweight to the United States, while Berlin views a strong Europe as a reliable partner of the United States. Germany wants to retain the Atlantic Alliance as a transatlantic framework for action and as an instrument for crisis management and peace enforcement.
>
> (Haftendorn and Kolkmann 2004: 476)

We believe that the existence of varying views among the most important members of the EU about both the future role of the Union as a global actor more generally, as well as of the proper nature of its relations with Washington, provides another reason for why a book such as ours ought to give more emphasis to the study of this actor than to the analysis of the other two actors.

Russia also is undergoing changes in its approaches to international relations in the transatlantic triangle. After a truly traumatic experience of national decline, Russian leaders are in the process of formulating their country's role in the world. The collapse of the Soviet Union was, of course, a major geopolitical shock, from which the much weaker successor state, the Russian Federation, is now trying to recover. President Vladimir Putin in April 2005 called it 'the biggest geopolitical catastrophe of the century'. While seeking to rebuild Russia as a great power and pursuing a long-term political strategy that is conceptually incompatible with the ambition of the current administration in Washington to preserve American primacy in world politics, the Russian leaders have decided to co-operate with the United States and the other democracies in the West in combating international terrorism. In this context, it was of central importance to US–Russian relations that President Putin reportedly was the first foreign leader to contact President Bush directly after the terrorist attacks of 11 September 2001 offering support. There are indications that the personal relationship between Presidents Bush and Putin was strengthened by Putin's actions on or just after 11 September and remains close. This is despite the fact that strains have recently been put on relations between Russia and the United States by the Iraq War, Russia's nuclear co-operation with Iran, its interference in the Presidential elections in the Ukraine in late 2004 to preserve the power of the autocrats, and the Kremlin's domestic political actions to limit democratic freedoms and centralize power in Russia, including its dismantling of the oil giant Yukos.

On the other side of the triangle, Russia also uses its ability to create linkages across issue areas. One example is where Moscow supplies a crucial EU country – Germany – with large amounts of natural gas. According to the *Financial Times*, 'Germany already imports 35 per cent of its oil and 40 per cent of its gas from Russia'.[13] It is hard not to see a link between this dependence on oil imports and the statement by German Chancellor Gerhard Schröder that Vladimir Putin is a 'dyed-in-the-wool democrat'.[14] One may intimate that Russia uses its energy assets to put the West European countries into a state of dependency which then decreases the ability of these countries to criticize the Russian Government, or otherwise act against Russia's interests. In addition, the example may indicate that the Kremlin uses the complex structure in the EU to sometimes interact with Brussels, other times with the national capitals.

An example of interest for this book where Russia has interacted more directly with Brussels is, we believe, the Russian decision to ratify the Kyoto Protocol on climate change, made in the autumn of 2004. It is hard not to see a connection between this decision on the part of the Russian leadership and the willingness of the EU to support Russian membership in the WTO. In a situation where the United States continued to refuse to adhere to the Kyoto Protocol, Russian accession became vital for the European countries, which very much want the Protocol to enter into effect. When Russia signed, the minimum threshold necessary for the Kyoto Protocol to come into force was passed.[15]

The United States of today is a very different actor from that of 30 years ago. It is, at the same time, uniquely powerful as the sole surviving superpower and, at least, if one considers the security situation of the past century, uniquely vulnerable. If the EU is an emergent actor trying to shape its security identity as it expands and increases its military co-operation, and Russia is attempting to find its footing as a much less powerful international actor than its predecessor the Soviet Union, then the United States is also, to some extent, searching for a new role in international security affairs, both globally and within the transatlantic strategic triangle. The global landscape in which the United States acts has been changed by at least two seminal events during the last 15 years: the collapse of the Soviet Union in 1991 and the terrorist attacks on New York and Washington in 2001.

The fall of the second superpower meant that the first, the United States, came to dominate the global scene, to the extent that some observers characterized it as the most powerful state in modern history. At the very apex of its power, however, the US giant was subject to what was perceived as the first military attack on the continental states since Great Britain burnt Washington in 1814. The 2001 terrorist attacks precipitated an American security policy of vigorous international engagement. A state that had seen itself as invulnerable within its shell – with the sole exception of the threat of extinction in a global nuclear war with the Soviet Union – thus went abroad to 'find monsters to slay,' so as to prove its continued power and to prevent, or, at least, to decrease significantly, the risk of further unconventional attacks on the American homeland. The US decision to go to war against the regime in Iraq in 2003 was a crucial security policy decision. This war and its implications for transatlantic security relations are treated in various chapters in this book.

We believe that the United States needs to be studied from several perspectives to determine what role it plays in today's transatlantic strategic triangle, and to discern what the important factors are that may influence its actions in this context in the future. One perceptive way of expressing the role of the transatlantic security relations for Washington in 2004/5 is stated by David M. Andrews: 'Absent the interlocking concerns that had once united Washington and Moscow in supporting a substantial armed American presence in Germany, Europe is no longer the centrepiece of American grand strategy.'[16] Given this fundamental starting-point, we endeavour to examine what role Europe plays in US global affairs in the early twenty-first century.

One such aspect that we believe we need to study is economic relations, particularly trade, among the three actors in the triangle. It is obvious that Washington has immensely strong links with Western Europe in this sphere, and less developed ties with Russia. In our view, economic relations form an increasingly important part of security policy today, both in their own right and as linked to other issues. These economic links form an absolutely vital bedrock of the relations between the United States and the EU, which is why it is necessary to explore their nature and their ramifications. Russia is not linked to the other two actors in the triangle to nearly the same extent in economic respects, even if Moscow's role in the delivery of oil and natural gas, particularly to some European countries, is not unimportant.

Other topics that need to be studied if one wishes to understand the role of Washington in the transatlantic strategic triangle are to what extent and in what ways US policy-makers seek to preserve the dominant global position of the United States and whether other international actors attempt to counterbalance the immense weight of the superpower. Counterbalancing reactions are discernible. In particular, we analyse the policies of Russia in this respect.

Economic issues and questions about military power come together in the US debate on Grand Strategy. The only overall superpower has been searching for overarching guidelines for its international posture ever since the Soviet Union collapsed in 1991. Instead of a broad political consensus on America's proper role in the world, there is an ongoing debate among American politicians and scholars featuring a number of contending grand strategy visions. This is the reason why we have included a chapter on the ramifications of this strategic debate after the terrorist attacks of 11 September. Due to our focus on the transatlantic strategic triangle, one crucial aspect of this chapter is that we analyse under what circumstances, or to put it differently, under the terms of which Grand Strategy the decision-makers in the United States would contemplate playing a strategic game such as the one postulated in this book.

The structure of the book

In this book, the transatlantic strategic triangle serves as the organizing principle. This means that our goal is to cover the most crucial issues for understanding the current status of transatlantic security relations, as well as address the issues that will determine the future of these relations. It also means that the chapters in our book share a few overriding themes, while they, at the same time, also delve deeper into issues that are specific to each chapter.

The following questions are thus the overriding ones that these chapters, to varying degrees, address: What is the significance of the issues covered in this chapter for the current status of relations in the transatlantic strategic triangle? What are the implications of the analysis in each chapter for the likely future development of the transatlantic strategic triangle, in terms of crucial developments for one actor, for the relations between two of the actors, or for the security relations between all three actors? What does our analyses of the 'actorness' of the European Union imply for the future of the transatlantic strategic triangle as a whole? And, finally, to what an extent, and on what issues, can the notion of the strategic triangle help understand current and future relations between the United States, Russia and the EU?

This book is divided into three sections following the introduction. Each section focuses on one of the actors in the strategic triangle, taking account of the actor's relations with the other two actors. In the first section, consisting of four chapters, we cover aspects of the development of the European Union. How can the enlarged EU of 25 members be characterized as an actor in the broader transatlantic region in the early part of the twenty-first century? That is one of the overriding analytical questions that this book wishes to address from different perspectives. Each individual chapter of the first section of our book covers a different aspect of this broader question.

The two first chapters in the section devoted to the EU, Chapters 2 and 3, examine the Union as a whole. Chapter 2, written by Magnus Ekengren and Kjell Engelbrekt, studies the enlargement of the Union from 15 members to 25 that took place in 2004, asking whether what may be gained in terms of capabilities in the sphere of foreign, security and defence policy may perhaps be lost to an even more important extent in terms of reduced cohesiveness? The consequences of the enlargement process of the Union are thus one crucial aspect of the further development of the EU as an actor in the strategic triangle.

In Chapter 3, Arita Eriksson studies how the military dimension has been developing in the EU since 1999. She discusses the implications of this development for the external and internal relations of the EU. She thus addresses the issue of what military capacity the EU has acquired during the last five years, and what its main plans are for the future in this field. The question of whether or not the development of the crisis management capacity that the EU has acquired really has any importance for its role in the greater transatlantic region is raised. In addition, she also illustrates another aspect of the development of the Union's defence policy: how this process interacts with and influences the defence policies of the Member States, in this case Sweden.

While Chapters 2 and 3 concentrate on developments within the European Union as a more or less unified actor, Chapters 4 and 5 are case studies of four individual members of the Union of 25. These studies illustrate a fundamental truth about EU member states in the early twenty-first century; namely, that they are grappling with issues of how to conduct their foreign, security and defence policy and where to anchor these policies: nationally, bilaterally, in NATO or in the European Union. The two chapters have the common theme of problematizing the relationship between the growing actor capacity of the Union in the security and defence sphere, and the implications that this has for carrying out security and defence policy, traditionally the preserve of the nation-state, in four European states in the future.

Chapter 4, written by Fredrik Bynander, asks the question: What makes some European states assume the role of 'trusted allies' of the United States in the war against terrorism in general and the Iraq War in particular, rather than align with the Franco-German axis that strongly opposes recent US policy in the Middle East? The chapter studies the cases of Poland and the Czech Republic in their processes of dual accession to NATO and the EU. The term 'instinctive atlanticism' has been used to describe their recent security policy, and their preoccupation with security guarantees from the United States through the enlarged NATO has been seen as the defining trait of its motivation. The author problematizes these unidimensional portraits of the two maturing democracies and their quests to find a place in a changing European security setting. This chapter thus provides us with another angle on an aspect that also preoccupies Ekengren and Engelbrekt in Chapter 2: What will enlargement mean for the EU as an actor in the strategic triangle? Poland and the Czech Republic can be seen as two case studies of this problem, but they may also represent tendencies among the other eight new members of the EU.

In Chapter 5, the final chapter of the EU section, Adrian Hyde-Price focuses on another aspect with clear relevance to the future of the European Union: strategic coercion.[17] He asks whether or not European nations, working as a collective in the EU, may be getting ready to contemplate the use of the threat of military force, as well as the practical application of such force, in situations, where diplomacy, economic policies and non-military sanctions have proved ineffective. Or instead will strategic coercion, to the extent that it still exists in Europe, remain the exclusive preserve of the independent nations, particularly the United Kingdom and France? If the British and French Governments in the future were both willing to devote real military resources to the further construction of the European Security and Defence Policy (ESDP), then this would mean the EU would become a very different actor in the strategic triangle of the future.

In the second section of our book, we study Russia from a triangular perspective. The broader analytical question that the two chapters in this section, combined, seek to address can be formulated as follows: What is the role that Russia under Vladimir Putin wants to play within the context of the new strategic triangle during the next five to ten years? Clearly, Russia cannot afford deteriorating relations with either the United States or the EU. In Moscow's view, the United States retains its historical role as Russia's primary counterpart in the global security arena. Washington's fierce battle against terrorism correlates well with Russia's uncompromising stance towards terrorists and separatists, and only serves to strengthen Moscow's impression that the United States counts more than any other state in the international security system. The EU is important to Moscow for partly other reasons. Cooperation between the EU and Russia is decisive since in the security sphere the two parties are mutually dependent. A range of motivating forces spur co-operation, most importantly interdependence both in the economic sphere and as regards 'soft threats' in Europe. Both economic interdependence and the need to co-operate to handle common threats to security increase with the eastern enlargement of the EU. However, several obstacles have served to delay a deepening of co-operation so far. This is further elaborated upon in Chapter 6, where Charlotte Wagnsson examines the relationship between Russia and the EU. While focusing on relations between two of the three actors in the triangle the chapter also has clear implications for the relationships between all three actors studied in this book. In this process of formulating their security strategies the two actors are acutely aware of the importance of their direct relationship, as well as of the crucial role for both of them played by the third party on the other side of the Atlantic Ocean.

In the seventh chapter of the book Bertil Nygren focuses on Russia and its relations with two of its most important neighbours, the Ukraine and Belarus. Relations among these three countries are strongly influenced by the two enlargement processes going on in Western Europe, in the EU and in NATO. The fact that none of these three countries has any realistic chance of entering either organization in the medium term, perhaps with the exception of the Ukraine, means that they will have to adjust their foreign and security policy to the developments in both organizations. A fundamental question asked in this chapter is whether Russia will use this changing situation to strengthen its ties with, as well as its dominance over, its two neighbours. A second important question for Chapter 7 is what the implications may be for the role of Russia in the strategic triangle as a result of the development of its relations with the Ukraine and Belarus. Together, the two chapters on Russia thus provide at least a partial answer to what type of role Russia wishes to play in the new strategic triangle, and, also, how Moscow envisions its role in relation to the EU.

In the book's third section, comprising three chapters, we focus upon the United States and its relations with the other two players in the new strategic triangle. The overriding theme that these three chapters have in common is an assessment of the United States as an actor in the greater transatlantic region. To what extent is the US conception of its role in global politics today consistent with the notion of the strategic triangle? Will Washington conduct important aspects of its foreign and security policy in the transatlantic region in a way that takes the relationships with Russia and the EU into consideration, or will what we earlier characterized as unilateralism continue to be the essence of US foreign and security policy in the global arena?

In Chapter 8, Peter Dombrowski and Andrew L. Ross assess the significance of the new strategic triangle in grand strategy options currently available to the United States. To what extent can this triangular relationship play any role in shaping global US commitments and interests after the end of the Cold War? Dombrowski and Ross place this question within the framework of the US debate on grand strategy, which has until now often been discussed in terms of four alternative visions: neo-isolationism, selective engagement, liberal internationalism and primacy. Dombrowski and Ross, in their analysis of how the new strategic triangle may be conceived in the United States, add a fifth alternative: empire. They outline the alternatives and assess the relative importance of the triangle in each alternative.

Jan Hallenberg in Chapter 9 focuses on the importance of economic ties among the three actors in the triangle. The strengths of the relations among them are assessed. In addition, the strains that the Iraq War put upon relations among actors in the strategic triangle are evaluated.

The tenth chapter in this book, by Håkan Karlsson, looks at the asymmetrical relations between the United States and Russia. It examines various manifestations of the grand strategy of primacy actually pursued by Washington in recent years, focusing primarily on the contentious international security issues of NATO enlargement, strategic nuclear force planning, strategic arms control, and missile defence, and studies the Russian perceptions of and responses to this US grand strategy. Washington's reaction to the efforts by Russia to resist US global domination is also explored.

In the final chapter (Chapter 11), the circumstances under which the new strategic triangle may exist are assessed on the basis of the results of the analyses in the previous chapters. The current status and prospects of the triangle are discussed, and we provide a tentative answer to the question whether the triangle concept in fact helps us understand the transforming security relations in the greater transatlantic region.

Notes

1 Apart from Kissinger the literature on the original strategic triangle includes G. Segal, *The Great Power Triangle*, New York: St Martin's Press, 1982. An example of using the notion of the triangle as the authors in this book have done is I.B. Neumann and S. Ulriksen (eds) *Sikkerhetspolitik: Norge i makttrianglet mellom EU, Russland och USA*, Oslo: Tane Aschehoug, 1996.

2 For the term 'greater transatlantic region', see A. Hyde-Price, ' "Burning a Path to Peace?" International Society, Europe and Coercive Military Power', paper presented at the British International Studies Association (BISA) Annual Conference, December 2002, p. 5.

3 In employing the concept of power, which is so notoriously difficult to define, we simply mean that it matters whether a state is weak or strong, and that it is indeed possible to assess the dimensions of this strength. In his overview of the use of the concept in international relations, D. Baldwin ('Power and International Relations', in W. Carlsnaes, T. Risse and B.A. Simmons (eds) *Handbook of International Relations*, London/Thousand Oaks, CA/New Delhi: Sage, 2002, p. 177) states that 'it is not surprising that power has been prominent in international interactions from Thucydides to the present'. For a recent treatment of the age-old power controversy in international relations, based on a rich vein of previous scholarly treatments of international relations, see T. Volgy and A. Bailin, *International Politics and State Strength*, Boulder, CO and London: Lynne Rienner, 2003 particularly pp. 18 and 35–42. We subscribe to their notion that 'state strength', which is their term for 'power' has three dimensions. The first *'Relational strength* refers to the capabilities of the state vis-à-vis other countries in the system' (p. 40). The second *'Structural strength* refers to the capability of the state to create essential rules, norms, and modes of operation for various dimensions of the international system' (p. 41). Their third dimension of 'state strength', *domestic strength* (p. 42) is roughly equivalent to our concept 'actorness', which is explained later in this chapter.

4 Some examples of this large literature are R.J. Art, *A Grand Strategy for America*, Ithaca, NY and London: Cornell University Press, 2003; A.J. Bacevich, *American Empire: The Realities and Consequences of US Diplomacy* Cambridge, MA: Harvard University Press, 2002; Z. Brzezinski, *The Choice: Global Domination or Global Leadership*, New York: Basic Books, 2004; I. Daalder and J. Lindsay, *America Unbound: The Bush Revolution in Foreign Policy*, Washington, DC: Brookings, 2003; N. Ferguson, *Colossus: The Price of America's Empire*, New York: Penguin, 2004; G. Friedman, *America's Secret War: Inside the Hidden Worldwide Struggle Between America and Its Enemies*, New York: Doubleday, 2004; J.L. Gaddis, *Surprise, Security, and the American Experience*, Cambridge, MA and London: Harvard University Press, 2003; J.B. Judis, *The Folly of Empire: What George Bush Could Learn from Theodore Roosevelt and Woodrow Wilson*, New York: Scribner, 2004; W.R. Mead *Power Terror Peace and War: America's Grand Strategy in a World At Risk*, New York: Knopf, 2004; W.E. Odom and R. Dujarric, *America's Inadvertent Empire*, New Haven, CN and London: Yale University Press, 2004.

5 The concept 'actorness' has two meanings in this volume. First, it attempts to capture the theoretical requirements that an entity needs to fulfil if it is to be a full actor in international relations. Second, in a more empirical political sense, it covers whether or not the EU is able to act coherently regarding a specific political issue, and if it is treated as a unified actor or not by the other two actors in the triangle.

6   The literature on the EU as a global actor includes: G. Sjöstedt, *The External Role of the European Community*, Westmead: Saxon House, 1977; R. Ginsberg, *The European Union in International Politics: Baptism by Fire*, Lanham, MD: Rowman & Littlefield, 2001; B. White, *Understanding European Foreign Policy*, Basingstoke: Palgrave, 2001; N. Gnessotto (ed.) *EU Security and Defence Policy: The First Five Years (1999–2004)* Paris: EU Institute for Security Studies, 2004. A US scholar advancing a view on the growing importance of the EU that is in many respects similar to the one made in this volume is Charles Kupchan. See Kupchan, *The End of the American Era: U.S. Foreign Policy and the Geopolitics of the Twenty-First Century*, New York: Knopf, 2002 for his extended argument about the growing role of the EU in international affairs and Kupchan, 'Hollow Hegemony or Stable Multipolarity?' in G.J. Ikenberry (ed.) *America Unrivaled: The Future of the Balance of Power*, Ithaca, NY and London: Cornell University Press, 2002, pp. 68–97 for a more focused argument on why the EU is likely to challenge the US's role as the only global superpower.

7   See Volgy and Bailin, *International Politics*, p. 10. The authors identify a growth in International Governmental Organizations from less than 1,000 in 1950 to about 5,000 in 1995.

8   Cf. on this point J.W. Garver, 'The China–India–US Triangle: Strategic Relations in the Post-Cold War Era', *NBR Analysis*, October 2002, vol. 13, no. 5, The National Bureau of Asian Research, p. 2.

9   R. Kagan, 'Embraceable EU', *Washington Post*, 5 December 2004, B07.

10 Article 1–40:1 in Treaty establishing a Constitution for Europe, as printed in *Official Journal of the European Union*, C310, 16 December 2004, vol. 47.

11 T. Blair, 'Speech at the Lord Mayor's Banquet', 15 November 2004, online.

12 J. Chirac, Speech given at the International Institute for Strategic Studies (IISS), London, 18 November 2004, online. In the same speech, President Chirac states: 'Building a credible European defence system is obviously not, as is sometimes said, about building up a Europe against the United States. It is about giving Europe the capabilities to assume its responsibilities either independently, in liaison with the Atlantic Alliance, or within it'.

13 B. Benoit and J. Thorhill. 'Fear that Gas Supply Gives Russia Too Much Power over Europe', *Financial Times*, 12 January 2005.

14 Ibid.

15 See F. Harvey, 'Now that Putin has Accepted Kyoto, the Real Work Can Start', *Financial Times*, 29 December 2004.

16 D.M. Andrews, 'The United States and Its Atlantic Partners: The Evolution of American Grand Strategy', *Cambridge Review of International Affairs*, October 2004, vol. 17 no. 3, p. 430.

17 The intellectual Godfather behind the notion of strategic coercion is the US economist Thomas Schelling, who called it 'compellence'. See Schelling, *Arms and Influence*, New Haven, CN: Yale University Press, 1966. Further applications of the notion of using military force, or the threat of the use of military force, to obtain diplomatic aims, include A. George, D. Hall and W. Simons, *The Limits of Coercive Diplomacy: Laos, Cambodia, Vietnam*, Boston: Little, Brown, 1971; L. Freedman (ed.) *Strategic Coercion: Concepts and Cases*, Oxford: Oxford University Press, 1998; and P.V. Jakobsen, *Western Use of Coercive Diplomacy after the Cold War: A Challenge for Theory and Practice*, New York: St Martin's Press, 1998.

2

THE IMPACT OF ENLARGEMENT ON EU ACTORNESS

Enhanced capacity, weakened cohesiveness

Magnus Ekengren and Kjell Engelbrekt

The purpose of this chapter is to discuss the impact of the latest European Union (EU) enlargement on actorness in an international environment. The question of EU actorness is of crucial importance for our understanding – and indeed the existence – of a triangular relationship between the USA, Russia and the EU. Can a Union of 25 member states think and act strategically, and will it be attributed strategic capacity by the two other actors making up the triangle? We begin looking for answers by considering eastward enlargement through the prism of new security threats, the changed significance of geography and geopolitics, the assets brought in by new member states, along with the dual role/identity of the Union as both a global network player and a more traditional actor. We conclude by elucidating implications of this somewhat intricate equation, as well as of the interplay between the EU and the other two players, in the form of four scenarios.

More than ten years have now passed since Christopher Hill raised the issue of the 'capabilities–expectations gap' and found flaws with the EU as an international actor.[1] In the meantime, the Union has gained a more robust mandate in external relations and a wider range of resources. In fact, it may be argued that several of the previously empty spaces in Gunnar Sjöstedt's evocative 1977 matrix, outlining structural prerequisites for full-fledged 'actorness', today can be pencilled in. A 'community of interests' has been formalized in the field of foreign and security policy, organizational units charged with the planning and execution of crisis operations are in place, and the routines guiding co-ordination between Council staff and the rotating presidency have been improved. On a variety of levels, that is, institutional elements have been added to augment the Union's ability to conduct itself internationally.[2]

Still, few consider this development as being satisfactory or believe the EU's overall ability to work the international scene matches the term 'actorness'. Except for a handful of issue-areas, most notably agricultural and trade policy, the elephant is not even run by an elephant boy, but by an ant. For a rough but mind-boggling comparison, the annual budget for the Common Foreign and Security Policy (CFSP) is 35 million euros, whereas the US State Department in 2004 alone spent 7.5 billion dollars on 'Administration of Foreign Policy and Other Appropriations'.[3] Besides the EU's tiny budget for foreign and security policy, major obstacles to joint action remain in terms of institutional complexity, a number of legal restrictions and the weakness of democratic oversight.[4]

The elusive character of EU actorness

On the output side, the old pattern of limited European co-operation persists. Development of joint policies has not been much advanced in recent years, despite obvious opportunities.[5] While there were as many 'joint decisions' in 2001 and 2002 as in the previous two years, there was in the same period a drop in 'common positions' from 35 (1999) and 33 (2000) to 19 (2001) and 16 (2002), respectively.[6] Among the new instruments created in the Amsterdam Treaty, 'enhanced co-operation' has not been used at all, and there are only a handful of instances of international agreements adopted via the concerted procedure under Article 24 of the Treaty. At any rate, the low level of activity testifies to an absence of active joint policy development and indirectly to failing actor cohesiveness. The same could be said about the voting patterns of EU member states in the United Nations General Assembly.[7]

To be sure, the term actorness has prompted a fair amount of confusion and misunderstanding in EU literature.[8] Countless analysts have noted that the underlying comparison with a powerful nation-state and its ability to operate in the global political environment is wrong-headed. In fact, even Hill and Sjöstedt hinted at an awareness of this problematic assumption. On the other hand, the alternative conceptualizations of the EU on the international stage advanced by scholars are plentiful, though not necessarily more appropriate. To recall only a few of them, the EU's external affairs policy has been described as 'post-national', 'post-modern', 'post-Westphalian' and characterized by 'network governance' or mere 'presence' rather than by agency.

While individually creative, the combined weight of these conceptual innovations also has a tendency to subvert or displace the original question. Instead of addressing the related issues, the literature has at times used the EU as a prop to discuss the nature of contemporary globalization, the pervasive influence of transnational flows, or trends of political and cultural fragmentation (or, conversely, homogenization). Arguments in the vein of the early discussion on actorness have been less common. Drawing on the well-established literature on principal–agent relations, Rittberger and Zelli usefully suggested that EU actorness can be derived from two sets of circumstances, namely that a mandate either has been delegated to an 'agent' (for instance to the Commission) or that it stems from a substantive agreement among the 'principals'.[9] Analytically pertinent too is the observation that the Union's international performance is increasingly characterized by the multi-level European polity, making the assessment of actorness dependent on the layer in focus.[10]

In a straightforward manner, this analysis will describe actorness as a function of *capacity* and *cohesiveness*. Capacity is understood as arising from the various resources the actor may be in a position to employ. Different from the term 'capability' applied in much earlier literature,[11] 'capacity' has an aggregate quality that its individual components may actually lack. Furthermore, capacity does not exclusively concern capabilities that are constantly at the disposal of an actor, but constitute resources that can potentially be mobilized for a particular end. Cohesiveness, meanwhile, is contingent on a significant degree of similarity in perceptions of values, identities, interests or threats. Needless to say, it is highly unlikely that all of the kinds of perceptions mentioned will ever fully coincide. Yet cohesiveness is therefore an appropriate term for that 'sticking-together' proclivity that actorness requires, not least when the going gets tough in world politics and other players seek to weaken the unity of EU member states.

The added complexity of enlargement

Whereas many in principle agree that implicit comparisons with Great Power actorness are misleading, much of the current debate about the implications of EU enlargement indicates that misconceptions are still deeply rooted in scholarly assumptions. By adding ten new member states, a common claim is that the EU will be significantly weakened as an international actor.[12] Besides a few references to the long-standing discussion on actorness, however, these claims are rarely explicated or systematically addressed. We would argue that, at the very least, such sweeping assertions regarding the repercussions of eastwards enlargement warrant serious scrutiny.

New members bring new capacity to the EU in part by adding areas of interest, history, geography, natural resources, population, economic assets, environmental problems, cultural values and political positions. However, they also contribute with their own skills and networks of external relations and diplomatic legacies, traditional bilateral ties and other constellations. For example, the first enlargement introduced a range of trade issues related to the British Commonwealth and Denmark, streamlining various areas of divergence between them arising out of the European Free Trade Agreement (EFTA) and the Common Commercial Policy of what was then the European Community (EC).

United Kingdom membership, in particular, implied a new dynamic in the EC's relations with the US and the developing countries. In one stroke the EC's external relations acquired both a Northern European and truly 'global' dimension. More recently, the fourth enlargement widened and deepened the geopolitical concerns on the part of the EU to Central and Eastern Europe and the Baltic region. Following the accession of Austria, Sweden and Finland, the Union notably came to share a common border with Russia.

Like the fifth enlargement, the (negotiated but not yet ratified) sixth and possibly seventh rounds of expansion will inevitably extend the EU's commitments all along its Eastern frontier. While the previous enlargement mainly precipitated the development of a 'Northern dimension' with significance for the approach to agriculture, fisheries and Russia,[13] it seems safe to assume that the new accessions will forge an 'Eastern dimension', which might transform the character of the entire Union. Judging from the May 2004 Commission strategy paper in particular, the eastwards enlargements ought to compel the EU to adopt more robust and elaborate policies with respect to all neighbouring countries, in the Mediterranean region as well as in the Black Sea area, the Caucasus and the part of Eastern Europe bordering on the new member states.[14]

As opposed to earlier enlargements, however, there are two extraordinary challenges to EU *cohesiveness* this time. First, the sheer number of new entrants is staggering. The inclusion of ten new member countries in May 2004 is far more than anything previously attempted, with implications ranging from steeply rising translation costs to the prospects of successfully applying the so-called Community method and traditional harmonization strategies. Second, the diversity of the individual countries has never been more overwhelming. Somehow the earlier expansions have tended to group countries with certain similarities in historical background, economic profile and political outlook. The 2004 accession, and those which may follow within the next decade, lack such facilitating conditions. What can Poland and Malta, or Estonia and Cyprus for that matter, be said to have in common other than their EU membership?

The unprecedented diversity among the new member states renders all predictions of common external policies of the future enlarged EU more difficult. True, the majority of new entrants are ex-communist countries. In terms of an Eastern dimension it is clear that the EU gains both knowledge and a complex heritage of entanglements when it comes to Russia and Ukraine, through the accession of the three Baltic states and Poland, and Turkey, via Cyprus. To the extent that Moscow and Ankara seriously pursue closer relations with the EU, this should be to their benefit. The same is presumably the case with applicant states in the Western Balkans and other countries in the Caucasus and the greater Black Sea area with, among others, Lithuania and Slovakia now on the inside.[15] But what are the likely consequences of enlargement on the external policies of the EU? In particular, what are the implications of EU ambitions to bolster its actorness in international affairs?

As in the case of earlier enlargements, the interplay between new capacity and challenges related to cohesiveness will to a high degree depend on the historical, global and institutional context. We hold that predictions of a dilution of EU actorness due to enlargement may be misconceived due to insufficient analysis of these contextual conditions. For example, the challenges to cohesiveness in the first enlargement were subsequently outweighed by a renewed partnership between the Community and the US. The same could be said for the challenges associated with the fourth enlargement, coinciding with fundamental transformations in world politics at the end of the Cold War. In order to pay sufficient attention to the context of world politics, we will therefore examine the possible effects of the most recent enlargement on EU actorness by answering the following three questions: What international environment will an enlarged Union be facing? What external policies will an enlarged Union pursue? What EU actorness and, indeed, what kind of international entity, will the new capacity and challenges of cohesiveness give birth to in a rapidly changing environment?

The outlook from Brussels

From the distinct vantage point of the EU and its key joint institutions, the present external environment could be described as characterized by three different factors. First, there is an incipient security landscape, born from the spoils of the Cold War arrangements and sharpened by the 11 September attacks and their consequences. Second, geography is taking on a new meaning, weakening the significance of borders and distance while inserting a novel geopolitical dynamic. Third, there is a transformed agenda of global issues facing all major actors and institutions operating on the international scene.

Against this backdrop, the enlargement has provided the EU with a powerful impetus in a forward direction. While still absorbing ten new members and adapting its routines, EU institutions appear to be exploring ways of translating the enlargement into additional capacity. At the same time, there is an intense quest for joint policy within an agenda that seems to be expanding at the same pace as enlargement itself.

The EU in a new security landscape

In recent years, scholars of international relations have criticized 'traditional' theories of the international system for depicting it as made up of autonomous actors among which the Union will take its place. Such approaches, they argue, fail to grasp today's transformed international environment and the new kind of entity that the EU constitutes.[16] Others hold that this may not be a problem when assessing the character and practices of the Union. The EU can be treated as an entity able both to further co-operation in networks and to possess traditional actor capabilities *vis-à-vis* other – national as well as international – players. It is perhaps even this combination, it is argued, which makes its experience unique. The EU's roles are simultaneously operational at two levels, or rather in two dimensions.[17]

Wæver argues that the EU is a security actor due to its four roles of 'keeping the core intact, ensuring there is one core rather than several in Western Europe; silent disciplining power of 'the near abroad'; the magnetism working already in East Central Europe; a potential role as direct intervenor in specific conflicts'.[18]

The first of these roles is closer to the Union's network character, the latter to the one of a traditional actor. William Wallace has defined the frontiers of Europe as 'boundaries of networks', within which the Deutschian 'sense of security community' is to be found.[19] A 'Network Europe' has been conceptualized as a region, a platform, a value space – as part of a network that is already becoming genuinely global. Here, the role of the EU consists in the creation of exchanges and interdependencies between poles or nodes *within* this network. On the basis of the growing collection of case studies of the Union's external actions,[20] it seems safe to assume that, due to its strong network character, the EU has been – and probably will remain – politically strongest within and on its own frontiers. In this perspective, the Union's greatest security value may be the European unity it can wield at the time of its biggest enlargement ever.

At the same time a remarkable development has, during the last decade, taken place with regard to the Union's actor capacity. After the horrifying Balkan experience, the Union set up a basic crisis management mechanism. This type of crisis, it was asserted, should never be allowed to recur. In the aftermath of 11 September 2001, and the wars of Afghanistan and Iraq, many in the Union began proposing an autonomous defence capability in order to be able to carry out the same type of global power politics and retaliation as the US. The unratified EU constitution would have opened up ways of introducing more flexibility into the actions of the Union outside its territory. The focus in that document is very much on the willingness and ability of member states. The EU is treated as an arena which provides suitable institutions for intergovernmental co-ordination. The Madrid terrorist attacks on 11 March 2004 displayed with brutal clarity the close inter-linkages between internal and external EU security. As an answer to this challenge, the Union in March 2004 adopted a solidarity clause for the prevention of and protection against terrorist attacks.

Thus, the new dynamics in global and European security have had a significant impact on the EU's Common Foreign and Security Policy and the European Security and Defence Policy (ESDP). This has been the case not only with regard to policy disagreements within the CFSP, such as the one over the Iraq conflict and the unipolar and US-led world. However, it has also taken place in terms of a more fundamental transformation in the form of new threats (above all terrorism), the erosion of the boundary between external and internal security and the decreasing importance of territorial defence. This dimension of change is now affecting the CFSP/ESDP just as it has affected national foreign and security policy.

The Security and Defence Articles that were planned to be included in a new EU Treaty establishing a Constitution for Europe would for the first time have implied a codification of the ESDP. Instead, the long-term development of the ESDP became more uncertain after the failure of the member states to ratify the Treaty in 2005–6. Even though many of the proposals in the Draft Treaty, such as the establishment of a European Defence Agency, can still be implemented within the framework of the existing Treaty, the issue of whether a 'common defence' still is the goal for the Union remains unsolved.

Meanwhile, the question is often raised: whose security are we referring to if not primarily the territorial security of the state? Many recent domestic reforms in the European states are a response to 9/11, such as the establishment of new bodies aimed at strengthening societal security in the field of emergency and vulnerability management. Tentatively labelled 'functional security',[21] such practices are aimed at minimizing a host of possible threats ranging from weapons of mass destruction (WMD) and dangerous materials in the former USSR, to transatlantic bioterrorism, container security, cyber-terrorism, power cuts and forest fires.[22] A vivid expression of this mental change is the blurring of the traditional border between internal and external national security. Analysis and planning are preoccupied with crisis situations and the prevention of conflicts and crimes rather than traditional wars.[23] European co-operation is becoming a prerequisite for functional security and national defence in the context of transnational threats and risks. The EU's objective within the broad sector of 'non-territorial' security – an objective developed in all three EU pillars – has been to minimize societal vulnerabilities and the number and impact of emergencies by establishing comprehensive systems of crisis management.

In December 2003, the Union adopted the European Security Strategy (ESS) proposed by CFSP High Representative Solana. The first threat mentioned in the security strategy is terrorism. The second is WMD proliferation, a scenario that might result in power cuts, water supply problems and a breakdown in basic infrastructure.[24] The other three threats are essentially structural and non-military: regional conflicts, failing states and organized crime. Discussions on whether or not to incorporate the realm of the Union's third pillar, justice and home affairs (for example personnel and threat identification), indicates wide acceptance for a broad security approach to the ESDP as well. For internal as well as external security reasons, many demand better co-ordination between civilian ESDP activities, Justice and Home Affairs (JHA) and the Commission. It has also been suggested that security thinking should be 'mainstreamed' into other areas of EU co-operation. The EU should, according to the solidarity clause, make the most of its multi-sectorial character – including military instruments – in action on its territory.[25]

Transcending geography

The EU is, according to many analysts, now acting in a transformed international system breeding new types of borders and identity, post-modern 'zones of peace and turmoil' and global network(s).[26] Some suggest that the system is likely to develop into a loose network of primarily economic co-operation between poles/regions.[27] The role of the EU would in this system be to strengthen the exchange and interdependence between the different poles. For example, the euro has, as a reserve currency, strengthened the position of the EC as the largest trading bloc. This is of great significance for the possible creation of a new world order based on a 'tripolar' monetary network (dollar, yen and euro zones, respectively) and an accompanying system of three trading regions (for further treatment see Chapter 9 of this volume). Former Commission President Delors saw as one of the goals of *la grande Europe* as becoming a 'geo-economic ensemble' in the globalization process.[28]

Internally, the EU is poised to begin dissolving the traditionally geographic or geopolitically oriented foreign policy of its member states. For example, the blurring of clear demarcations between national and EU affairs, due to the evolving EU polity, alters the very nature of foreign policy in Europe.[29] The development is basically a result of pragmatic, result-oriented sector policies and horizontal problem-solving. One may predict that also the Union's *external* policies will be similarly characterized by horizontal issues that bypass the geopolitical logic. The Union presently stands for a multilateral approach projecting civilian influence rather than (military) power to the outside world.[30] Even though this role has been questioned due to the large number of troops deployed abroad by the EU member states,[31] the main instruments of the EU in global affairs remain economic and 'soft' instruments, such as humanitarian aid and environment policies. Some believe that only by preserving its civilian character will the Union continue to exercise its 'normative power' and project its role as a model for other regions in the world.[32]

Some observers envisage that an enlarged Union to an increasing degree may also transform the European and international environment. Precisely the Union's internal structure and its lack of traditional foreign policy means is thought to engender a new outlook that goes beyond the traditional nation-state way of assessing the global challenges.[33] On this view the Union's external policies would help shape the international environment and decrease the importance of geo-politics in the Union's relations with other parts of the world. One question is to what extent security, economic and monetary systems actually can be 'regionalized'.[34] For instance, the security and economic wealth of Europe will continue to largely depend on political stability and oil imports from the Mediterranean area and the Middle East. Another issue is how the Union would actually go about bolstering its influence in global networks, given the existence of more than one global power-centre.[35] In this vein, the prime minister of Luxembourg, Jean-Claude Juncker, has called on Europe to 'invent a new atlas, not just reform the road map'.[36]

The widened global agenda

Globalization is likely to continue to alter the structure and functioning of European economies, the way of preparing and making policy and moulding our societies. The EU is at the same time an expression, a promoter and a regulator of economic globalization. Even if national policies and domestic economies remain critical, European economic regionalism has increased the EU bargaining leverage in global economic negotiations, increased the competitiveness of European firms and facilitated the pooling of resources and formation of regional corporate alliances. The inter-relationships among the three major economic regions – the EU, the North American Free Trade Agreement (NAFTA) and the Asia-Pacific Economic Co-operation (APEC) – will presumably be increasingly decisive for the global political economy, although individual players such as China and India are also likely to assert themselves. The question is to what extent the three economic regions could found a sufficiently robust common ground for the building of governance structures and international institutions able to govern the global economy.[37] The weakness of the EU in this game is that the gap between economic and political integration has been growing wider during recent years.[38]

The global agenda also encompasses climate change and global warming, which could precipitate expansion of deserts and increase the number of people in the world that are exposed to extreme weather conditions. As a result, the number of humanitarian crises around the globe is likely to rise, in their turn triggering large-scale migratory movements. Sustained high population growth rates may cause an increasing number of people to compete for food, energy, water, land and clean air – and thus pose a major potential for conflict. By the same token, global health concerns are likely to gain increasing importance; the spread of transmittable diseases is already causing concerns. This can only increase in the future, as epidemics such as HIV/AIDS cause life expectancy to plummet and to hollow out the productive classes, in particular in developing countries, with important implications for long-term stability.

More so than individual member states, the EU has the potential to effectively address several of these global challenges. Its external policy areas can today be said to include: trade policy, the external dimension of financial and economic policy (the external dimension of Economic and Monetary Union (EMU)), aid and development co-operation, common foreign and security policy, the external dimension of policy on police and judicial affairs, and the external dimension of asylum and migration policy. In one way or another, on a global scale the EU has to respond to growing income inequalities, persisting poverty, the spread of transmittable diseases, the need to create a level playing field for our industries to compete internationally, and the risk of 'downward' regulatory competition (taxation, environmental or labour standards).

Closely linked to these challenges is the need to help reshape the global institutional architecture to new realities, reducing the risk of regional economic crises impacting on Europe's economy, responding to international terrorism, illicit drugs and arms trade, illegal immigration, cyber warfare, and the threat of nuclear proliferation.[39] In a sense, these are all defensive measures necessitated by the vulnerabilities of modern European societies. Another institutional agenda is more offensive, benefiting from new technologies and opportunities created by democratizing societies and free markets. The latter includes the need for the EU to lower its tariffs and make other rich countries follow suit, but also to help build international coalitions to fight poverty, to develop novel approaches to aid (embracing good governance, the rule of law and basic human rights), to sustain energy security, to halt environmental degradation (natural disasters, energy consumption, migratory movements) and to develop the concept of 'humanitarian intervention').

The impact of enlargement: readjusting external policies

In this section we revisit the three dimensions of the EU's external environment outlined in the previous section, focusing on the policy agenda of the newcomers and prospects for applying the new skills and resources to external challenges in the coming years. But before turning back to foreign and security policy, a few remarks on diplomatic practice and economic interests may be in order.

Once outside the orbit of Moscow domination, the Central and East European (CEE) states rapidly rebuilt their skills in the realm of multilateral diplomacy. If the room for manoeuvring had been severely limited under constraints imposed under commitments to the Warsaw Pact and the Council of Mutual Economic Assistance (CMEA), post-1989 realities opened new opportunities for bargaining on the international scene. CEE activism contributed to revitalizing several branches of the United Nations family of international organizations, with the IMF, the World Bank and the United Nations Development Program (UNDP) assuming a direct interest in the problems of transition societies. With the exception of accession negotiations – which remained bilateral in the formal sense – the multilateral activities of CEE states in Europe spawned into most aspects of foreign policy. The Organization for Economic Cooperation and Development (OECD), the Council of Europe, NATO, the Organization for Security and Cooperation in Europe (OSCE) and the EU provided new venues for diplomatic and political co-operation and, given the widespread interest in problems of transition societies in the early 1990s, CEE governments found themselves in a position to influence the agenda of international organizations.

From the outset, the EU influenced candidate countries towards a less legalistic approach with a distinctly regional and multilateral flavour. As 'objects' of the common policy emanating out of the 1993 Copenhagen Council, CEE governments found that it was in their mutual interest to co-ordinate some of their actions *vis-à-vis* the powerful Union. Moreover, Brussels openly encouraged formal co-operation among candidate countries, such as the so-called Visegrad group drawing on an historic experience of co-operation between Poland, Hungary, the Czech Republic and Slovakia. The Central European Initiative, the Council of Baltic Sea States, the Quadrilaterale, the Black Sea co-operation group and others, can be added to the list. On the other hand, due to the polarization of international relations in the Cold War era, post-communist countries often maintained connections in precisely those parts of the Middle East, Latin America, Africa and Asia where West European governments kept a modest presence. So even if some post-communist governments wished to thoroughly overhaul their countries' foreign policy, such ties proved simply too useful to be discarded and could now be mobilized for EU purposes.

Some continuity in 'substance' is thus likely to carry over into Europeanized CEE positions. When it comes to the economy, it similarly appears probable that the Union's emphasis will, at least temporarily, tilt towards agriculture, due to the lower level of urbanization in the majority of new member states. Poland, and in the next round Romania, represent the main cause of that shift as eight million farmers will be added to the Union's current seven million.[40] The widespread reliance on Russian oil and gas deliveries will accentuate vulnerabilities in energy supply for the Union as a whole, though with Poland as a major consumer. Meanwhile, the higher rates of economic growth throughout Central and Eastern Europe will somewhat help offset stagnating figures in the western portions of the continent.[41] Levels of foreign investment are also comparatively high in, above all, the Baltic countries, Hungary and Slovakia. Overall, prices, wages and costs are growing but will remain substantially below those of Western Europe for the foreseeable future.

However, these are aggregate effects and do not always reflect common features or interests on the part of the acceding states. For instance, the economic structure of Cyprus and Malta has little in common with that of the former communist countries in Central Europe. But even among the CEE countries, there are both historically contingent variations and cleavages resulting from post-1989 flows of foreign investment, government or NGO aid, as well as enrichment or depletion of human capital resources. For example, Romania's initial advantage in lacking a significant foreign debt was swiftly dwarfed by the vast inflow of foreign capital in neighbouring Hungary. Also, the absence of a range of economic and political institutions in newly independent Estonia, Latvia and Lithuania may in retrospect be regarded as a blessing, as entirely novel modern structures could be created from scratch after 1991.

Security: new and old conceptions

While reforming the defence and security forces in Central and East European countries in connection with EU and NATO enlargements, post-communist governments embraced a broader security agenda. Defence forces were given a broader mandate so as to be able to assist civil emergency units in case of natural disasters, but also for general emergency planning purposes. In readying for NATO enlargement in particular, border disputes and other bilateral issues were solved or permanently set aside. Working with EU bodies such as the Commission, the European Parliament and the Council, a wider conceptualization of security and of threat was gradually integrated into the foreign policy of candidate countries. Supporting roles were played by the OSCE and the Council of Europe.

The new threat perceptions derived from mass-scale terrorist attacks challenged the foreign and security policies of all European states (albeit not as massively as in the US). Several of the new EU members were in fact quite responsive to calls on counteracting terrorism and to do so by coercive, partly military means. It could be argued that an initial incentive to do so was the unfinished US ratification process regarding NATO accession. Others, though, argued that the experience of post-communist societies is different from that of Western Europe in that many believe the defence of liberty may require sacrifices. Despite ambivalence among the population as to the rightfulness and effectiveness of military intervention as a tool, some new member states – notably Poland – assumed important commitments in Afghanistan as well as in Iraq.

An obvious sign that most CEE governments are more concerned about classic military, territorially based, threats is the unambiguous preference for NATO as a security instrument on European soil (on conflicting loyalties of CEE countries see Chapter 4 of this volume). Some simply view it as the only truly effective security organization in the region, unrivalled by any new acronyms the EU has thought up over the past years. Others equate NATO to US security guarantees, which they believe are useful not only to prevent a future Russian threat but something that keeps Germany at bay. The mixture of confusion and anxiety on the part of all CEE governments when the ESDP was launched in the late 1990s seems symptomatic; all immediately declared that they were deeply opposed if this new co-operation in any way threatened to undermine NATO and US involvement in European matters.[42] In accordance with the same logic, with Warsaw leading the way they have as EU members made the Union 'tougher' *vis-à-vis* Russia and Belarus but been careful not to harm the US–Russia relationship, which in turn might have repercussions on their own ties with Washington.[43]

Still, the traditionalist views are not matched by adequate military resources. All new member states spend well below 2 per cent of GDP on defence. Due to NATO commitments, a slow rise should be expected over the next couple of years. Some of the countries are nevertheless starting from (literally) zero. The Baltic states have in fact built up a defence force with equipment and advice from, above all, the Nordic countries. Looking at the modest pledges made to the European Rapid Reaction Force (and in some cases 'double-hatted' to NATO Rapid Reaction Forces), the newcomers are hardly poised to assume major commitments under the ESDP, for the most part offering to dispatch a company or a battalion. Poland, with a population larger than the other nine accession states put together, stands out in earmarking an entire framework brigade, along with police and search and rescue units.[44]

Anyway, it seems uncertain whether the widened notion of security always translates into a deeper recognition, or appropriate conclusions being drawn, among the new member states. It also remains to be seen if the lack of implementation stems from lack of knowledge of deeper EU values and methods, or if the new members simply differ in their foreign policy 'disposition'. The same uncertainty applies to the 'national bias' of foreign policies in several countries. Poland's 'Nice or Death' slogan during the December 2003 European Council may have stunned West European governments, but expressions of similarly assertive and 'self-centrist' policies are not uncommon among the newcomers.[45] The rejection of the UN plan to unite Cyprus by the Greek population in the south of the island, on the eve of the republic's accession, represented an analogous disappointment to many EU officials. Sensitivities on minority issues clearly linger in several new member states and most governments pursue an active relationship with the Diaspora community. For example, Hungary, despite international criticism, persists in its protective stance with respect to Hungarians in neighbouring territories, and Latvia has declared ties with the national Diaspora as one of its five top foreign policy priorities.[46]

A 'post-national' EU less likely?

It may therefore be said that the majority of new entrants share certain distinct features of a more 'traditionalist' foreign and security policy than that of the West European states. Having gained real sovereignty and autonomy some fifteen years ago, and experiencing a form of national rebirth in the meantime, it would probably be strange if most of the new members did not feel a wish to bolster both state and nation.[47] The 'Back to Europe' slogan partly means 'away from communism and Russian dominance', though partly 'Back to Normalcy'. With normalcy, a prosperous, democratic, but also sovereign condition is intended.

Nationalism remains a powerful force in Central and Eastern Europe, and right-wing political parties – viewing themselves as the guardians of national dignity and integrity – will continue to be sensitive to any perceived retreat from sovereign positions.[48] They will help keep alive, beyond formal agreements, what they view as historical injustices and skewed power relationships between majorities and minorities. To the extent that disputes between ethnic and religious groups cannot be solved or are aggravated, these national sentiments could be mobilized anew. More than the persistence of geopolitical reasoning in European politics, it is a legacy of geopolitical rivalries in the nineteenth century and the first half of the twentieth century.

The lingering of 'national issues' may evidently make the transition to a 'post-modern' or 'post-national' state of EU regional or global policy less likely. The intricate multilateralism of European politics is something the new members already have become accustomed to. But the experience is more of inter-governmentalism than of political forms oblivious of borders, space and ethnic identity. The kind of activism which Spanish, German or Italian regions display in EU settings will take time to develop in the new member countries, not least because of their communist centralist legacy. Like most small EU countries, they are likely to be assertive about safeguarding the standing of their language and culture.

Conversely, there are, as of yet, few signs that the new members will be comfortable in pursuing ideas of the EU as a model, or a 'normative power', in conducting foreign and security policy. First, the high-strung rhetoric of the communist predecessors has made the ground particularly weak for 'model' idealism. Second, the sometimes useful but rather annoying paternalism of the EU Commission towards the former candidate countries is presumably not something they would want to emulate.[49] Third, for several of the CEE governments the US provides a better model in some policy-making areas. Fourth, there is principled disagreement as to the effectiveness of the EU's institutional capabilities to match the rhetoric, as well as to the political desires which might ensue from such self-praise.

Fitting the global suit

As in the case of previous enlargements, it will take some time before the ten new member countries, all 'small or middle' powers in realist theory terminology, get used to wearing the new global suit. It is not the suit of a 'great power' actor in the sense that heads of government can exert the kind of direct influence that they are familiar with from the domestic context. The newcomers, however, will now be sitting at a table, with a voice among several others, at which policies with, at times, global repercussions are actually forged. By comparison, CFSP policies have a much wider scope than those of NATO, where Hungary, Poland and the Czech Republic already have several years of experience. To the extent that the new member states have ambitions to be part of that process, they will need to rapidly develop skills and competences on issues and about parts of the world which so far have been of marginal interest to them. Considering problems more close to home, on the other hand, accession will multiply the opportunities to yield influence through that of the EU's overall stance.

In terms of the EU's present and future global agenda we have already noted that the new members are positive towards free trade but may strengthen the conservative position of the Union on the important question of the Common Agricultural Policy (CAP) and trade in agricultural products. The greater reliance on the farming and foodstuffs sector in Central and Eastern Europe is likely to make countries like Poland, Slovakia, and later, Romania and Bulgaria potential allies of France and protectionist lobby groups in Brussels in this subsection of Union trade policy.[50] Combined with a fear of further social dislocation and higher unemployment resulting from additional waves of economic restructuring, the possibility cannot be excluded that this conservative bias under certain conditions may weaken overall EU support for liberal world trade arrangements.

More likely, however, is that the new members will continue to benefit greatly from growing trade within and outside the internal market, and therefore work with Western European governments to restructure their economies and modernize the farming sector so as to reduce its dependence on subsidies. Several countries, such as the Baltic states, Hungary and Cyprus, have economies which are already deeply intertwined with the rest of Europe and they will no doubt be forceful proponents of further liberalization of international trade. Even if the EU through the Eastern enlargement will become more self-sufficient in trade terms, from 19.4 to 17.7 per cent share exchange with non-EU partners,[51] most governments tend to maintain a position on global trade arrangements which is consistent with their stance on free trade within the internal market.

More of a contradiction between old and new EU members is likely on environmental issues. It is true that basically all post-communist states have activated a number of the international conventions and other agreements which their predecessors had, typically, signed but not ratified or effectively implemented. Symptomatically, despite their alleged sympathies for US foreign policy, all new members and candidate countries have both signed and ratified the Kyoto Protocol on reducing carbon dioxide emissions.[52] Overall, though, the commitment to environment-friendly policies is shallower than that of many 'old' EU members.[53] All new member states negotiated long phase-in periods in this area of the *acquis communautaire*, and environmentalism as a social movement only gained ground in Central and Eastern Europe in the late 1980s (and at first mainly as a relatively safe channel of political protest).

The same can be said about the prospects of new member states becoming deeply involved in the health approach pursued globally by the EU in recent years. Unaccustomed to active participation in the richly woven fabric of international co-operation on welfare matters, not least due to the fact that the EU, the US and Japan in the past set the agenda in this realm, there is limited experience and political energy to mobilize on global health issues. On certain concrete problems, which concern the region more directly, co-operation prospects are brighter. While the HIV/AIDS issue only recently began to seriously affect CEE countries,[54] trafficking in women and teenage girls and boys already constitutes an acute problem. A related issue, which is beginning to impact new members, is immigration. Whereas West Europeans mainly fear a large-scale labour force influx from Central and Eastern Europe, immigration into the new member states is in some cases rising steeply.[55] This increase should represent a powerful incentive to help forge an effective EU policy on immigration and migration, regionally as well as globally.

The nature of the (actions of the) beast

The latest EU enlargement should, as mentioned above, result in a new balance between capacity and cohesiveness, which does not necessarily translate into weakened actorness, though it might change the *nature* of the EU's character and actions. The capacity of the Union draws strength from knowledge and assets brought in by new members, but it is also bolstered as a consequence of extending economic co-operation, trade and network governance beyond the EU's formal borders. At the same time, cohesiveness could weaken through the internalization of an increased number of 'national issues' and be additionally undermined by the establishment of a new set of demanding security and defence aims. The overall implication is that the contours of the enlarged Union appear differently in each of the three dimensions – or 'historical trends' – that we have extrapolated and then allowed to inform our study.

European capacity augmented

By extending and enhancing the importance of European networks through enlargement, the Union is extending the frontiers within which it is at its strongest. It extends the level playing field where it is profoundly influential, i.e. within European and global networks. In this way, the EU acts a promoter of the exchanges and regulations in European networks for dealing with 'horizontal' questions, such as environmental degradation and organized crime. The Union projects its 'internal' functional approach to security 'externally' in a system with no clear apex or centre.[56] The blurring of the internal/external security division is expected for the EU itself (not only between the member states) as a consequence of the extended co-operation with new candidate and neighbouring states beyond the new circle of members.[57] The European Neighbourhood Policy launched in May 2004 is a good illustration of how the EU operates in this vein to build relationships and project stability in its vicinity.[58]

On the other hand, failures and problems for enlargement would challenge the Union's identity as a model for regional co-operation. In the light of the preceding section, it seems as if actor capacity will be bolstered due to increased resources and greater weight in multilateralism and international organizations. In the European Security Strategy adopted in December 2003, Javier Solana put the total number of foreign affairs professionals working for the then 15 member states at 45,000.[59] To the degree that the world's largest 'army' of diplomats can be mobilized for a particular purpose, the Union is indeed a traditional world actor, since mid-2004 gathering 25 states behind its negotiation and bargaining positions. Add to that, EU Commission delegations in 125 countries. In this dimension, the Union has an awesome capacity – agency – to move issues. Moreover, it provides a powerful platform for common or co-ordinated actions of an increasing number of member states *vis-à-vis* other actors.

Will the Union then be able to speak with one voice and act cohesively in the world through a 'single machinery'?[60] Clearly it will not be able to do so on every issue, or all the time. According to many observers, there has until now been too much of a focus on the actor side – and its shortcomings – shadowing the Union's long-term stability promotion through the creation of international networks. The expectations have been based on a conception that the EU would develop traditional foreign and security policy aims and instruments: it was expected to become a nation-state on a larger scale.

Perhaps a more pertinent question is whether one of the two dimensions of the Union – actor or structure – will become more important than the other in an enlarged Union and an increasingly globalized world. The Union will presumably continue to promote the two as complementary tracks. Can the Union, though, explain to other international actors and to public opinion what it does at both levels, and to the US and Russia in particular? Here, the serious image problem of the Union may become greater due to enlargement and weakened cohesiveness. At least for the purposes of political symbolism, larger organizations tend to demand a stronger centre.

Recent research suggests, however, that a 'Europe of several layers' is developing and that it generates a new type of international relations where the EU is involved. At the 'lower' level, there is a Union that conducts networking activities on a global scale (related to trade, co-operation and governance structures). At a 'higher' level, this work is supplemented by common (foreign) policies, bilateral relations between EU member states and non-governmental external relations. If sufficiently influential, 'EU visionaries' feel, this multi-layered external identity might be promoting a paradigmatic shift in international relations, towards a situation in which the balance of power logic between autonomous units will be downplayed.[61]

The challenge of cohesiveness

With regard to the CFSP, the second enlargement (Spain and Portugal) complicated the EC's discussions on Eastern Mediterranean issues, given Turkey's membership aspirations. The fourth enlargement meant a new emphasis on crisis management and conflict prevention – the Petersberg tasks – in the CFSP, introduced by new non-aligned member states (Austria, Finland and Sweden). This brought about a new focus for the security policy of the EU: from defence matters to crisis management. Between 1998 and 2001 the institutions of the CFSP evolved at a rapid pace, further leading to the establishment of the ESDP, military and civilian crisis management capabilities, and a conflict prevention policy (on the military dimension see Chapter 3 of this volume).[62] So far the increase in the number of members has not, defying many predictions, resulted in EU bodies becoming bogged down in endless discussions and inefficiency. In fact, the early experience suggests that stricter rules for interventions are applied in order to allot representatives of all 25 member states a fair share of the total meeting time.[63]

This does not mean that there are not substantial forces of divergence at work. The failure to ratify the Draft Constitution in 2005 also implied a missed chance to establish the post of a Foreign Minister for Europe. This will most probably have negative repercussions on the cohesiveness of Union foreign and security policy, not least on the intra-institutional relations between the member state-oriented Council and the supranational European Commission. Moreover, it has been suggested above that most CEE governments are more concerned with military instruments and collective defence than were the EU15.

In order to depict the emerging security identity more clearly, it is nevertheless important to link such policy preferences to the overall constitutional developments of the Union. The possibility of including a mutual defence clause in the Treaty has repeatedly been discussed in the EU. However, it was never realized due to strong resistance from many member states. The enlargement has now inserted a new dynamic into this matter. The focus on strong conditionality of a possible mutual defence clause in the 2003–2004 discussions on a new Constitution may have begun to shift the debate in a new direction. The CEE members, first and foremost firmly committed to NATO's Article 5 security guarantees, would be in a position to change the balance in favour of so-called flexible integration and unconditional mutual defence obligations among a subset of members. They are unlikely to do so by engendering consensus on autonomous EU defence, but rather by restating the negative argument for flexibility: we can't wait for all 25'.

This development could already be seen in the drafting of a 'structured co-operation' Article during the elaboration of a new Treaty in 2003–4. The aim of this Article was to provide for a framework for those member states that are both willing and able to participate in more demanding military capability co-operation. Here the EMU is the model, with its convergence criteria for membership (i.e. with corresponding requirements for military equipment and crisis management readiness) which have to be fulfilled by the member states wanting to participate. The model generates pressure on all states to strengthen their military crisis management capacity and to create a better trustworthiness and efficiency for Petersberg missions (peace enforcement, peace-keeping, crisis management). The underlying rationale is an implicit expectation that member states will increase spending on new military equipment (satellites, combat aircraft, aircraft carriers) and an improved division of labour between the member states based on their comparative advantages regarding the production of needed material. The overall aim is a genuinely European crisis management capability.

A possible structured co-operation on defence capabilities in the future could be seen as 'back-door' erosion of national autonomy. No country wants to be denied participation in any future operation in which it might want to participate. The new form of co-operation will compel member states to fulfil the EU capacity criteria in order to retain their freedom of manoeuvre for possible participation in future EU missions. The CEE states will ask themselves to what extent they want to allocate resources to both NATO's rapid reaction forces and the EU's military crisis management, including structured co-operation. It requires little imagination to forecast that this new form of flexible integration may also, in the medium term, precipitate new divisions among the EU member states.

Thus, the new trends in the area of defence could potentially weaken cohesiveness and lead to differentiation and possibly even rifts among the member states. One can discuss whether this is a natural development or something prompted by an enlarged Union of 25 to 30 member states. What seems clear is that the issue of flexible integration in EU defence matters will always trigger debate among the member states. EU25 will probably be as sceptical about the idea as EU15. The question is whether strong division over the issue will add another dynamic to a larger circle of members with a variety of security traditions and preferences. The UK and non-aligned EU member states will always have difficulties with differentiation in this area, as they see no need for flexibility clauses. Other states want to see a more autonomous European defence and military crisis management power on the world scene.

However, there are also signs of counteracting developments in the area of security and defence, of significant forces of convergence. The Solidarity Clause – a political declaration adopted in the aftermath of the Madrid bombings in 2004 – could be a way forward to forge a sense of unity among 25 member states. Also, the clause indicates that the Union, due to its transnational character, is able to think about transboundary threats in a way that is difficult for nation-states. It states that the Union shall mobilize all the instruments at its disposal, including military resources, in order to: prevent terrorist threats; protect democratic institutions and civilians from terrorist attacks; on request, assist member states on their own territories in the event of a terrorist attack. To that end member states need to co-ordinate their actions in the Council. In turn, the Council will be assisted by the Political and Security Committee and by a new standing Committee on Internal Security. The European Council, finally, is tasked with regularly assessing the threats facing the Union. In that sense the Solidarity Clause has the potential of bridging the two main views on EU defence: collective defence, on the one hand, and crisis management and security through networks on the other.

Geopolitical object/subject

Many observers estimate that the eastwards enlargement will pose formidable problems for EU actorness, since there lies a crucial difference between the fifth and previous enlargements in the *number* of candidates. We question the logic behind the reasoning about the importance of the number of actors, and possible dilution of integration, by dividing up the actorness concept into capacity and cohesiveness. Thus, we should now be able to make distinctions on the basis of the dichotomy with regard to the impact of numbers. Do, for example, numbers matter in the global networks of primarily economic co-operation between poles/regions, as envisaged by some? Maybe on the contrary: the extension of the European 'pole' of the global network into Eastern and Central Europe, which also radiates into Russia, can be advantageous for the EU's external role. It will bind the continent together into a web of contacts, exchange and common rules.

It is more difficult to discuss the possible problems of numbers when focusing on the cohesiveness of the EU as an actor *vis-à-vis* other global players, including the triangular constellation explored in this volume. Here it may be fruitful to try and understand the *net effect* in terms of centrifugal forces, affecting the cohesiveness in a negative way, whereas others are centripetal forces, working to promote common external policies. Strömvik believes that the net effect of enlargements is determined by, among other things, the 'shadow of enlargement' and 'size adjustment'. The fear of a greater difficulty in reaching decisions after enlargement would then have persuaded old member state governments to finally decide on matters that without the 'shadow of enlargement' were nearly impossible to solve, such as institutional reform (as illustrated by the Draft Constitution provisionally adopted in June 2004 but not accepted by French and Dutch voters). There have actually been steps towards developing the procedural framework for the EPC/CFSP in connection with each enlargement.[64]

An alternative way of approaching the problem of cohesiveness is to follow Rittberger and Zelli in framing it as a principal–agent relationship.[65] The entire integration project can be couched in the principal–agent theory by highlighting the role of the Commission as an agent, mandated and acting on behalf of member state governments and legislatures, in executing jointly decided policies. In the field of foreign and security policy, however, this analogy has become more relevant as a result of the opportunities provided by current treaties to charge the CFSP High Representative with important tasks on a case-by-case basis, as well as by the (still unexploited) possibilities of applying qualified majority voting. Given the political will of principals, the shrewdness of the High Representative, and a big enough crisis or threat to European interests, it is no longer so difficult to imagine a situation in which EU bodies are granted a robust mandate to resolve a specific problem. With 25 member states instead of 15, arguably, this prospect may in fact appear closer at hand.

As mentioned, the EU has most effectively responded to its boundary area not as a traditional foreign policy actor, but by extending its internal structure ('network governance') and integrating external actors and resources into the policy-making processes.[66] In other words, it has done so by projecting the Union's 'internal' methods of crisis and conflict prevention externally. Thus, one of the tasks of the new actor capabilities of the Union is to manage crisis and conflict in an area where it is already functioning as a transboundary network. The EU aims at being a better-equipped foreign policy (external) actor in the same boundary realm as it increasingly constitutes a domestic (internal) European structure. The forthcoming enlargements of the Union only serve to underline the complex EU security role in a boundary realm 'moving' eastward.[67]

One implication of this is that numbers may matter less than commonly expected when considering our definition of actorness. Thus, EU enlargement is perhaps rather a question of 'the more the merrier' than 'wider but weaker'. If economic co-operation is the main feature of the EU's external relations, enlargement is likely to strengthen the position and influence of the CFSP as well. The problem remains that the lack of strong political leadership may even be aggravated in a more diversified union. Will the enlarged EU develop into an international actor able to make *strategic* choices, for example *vis-à-vis* Russia? Will it be an actor with political autonomy reflecting at least part of the aggregate capacity that EU member states possess individually? That is, is the EU able to begin to change from a geo-political object or presence on the international scene, to a subject?[68]

As a civil world power and defence union, the EU will perhaps not contribute to a multipolar world. Instead, a theoretical possibility is that the Union's successful internal dissolution of a geopolitically oriented foreign policy, and of balance of power behaviour between member states, will be transposed into the international environment of its extensive relations. Like European foreign policy in general, EU defence might be set up according to a functional approach. Its focus will continue to be 'horizontal' questions, such as environmental degradation, human rights, and international terrorism and information warfare. The Union can in this context be described as an innovative 'platform' for international co-operation, a 'network' and a 'democratic space'. This is demonstrated by the fact that it is strongest within, and on, its own frontiers. The Union's enlargement policy may in this respect be its optimal external strategy.

The EU may therefore not need not to resolve the tension between Network Europe and *'l'Europe Puissance'*. Instead it should try to exploit the duality to a maximum. In this way the Union may contribute to a redefinition of the global security landscape. The new outlook goes beyond the traditional nation-state's way of assessing the global security challenges and can be conceived as a truly European 'post-nation-state' outlook. Given this admittedly ambitious objective, one of the EU's primary tasks would be to comprehensively understand and explain – to public opinion and its partners in the world – the innovative value and inherent potential of this duality. In other words, EU institutions would be shaped so as to reframe globalization from being perceived as a threat to looking at it as a structured, regulated network based on multilateral organizations with the Union itself as one possible model.

Four scenarios

The fear that actorness would be undermined by eastwards enlargement seems exaggerated. The overall capacity of the EU will grow even though many of the individual capabilities are not substantially enhanced. This is not well understood by political scientists, but perhaps better by decision-makers. In a poll taken at the Davos summit in 2004, only 4.7 per cent of the participants believed the latest EU enlargement would weaken the influence of the Union in the world; 69.8 per cent of the participants responded that it would be strengthened.[69] Cohesiveness is clearly the major challenge, but it remains to be seen to what degree political differentiation will represent an actual impediment to the Union's political autonomy. For instance, it is striking how extraordinarily few exceptions were made by the new entrants when they acceded to the CFSP *acquis* and policy positions.

The level of cohesiveness may very well depend on what concrete issues the Union is confronted with over the next few years. Politically, it would appear that two aspects are likely to have overarching significance. First, will the EU face serious security threats which require military responses? Second, will the US be intimately engaged in the most important external relations challenges of the EU?

Regardless of all other circumstances, the persistence of the *status quo* appears unrealistic. Considering the huge aggregate capacity amassed by the enlarged Union, the 'capabilities–expectations gap' has grown accordingly. The expectations of the new members are not necessarily oriented in a particular direction, or focused on a specific set of issues, but the historical opportunity of 'returning to Europe' implies that people inevitably pin hopes on European institutions. Not applying the capabilities at the disposal of each member of this group of states, at least in part forged as a value community, would sooner or later undermine the EU as a political project. Therefore, with regard to EU actorness and its implications on the strategic triangle discussed in this volume, four different scenarios appear feasible.

The first scenario can be termed *modest Europe*. The EU and its external relations objectives revert back to a situation similar to that before the Balkan wars of the 1990s. The Union scales back ambitions to shape the global agenda in the fields of trade, environment, health and others. It is induced by the new member states, as well as by the threat of mass terrorism, to work with a narrower conception of security and to reaffirm bilateral ties to the US. Most probably, Europe revitalizes the transatlantic link, but this also allows for a partial 'renationalization' of the ESDP and the CFSP. Traditional geopolitical thinking may linger and negatively affect ties with Russia, though global trends in economic relations and technology will not permit international relations in Europe or elsewhere to shift back to the forms of the twentieth century. The Union remains, above all, the world's largest marketplace.

The second scenario may be labelled *assertive Europe*. The EU develops security and defence capabilities and, in parallel, the decision-making structures and procedures which allow them to be used. Put differently, the Union forges interrelated foreign, security and defence policies for EU25 (plus). It increases its activities in a number of global policy fields and reinforces its reputation as a powerful promoter of international justice, prosperity, welfare and human rights. In the realm of security, the Union continues to operate with a broad understanding of security, but this notion is supplemented by development of a substantial military capability. Building on the aggregate capacity which in several policy areas and in crisis situations can be mobilized for common actions, the EU for the most part continues to be supportive of US strategy. Yet as Washington is turning its attention towards Asia, the EU is, in its own proximity, sometimes also able to more or less offset the influence of the world's remaining superpower. The latter is a development which Russia, under its present leadership, is likely to embrace.

The third scenario is called *ambivalent Europe*. It entails a Union which has developed a range of external relations capabilities, including military instruments, as well as the relevant decision-making procedures, but remains deeply divided about how and when to apply them. It has gone along part of the path outlined in the assertive Europe scenario, but stopped short of reaching consensus on the policy implications. The result is a vacillating Europe which has problems finding a workable equilibrium. One outcome may be to stick primarily with the Union's considerable 'soft power' instruments, but with the danger of several of the larger countries temporarily breaking off collaboration to launch their own missions. Either the Union's formal unity retains priority for all and 'ambivalent Europe' is more or less entrenched, or a smaller number of activist, transatlanticist or 'you-have-to-crack-eggs-to-make-an-omelette-minded' member states will eventually forge a federation – a United States of Europe. European ambivalence would then have been institutionalized. Meanwhile, the US, Russia and other international actors will have to live with the unpredictability of EU policy-making.

The fourth scenario can, for lack of a better term, be entitled *New Atlas Europe*. As in the vision of Prime Minister Juncker, the Union invents a new set of instruments and approaches altogether, drawing on its unique experience and character. 'New Atlas Europe' no doubt envisages a high profile in most realms of global governance and norm-setting. It includes a focus or 'specialization' of EU security policy on stability-projection, echoing the first point of the 2003 strategy document developed by Solana's team. Whereas stability-projection has a clear geographical element, the Union will go on working to pull out the rug from beneath traditional security conflicts over military capabilities, territories and borders, ethnic tensions and so forth, by manipulating political and economic incentive structures. It will also try and do so at an early stage, by preventive action, instead of putting out the fire afterwards. Since there is no historical precedent of such actorness, it is exceedingly difficult to predict the repercussions of this scenario on the other key entities in world politics. Suffice it to say that New Atlas Europe will have to create its own, novel diplomacy to go with its innovative external relations approach.

At this point we leave the reader to consider the feasibility of the four scenarios. Throughout the investigation, we have tried to suppress biases, except in one limited respect. In developing the four dimensions above, a theoretical goal of ours has admittedly been to explore the feasibility of the fourth path. This does not mean that we believe it more likely than the others; actually, rather the contrary. But in case 'New Atlas Europe' should have any relevance beyond rhetoric, it will need to be developed at the conceptual and political levels. What kind of actorness is envisaged by advocates of a stronger EU presence on the international stage? Given that several members are wary of the Union becoming a nation-state on a grand scale, what does their vision really look like?

It may seem unsatisfactory to end the analysis with another set of questions, although this is unavoidable. The EU is arguably the world's biggest 'work-in-progress', today just as in the past decades. Given the tremendous weight of some of its policies and its still unexploited aggregate capacity, the Union must sooner or later come to grips with the growing role it is playing in its own neighbourhood as well as in the world at large.

Notes

1 C. Hill, 'The Capability-Expectations Gap, or Conceptualising Europe's International Role', *Journal of Common Market Studies*, 1993, vol. 31, pp. 305–28.
2 M.E. Smith, *Europe's Foreign and Security Policy: The Institutionalization of Cooperation*, Cambridge: Cambridge University Press, 2004, pp. 176–206; and K. Hughes, 'European Foreign Policy under Pressure', *The Brown Journal of World Affairs*, 2003, vol. IX, issue 2, p. 127.
3 U.S. Department of State, 'Performance and Accountability Highlights Fiscal Year 2004', online.
4 M.E. Smith, *Europe's Foreign and Security Policy*, pp. 214–20.
5 J. Zielonka, 'Challenges of EU Enlargement', *Journal of Democracy*, 2004, vol. 15, pp. 26, 31.
6 U. Diedrichs and W. Wessels, 'Die erweiterte EU als internationaler Akteur', *Internationale Politik*, 2003, vol. 58, no. 1, pp. 11–18.
7 P. Luif, 'EU Cohesion in the UN General Assembly', *Occasional Paper*, no. 49, Paris: European Union Institute for Security Studies, 2003.
8 B. White, *Understanding European Foreign Policy*, Basingstoke: Palgrave, 2001.
9 V. Rittberger and F. Zelli, 'Europa in der Weltpolitik: Juniorpartner der USA oder antihegemoniale Alternative?', *Tübinger Arbeitspapiere zur Internationale Politik und Friedensforschung*, 2003, no. 41, Eberhard-Karls-Universität Tübingen.
10 W. Carlsnaes, H. Sjursen and B. White (eds), *Contemporary European Foreign Policy*, London: Sage, 2004.
11 K. Goldmann and G. Sjöstedt (eds), *Power, Capabilities, Interdependence: Problems in the Study of International Influence*, London: Sage, 1979; K. N. Waltz, *Theory of International Politics*, Reading, MA: Addison Wesley, 1979, p. 98; and Hill, 'The Capability–Expectations Gap, or Conceptualising Europe's International Role'.
12 Stratfor, *Annual Forecast: When Other Things Start to Matter – Part II*, 17 January 2005; C. Hill, 'Renationalizing or Regrouping? EU Foreign Policy since 11 September 2001', *Journal of Common Market Studies*, 2004, vol. 42, pp. 138–60, and K.E. Smith, 'The European Union: A Distinctive Actor in International Relations', *Brown Journal of World Affairs*, 2003, vol. IX, issue 2, pp. 103–13.
13 C. Preston, *Enlargement and Integration in the European Union*, London: Routledge, 1997, pp. 157–74.
14 'Beyond Enlargement: Commission Shifts European Neighbourhood Policy into Higher Gear', IP/04/632, Brussels, 12 May 2004.

15 'Towards a Wider Europe: The New Agenda', Bratislava document adopted by the prime ministers of Albania, Bulgaria, Croatia, Estonia, Latvia, Lithuania, Macedonia, Romania and Slovakia, 19 March 2004.

16 R.B.J. Walker, 'Europe Is Not Where It Is Supposed To Be', in M. Kelstrup and M.C. Williams (eds) *International Relations and the Politics of European Integration – Power, Security and Community*, London: Routledge, 2000; N. Rengger, *International Relations, Political Theory, and the Problem of Order beyond International Relations Theory?* London: Routledge, 2000.

17 C. Bretherton and J. Vogler, *The European Union as a Global Actor*, London: Routledge, 1999.

18 O. Wæver, 'The EU as a Security Actor: Reflections from a Pessimistic Constructivist on Post-Sovereign Security Orders', in M. Kelstrup and M.C. Williams (eds) *International Relations Theory and the Politics of European Integration: Power, Security and Community*. London: Routledge, 2000, p. 260.

19 W. Wallace, *The Dynamics of European Integration*, London and New York: Pinter Publishers, 1990; and K. Deutsch et al., *Political Community and the North Atlantic Area*, Princeton, NJ: Princeton University Press, 1957.

20 C. Rhodes, *The European Union in the World Community*, London: Lynne Rienner Publishers, 1998; and C. Piening, *Global Europe: The European Union in World Affairs*, Boulder, CO: Lynne Rienner, 1997.

21 B. Sundelius, 'Functional Security', in M. Ekengren (ed.) *Functional Security – A Forward Looking Approach to European and Nordic Security and Defence Policy*, Proceedings of the Conference held at the Swedish National Defence College, 5–6 December 2003, Stockholm: Swedish National Defence College, ACTA B30, 2004; and S. Myrdal (ed.) *EU som civil krishanterare*, Stockholm: Utrikespolitiska institutet/ Säkerhetspolitiska rådet, 2002.

22 A. Dalgaard-Nielsen and K. Søby Kristensen, *Catalogue of Ideas. Homeland Security – Bridging the Transatlantic Gap*, Report of the Conference, 19–21 September 2003, Copenhagen, Danish Institute for International Studies (DIIS).

23 D. Bigo, 'When Two Become One – Internal and External Securitisations in Europe', in M. Kelstrup and M.C. Williams (eds) *International Relations and the Politics of European Integration – Power, Security and Community*, London: Routledge, 2000, pp. 171–204; and D. Bigo, 'The Möbius Ribbon of Internal and External Security(ies)', in M. Albert, D. Jacobson and Y. Lapid (eds) *Identities, Borders, Orders – Rethinking International Relations Theory*, Minneapolis, MN: University of Minnesota Press, 2001, pp. 91–136.

24 Note pour le Haut Representant, Strategie de securité de l'Union européenne. Compte rendu du séminaire sur les menaces 'Identifying and understanding threats', Rome, 19 September 2003, Institute for Security Studies, 23 September 2003.

25 M. Ekengren, 'The Interface of External and Internal Security in the EU and in the Nordic Policies', in A. Bailes, G. Herolt and B. Sundelius (eds) *The Nordic Countries and the European Security Defence Policy*, Oxford: Oxford University Press, 2006.

26 M. Albert, D. Jacobson and Y. Lapid, *Identities, Borders, Orders – Rethinking International Relations Theory*, Minneapolis, MN: University of Minnesota Press, 2001; and M. Singer and A. Wildawsky, *The Real World Order: Zones of Peace/Zones of Turmoil*, Chatham: Chatham House, 1993.

27 B. Hettne, A. Inotai and O. Sunkel, *Comparing Regionalisms: Implications for Global Development*, Basingstoke, Palgrave/Macmillan, 2001.

28 J. Delors, 'A la recherche du miracle', speech at L'Académie des sciences morales et politiques, Paris, 7 January 2004, online.

29 W. Carlsnaes, 'Introduction', in W. Carlsnaes, H. Sjursen and B. White (eds), *Contemporary European Foreign Policy*, London: Sage, 2004; and M. Ekengren,

'National Foreign Policy Co-ordination: The Swedish EU Presidency', in H. Sjursen, W. Carlsnaes and B. White (eds) *Contemporary European Foreign Policy*, London: Sage, 2004.

30 Two good examples of this EU thinking are: 'A Secure Europe in a Better World – The European Security Strategy', approved by the European Council in Brussels on 12 December and adopted in December 2003, online; and the Commission proposals to establish the 'European Neighbourhood Policy', ENP (formerly called 'Wider Europe') (Commission of the European Communities, *Communication from the Commission – Paving the Way for a New Neighbourhood Instrument*, Brussels, 1 July 2003, COM (2003) 393 final).

31 B. Giegerich and W. Wallace, 'Not Such a Soft Power: The External Deployment of European Forces', *Survival*, 2004, vol. 46.

32 I. Manners, 'Normative Power Europe: A Contradiction in Terms?', *Journal of Common Market Studies*, 2002, vol. 40; and R.G. Whitman, *From Civilian Power to Superpower? The International Identity of the European Union*, Basingstoke: Macmillan, 1998.

33 R. Cooper, *The Breaking of Nations: Order and Chaos in the Twenty-First Century*, London: Atlantic, 2003; and T. Diez, *The European Union and the Cyprus Conflict – Modern Conflict, Postmodern Union*, Manchester: Manchester University Press, 2002.

34 L. Tsoukalis, *The European Economy Revisited*, Oxford: Oxford University Press, 1997.

35 O. Wæver, 'The EU as a Security Actor: Reflections from a Pessimistic Constructivist on Post-Sovereign Security Orders', in M. Kelstrup and M.C. Williams (eds) *International Relations Theory and the Politics of European Integration: Power, Security and Community*, London: Routledge, 2000, pp. 258–65.

36 J.-C. Juncker, 'Nous agissons comme si nous réformions le Code de la route alors que nous devons inventer un nouvel atlas', *Les Echos*, 19 September 2000.

37 R. Gilpin, *Global Political Economy – Understanding the International Economic Order*, Princeton, NJ and Oxford: Princeton University Press, 2001.

38 Tsoukalis, *The European Economy Revisited*.

39 Gilpin, *Global Political Economy*.

40 T. Kreyenbühl, 'Ostmitteleuropas Bauern in Erwartung des EU-Shocks', *Neue Zürcher Zeitung*, 7/8 February 2004.

41 T. Kreyenbühl, 'Die Osterweiterung ist ein voller Erfolg', *Neue Zürcher Zeitung*, 8 March 2005.

42 A. Missiroli (ed.) 'Bigger EU, Wider CFSP, Stronger ESDP? The View from Central Europe', *Occasional Paper*, no. 34, Paris: European Union Institute for Security Studies, April 2002.

43 Authors' interview with an anonymous national civil servant and member of the Political and Security Committee of the Union, 21 September 2004.

44 Missiroli, 'Bigger EU', p. 21.

45 Warsaw surprised Western European governments by its relentless negotiating stance, refusing to relinquish the voting rights compromise struck at the Nice European Council in December 1999. In contrast, almost all existing EU members regarded the Nice agreement as a temporary, suboptimal deal.

46 S. Kalniete, 'Latvia's Foreign Policy at the Crossroads', speech by Latvia's Minister of Foreign Affairs, Sandra Kalniete, at the 62nd Scientific Conference, University of Latvia, 27 January 2004.

47 J. Zielonka, 'Challenges of EU Enlargement', *Journal of Democracy*, 2004, vol. 15, p. 26.

48 P. Kopecký and C. Mudde, *Uncivil Society? Contentious Politics in Post-Communist Europe*, London: Routledge, 2003; and G. Schopflin, *Nations, Identity, Power*, London: C. Hurst & Co, 2000.

49 K. Engelbrekt, 'Multiple Asymmetries: The European Union's Neo-Byzantine Approach to Eastern Enlargement', *International Politics*, 2002, vol. 39.
50 *The Economist*, 29 May 2004.
51 R. Höltschi, 'Die EU-Erweiterung weckt russische Sorgen', *Neue Zürcher Zeitung*, 6 February 2004.
52 For further assessments of 'organizations, providers and research involved in the effort to understand and deal with climate change' see the Kyoto Protocol, online.
53 On the institutionalization of EU policy in this field, see A. Weale et al., *Environmental Governance in Europe*, Oxford: Oxford University Press, 2000.
54 EU Background Paper, 'Breaking the Barriers', Ministerial Conference, Dublin, 23–24 February 2004.
55 International Organization for Migration (IOM), 'EU Enlargement Will Pose Migration Challenge in Accession States', news release, 30 April 2004, no. 868.
56 A. von Bogdandy, 'The Contours of Integrated Europe', *Futures*, 1993, vol. 25, no. 1, 22–7.
57 L. Friis and A. Murphy, 'The European Union and Central and Eastern Europe: Governance and Boundaries', *Journal of Common Market Studies*, 1999, vol. 37, issue 2, 211–32.
58 T. Bleichelt, 'The Impact of the Eastern Enlargement on the Common Foreign and Security Policy of the Union', paper presented at the Annual Convention of the International Studies Association, Honolulu, USA, 1–5 March 2005.
59 'A Secure Europe in a Better World – The European Security Strategy'.
60 C. Hill, 'Closing the Capabilities–Expectations Gap?', in J. Peterson and H. Sjursen (eds) *A Common Foreign Policy for Europe? Competing Visions of the CFSP*, London: Routledge, 1998, pp. 40–1.
61 R. Cooper, *The Breaking of Nations*; J. Nye, *Soft Power: The Means to Success in World Politics*, New York: Public Affairs, 2004.
62 Smith, *Europe's Foreign and Security Policy*, pp. 176–206.
63 Authors' interview with national civil servant.
64 M. Strömvik, 'Fifteen Votes and One Voice? The CFSP and Changing Voting Alignments in the UN', *Statsvetenskaplig Tidsskrift*, 1998, vol. 101, no. 2, pp. 181–97.
65 Rittberger and Zelli, 'Europa in der Weltpolitik: Juniorpartner der USA oder antihegemoniale Alternative?'
66 M.S. Filtenborg, S. Gänzle and E. Johansson, 'An Alternative Theoretical Approach to EU Foreign Policy – Network Governance and the Case of the Northern Dimension Initiative', *Cooperation and Conflict*, 2002, vol. 37.
67 M. Ekengren, 'The Interface of External and Internal Security in the EU and in the Nordic Policies'.
68 G. Sjöstedt, *The External Role of the European Community*, Westmead: Saxon House, 1977.
69 D. Rienstra and P. Hulm, 'New EU Countries Expand Market Horizons', *International Trade Forum*, 2004, issue 1, online.

3

THE BUILDING OF A MILITARY CAPABILITY IN THE EUROPEAN UNION

Some internal and external implications

Arita Eriksson

Introduction

One of the main questions for the assessment of the usefulness of a strategic triangle as an analytical concept for understanding security relationships in the transatlantic area concerns the role of the European Union. The aim of this chapter is to provide some insights for understanding the role of the EU, in particular concerning the development of its military capability. In order to do this, we first need to investigate how member states within the EU view this process and what role it plays in the national context. Only with an understanding of the internal significance of the EU in this area may we assess its external importance.

The development of the European Security and Defence Policy (ESDP) has made the EU an actor with a military capability. Thus, the EU may be said to have reached a higher level of actorness.[1] The purpose here is to give an empirical overview of key aspects of the process within the EU and to discuss some internal and external implications of it. For the assessment of internal implications, Sweden will be used as an illustrative example. The process, which will be analysed in terms of Europeanization, focuses on the period 1999–2004.[2]

Since the decisions in Helsinki in 1999 the developments have been remarkable.[3] What in the beginning of the 1990s was only a vision in the Maastricht Treaty has, since Helsinki, been filled with more and more substantial policy, structure and common action in the form of military operations. It may therefore be argued that a process of Europeanization is taking place within the area of security and defence policy.[4] The extent of and the pace at which this development has taken place is perhaps unique in the history of European integration.

The Europeanization perspective is used here in order to analyse the ESDP process and its consequences. Traditionally, security and defence have been policy areas dealt with mainly within (national) public policy or international relations.

With security and defence policy brought into the European Union, new theoretical and analytical perspectives may become applicable for studying this policy area. The Europeanization perspective is one such perspective.[5] In particular, Europeanization allows a focus upon the embeddedness of the member state, and an analysis of the 'internal' consequences of the ESDP, that is, within the European Union and within member states. The analysis of external consequences is usually not part of the research on Europeanization,[6] though this process may have important external effects. External consequences will here be elaborated upon on the basis of the results of the analysis of the Europeanization process and its internal significance.

Many different definitions of Europeanization exist in the literature of this area. The focus might lie either on the effects on domestic structures and polices, and/or on the effects on the European process that has been developed.[7] Within the area of security and defence Europeanization is (or at least was up until 2004) at a stage with few formal demands and where co-ordination, harmonization and adaptation may take place informally and without evident governance from the European level. EU member states are themselves taking part in developing a policy process: it is not something that is imposed upon them from 'above'. Therefore, a Europeanization process is here viewed as a constant, dynamic interaction between these levels, which implies an embeddedness that has different types of effects on the state.[8] The content and form of the interaction in a Europeanized policy process is seen as an empirical question.

The literature considers the following domains of Europeanization:[9] domestic structures (political structures and structures of representation and cleavages), public policy and cognitive and normative structures. Three means by which transformation is driven are identified by Radaelli. First, the existence of a 'European model' may be understood as positive integration, which may spur change through coercion or mimetism by its adaptational pressure. Second, negative integration occurs when no model exists but change is driven by regulatory competition or domestic opportunity structures. Finally, framing mechanisms may be at work in the form of 'minimalist' directives, which confer legitimacy on change, by convergence around policy paradigms and, if the balance of power does not exist, through an understanding of governance.[10]

In this chapter it is not possible to go into detail on the claims by the literature on Europeanization presented above. However, some of the domains of Europeanization in the area of security and defence will be described together with an attempt at identifying the mechanisms present in the process. Indications of effects upon member states are also made.

The content of the Helsinki decisions

The decision in Cologne (summer 1999) to develop a European crisis management force was developed further in Helsinki on 10–11 December 1999. The European Council in Helsinki took on the task of creating a crisis management force in a comprehensive manner, providing political direction on aims and capabilities, the institutional framework to be established and general guidelines for further work. The tasks of defining and implementing this decision would prove to be great and it took several years before the EU's crisis management capability could finally be declared (more or less) fully operational in May 2003.[11]

Concerning military capabilities for the Petersberg tasks,[12] it was decided that the EU member states should work towards being able, by 2003, to put together (on a voluntary basis) an EU-led military self-sustaining force consisting of 50–60,000 men. The force should be able to deploy within 60 days' notice and be capable of functioning for at least one year. This political goal constitutes what would be called the Helsinki Headline Goal (HHG). Besides the HHG, it was also decided in Helsinki to develop collective capability goals, for example strategic airlift. The HHG has constituted a basis for further work within the ESDP since its adoption up until 2003, and most policies within the policy area are more or less connected to the defining and implementation of it. It was in the summer of 2004 followed by a second one, Headline Goal 2010 (discussed below).

The EU's new ambitions in this area required an autonomous decision-making capacity. Appropriate political and military structures needed to be set up within the EU system. Therefore, it was decided that permanent political and military bodies should be established within the Council structures; a standing Political and Security Committee (PSC), a European Union Military Committee (EUMC), and a European Union Military Staff (EUMS). For several years, the newly formed actors were occupied with the task of developing the structures and procedures necessary for an autonomous EU decision-making capacity in this field.

The development of military capabilities

The implementation of the Headline Goal started soon after the Helsinki decision. The Headline Task Force (HTF),[13] supported by the interim military body (future EUMC), produced a document outlining the military strengths necessary in relation to crisis management scenarios. This document, indicating the overall capability needs, was presented in the late autumn of 2000. Next, a Capabilities Commitment Conference was held, where member states committed national military resources to the EU – capabilities that were collected in a force catalogue. At this time over 100,000 soldiers, 400 combat aircraft and 100 vessels were listed. However, it seemed that the EU would be in need of more qualitative assets such as strategic intelligence, strategic air and naval transport capabilities.[14] As a starting point, a progress catalogue was created and work on developing capacities was initiated. A Capabilities Improvement Conference was held in November 2001.

The issue of how to deal with the problems concerning capabilities was difficult. The need for an evaluation mechanism was discussed but no agreement was found. It would take almost a year until concrete work on dealing with the shortfalls was initiated – within the framework of the European Capability Action Plan (ECAP). The principles of this plan were:

- Enhanced effectiveness and efficiency of European military capability efforts;
- A 'bottom-up' approach to European defence cooperation;
- Coordination between EU member states and cooperation with NATO;
- Importance of broad public support.[15]

In the beginning of 2002, the ECAP started its work within the framework of the HTF in order to provide a more organized framework for dealing with capability shortfalls from a military expert viewpoint. All possible solutions were to be investigated, including, for example, the leasing of capabilities. Within ECAP, 19 panels were activated (as of December 2002), each dealing with one specific shortfall. The ECAP produced a report on the progress of its work, consisting of recommendations, by 1 March 2003. In NATO a process parallel to ECAP was also initiated, called the Prague Capabilities Commitment (PCC). The PCC builds on national commitments and is being handled in working groups. The shortfalls are to a large extent the same for the two organizations. Not until the spring of 2003 was an agreement finally reached on a capabilities development/evaluation mechanism within the EU. By then, the capabilities process had already been informally institutionalized. However, the Capabilities Development Mechanism (CDM) was important as it regulated the interrelationships between the actors in the process and also between the EU and NATO.[16]

The next phase of the ECAP concerned implementation of the solutions drawn up by the panels. To this end, ECAP project groups (PG) were started. Since spring of 2003, 15 ECAP project groups have been established.[17] Several ECAP project groups cooperated very closely with corresponding groups within NATO's PCC. Activities included, for example, the NBC PG which aimed at the creation of a multinational NBC battalion and the Strategic Air Lift PG which aimed at the creation, in 2005, of a multinationally coordinated air transport resource. A Memorandum of Understanding on this was signed in June 2004. Different types of EU Coordination Centres, for example regarding strategic sealift, were also discussed as well as a pool of experienced staff officers.[18] This shows that by 2004, the capabilities issue was moving not only from being a national problem to a European one, but from a problem with many separate national solutions to common European solutions. However, the ECAP project groups would not be able to deliver all shortfall capabilities, instead work had focused on qualitative aspects such as defining concepts, organizations and procedures. By 2004 some of the project groups were closed, as no further progress was considered possible.

The capabilities issue is closely connected to other policy areas, in particular the defence industrial area, in which economic and industrial interests, both national and European, are at stake. This related dimension seems, by 2003, to have become actively involved in the capabilities development process, although the first part of the ECAP did not involve the defence industry. The capabilities issue within the ESDP thus seems to have contributed to the spread of the armaments issue across policy areas within the EU, from the market field within the Commission where the defence industry policy area had been located so far, to the defence field of the

ESDP. The armaments and defence industry issue within the defence field has earlier been Europeanized primarily outside of the EU.[19]

Following the first phase of the capabilities issue within the EU, where the focus was set on harmonizing requirements and finding national or common solutions to current problems, actors within the process seemed to realize that forward-looking political decisions on the capabilities issue are important, considering the long timeframes in this area. In most cases it will take years before the capabilities decided upon today are operational. The capabilities issue also gives rise to more general strategic questions that need to be dealt with at the political level. Finding forms for the future development of capabilities was complicated. Something more needed to be done in order to achieve a common approach in this area. The idea of the creation of a European Defence Agency appeared at this moment, first within the context of the work of the European Convention, working on a future European Constitution. In July 2004 the European Council adopted a Joint Action on the establishment of the European Defence Agency.

The Agency is to deal with defence capabilities development, research, acquisition and armaments. Headed by Javier Solana, it will receive political guidance from the defence ministers of the Council and cooperate both with the Commission, defence industries and existing defence industrial structures in Europe. In the 2005 work programme, a number of areas are set up in which the Steering Board expects to see the Agency handle initiatives by the end of 2005, for example Unmanned Aerial Vehicles (UAVs) and Intelligence, Surveillance, Target Acquisition and Reconnaissance Equipment (ISTAR), advanced European jet pilot training, command control and communications, defence test and evaluation base rationalization and armoured fighting vehicles (initiatives already exist for some of these issues). The Agency should also look into possibilities for a role in areas such as the development of a future naval defence technological and industrial base, air-to-air refuelling and the A400M (a major project concerning strategic transport).[20] It remains to be seen what effect the Agency will have on the issues it is set to develop and how it will be able to incorporate or cooperate with existing structures in Europe. It also remains to be seen what effect the Agency will have on NATO. It could be assumed that from the point of member states, the importance of the EU as a capabilities development institution will grow. The question of a future common market in the area of defence equipment is also important in relation to this development.

The EU goes operational

In January 2003, the ESDP process entered its operational phase, which finally transformed the ESDP into a practical instrument of the CFSP. Joint action in military crisis management now made the EU an external actor in this sphere.[21] This phase began with a civilian police operation, the European Union Police Mission (EUPM) in Bosnia and Herzegovina. On 31 March 2003 the first EU military operation followed, Operation Concordia in the Former Yugoslav Republic of Macedonia (FYROM). The operation was taken over from NATO. Small, but symbolic, the operation in FYROM was followed by a more demanding military rapid reaction operation in the Democratic Republic of Congo (DRC) in June 2003 (until August 2003). In this operation, named Artemis, France acted as 'Framework Nation'. In this role, France provided the nucleus operational planning capacity and exercised military leadership under the political and strategic control of the EU. In June 2004, a rule of law mission was set up in Georgia. In December 2004 the EU took over the SFOR from NATO in Bosnia Herzegovina (named Operation Althea). This was the largest EU operation thus far, making the EU involved in the country with both civil and military means. Operation Althea makes use of NATO assets through the Berlin Plus arrangements and has eleven contributing third states. In December 2004 the EU launched a police mission in the DRC, and further initiatives were taken concerning the DRC in the spring of 2005.[22] Other possible missions include a takeover of KFOR in Kosovo and a joint EU/Russia mission to Moldova.[23] In the case of Kosovo the role and ability of the EU as a strategic actor in the transatlantic arena might really come to be tested, and in the case of Moldova the relationship with Russia will have to be substantially developed for the first time in relation to ESDP. With respect to Iraq, the European Council has agreed that the EU could contribute with an integrated police, rule of law and civilian administration mission.[24]

The EU's operational phase started out quite intensely with three rather different civil and military operations in only about six months. Following these initial operations there will be continuous evaluations and 'lessons learned' that will probably lead to a revision of structures and procedures. Indeed, there seems to be great pressure upon the EU to take on tasks in the field of civil and military crisis management. The EU has a particular role to play in the area where future member states are situated, in particular the Balkans. Here, its involvement is likely to intensify. The other area of interest for the EU is Africa. In December 2004 an action plan for ESDP support to peace and security in Africa was adopted, and involvement is likely to grow here as well.

It remains to be seen in each situation whether it will be possible to use the EU military capacity for substantive joint policy. So far, member states have been able to agree on the establishment of operations and have been willing to submit the forces and resources necessary. In the end, it is a question of national decisions although well-functioning ESDP structures may help in other ways. The Headline Goal 2010 (see below) indicates that a development has taken place as regards the view on which capabilities that are needed for EU crisis management as well as the conditions for deployment. The lessons learned from the initial operational phase have probably contributed to these conclusions. Some kind of informal flexibility system may develop among member states related to these kinds of operations, as some countries are more eager and capable to supply rapid reaction and planning capacity than others. The conduct of more EU operations may result in common understandings and experiences that in the long term may produce more European convergence across the spectrum of strategic levels.

A new phase

During the spring of 2004, the ESDP found itself in a transitional period, further developing structures, awaiting new initiatives in the area of ESDP and new member states. These important events together with developments in autumn 2003, for example the adoption of the EU Security Strategy,[25] indicate that the CFSP/ESDP is entering a new phase.

With the ESDP operational, there is a tendency for a shift in power from the member states to the Council Secretariat. The entering into an operational phase also suggests that more informal flexibility will be seen within the ESDP process. The development within the capabilities area and the enlargement strengthen this impression.

The adoption of the EU security strategy in December 2003 suggests the development within the ESDP not only consists of regulatory norms (that define standards of appropriate behaviour), but also of constitutive norms (that express identities and define interests and through these affect behaviour).[26]

Capability requirement goals changed during the spring of 2004. In the winter of 2003–4, the ESDP structures started working on the development of a new rapid response element, based on the so-called 'Battle Group' concept. A Battle Group is:

> a specific form of rapid response. It is the minimum military effective, credible, rapidly deployable, coherent force package capable of stand-alone operations, or for the initial phase of larger operations. The Battlegroup is based on a combined arms, battalion sized force and reinforced with Combat Support and Combat Service Support elements. A Battlegroup could be formed by a Framework Nation or by a multinational coalition of Member States. In all cases, interoperability and military effectiveness will be key criteria. A Battlegroup must be associated with a Force Headquarters and pre-identified operational and strategic enablers, such as strategic lift and logistics.
>
> (Military Capability Commitment Conference, Brussels, 22 November 2004, paragraph 9)

The Battle Group would become an important element of a new capability goal, the so-called Headline Goal 2010. Headline Goal 2010 emphasized qualitative aspects, compared to the Helsinki Headline Goal, which was very much focused on the quantitative dimension. The need for further elements of pooling and possibilities for the sharing of assets was also introduced.[27] It is stated in the Headline Goal 2010 outline that:

> This approach requires Member States to voluntarily transform their forces by progressively developing a high degree of interoperability, both at technical, procedural and conceptual levels. Without prejudice

to the prerogatives of Member States over defence matters, a co-ordinated and coherent development of equipment compatibility, procedures, concepts, command arrangements and defence planning is a primary objective. In this regard, commonality of security culture should also be promoted. Deployability, sustainability and other crucial requirements such as force availability, information superiority, engage-ment effectiveness and survivability will play an immediate pivotal role.

(European Council 2004a: B8)

With the new capability goals, a new phase of implementation starts all over again. This time the EDA will be engaged together with Council bodies. At the military capabilities commitment conference in November 2004, it was stated that the EU would have initial operational capability in 2005 and full capability in 2007. Member states indicated their commitment to form a total of 13 Battle Groups and several states announced that they would offer niche capabilities.[28]

Another aspect of this new phase is that the new Headline Goal also took a broader approach to EU crisis management tasks, involving, beyond the original Petersberg tasks, joint disarmament operations, the support for third countries in combating terrorism and security sector reform.[29] The European Security Strategy inspired the adoption of these tasks. The new rapid reaction forces for fast crisis management will function in parallel with the old requirements of the HHG and tasks such as post-conflict management.

The EU's transformation into a military power/actor in the wider transatlantic region and on the European and global scene has not been finalized. It could be argued that the EU is still very much in a process of change in this respect, and that the main development of the military dimension within the EU may not be seen for several years yet.

A process of Europeanization

As has been shown, a dynamic policy process has been firmly established at the European level. Member states take active part in an intense cooperation at different levels, involving different national actors and domestic structures. As the process started, it was goal- and policy-oriented. However, the initial political guidelines have been rather vague, as no substantial guiding document has existed. In principle, European Council conclusions and the Petersberg tasks have been the main guiding principles. Europeanization of policy gradually expanded and the need for further related policies due to the first one was identified. This dimension can therefore be said to have 'grown', increased in scope and been filled with more aspects of security and defence policy during the period 1999–2004. The movement from regulative norms to constitutive norms that may be a result of the EU Security Strategy could have implications for Europeanization, which may be deepened. Possibly, this will change the impression of the ESDP as an ad hoc, practice-driven process, as the security strategy will become a basis for the development of policy.

The security and defence issue within the EU has been framed (on framing, see also Wagnsson, Chapter 6)[30] as crisis management, concerned with Petersberg tasks. At the time of the Amsterdam Treaty, and perhaps still today, framing ESDP as dealing solely with crisis management was probably the only way forward for the EU in order not to duplicate NATO. However, one may ask if and to what extent the content and practice of Europeanization within this area in the EU is indeed qualitatively different from non-Article 5 issues in NATO.

Another domain of Europeanization is the creation of structures that have institutionalized interaction between member states. Structures have been a prerequisite for the continued Europeanization of security and defence policy and for the implementation of the Helsinki process. New actors have been created that have become players in the new defence policy arena.

The capability development process, in particular the ECAP project groups, contains efforts to harmonize military requirements. With the Agency functioning common acquisition may be undertaken. This is a form of regulative effort at the European level – a mechanism of Europeanization – although it is definitely very 'soft' and bottom-up in its approach. The Helsinki Headline Goal did not contain any formal obligation to submit forces to the EU registers. The pressure to take part in the development of capabilities, and to eventually deploy forces, was instead political. Force requirements were broadly defined, and member states could offer what they wanted to submit to the EU registers. Commitments did not contain any assurance that the forces submitted to registers would actually be available and able for deployment. The new Headline Goal 2010 is much more closely specified, both when it comes to force and deployment requirements. Indeed, the term 'benchmark' is used repeatedly in the document, indicating stronger pressure upon member states. As will be discussed below, the Battle Group concept is likely to have effects upon the force planning of small and medium-sized member states. This makes it possible to argue that in terms of Europeanization mechanisms, a 'European model' is being established. This would indicate a new phase in the Europeanization of security and defence policy where negative integration increasingly seems to be transforming into positive integration.

With the ESDP becoming operational in 2003, Europeanization has reached a stage where it results in common action. This has, in different ways, reinforced policy and structures and thus it has become a dimension of the ESDP dynamic. The EU operations are a domain of Europeanization, of 'common practice and experiences', that might be added to Radaelli's list.[31] This domain is, however, not only driven by an internal logic – external events with security implications are important sources of pressure.

Another aspect, addressing the external dimension of Europeanization is that the whole process can be seen as the result of careful triangular diplomacy (see Chapter 1). The inescapable relationship with the US and NATO is evident in the process studied. Russia does not seem to have the same place in this context as concerns the development of the ESDP and a EU military capability; however, it may become more important as the focus of the EU moves eastward. The relationship to NATO has, however, been crucial. Politically, it has affected the development of ESDP and its structures and on an operational, 'military level' it has constituted something of a model – the EU in the development of its crisis management capability has used many of NATO's standards.[32] Europeanization within this area thus contains obvious elements of institutional copying, something that has been called mimetic isomorphism.[33] Sometimes, for example as regards the use of NATO standards, this method has been used in order to legitimize Europeanization and avoid duplication. In other cases, as regards institutional structures, it has been a natural starting point, but realities have shown that changes are sometimes necessary in order for the structures to fit into the EU context.[34]

Internal implications – the example of Sweden

Since the end of the Cold War, security and defence policy has changed in all European states. Transformations of the military forces have started in order to face a new reality. To what extent has the growth of the EU as an actor been important for member states in the development of new defence policies? In this section implications of Europeanization within security and defence policy for EU member states are discussed, with Sweden as an illustrative example. The analysis builds upon some of the preliminary results from a research project on the Europeanization of Swedish defence policy 1999–2004.[35]

Swedish security policy has, during most of the post-Second World War period, been characterized by a policy of neutrality and non-alignment. The policy of neutrality was officially considered as being dependent upon three factors: national defence, public support and general foreign policy orientation.[36] Sweden has hence maintained a strong defence during the Cold War, and worked in order to keep a national defence industry to supply this force with materiel in case of war.

The events taking place in the second half of the 1980s and at the beginning of the 1990s fundamentally changed the conditions for Sweden's security policy. Non-alignment turned into military non-alignment and Sweden joined the EU in 1995. During the same period of time cooperation with NATO intensified, mainly within the framework of Partnership for Peace (PfP) and the Planning and Review Process (PARP). This development was of great political importance, and a significant international influence on the military forces. It helped Sweden develop inter-operable forces for multinational peacekeeping missions.

From the beginning of the 1990s and in particular since 1999–2000, the Swedish military forces have been going through a process of reorientation and reform. In 1999, the Parliament decided that the threat of invasion was so low and the security policy situation so fundamentally changed that the defence could reorient, from being focused on countering an invasion threat, towards having international operations as one of its main tasks.[37] At the time of the commencement of the development of ESDP in 1999, Swedish defence policy was a strictly national business. International influences only affected small parts of the defence policy and the defence structures. The internationalization envisaged for 2000–4 in the 1999

Defence Review was to take place mainly on national terms. The EU dimension had no prominent place in this decision.

However, the Europeanization process that started due to the ESDP increased the embeddedness of policy and structures in the European process. Initially, a small core of people in the Permanent Representation to the EU, the Foreign Ministry, the Defence Ministry and the Swedish Armed Forces handled ESDP issues more or less separately from other issues in the policy area. Soon, however, the deepening and pace of the process made integration of EU issues in the ordinary policy process necessary.[38] In terms of practical influence on the military forces, the first years with the ESDP were focused on contributions for fulfilling the Helsinki Headline Goal by 2003. The government committed military forces from all defence branches. Large costs were associated with this commitment, in terms of making the units interoperable and maintaining the necessary readiness. Participation in the ESDP became an important driving force for the internationalization of the Swedish Armed Forces.[39] Sweden also played an active role in the capability development process, in areas where a particular interest was identified.[40] As the first EU operations were launched, Swedish participation was considered very important. In the summer of 2003, Swedish Special Forces were sent on a demanding mission to Congo in Operation Artemis, something that has since been assessed as being of great importance, both within the political and the military sphere in Sweden.

In 2004, a significant shift may be seen in Swedish defence policy when it comes to the importance of the EU to Sweden. For the first time since the Europeanization process started, the national and international (EU) starting-points and requirements seem to become more or less fully integrated.[41] The report issued by the Defence Commission in the summer of 2003 indicated an increased international influence, but not to the extent that it did a year later.[42] In 2004, civil servants felt that the ESDP had become 'mainstream'.[43] Only about six months before the Swedish defence review that was planned for December 2004, the Battle Group concept was launched and the Headline Goal 2010 developed. In February 2004, the Swedish Armed Forces were just about to submit to the Ministry an evaluation of estimated consequences given certain economic levels and had to bring this development into calculations.[44] In presenting the main content of a complementary evaluation in late April, the Chief of Defence, General Håkan Syrén, said that development at the European level had reached very far beyond what he could imagine only two months previously. The Chief of Defence made the estimation that EU requirements would become the most important factor in developing the Swedish military forces during the next couple of years and that the whole body of the Swedish Armed Forces needed to become adapted to the EU concept in order to make participation possible.[45] This understanding seems to be shared also by the political establishment. According to the Swedish Minister of Defence, the development within the EU is a driving force in the process of transformation of the Swedish Armed Forces.[46] Thus, it can be said that ESDP has begun to affect not only aspects of policy but also substantially influence the development of defence structures. In addition, the

Europeanization process becomes part of the national logic and has effects upon all aspects of policy.

It is reasonable to conclude that the ESDP has had influence in the Swedish case. It provides a tool for participation and influence. Increasingly, it is also an instrument for reforming the military forces, and it could be said to have promoted an integration of the national and international dimension of the military forces. Europeanization concerns not only policy, structures and implementation of related issues, such as capabilities at a political-strategic level, but also political and military leadership of operations, operational planning and military personnel acting together at a military strategic and operational level. For those EU members that are not members of NATO, this is a new dimension, taking part in the whole multi-level chain of work concerning crisis management.[47]

Given the development and implementation of the Battle Group concept small and medium-sized member states are likely to become even more integrated with respect to defence policy, not only with the European level process, but also with each other. As these states will have difficulties setting up an autonomous Battle Group, multi-national cooperation will be necessary, which in practice will imply long-term, close cooperation with other member states in the development of military units. Inherent in this concept are both political and military requirements, and its implementation is likely to have integrative effects. The effect will perhaps not be as great on the large EU states that do not have to set up multinational Battle Groups in order to be able to participate. However, the larger EU states may set up Battle Groups in cooperation with other member states as well, in order to achieve legitimacy. Taken altogether, this development suggests that in the long term multilateralism in defence cooperation, as well as at the military strategic and operational levels, may become settled as a feature of the military dimension within the EU.

External implications in the context of the strategic triangle

As has been shown by Ginsberg the EU's foreign policy has an external impact far beyond what is usually assumed, even on the superpower the United States.[48] What external implications can follow from the development of EU's military capability? It is still too early to fully assess these questions, though some indications may be discussed. The most apparent consequence of the EU becoming a military actor is the new, closer relationship between the EU and NATO.

EU–NATO relations are central for the development of an EU military capability. Most states agree that the organizations should be complementary and not competitive. There are, however, several dimensions of this relationship and it has been a constant theme in the development of the ESDP, as some states disagree in their interpretation of particular aspects of this problem. Dialogue with the US has been important in the development process, and Britain has had a crucial role in this context, as a bridge between Europe and America.[49] The fact that membership in the two organizations is not similar also causes difficulties, with new problems to solve as institutional cooperation becomes operational.

The most important agreements regarding practical EU relations with NATO is called Berlin Plus. For several years negotiations on this agreement were stopped from being concluded by the US and France, as well as there were divisions between Greece and Turkey. The contents of Berlin Plus were formulated in Washington. More detailed negotiations on the arrangements followed and the agreement could be finalized in time for the launching of the EU's first military crisis management operation in March 2003.

The issue of capabilities and the development of capabilities are also important. The problems concerning shortfalls have been similar, and efforts to deal with the shortfalls have also been conducted in close cooperation. A question for the future is what function the Agency will have in this respect and what a possibly tighter EU process of capability development will mean for the process within NATO. It is possible that the development process within the EU will become more focused and dynamic than the one within NATO. However, benefits from either of the processes should enhance both organizations with respect to capabilities. Essential to the capabilities development are the new requirements of the Headline Goal 2010 and the NATO Response Force (NRF).[50] To what extent are these requirements compatible and what is the difference between the two approaches? What will be the inter-relationship between them? It is still too soon to fully answer these questions, as these new targets have only recently been defined. Views may also differ as regards these issues.

Although NATO's assets are important, especially in planning and command and control, the EU has shown that it may conduct autonomous operations such as Artemis. Furthermore, the 'NATO' option does not seem to be the main choice in the Battle Group concept, but instead it appears to rely on the EU Framework Nation concept. Perhaps NATO had a more important function as a model in the build-up phase and the EU is now ready to act more autonomously in the development of its military capability. If this is correct, the future relationship between the two organizations will perhaps not so much be characterized by EU dependence on NATO, but on mutual interdependence.

US Strategy and the role of NATO in this is a decisive factor in determining the future role of NATO. Indirectly, this also affects the EU, as the functioning of NATO will have repercussions on the development of the EU's role as a military actor. If NATO is not used in situations where a common transatlantic interest may be identified, the EU option is likely to grow in importance for the Europeans. Here, important dynamics between two of the poles in the triangle are at work. As demonstrated by Smith,[51] external factors have been important for the development of European foreign policy cooperation. It is reasonable to assume that the same factors may be at work in the defence area. Furthermore, the increasing relevance of the CFSP and the multinational cooperation in defence that is the likely outcome of further Europeanization within the EU will also create European demands for multilateral solutions. These demands may, if they are not embraced by the US within the framework of NATO or in dialogue with the EU, lead to a situation where the US and the EU will both increasingly be acting alone.

It is clear that in the development of an EU military capability the relationship between the EU and Russia has not had the same importance as the one between the EU and the US. Politically as well as practically, Russia seems to have been little engaged in this process – though a framework for dialogue has been established (see also Wagnsson, Chapter 6). This lack of interest has probably been mutual; the EU has not considered Russia very important for the development of its military dimension, at least not in the first phase that was concerned with policy, structures and capabilities. Russia has been more concerned with the enlargement of NATO, and developing relations with the US through NATO. Perhaps Russia has seen the EU as a military midget, not worthy of its attention. However, as shown by Bynander (Chapter 4), Russia has had an indirect effect on the ESDP through its relationship to some of the new member states. This relationship has led these member states to prioritize NATO over the EU in this area, although they seem to have stepped on to the EU track after having become members in 2004. The relationship between the EU and Russia may change in the future, however. As the EU grows to become a more important actor, in particular with regard to its eastern neighbours, it may have to act also with military means and thus would have to become engaged together with Russia. The growing responsibility that the EU shows in the Balkans may also make the two actors more inclined to interact (see also Wagnsson, Chapter 6). The relationship between the EU and Russia will probably grow more strategic in the years to come. This may make the EU and Russia poles of the triangle on the transatlantic area more important to the United States as well.

Conclusion

The aim of this chapter was to shed some light on the role of the development of EU military capacities within the strategic triangle. It was argued in the introduction that in order to do this, it is vital to assess what importance EU member states attach to this Europeanization process. Europeanization has taken different forms within this area. First, it has consisted of the establishment of policy. Second, it has taken the form of a structural build-up and institutionalization of security and defence policy at the European level. Finally, the ESDP has reached a stage where it consists of joint operations.

The internal consequences of this Europeanization process have been discussed here on the basis of the Swedish example. It is important to note that it is complicated to generalize from this case only, given the increasing diversity between member states, new and old, large and small. The results should be seen as an indication of one way of approaching these issues, though there may be other ways, as shown for example by Bynander in Chapter 4 in this book. The Swedish case shows that though this member state has not had a history of international cooperation in this area; the ESDP has gradually been adopted more and more into the national logic. Participation in this process seems, at least from 2004, increasingly to have been used as a tool, a model, for reorienting and developing the armed forces. This tendency is likely to increase as the process deepens with the implementation of the Battle Group concept. Given the importance of the defence industry in the Swedish context, it will be interesting to see what role the European Defence Agency will have in the future. However, it is quite clear that the ESDP and the building of an EU military capability are very important to Sweden, both as an internal process in the EU and as a tool for enhancing the EU's overall capacity in reaching out beyond the borders of the EU.

What can be said about the external implications of this process for the relations within the transatlantic area and the strategic triangle? From the above it is clear that the EU is an actor of importance to its member states, and that Europeanization seems to deepen. Externally, the EU has only recently become an actor with a military capability. The EU's actorness in this area is certainly a problem, as it does not fit into the traditional conception of an actor with a military capability. Numerous essays and articles have criticized the EU's military dimension, pointing towards its flaws and inefficiency.[52] The EU is often judged on either the criteria of a military organization, with NATO standing as a model, or a nation-state – with the United States as a comparison. The development of the ESDP and a military capability of the European Union, do not, however, make it a military organization in the traditional sense. Neither is the EU a nation-state that has the same interests and uses force in the same way as the USA.

For analytical purposes this chapter has, in a sense, brought the military dimension out of its overall EU context. Foremost, at the strategic level, an EU military capability should be seen as one of several tools in a toolbox. It will increase the possibilities of conducting an effective CFSP. For the time being, the military capability of the EU should be seen mainly within this context, and the EU should not be seen as a military actor equal to the US or Russia. The seed for creating, in the long term, a military organization is part of the larger integration force of the European Union. This process may, however, very well earn support from the Europeanization process currently taking place, in particular the closer cooperation concerning the development and acquisition of armaments that may be a consequence of the European Defence Agency.

The above concerns the special character of the EU as a military actor. The other question is how does this process of developing a military capability affect the relationships within the strategic triangle? The role of NATO has been highlighted in this chapter as the most obvious concern. However, the build-up of an EU military capability does not in itself constitute a threat to NATO in terms of capabilities. The Europeanization of security and defence within the EU may, through the reform of the European Armed Forces it spurs, also serve to strengthen the European pillar of NATO (though some say it doesn't,[53] and others that it is the other way round[54]). However, in the long run the fact that the EU, and not NATO, aims at creating a *common* security and defence policy may be of importance. This is perhaps primarily because it may shift the focus within member states from NATO to the EU. Thus, it could be said that the Europeanization *process* itself is threatening to NATO – as it may lead to integration closer than ever achieved within the Atlantic Alliance, something that may in the future decrease the importance of the latter.

Concerning the issue of task-sharing the greatest challenge for NATO is probably to become used as a political tool. If an organization is not used, it will in the long run inevitably lose importance. Here, US policy plays an important role. The military capability of the EU (and thus its member states, perhaps with the exception of Britain and France) is growing distinctly multinational in composition. In order to make use of this force, political legitimacy is likely to require a multi-lateral setting.

Neither the US nor Russia currently seems to place much emphasis on the EU as a military actor. The enlargement of the EU and new ambitions within the framework of the ESDP may, however, change this picture. The EU may grow to become a partner both to the US and Russia in security matters of concern, in the short run probably mainly within the transatlantic area, but in the long run also on a global scale.

Notes

1 G. Sjöstedt, *The External Role of the European Community*, Swedish Studies in International Relations 7, Westmead: Saxon House, 1977; C. Hill, 'The Capability-Expectations Gap, or Conceptualizing Europe's International Role', *Journal of Common Market Studies*, 1993, vol. 31, pp. 305–28.

2 The ESDP process has been analysed in a similar fashion in M. Britz and A. Eriksson: 'The European Security and Defence Policy: A Fourth System of European Foreign Policy?', *Politique européenne*, 2005, no. 17, pp. 35–62. This chapter deals with EU military capabilities. It does not investigate the overall EU toolbox when it comes to crisis management, and also does not discuss the wider Common Foreign and Security Policy (CFSP). Neither are the contents of the European Constitution assessed. It should be noted that the example of Sweden implies much of a small-state perspective. Taking this into account, it should be noted that there may be problems associated with trying to generalize from the results concerning internal implications.

3 The Amsterdam Treaty substantially developed the CFSP and set a framework for the ESDP. The British–French St Malo summit on 3–4 December 1998 could be seen, however, as the political window opening up for the ESDP process within the EU. Part of the British reluctance to allow the EU to develop a European defence capability apart from that of NATO was then removed. At St Malo it was stated that the EU needed a crisis management capacity of its own. Among the Europeans the debate on the proper forms of European defence integration has been connected to diverging views and interpretations of the relationship with the US and NATO. The issue of competition between the two organizations is an element that is always present and fundamental to the development of the ESDP.

4 P. Rieker, *Europeanisation of Nordic Security: The EU and Changing Security Identities of the Nordic States*, Oslo: Department of Political Science, Faculty of Social Sciences, University of Oslo, 2003; A. Eriksson, 'Sweden and the Europeanisation of Security and Defence Policy', in B. Huldt, T. Ries, J. Mörtberg, and E. Davidson (eds) *The New Northern Security Agenda – Perspectives from Finland and Sweden*, Strategic Yearbook 2004, Stockholm: Swedish National Defence College, 2003; A. Eriksson, Ph.D. Dissertation at Department of Political Science, Stockholm University, forthcoming.

5 On the relationship between Europeanization and European integration Radaelli writes, 'Europeanization would not exist without European integration. But the latter concept belongs to the ontological stage of research, that is, the understanding of a

process in which countries pool sovereignty, whereas the former is post-ontological, being concerned with what happens once EU institutions are in place and produce their effects . . .' (C. Radaelli, 'Europeanization of Public Policy', in K. Featherstone and C. Radaelli (eds) *The Politics of Europeanization*, Oxford: Oxford University Press, 2003, p. 33).

6 It has, however, appeared in studies on the EU and NATO accessions: see for example H. Grabbe, 'Europeanization Goes East: Power and Uncertainty in the EU Accession Process', in K. Featherstone and C. Radaelli (eds) *The Politics of Europeanization*, Oxford: Oxford University Press, 2003.

7 K. Featherstone, 'Introduction: In the Name of Europe', in K. Featherstone and C. Radaelli (eds) *The Politics of Europeanization*, Oxford: Oxford University Press, 2003.

8 A similar definition is used by B. Jacobsson, 'Europeiseringen och statens omvandling', SCORE Rapportserie 1999, no. 2.

9 Radaelli, 'Europeanization of Public Policy', p. 35.

10 Radaelli, 'Europeanization of Public Policy', pp. 40–4.

11 Council of the European Union, 2509th Council Meeting (External Relations), 'Declaration on EU Military Capabilities', press release, no. 9379/03 (Presse 138), Brussels, 19–20 May 2003b. It had already been declared at Laeken that the EU was capable of conducting certain crisis management tasks, including civilian tasks.

12 The Petersberg tasks include: humanitarian and rescue tasks, peacekeeping tasks, tasks of combat forces in crisis management, including peacemaking (WEU Council of Ministers, *Western European Union Council of Ministers Petersberg Declaration*, Bonn, 19 June 1992, online).

13 The HTF is a sub-group to the EUMC, composed of military experts from the member states, regularly convening in Brussels under the leadership of the Presidency.

14 Council of the European Union, General Affairs/Defence, 'Military Capabilities Commitment Declaration', press release, no. 13427/2/00, Brussels, 20 November 2000.

15 Conference on EU Capability Improvement, Brussels, 19 November 2001 – Statement on Improving European Military Capabilities, reproduced in M. Rutten, 'From Nice to Laeken, European Defence: core documents, Volume II', *Chaillot Paper*, no. 51, Paris: European Union Institute for Security Studies, April 2002.

16 The CDM was actually part of the Berlin Plus package, which also explains its delay. Berlin Plus consists of:
'a. Assured EU access to NATO planning capabilities able to contribute to military planning for EU-led operations;
b. The presumption of availability to the EU of pre-identified NATO capabilities and common assets for use in EU-led operations;
c. Identification of a range of European command options for EU-led operations, further developing the role of DSACEUR (Deputy Supreme Allied Commander, Europe) in order for him to assume fully and effectively his European responsibilities;
d. The further adaptation of NATO's defence planning system to incorporate more comprehensively the availability of forces for EU-led operations' (NATO, Washington Summit Communiqué 24 April 1999, Press Release NAC-S(99)64, 1999, paragraph 10)

17 The project groups (PGs) concerned the following areas (some project groups were also divided into subgroups): Headquarters (HQ), Unmanned Aerial Vehicles (UAV), Air to Air Refueling (AAR), Special Operation Forces (SOF), Nuclear, Bacteriological and Chemical Weapons (NBC), Intelligence, Surveillance, Target Acquisition and Reconnaissance (ISTAR Information Exchange Framework), Combat Search and Rescue (CSAR), Interoperability for Humanitarian and Evacuation Operations, Tactical Ballistic Missile Defence (TBMD), Strategic Air Lift, Strategic Sea Lift, Space Assets,

Medical Group, Attack Helicopters and Support Helicopters. All shortfalls were not dealt with in PGs.

18 Försvarsmakten, HKV/PLANS INT PM 2004–03–31 L-O Roos, 2004a; Council of the European Union, 'The Way Forward on the European Capabilities Action Plan', paper, spring 2003a; Council, 'Declaration on EU Military Capabilities'.

19 U. Mörth, *Organizing European Cooperation – the Case of Armaments*, Lanham, MD: Rowman & Littlefield, 2003; M. Britz, 'The Europeanization of Defence Industry Policy', Ph.D. Thesis, Stockholm: Department of Political Science, Stockholm University, 2004.

20 European Defence Agency, 'Second Meeting of the European Defence Agency's Steering Board', press release, Brussels, 22 November 2004.

21 The EU does not have an autonomous capability for operational planning – this has to be conducted either at NATO Headquarters within the framework of Berlin Plus or at the national level with a member state adopting the role of 'Framework Nation'. In order to prepare for situations like the first case, it was agreed in December 2003 that a small EU cell would be established within the Supreme Headquarters Allied Powers Europe (SHAPE). At the same time, it was also decided that in order to make the second case possible, the capacity of the EUMS needed to be enhanced (Council of the European Union, 'European Defence: NATO/EU Consultation, Planning and Operations', press release, 15 December 2003, reproduced in A. Missiroli, 'From Copenhagen to Brussels. European Defence: Core Documents, Volume IV', *Chaillot Paper*, no. 67, Paris: European Union Institute for Security Studies, December 2003c).

22 Council of the European Union, 'The European Union Launches a Police Mission to Kinshasa in the Democratic Republic of Congo (DRC) (EUPOL KINSHASA)', press release, no. 15855/04 (Presse 349), Brussels, 9 December 2004b; Council of the European Union, 'Council Establishes Mission to Provide Advice and Assistance for Security Sector Reform in the DRC', press release, no. 8644/05 (Presse 105), Brussels, 2 May 2005.

23 Comment to question by Dr Christoph Heusgen, Director, Policy Planning Unit, Secretariat General of the Council of the European Union, Brussels at the Young Faces Conference 'The New Security Challenges and Europe's International Role', Berlin, 20–22 January 2005.

24 Council of the European Union, 'ESDP Presidency Report', endorsed by the European Council of 17 December 2004c.

25 'A Secure Europe in a Better World – The European Security Strategy', Brussels, 12 December 2003, Council of the European Union.

26 P. J. Katzenstein, 'Same War – Different Views: Germany, Japan, and Counter-terrorism', *International Organization*, Fall 2003, vol. 57, p. 737.

27 Council of the European Union, 'Headline Goal 2010', as finalized by PSC, Brussels, 4 May 2004a, 6309/6/04.

28 Military Capability Commitment Conference, Brussels, 22 November 2004

29 Council, 'Headline Goal 2010', A2.

30 According to Mörth, framing is about how an issue is labelled. It may be diagnostic (identification of an issue or problem as well as its source) or prognostic (focusing on solutions and strategies to dealing with the problem). How an issue is framed may be important for the construction of identities, and it is an important political instrument in organizing cooperation (Mörth, *Organizing European Cooperation,* pp. 23–4).

31 Radaelli, 'Europeanization of Public Policy'.

32 L. Wedin, 'Tre år i EU:s militära stab', in *Kungliga Krigsvetenskapsakademiens Handlingar och Tidskrift*, 2004, no. 1, p. 133.

33 C. Radaelli, 'Policy Transfer in the European Union: Institutional Isomorphism as a source of legitimacy', *Governance: An International Journal of Policy and Administration*, January 2000, vol. 13, no. 1, pp. 25–43.

34 Wedin, 'Tre år i EU:s militära stab', pp. 127, 131–2.
35 Eriksson, Ph.D. Dissertation.
36 K. Goldmann, 'The Swedish Model of Security Policy', in J.-E. Lane (ed.) *Understanding the Swedish Model*, London: Frank Cass, 1991, p. 123.
37 Swedish Government, Regeringens proposition 1999/2000:30, *Det nya försvaret*, 2000, p. 13.
38 Interviews with officials at Department for International Security Affairs, Swedish Ministry of Defence (MoD), 17 February 2003; and at Joint Strategic Plans and Policy, Swedish Armed Forces (SAF), 2 June 2004.
39 Interviews with General J. Kihl, Chief of Joint Strategic Plans and Policy, SAF, 4 February 2004; and General J. Hederstedt, former Supreme Commander, SAF, 13 February 2004.
40 Interviews with officials at Joint Strategic Plans and Policy, SAF, on 22 April 2003; and 23 April 2004.
41 Interview, General J. Hederstedt.
42 Defence Commission, *Försvar för en ny tid*, Departementsserien, 2004:30.
43 Interview with official at Secretariat of Strategic Planning, Swedish MoD, 2 April 2004.
44 Försvarsmakten, Försvarsmaktens Budgetunderlag för år 2005 med särskilda redovisningar, HKV beteckning 23 383:62995, 27 February 2004b.
45 H. Syrén, Internal Television Broadcast, 29 April 2004a; and H. Syrén, 'ÖB föreslår Svenskt försvar för Europa', *Insats & Försvar*, 2004b, no. 2. At the military commitment conference in November 2004, Sweden announced its willingness to serve as a Framework Nation in the setting up of a Swedish-Finnish-Norwegian Battle Group. Later, it was announced that Estonia would also be part of this constellation.
46 Swedish Ministry of Defence, Leni Björklund, Swedish Defence Minister, press release, 17 May 2004.
47 L. Wedin, *Reflektioner över ämnet strategi*, Stockholm: Swedish National Defence College, 2002, p. 16.
48 R. H. Ginsberg, *The European Union in International Politics – Baptism by Fire*, Lanham, MD: Rowman & Littlefield, 2001.
49 C. Grant, 'Conclusion: The Significance of European Defence', in L. Freedman, F. Heisbourg and M. O'Hanlon, *A European Way of War*, Centre for European Reform, 2004, p. 64.
50 NRF was decided upon at Prague, see NATO, 'Prague Summit Declaration', press release, no. 127, 21 November 2002.
51 M. E. Smith, *Europe's Foreign and Security Policy – The Institutionalization of Cooperation*, Cambridge and New York: Cambridge University Press, 2004.
52 See for example L. Freedman, 'Can the EU Develop an Effective Military Doctrine?', in Freedman, Heisbourg and O'Hanlon, *A European Way of War*.
53 A. Menon, 'Why ESDP is Misguided and Dangerous for the Alliance', in J. Howorth and J. T. S. Keeler (eds) *Defending Europe: The EU, NATO and the Quest for European Autonomy*, New York: Palgrave/Macmillan, 2003.
54 S. Everts and D. Keohane, 'Introduction', in Freedman, Heisbourg and O'Hanlon, *A European Way of War*.

4

POLAND AND THE CZECH REPUBLIC

New members torn between the EU and NATO

Fredrik Bynander

Introduction[1]

What makes some European transitional states assume the role as 'trusted allies' to the United States in the war against terrorism in general and the Iraq war in particular, in sharp contrast to the Franco-German axis that vehemently opposes recent US policy in the Middle East? Why was Europe not more closely knit as a political entity than to allow the disarray that followed the US and UK initiatives regarding Iraq, which seriously damaged the cohesion of NATO and the EU's Common Foreign and Security Policy?[2] In order to begin answering these questions, this study investigates the basic principles and policy ideas underlying the foreign policy of two increasingly central, yet surprisingly overlooked, actors in modern European politics – Poland and the Czech Republic.[3]

This chapter is exploratory in the sense that several possible sources of Polish and Czech foreign policy decision-making are being probed and juxtaposed against contextual factors that may affect the outcome of the policy-making process.[4] The aim of this chapter is to explicate the actual choices made under the pressure of 'Western' disagreement on the way forward concerning Iraq. A secondary aim, which is allowed to guide the presentation throughout the study at hand, is to describe the dilemma faced by Poland and the Czech Republic (along with other fellow accession states) in the simultaneous adaptation to two separate institutions with partly overlapping competencies, and partly opposite policy agendas. Of course, describing the differences as having sprung out of the institutions themselves is a gross simplification and the complexity of national positions and intersecting bilateral relations are elaborated. The third aim is to use a comparison between the countries as a tool for analysing the factors that drive foreign policy in institutional cross-pressure. Ultimately, this practice adds to the unfolding tale of the EU as a foreign policy actor and thus a leg of the strategic triangle envisioned in this edited volume. It also directly targets the complex relationship with the two 'significant others' in the triangle by emphasizing the national view of the triangular relationship and its strategic component.

Nevertheless, the EU/NATO institutional divide exists, and it is especially troublesome for the new members, and this fact grants opportunities to find clearer evidence of its repercussions in the policies (and policy debates) of those countries. For the accession states, a very concrete issue where they have come to consider themselves between a rock and a hard place is the strong conflict between NATO's calls for higher defence expenditure and EU's demands for budget deficit reductions. In the Czech Republic, this has caused severe criticism from NATO, as the government is planning to cut the defence budget in nominal terms.[5] Another issue is the development of EU capabilities in areas that have traditionally been the sole responsibility of NATO, such as the EU rapid reaction mechanism or the proposal of a European military planning unit, both opposed (to some degree) by the United States. The pressure in these areas usually emanates bilaterally from the US, but the repercussions for the accession states are institutional, as their bargaining positions are generally weak and they are in need of flexibility from both organizations to be considered in accordance with their respective central regulations.[6]

In addition, there is a distinct difference of institutional political logic between the two organizations. NATO is a military alliance created at the dawn of the Cold War to counter the Soviet threat, now transforming to meet new threats, but essentially geared to foster effective military cooperation and resolve hard security problems. The EU approached the continent's age-old security dilemma from another direction by founding the Coal and Steel Union on cooperation outside the core of national security, hoping that collaborative solutions would spill over and tie the European states into a strong institutional framework of cooperation. The EU thus became an 'issue magnet' ever incorporating new policy areas into its sphere of regulation, whereas NATO's military security core was diligently protected from dilution by its largest power, the United States.

As NATO is now starting to look beyond a major war as its principal contingency, considering the terrorist threat and potentially other major cross-boundary sources of instability and with France and others pushing for a higher security profile for the EU, clashes are inevitable. The EU tends to agree generally on and announce grand ambitions first, and only then starts to worry about how to realize them. This is primarily the case for putting in place the EU rapid reaction force, and this has been the general development of its Common Foreign and Security Policy.[7] NATO usually works by different standards. The Cold War lesson of guarantees for member states to deliver its required resources has produced strong pressure and strict codes to ensure the performance of its member states, although the end of the Cold War led to large cuts in defence expenditure.[8] In security terms, and especially with the accession states, this produces expectations that NATO is more likely to withstand serious security challenges. The EU's ambitions are viewed with more scepticism, in terms of the collective political will to face military threats, as well as the complicated decision-making process required to manifest that will. However, the structure of EU commitments in this area is changing, and the strengths of the Union in other areas may also make it an increasingly attractive tool for security needs.

We cannot understand Polish or Czech political influence and decision-making within the European security structures without a broad outline of how the latter are constituted, which is why this chapter will cast the national cases against the emerging regional security climate and its linkages to the global scene. It considers the tensions that have been apparent in transatlantic relations since the run-up to the Iraq war, but that has reasons and repercussions broader than that conflict. Most involved states can discern scenarios for their own positions directly tied to increasing discord across the Atlantic and within Europe, which can certainly feed risk perceptions of marginalization as well as opportunity incentives for increased influence by, for example, strategies of bandwagoning or aggressive bargaining on key political issues.[9] These perceptions can partly be based on the careful assessment of what is in each state's national interest,[10] but also on ideas of political belonging, the strength of various bilateral relationships, domestic political dynamics, and attempted contributions to the long-term political stability and integration in Europe. Needless to say, the stakes are seen as high and the situation as pivotal for some of the newly inaugurated Central and Eastern European states in their quest to secure influence, legitimacy and trust as actors on the European arena.

The consequences of the institutional ambiguity for security in these countries make them uneasy participants in a strategic triangle. For many reasons, a strategic dyad with their own states firmly embedded in the Western node would be preferable. Nevertheless, forced to take part in a transatlantic interaction of both cooperation and conflict, their strategies have varied over time and the EU/NATO balance has been struck differently as the countries have gone through quite distinct phases of membership negotiations and accession procedures. This chapter illuminates those national deliberations under pressure. But it also shines a light on the triangle from an angle often overlooked. The common Western European perspective is that the new members have much to learn and that, once they are 'educated', their long-term policies will not differ much from their Western counterparts. This chapter makes credible that this may not be the case and that, in fact, the Western security communities may be what are changing in order to correspond to new realities, as Russia and its 'near abroad' become the primary counterparts in building European security.

The Czech Republic

The turbulence of the demise of the Soviet empire in Central and Eastern Europe (CEE) came to mean more to Czechoslovakia than emancipation, self-rule, and the gradual reintegration with Western economic and political institutions. It became the trigger for a largely amicable secession process, where Slovakia slipped out of the federation creating few objections from the Czech majority – the 'velvet divorce'.[11] The remaining Czech state possessed the lion's share of the federation's industrial capacity, its armed forces and financial resources. With just over 10 million in population, and an economy second only to Poland's among the accession states, the Czech Republic is set to find itself in the middle range of EU members.[12]

It looked immediately to the West for both opportunities for economic growth as well as military security – there was no doubt that the Czech Republic was on a path to integration.

Czechoslovakia had had a slower start to the rapprochement to Western Europe than the early frontrunners Poland and Hungary, partly due to the scepticism of the highly conservative communist regime up to 1989, and it was left out of the PHARE programme for technical assistance, signed between the EC and the reforming regimes of Poland and Hungary. Rather soon after the first euphoria over self-rule had stabilized, however, Czechoslovakia approached the EC, concluding a Trade Cooperation Agreement in March of 1990 and soon after joining PHARE. The forming of the Visegrad group with Poland and Hungary (and eventually Slovakia), designed to foster a coordinated approach to European integration, cemented the Czech position as a leading reformist in Central Europe.[13]

The Václav Klaus government that came to power in 1993 changed the face of Czech politics forever. Within months, the Czechoslovak federation had split into two sovereign states, and the Klaus government came to rule a republic on the fast track to NATO and the EU. The image portrayed was that of having lost a shackle in spawning off Slovakia, and the lightning reform period that followed was designed to establish the Czech Republic as a candidate for early accession to the EU. Klaus brought the country into the OECD and GATT/WTO. The idea was not to knock ceaselessly on the EU front door like some other CEE countries, but to become a political asset for the main EU states quickly and slip through the back door as a future European political power. Klaus abandoned the Visegrad strategy as a means of approaching the membership negotiations concertedly with the others, and pursued a more exceptionalist policy that included a harder line in negotiations with Germany over border issues and criticism of the EU for being overregulated and inefficient.[14]

The withdrawal from the Visegrad collaboration and the new hard line of the Klaus government was met with forceful reactions from the other Visegrad members as well as from leading EU and NATO members. Klaus softened his approach somewhat, but kept stating the ambition to be the first former Warsaw Pact (successor) state in the EU. Klaus's success was evident when the Czech Republic joined the OECD as the first former communist member in 1995 and as it was invited for accession negotiations with the EU in 1998 along with five other states.

In terms of security, successive governments in the 1990s were modestly committed to early accession into NATO. There was no great sense of urgency, since the break-up of both the Soviet Union and Czechoslovakia had left the Czech Republic geographically removed from Russia and increasingly close to the unified Germany. However, the prospect of early NATO entry was not squandered as the country joined Partnership for Peace on its initiation and serious security cooperation with Germany and the US commenced. This lined the Czech Republic up for a strong position in the early enlargement talks in 1995–6, further reinforced by a Czech rapprochement to Poland, which had been lent further security importance by the velvet divorce.[15] The last achievement of a fragmenting and electorally weakened Klaus government in 1997 was to receive an invitation to join NATO at the Madrid summit. Since then, social democratic governments have succeeded one another in promoting integration through the accession processes.

In 2003, Václav Klaus succeeded Václav Havel as President and brought his Eurosceptic agenda to the highest, but largely symbolic, office of the Czech Republic.[16] He has, since then, continued his firebrand rhetoric against further EU integration and is set against the adoption of the EU constitution, which he feels will extend Brussels' power too far into the affairs of the member states. The image of a Eurosceptic Czech Republic created by its President is to some extent balanced by a much more cautious cabinet. Under the past three social democratic premiers, Zeman, Spindla and Gross, EU integration has been a major priority and deficit reduction measures have taken precedence over NATO requirements on defence spending. The Social Democrats have opposed Klaus's Civic Democrats on their EU-sceptic policy proposals and have been more lukewarm about NATO accession.[17]

Poland

Poland's ascendancy as a regional European power, as well as member of NATO and the EU, is a source of political change in Central and Eastern Europe, and a marker of the shift in security cooperation towards the east within the previously Western security complex.[18] With 38.5 million citizens and one of Eastern Europe's largest economies, Poland is potentially a major player now that the political map of Europe is being redrawn after the Iraq war of 2003, partly by the parallel processes of the ESDP and NATO's Membership Action Plan.[19] Its rapprochement with the United States, and its open disagreements with major continental European powers over the logic and legitimacy of the Iraq intervention has cast Poland as a politically autonomous actor, not readily intimidated under the auspices of European unity or the dominance of the Franco-German axis in European politics. The possibility of what US Secretary of Defence, Donald Rumsfeld, has labelled a 'new' Europe, and Poland's leadership status within it, could be seen as a divide in European political worldviews, intimately connected to concerns regarding American projection of power and the basic principles of the European security structure. Of course, we have only seen the first major ripples of such a wave and much can still happen to reconcile the main players in Europe.

Historically, Poland's location between Russia/the Soviet Union and Germany has been its defining feature as a regional actor and the root to most (or all) of its security problems. When Poland gradually forced its way out of authoritarian rule and claimed full independence from Moscow, several old issues surfaced that had been contained by the Cold War and by the inclusion of East Germany in the Warsaw Pact. With German reunification, the old border issues were again polit-ically viable, and the position of the German minority in Poland became politically burdensome. Polish suspicion of a united Germany was initially rather high, but quickly subsided as several potentially thorny issues were handled diplomatically (such as the German acceptance of the Oder–Neisse line), and the problems of reunification came to the fore, calming some fears of an instantly successful and powerful juggernaut in the centre of Europe.[20] Germany's continued commitment to NATO and the EU, including the process which produced widespread support across Western Europe of its reunification, reassured the Polish government that German dominance of the region would be at most economic, but never military. This led to a policy of engagement with Germany and the rest of Western Europe, as well as vigorous Polish attempts to secure EU and NATO membership. The enlargement of those organizations seemed to many Poles to be a way of embedding Germany further into the confines of European integration.[21]

The relations to Russia were more painstakingly thawed as the new Polish democracy aimed at ridding itself of debilitating political and economic ties parallel to the internal reform process, which at times created turbulence domestically.[22] The failed Moscow coup attempt in 1991, the sometimes difficult negotiations over troop withdrawals, and the fate of Russian 'near abroad' on Poland's borders, all caused Polish governments to balance their policies towards the nation's large neighbour carefully.

Shifting to the West

The domestic urges in Poland to seek security by approaching the Western political structures were not unopposed during the nineties, although they proved convincing as the reformed socialists slowly accepted the call for NATO membership. In February of 1992, Polish Defence Minister Jan Parys had declared Poland's intention to seek membership and the process was increasingly cast as depending on the willingness of core NATO countries to welcome members from the former Warsaw Pact. The Czechs had achieved a greater sense of security by the secession of Slovakia as it no longer bordered to the former USSR (Ukraine), but when the alliance moved towards enlargement, Czech governments intensified their political efforts to be included in the first round of accession. In this light, the creation of the Partnership for Peace in early 1994 was widely seen as a way by NATO members to postpone enlargement.

However, the integration and coordination that followed PfP membership has since proved vital for the reform of both the Polish and Czech armed forces, which paved the way to full membership. When the 1995 'Study about NATO Enlargement' was presented, opportune reform was already under way in Poland to modernize and strengthen the military to meet NATO standards. The most important change was a division of the forces into mobile units for NATO operations and traditional territorial defence units.[23] The Czechs have typically moved with less urgency, partly because their military forces were more updated to begin with, partly because they felt that their position was too good for NATO to exclude them.[24]

Surprisingly, perhaps, throughout these trials and tribulations over domestic politics, the mainstream of Polish and Czech politics steered straight for NATO and EU accession. One reason for élite attraction to Western integration was the externally imposed discipline it brought regarding, for example, the deregulation of important domestic markets and remaining commitments to large public expenditure. The other major reason for Poland was, quite clearly, a sense of urgency to escape the strategic void that had been created with the collapse of the Warsaw Pact in 1991 into the warmth of the Article V security guarantee.

Of course, reforming the armed forces to become compatible with NATO missions and coordinated with NATO standards is an enormous undertaking, especially considering that both economies can still be considered transitional. The Polish conscript defence of 1989 counted 400,000 standing troops. In radical cuts over the years that number has been lowered to 165,000 in 2002, with a further reduction of 15,000 in the works for 2006.[25] More troubling is the fulfilment of NATO requests that defence expenditure should equal 3 per cent of GNP. The real figure has hovered around 1.95 per cent and it is showing no sign of rising in the near future.[26] The military budget is bogged down by sizable costs for salaries and pensions, preventing further modernization of the defence structures and acquisition of modern weapon systems. The 2001–6 reform programme designed to meet NATO standards is increasingly looking like a failure.[27]

The Social Democrats in the Czech Republic are, for various reasons, one of them being their domestically focused constituency, not a security- and defence-oriented party. In the choice between easing social disruptions in their transitional economy and spending scarce resources on reforming their defence forces, they will opt for the former every time. This tendency has been reinforced by the economic difficulties that started in 1997, which have further slowed down reform. Also, the Czech Republic has a strong tradition of pacifism, often cited as deriving from the fact that the last Czech/Bohemian army to fight a battle in defence of its homeland was in the Thirty Years' War. After the 1993 break-up of Czechoslovakia, the Czech Republic embraced a 'shock therapy' approach to defence reform and became the first Central European state to place its military fully under civilian control, which it accomplished by the summer of 1994.[28] Its troops have been reduced from 107,000 in 1993 to 61,000 in 1999. The projection for 2007 is 35,000 soldiers.[29] In terms of military spending, the Czech military budget has been stable for years at 2.0–2.1 per cent of GDP, which is in line with the 2 per cent goal that was declared upon membership negotiations, but it is down from 2.2 per cent in 2000 and it is causing criticism from the NATO secretariat. The situation is not improving according to many observers and indeed according to Minister of Defence Tvrdik, who resigned in June 2003:

> The Czech defence minister has resigned after the government decided to scale back plans for defence spending in the face of mounting deficit in public finances. 'I know I look like an idiot, but better [to be an idiot] for one day than for the rest of my life.
>
> (Zapletnyuk 2003)

In Poland, the eagerness to contribute to operations in Kosovo, Afghanistan, and, by assuming responsibility for an occupation zone, in Iraq, has overcome the shortcomings of the modernization of its armed forces, to a large degree with direct American aid. Although other Central European states, like the Czech Republic and Slovenia, may be further ahead in reforming and supplying their militaries, Poland's mere size and strategic location makes it, alongside Turkey, NATO's most important member state to the East, which guarantees the continuing support from important allies.

US shifting to the East

With the deterioration of NATO unity on the handling of the Iraq problem and the creation of a 'coalition of the willing' to oust Saddam Hussein from power and install a US-led occupation force in Baghdad, the future of NATO as the institution of choice for US security policy is unclear. With US interests increasingly turned towards the Middle East and the Eastern European allies rallying to aid American efforts in Afghanistan and Iraq, even as Germany is a reluctant host to the bulk of US troops in Europe, the United States is shifting its military weight in Europe eastwards.[30] The reform pace of NATO and US military capabilities pushed by Secretary of Defence Rumsfeld, and represented by the establishment of the NATO Response Force, is causing drastic cut-backs in the large numbers of troops based in Germany.

An accompanying development is the adoption of wider responsibilities for the armed forces, notably in the 'war on terrorism'. The 'wider security concept', previously thought to mean a move towards 'softer' security issues, has become an important part of the strategy for fighting terrorism as well as the geopolitical ('hard' security) push in the Middle East that the Bush administration has initiated. To a large extent, Central and Eastern European countries have answered the call to contribute troops to Afghanistan and Iraq, including Poland and the Czech Republic, but also Albania, Azerbaijan, Bulgaria, Estonia, Georgia, Hungary, Kazakhstan, Latvia, Lithuania, Macedonia, Moldova, Mongolia, Romania, Slovakia and Ukraine.[31] This is a stark picture of a shift to the East of US military cooperation if anything. In the effort to portray international support, the former Warsaw Pact countries deliver – the Western allies do not with a few exceptions.

The new situation gives Warsaw some hope of becoming a prominent regional actor, providing the institutional and geographical link to the East. It seems the main obstacle is the continued suspicion in the relations with Russia. In order to be the go-to option in the war on terror for the United States, an important characteristic is to be able to work with Moscow, thus relieving friction in the region by furthering NATO interests in Eastern Europe.[32]

However, Polish unease with Russian regional advances is deep-seated and cooperation does not come easy. This is the core of what some experts call 'the double catch',[33] – the paradox that appeared as several Eastern European states joined NATO to enjoy Article V as a deterrent and protection from Russian domination, only to find that 'new NATO' was more complex in several respects, partly as a consequence of the enlargement.[34] The 11 September attacks had several consequences for the alliance, not least being the first ones ever to invoke Article V. However, the lukewarm US response, and its subsequent preference for 'coalitions of the willing' in Afghanistan and Iraq, sent the signal that the war on terror was different from the collective defence situation that NATO was created for. The choice for those states was between joining America in the campaign against terrorism, or going along with the more cautious approach of Germany and France – risking US disengagement from Europe and increased Russian influence in the region.[35]

For Poland to cooperate so fully with the US as to send a substantial force to the Persian Gulf is a recognition of the need for an American presence in Central and Eastern Europe, and a clear signal that the Franco-German approach does not extend beyond the Oder–Neisse line. Even though out-of-area operations are not what Poland signed up for, and though their military structures are not designed for deploying Special Forces in unfamiliar terrain such as Afghanistan or Iraq,[36] this is a price that the country seems very willing to pay for continued US commitment to European security. It seems that the logic is one of bargaining with the superpower, exchanging international legitimacy in Iraq for a strengthening of Article V relevance in the face of serious tension within the alliance. Also, American ad hoc partnerships in the Caucasus and Central Asia are tolerated by Russia at a political cost – for Poland this may be another reason for keeping in step as a reliable ally. Having stated the high level of commitment by the Polish government to the Iraq operations in particular, it is necessary to point out the new signals communicated by the Belka government in 2004. Domestic pressure and the lack of constraints on a new cabinet led to the announcement of reductions of Polish troops in Iraq during 2004, possibly phasing them out altogether by the end of 2005. This is quite disturbing news for the Bush administration, adding to its woes in the run-up to the US presidential election, and creating more security concerns with an Iraqi election already called into question by the widespread insurgency on the ground.

At the core, still, are the relations with Russia with whom Poland shares only the border to the Kaliningrad Oblast, but which is the looming presence in Polish security concerns. Not only does that relate to classic threat perceptions of Russia as an expansive state, but also to a host of potential new threats that may diffuse out of its vast territories and the dominated small states that it calls its 'near abroad'.[37] For Poland, regional stability requires a possible development in Ukraine and Belarus, both of which are subjected to heavy Russian influence.[38] The pressures of guarding the external border of the European Union towards Ukraine and Belarus will weigh heavily on a country used to looking in the other direction. With Belarus in decline and isolating itself from Western influence and Ukraine partly retreating after disappointing signals regarding NATO and EU integration, Poland has reason to worry about its position as the last outpost for those institutions.[39] The emerging EU focus on soft security and the trafficking of drugs, arms and illegal aliens will not be easily maintained in these border regions. It is also apparent that Russia will be needed as a stabilizing factor, especially with regard to Belarus, in a way that will require Polish diplomatic skills and possibly concessions in regional affairs.

The Czech position on these issues is considerably more complex. The small degree of attention to external security paid among Czech voters is causing leaders to play down military cooperation and stay clear of unpopular foreign policy adventures. Simultaneously, the strong pressure to be a reliable ally to the United States in Afghanistan and Iraq has forced consecutive Czech governments to strike a fine balance in providing symbolic troop contributions and political support for those missions, yet staying clear of all-out commitment that would alienate domestic support as well as important European partners. The deployment of 110 troops in Iraq makes the Czech Republic number 19 on the list of contributors to the US-led operation (for which countries such as Ukraine, Georgia, and Mongolia committed larger numbers of troops).

There is, however, a strong sense of commitment to coalition stability and Czech officials often echo US sentiments on terrorism and the conflict in Iraq as in Foreign Minister Cyril Svoboda's speech to the UN General Assembly:

> [The terrorists'] ideology is aggressive and expansive and they do not recognize terms such as 'conciliation' or 'co-existence'. Therefore each offer we make to negotiate, each sign of unwillingness to defend ourselves is seen by them as further proof of our weakness and, by extension, their 'right' to assume control of a declining society. In the fight against terrorism, nobody can stay neutral.
>
> (Czech Embassy to the United States 2004)

After the Spanish Zapatero government had decided to withdraw Spanish troops from Iraq, then Minister of Interior Stanislav Gross argued: 'Spain's decision to pull its soldiers out of Iraq would only support the idea that goals can be reached through terrorism.'[40]

Czech foreign policy is thus increasingly under fire for being evasive and often inconclusive, especially from the sizable leftist opposition, but also from several continental European states. A major row followed the exclusion of the accession states from the 17 February, 2003, EU emergency summit meeting to discuss the growing crisis over Iraq. Outgoing President Havel had recently co-signed the first open letter by European leaders in support of the US effort in Iraq,[41] and French and German leaders clearly wanted to punish the CEE countries for their overt pro-Americanism. Foreign Minister Svoboda added insult to injury at a Czech–German forum on 15 February by stating that he was 'not sure Germany had staked out a good path by insisting on more weapons inspectors [in Iraq]'.[42]

The continued relevance of Europe

Any talk of a shift of military weight is incomplete without the mention of the North–South dimension that has become apparent after the cessation of large-scale hostilities in the Balkans. Remaining forces have entered the twilight of post-conflict inertia, with the political focus moving elsewhere, and costs for troop deployments becoming less attractive to bear. The new theatres in the Middle East are significantly more 'acute' and the security problems that the forces are to address more pressing to the coalition(s) they represent. The military focus of attention is thus also moving South.[43] Having cited Poland's and other Eastern European states' desire to keep the United States engaged in the region, this is also a factor that is diluting the perceived essence of Central and Eastern European security. The continued global relevance of European security issues being narrowly defined, and Central and Eastern European ones in particular, is in the interest of several of the weaker actors in those areas.

Neither the Czech Republic nor Poland have been completely opposed to the growing of soft security items on the European security agenda, at times citing the Petersberg tasks as important for the integration of CEE into a more robust pattern of security cooperation at a societal level.[44] To the extent that these can be attributed with some weight within NATO, other small states in the region are interesting partners in furthering them. Especially with regard to the problem that was previously defined as central to Polish success as a partner of the US in Europe and the evolving relationship with Russia, the soft security matters can be used to make progress and create bilateral trust. They can be functional in the effort of developing ties that are far from the delicate substance of hard security dealings with Russia, possibly facilitating a more constructive dialogue and creating the impression of benevolence in Polish–Russian relations.[45] It is, however, a complex issue for all former Warsaw pact states to allow Russia into cooperative structures, which was manifested as Western NATO states sent conciliatory signals to Russia after 11 September; and Prague, Warsaw and Budapest had clear misgivings, fearing NATO concessions in the accession process. The United States came to the aid of the Visegrad three, and the 2001 North Atlantic Council meeting toned down the proposed radical cooperative approach to Russia.[46]

For Poland the Baltic Sea dimension is the most natural hub for such an approach, especially since a greater sense of stability has already been reached there with the imminent accession of the Baltic States into NATO. Also, this is aided by the fact that far-reaching cooperation between those states and the neutrals on soft security is already underway and also by the fact that Poland has access to most of the institutional arrangements that are being used to further these ambitions. The mid-term great bounty for Poland – better relations with Russia – is also in accord with most of those states. As long as one does not expect to see Poland as fully committed to the all-out soft security agenda, relying on international cooperation over societal 'strains' as a reliable path to military security, it is reasonable to expect a higher level of attention to such matters. After all, Poland knows Russia and the workings of Kremlin power politics, suggesting an ever-sceptical approach when it comes to national security.

An especially delicate matter for Poland is the Kaliningrad enclave that has been the source of serious disagreement between Russia and the EU, with potentially great consequences for Lithuania and Poland encircling the enclave. Russian concerns have been grave, as the EU has refused special arrangements for allowing

Kaliningrad free access to Schengen territory, effectively cutting it off from Russia proper. Kaliningrad's already weak economy and social disarray would probably further deteriorate in a EU-enforced isolation from Russia.[47]

Poland and the Czech Republic in the Union

When Poland and the Czech Republic joined the European Union as full members in May 2004, it was still unclear what that Union was, pending the postponed final negotiation of the EU constitution. Although the new members have full disclosure of that process, it is likely that they will not be entirely happy with the result, nor with the other concessions forced upon them in last-minute membership negotiations that ultimately led to the Copenhagen summit accession decision.[48] For those states, and particularly for Poland being the largest among them, the EU as a result of second-best compromises and clashes of strong national sectoral interests is not an ideal organization to join or an organization to which it has long-standing commitments that need defending. It is therefore likely that the approach of the new members will be considerably less sentimental and more status quo-oriented than those of the founding members of the Union. The burden of proof may, considering the relatively large addition of states, shift towards justifying the legitimacy of separate policies, rather than the relative acceptability of the whole cobweb known as EU institutions to a variety of national interests.

It is likely that Poland will assume a leading role in such advocacy of re-examination of EU policy. This policy of scepticism is combined with a staunch stance on the voting structure in the Council, trying to preserve the relatively large proportion of votes allotted to the medium-sized states Poland and Spain.[49] In these and other areas, Poland has not made many friends over the period of accession, which has at once cast the country as an uncooperative and an influential tough negotiator.[50]

On areas relating to the ESDP, the two states have had similar reservations to some EU developments, even if Poland had the more extreme view. The proposed incorporation of the West European Union (WEU) functions into the EU and misgivings about the St Malo initiative caused the two countries, together with Hungary, to try to negotiate a common standpoint. The talks broke down because Poland wanted to try to completely block the WEU-EU process and veto any EU access to NATO assets, which was too tall an order for the Czech Republic. Eventually, all three moderated their views as EU membership approached and a more comprehensive influence on these processes was anticipated.[51]

The Czech Republic is more amicable in its EU strategy, having secured most of its core objectives in the membership negotiations and expecting to achieve rapid economic success as a result of joining the Common Market and the EU subsidy system. The main problem for the country in the run-up to the accession was a public argument with Germany over the so-called Benes decrees. President Benes of Czechoslovakia expelled between 2 and 3 million Sudeten Germans after the Second World War, and Germany has advocated reparations to the descendants of those displaced. An agreement with Germany and Austria was hindered for many years by the Czech Communist Party's success in playing the 'German scare' card, especially in the election of 2002, forcing a harder stance by the democratic parties (Klaus's Civic Democrats in particular).[52] A European Parliament legal opinion in October 2002 concluded that the decree should not be an obstacle for the Czech Republic to join the EU, and the issue was transferred to the diplomatic back-burner.[53]

When it comes to security policy and the relationship of the ESDP to NATO, a similar approach can already be seen as commented on above. The fact that several large Western European countries are also critical of plans for a more autonomous European posture in defence matters adds weight to the integration sceptics, and pressures the Europeanists in Paris, Berlin and Brussels to forge stronger alliances in the centre-field of EU security cooperation.[54] With EU accession completed, the threat of membership negotiation trouble is out of the way, and several CEE countries are basically free to promote an Atlanticist agenda if they want to. The US influence on several of the new member states erects a large barrier for the EU to expand its cooperation and autonomy in terms of security and defence. Negotiating a further deepening of the security dimension will almost certainly have to include a considerable measure of voluntary commitment and multiple-track solutions that imply large risks for the main integrationists.[55]

The danger of dividing the Union on security issues and creating a tug-of-war with NATO is real and may cause major ripple effects in other areas for cooperation.[56] For example, persuading Poland to accept reform of the Common Agricultural Policy that would mean significant cuts in the prospected support to its large agricultural sector, in a situation where it is under pressure to accept larger European security autonomy, will be a very tall order for the integrationists in Paris and Berlin. A further complication is represented by other causes for resistance such as the reluctance of the (former) neutrals to join far-reaching defence initiatives, or states enjoying special NATO attention, such as Greece, to accept further dilution of NATO political cohesion. To continue pushing for policy change in this environment, which is primarily directed against US dominance and designed to increase the influence of the Franco-German axis, must be deemed risky and doomed to fail.[57]

Furthermore, the bargaining structure that has emerged since the enlargement is not fully understood yet. Traditionally, even a shaky alliance between Germany, France and the UK would be certain to carry the day. Now, the Blair government's uneasy endorsement of a European military planning unit separate from NATO may not be enough to sell it to sceptical CEE allies. The latter can elect to work inside both the EU and NATO to foil such plans, making far-reaching demands on the activist Western governments to safeguard NATO commitment in Europe, ultimately making an autonomous capacity impossible or so watered down that it becomes irrelevant.

Poland and the Czech Republic as European security actors

At the core of the items probed here as pertinent for assessing Polish and Czech foreign policy seems to be the prospect of how it will 'fit' into the previously Western conceptual thinking on security and its relation to Russia. The short answer is that Poland is on much more familiar terrain with the recent unilateral tendencies of the United States and the increased transparency regarding regional power structures it has created. For a country squeezed between two large neighbours for the best part of the last 500 years, EU-style multilateralism may be attractive as a model for economic growth and social development, but it is hardly a reassuring foundation for national security. NATO, on the other hand, is. Considering Poland's outlook on European security based on Russia as a remaining potential security threat and continental Europe as politically and militarily uncommitted to Central and Eastern European security, American involvement under the binding conditions of Article V is the sole guarantee for long-term stability. This is why Polish interests are focused on creating incentives for deeper US engagement in Eastern Europe by providing political and (modest) military support for out-of-area missions in Iraq and Afghanistan.

The difference between this dimension of Polish security thinking and the participation in emerging frameworks for soft security cooperation and regional development schemes designed to further security is real and should not be under-estimated. Recent political experiences of the European states put different emphasis on power capabilities and integration factors, affecting expectations of other actors' behaviour and substantial issues of regional stability. The newly independent states can reasonably be anticipated to be suspicious of EU-style non-security integration as a safeguard of national security, yet gladly participate in it as long as it can deliver other benefits without posing a threat to perceived core interests. To the extent that the EU can act as a united force in European affairs, Poland seems willing to participate all-out, but its focus on regional stability in combination with the opening transatlantic rift and its secondary effects on European unity provokes caution on the part of several incoming members of the Union.

In terms of regional cooperative structures, the outlook for Polish involvement with Russia seems reasonable given a continued substantial US presence in Central and Eastern Europe. The EU's Northern Dimension can be a vehicle for creating essence in those structures, provided that basic political and financial requirements are being met – a responsibility mainly located with the central institutions of the EU. In this sense the opportunity costs seem rather low, and the chances high, of reaching progress in a complex area of EU external relations, which is increasingly important as the enlargement process proceeds. A more direct approach on the Kaliningrad issue could bolster the likelihood for success and upgrade the agenda to focus on more important tasks in stabilizing the Baltic Sea region by calming Russian concerns about EU heavy-handedness in its Schengen work. The mere style of EU politics, with its multi-faceted ambitions and ambiguous wordings of agreements, is an obstacle to progress in its relations with Russia. Here also, the new member states can be of service, making EU initiatives transparent, and brokering deals with a tighter focus and less 'meandering' consequences.

The Czech Republic shares much of the basic analysis of the Polish political élite, but it has several shock-absorbing factors at play. Clearly, being removed from Russia, geographically, politically and psychologically has been a major factor in its more growth-oriented, EU-centred policy. The NATO insurance was thus not passed over, but the economic incentives inherent in the European Union have long been the big price for Prague. A second factor that has been of growing influence is domestic public opinion. The Czech public attitudes towards a host of political and economic issues have steeply converged with those of a consolidated democracy over the past few years to a much larger extent than is the case for Poland and other CEE countries, with the exception of Slovenia. This has produced a political climate regarding the role of the US, NATO and the legitimacy of the Iraq war that is similar to that of Western Europe. For example, when asked by the Pew Global Attitudes Project about preferences for 'democratic government' or a 'strong leader', the Czech replies came in at 91 per cent and 7 per cent, whereas the Polish numbers were 41 per cent and 44 per cent.[58] In every similar category, dealing with the preference for political freedoms, market economy and globalization over political stability and government intervention, the Czech public scores higher on the former than other CEE countries.

This development has generated a much higher sense of élite vulnerability to anti-war sentiments in the Czech Republic. Leading up to the Iraq invasion, public support in the Czech Republic for the war fell from an even split to a 12 per cent support for an invasion without a UN Security Council resolution and 22 per cent with such a resolution.[59] The overwhelming numbers apparently helped turn incoming Prime Minister Spidla around on the question of whether to authorize NATO commitments in Iraq in May 2004.[60] For Prague, the political cost of paying tribute to the transatlantic link has become too high domestically as well as in the EU context. The Czech Republic has scheduled its withdrawal of the 100 police officers in Iraq for February 2005. Poland, with its 2,400 soldiers, started reducing its presence in January and intends to completely withdraw its troops by the end of 2005.[61]

Which Europe?

The distinct differences between the respective 'institutional option packages' of our two study objects has some easily identified explanations. The Czech Republic lies geographically sheltered between benign neighbours in a largely tranquil part of Central Europe. It is a small state with its ambitions for influence over the European political space lying exclusively in becoming a rapidly modernizing state, which serves as an example for other transitional East and Central Europeans. Poland's sense of vulnerability towards its Russian-dominated north-eastern areas produces a very different political environment that emphasizes more classical security issues. Its size and economic potential breeds an element of entitlement as it acts on the EU stage.

The Polish orientation towards NATO at the expense of the EU is a product of the EU's low credibility on military security. ESDP and CSFP notwithstanding, historical reference in Poland advises against trusting Western European allies over the US. The Second World War analogy is alive and well in Polish politics and putting the security 'eggs' in the exclusively European basket seems risky from that perspective. The US has brought stability to Western Europe during the post-war era and Poland works actively to tie the superpower into the continent for the foreseeable future by being a reliable ally. An autonomous EU security identity would be detrimental to transatlantic cooperation and undermine the legitimacy of any military solidarity clause *sans les Américains* from this standpoint.

One might ask what the EU would have to prove politically to be the credible first choice for a state in Poland's position. It would not be enough to have the military hardware accessible (which arguably is being assembled under the auspices of the ESDP, see the analysis in Chapter 3 in this volume) – it would have to be legitimate in terms of rapid decisions in the event of severe regional discord, which would be part of any crisis involving Russia, including a reasonable possibility of forcing reluctant large European powers to commit politically and militarily to a decisive policy in support of a common objective. In the eyes of sceptical Central and Eastern Europeans, this is a pipedream. The gap in military capability between the EU and the US only serves to weaken the attraction of such an option, as any larger crisis in Europe's periphery would have to include US involvement at some level. So, as long as the US has a remote interest in Europe, it will be one of the continent's main players in security terms – at least until the major powers of Europe form a stronger alliance than present-day NATO and start to close the enormous divide in military spending between Europe and the US significantly.

Correspondingly, as long as Poland strives for security guarantees, the association with the US will be more important than the EU link in this area. However, if integration (and developments in Russia, Ukraine and Belarus) transforms Polish expectations to downgrade threat perceptions and upgrade the anticipation of security effects of European integration, then Poland is likely to move towards a more activist stance on European cooperation as well as on hard security issues. If that scenario carries worsened transatlantic trade relations, Poland's choice may well look very different from today and geo-economics could prove more convincing than geo-strategy as the underlying rationale for the 'new' European (on this point, see also Chapter 7 in this volume).

The Czech Republic's stance is similar to that of many other small members of the Union, partly due to the lack of a realistic security threat, partly due to the economic realities of small industrialized countries that emphasize market opportunities over traditional 'national interest'-based considerations. The Czech attempts to have it both ways on Iraq are symptomatic of the small state's preference for institutional stability. In the forced choice between two political extremes, the small state is surprisingly likely to choose both in an effort to avoid disloyalty to institutional partners. Of course, this is a political act of (self-) deception, and in the Czech case the chips ultimately landed in the interventionist corner, even though it made concerted efforts to soften that image by criticizing the war and trying to exclude itself from the list of active partners of the US and UK.

Given that the Czech Republic is a reluctant ally of the US in the Iraq war, the inclusion of former neutrals and the traditionally coy NATO allies Denmark and Norway in the ESDP (Norway being an associate member), is a reason for the Czech preference for intensified integration there. Increasingly, the Czech Republic is finding its closest partners in that group, choosing the Swedish combat aircraft Gripen over the US F-16 to modernize its air force and teaming up with Austria (and Hungary and Italy) to form the Central European Initiative designed to help pull the Balkans back into economic growth. From this perspective, the EU path is desirable, not only for the furthering of core economic interests, but also for building a coherent security policy under an institutional umbrella that includes likeminded states.

However, one threat to the perceived efficacy of the Czech approach is the risk associated with long-standing rifts in the European security community. The main tool for the small and medium-sized states is deliberation in conditions of political stability, especially in the EU framework where the negotiation framework is conducive for small-state influence when they can present middle-of-the-road alternatives under benign circumstances. When the larger powers are at odds, small states generally find themselves on the sideline. Nevertheless, it is unlikely that this logic would fundamentally challenge the Czech strategy of finding broad coalitions within the EU camp rather than narrow ones in NATO, although conflict-ridden issues may be compartmentalized in the same manner as the Iraq intervention.

In comparison, the two Central Europeans are deeply influenced by their respective focus powers – for Poland Russia, and for the Czech Republic Germany – which alter their commitment to a distinct European security identity, and thus their interest in a fully fledged triangular alignment of the transatlantic security structure. Dealing with Russia as a potential threat is perceived as requiring hard security safeguards that only NATO's Article 5 can bring in the short term and medium term. Coupling that with a Polish sense of opportunity in increasing its NATO influence by participating in out-of-area missions, while old-member resistance and relative economic weakness in the EU context dampens its prospects there, the logic seems to clearly stake out a NATO/US emphasis for now. For the Czechs, Germany is the influential actor most likely to affect their political situation. The one instrument deemed to be effective in keeping German national ambitions low is the European Union, and it is natural that Czech policy will rest on that institution rather than on a NATO that constantly forces domestically controversial decisions regarding defence spending and coalition participation. Balancing Russia in Central and Eastern Europe is certainly perceived as important from the Czech perspective, but seen as beyond Czech political resources and thus left to more influential actors within the region and outside it.[62]

In sum, the dual integration seems to foster a movement away from traditional security concerns across the continent, disrupted at times by acute international crises that create discord across Europe but not significantly altering the path towards a more institutionalized Union. For the more recent members, this process is volatile, since they lack a track record that fosters stable expectations of how the state and its immediate environment will act. Thus, balancing the numerous interlinkages in the forming security community of the Northern Hemisphere is especially difficult and ridden with many traps. As the transitional phase is coming to an end for these countries and the actorness of the EU is changing, the logic of being a Central European member state will certainly transform as well. It would not be shocking if the states with the fewest vested interests in the legacy of traditional EU and NATO values were the ones to succeed in modernizing both institutions to reflect the demands of a post-enlargement world. For the European Union as a leg in a strategic triangle, cohesion may not be all that it is cracked up to be as the mere strength of the common market grows and European commitment to the Middle East and other important regions rises. However, the EU as a distinct actor in a strategic triangle, acting independently on all transatlantic security areas, requires a common distancing from the bilateral embraces of the United States. For Poland, this is not likely any time soon.

Notes

1 The author would like to thank the Swedish Institute for European Policy Studies (SIEPS) for generous support in finalizing this chapter.
2 The grand debate that this refers to will not be resolved in this chapter. Instead, it will be framed from a different angle, seen from the perspective of two aspiring major players, and possibly shedding a different light on its core problems. See, for example, R. Kagan, 'Power and Weakness,' *Policy Review*, 2002, vol. 113, 3–28; D. Yost, 'The NATO Capabilities Gap and the European Union', *Survival*, 2001, vol. 33, no. 4, 327–51; T. Risse, 'Beyond Iraq: The Crisis of the Transatlantic Security Community,' *Die Friedenswarte*, 2003, vol. 78, no. 2–3, 173–94.
3 Of course, in recycling the old claim of dealing with an overlooked problem, some moderation is in order. See for example J. Sedivy, P. Dunay and J. Saryusz-Wolski, 'Enlargement and European Defense after 11 September', *Chaillot Paper*, no. 53, Paris: European Union Institute for Security Studies, 2002; A. Michta (ed.) *America's New Allies: Poland, Hungary, and the Czech Republic in NATO*, Seattle, WA: University of Washington Press, 1999. In addition, vibrant domestic debate in both countries as well as regional analysis, should be noted.
4 This is not to say that the selection of empirical facts presented is 'objective', but rather that it is open-ended in regard to what determines foreign policy choices. See C. Hermann, C. Kegley and J. Rosenau (eds) *New Directions in the Study of Foreign Policy*, Boston, MA: Allen & Unwin, 1987; L. Neack, J. Hey and P. Haney, *Foreign Policy Analysis: Continuity and Change in its Second Generation*. Englewood Cliffs, NJ: Prentice Hall, 1995.
5 'Mr Gross goes to Brussels', *Radio Prague*, 10 June 2004, online; S. Vaknin, 'Commentary: The Euro Atlantic Divide', *United Press International*, 18 February 2003, online.
6 See F. Schimmelfennig, *The EU, NATO and the Integration of Europe*, Cambridge: Cambridge University Press, 2003.
7 See R. Ginsberg, 'The EU's CFSP: the Politics of Procedure', in M. Holland (ed.) *Common Foreign and Security Policy. The Records and Reforms*, London: Pinter, 1997, 12–33; C. Hill, 'Renationalising or Regrouping? EU Foreign Policy since 11 September, 2001', *Journal of Common Market Studies*, 2004, vol. 42, 143–64.

8 Of course, portraying NATO as a wonder of efficiency is a violation of historical facts. There have been enough recurring scandals and examples of mismanagement within the NATO bureaucracy and in the member countries' NATO-related activities to challenge its effectiveness. However, it is clear that the member states attach a high level of importance to the functioning of the organization as a 'hardware' operation with clear and unambiguous capacities and goals – much more so than is the case with the European Union. See S. Cambone, *The Debate in the US Senate on NATO Enlargement*, Brussels: NATO Academic Forum, 1997; Schimmelfennig, *The EU.*

9 R.L. Schweller, 'Bandwagoning for Profit. Bringing the Revisionist State Back In', *International Security*, 1994, vol. 19, 72–107.

10 For an overview of power politics in International relations, see D. Baldwin, 'Power and International Relations', in W. Carlsnaes, T. Risse and B. Simmons (eds) *Handbook of International Relations*, London: Sage, 2002.

11 See J. Simon, *Czechoslovakia's 'Velvet Divorce', Visegrad Cohesion, and European Fault Lines*, Washington, DC: National Defense University, 1994.

12 CIA World Factbook: The Czech Republic, online.

13 See S. Hanley, 'The Political Context of EU Accession in the Czech Republic', Royal Institute of International Affairs Briefing Paper, 2002; A. Hyde-Price, *The International Politics of East Central Europe*, Manchester: Manchester University Press, 1996.

14 See T. Szayna, 'The Czech Republic', in A. Michta (ed.) *America's New Allies: Poland, Hungary, and the Czech Republic in NATO*, Seattle, WA: University of Washington Press, 1999.

15 J. Sedivy, et al., *Enlargement*; J. Simon, *Czechoslovakia's 'Velvet Divorce', Visegrad Cohesion, and European Fault Lines*, Washington, DC: National Defense University, 1994.

16 V. Klaus, 'The Importance of NATO Enlargement to the Czech Republic', speech to The Heritage Foundation, 21 October 1997, online; 'President Klaus Slams EU Integration on a Visit to Spain', *Radio Prague*, 30 November 2004, online.

17 European Parliament/Directorate General for Research, 'Information Note on the Economic and Political Situation of the Czech Republic and Its Relations with the EU. 2003', online; Szayna, 'The Czech Republic'.

18 See D. Bereuter and J. Lis, 'Broadening the Transatlantic Relationship', *The Washington Quarterly,* 2003, vol. 27, no. 1, 147–62; K. Longhurst, 'From Security Consumer to Security Provider – Poland and Transatlantic Security in the Twenty-First Century,' *Defence Studies*, Summer 2002, vol. 2, no. 2, 50–63.

19 See E. Rhodes, 'Transforming the Alliance: The Bush Administration's Vision of NATO,' CIAO Working Papers, November 2003.

20 G. Gromadzki and O. Osica, *An Overview of European (In)Security*, Policy Papers, no. 7, Warsaw: Stefan Batory Foundation, 2002.

21 See R. Trzaskowski, 'From Candidate to Member State: Poland and the Future of the EU', *Occasional Paper*, no. 37, Paris: European Union Institute for Security Studies, 2002.

22 F. Bynander, P. Chmielewski and G. Simons (eds) *The Politics of Crisis Management in Transitional Poland*, Stockholm: Crismart/Swedish National Defence College, forthcoming.

23 See Longhurst, 'From Security Consumer to Security Provider'.

24 Szayna, 'The Czech Republic'.

25 M. Zabrowski and K. Longhurst, 'America's Protégé in the East? The Emergence of Poland as a Regional Leader', *International Affairs*, 1993, vol. 79, no. 5, 1009–28.

26 The original figures quoted by the Polish government and by the US Congressional Budget Office are higher, for 2003 they are 2.3 per cent.

27 W. Patoka, 'Victims of Geopolitical Legacy: An Analysis of Security Policy and Army Transformation in Poland 1989–2002', Mimeo, February 2003.

28 US Congressional Budget Office Report, *Integrating New Allies into NATO,* Washington DC, October 2000.

29 'Reforming the Czech Armed Forces', *Radio Prague,* 30 November 2002, online.

30 J. Garamone, 'Jones Discusses Changing Troops' 'Footprint' in Europe', *American Forces Press Service,* 10 October 2003.

31 J.D. Banusiewicz, 'Rumsfeld: Reagan Legacy Present in Iraq Today,' *American Forces Press Service,* 10 October 2003.

32 See E. Stadtmuller, *The Issue of NATO Enlargement in Polish – Russian Relations,* NATO Research Fellowship Report, Brussels: NATO-EAPC, 2001.

33 Patoka, 'Victims of Geopolitical Legacy'.

34 See *The National Security Strategy of the United States of America,* 17 September 2002.

35 J. Sokolsky, 'The Power of Values or the Value of Power? America and Europe in a Post-9/11 World', CIAO Working Papers, online.

36 Patoka, 'Victims of Geopolitical Legacy'.

37 See D. Kelley, *Politics in Russia and the Successor States,* Fort Worth, TX: Harcourt Brace, 1999; C. Wagnsson, this volume; M. Webber, *The International Politics of Russia and Its Successor States,* Manchester: Manchester University Press, 1996.

38 See B. Nygren, this volume.

39 K. Mihalisko, 'Belarus: Retreat to Authoritarianism', in K. Dawisha and B. Parrot (eds) *Democratic Changes and Authoritarian Reactions in Russia, Ukraine, Belarus, and Moldova,* Cambridge: Cambridge University Press, 1997.

40 'Press Review', *Radio Prague,* 16 March 2004, online.

41 J.M. Aznar, et al., 'Europe and America Must Stand United', *The Wall Street Journal,* 30 January 2003.

42 K. Livingston, 'EU Bars Czechs from Iraq Summit', *Prague Post,* 19 February 2003.

43 D. Kaye, 'Bound to Cooperate? Transatlantic Policy in the Middle East,' *The Washington Quarterly,* 2003, vol. 27, no. 1, 179–95; 'Bush Plans to Cut Forces in Europe, Asia', *Fox News Online,* 15 August 2004, online.

44 H.-G. Ehrhart, 'What Model for CFSP?', *Chaillot Paper,* no. 55, Paris: European Union Institute for Security Studies, 2002.

45 E. Stadtmuller, *The Issue of NATO Enlargement in Polish–Russian Relations,* NATO Research Fellowship Report, Brussels: NATO-EAPC, 2001.

46 J. Sedivy, 'The Constraints and the Opportunities' in 'Enlargement and European Defence after 11 September', *Chaillot Paper,* no. 53, Paris: European Union Institute for Security Studies, 2002.

47 J. Moses, 'The Politics of Kaliningrad Oblast: A Borderland of the Russian Federation', *Russian Review,* 2004, vol. 63, no. 1, 107–30.

48 The internal debates in both countries surrounding the Copenhagen summit were massive, and the general impression is that Czech opinions were largely very positive, whereas in Poland there was criticism towards both the old EU states and the Polish government mixed in with celebration of the accession decision (P. Horakova, 'Czech Republic Reaches Agreement at Copenhagen Summit', *Radio Prague,* 17 December 2002; R. Cameron and D. Asiedu, 'EU Summit: No More Cash for Candidate Countries', *Radio Prague,* 13 December 2002; M. Kaczorowska, 'Commenting on Copenhagen', *Polish Voice,* 31 January 2003; 'Triumph of the Will', *The Warsaw Voice,* 22 December 2002).

49 'Europe in a Spin,' *Economist,* 10 June 2004.

50 See Hyde-Price, *The International Politics*; Stratfor, 'Fourth Quarter Forecast: Gaining Traction and Reclaiming the Initiative', 2003, online.

51 Sedivy, 'The Constraints and the Opportunities'.

52 'Czech Republic: Rough Patches on Way to the EU', *Deutsche Welle,* 12 October 2002.

53 J. Frowein, U. Bernitz and Lord Kingsland, 'Legal Opinion on the Beneš-Decrees and the Accession of the Czech Republic to the European Union', European Parliament/ Directorate-General for Research, 2002, online.
54 See D. Král, *The Czech Republic and the Iraq Crisis: Oscillating between the Two Sides of the Atlantic*, Prague: Europeum Institute for European Policy, 2003.
55 Cf. J. Saryusz-Wolski, 'Looking to the Future', in 'Enlargement and European Defence after 11 September', *Chaillot Paper*, no. 53, Paris: European Union Institute for Security Studies, 2002.
56 J. Smith, 'Introduction: The Future of the European Union and the Transatlantic Relationship', *International Affairs*, 2003, vol. 79, no. 5, 943–9.
57 See Council on Foreign Relations, 'Transcript: France, Germany and the US: Putting the Pieces Back Together, a Debate between Jean-David Levitte, Richard Holbrooke and Wolfgang Ischinger', CIAO Working Papers, March 2003.
58 Report from the Pew Global Attitudes Project, *Views of a Changing World*, Washington, DC: The Pew Research Center for the People and the Press, June 2003.
59 M. Hrobsky, 'Support among Czech Public for War in Iraq Running Thin', *Radio Prague*, 14 March 2003.
60 D. Asiedu, 'Spidla: Czech Republic Will Not Support NATO Engagement in Iraq', *Radio Prague*, 25 May 2004; V. Tax, 'Spidla Supports NATO Mission to Iraq', *Radio Prague*, 15 February 2004.
61 J. Dempsey, 'Poland Sets Pullout in Iraq for 2005', *International Herald Tribune,* 10 April 2004.
62 See Szayna, 'The Czech Republic'.

5

STRATEGIC COERCION

A tool for the EU or for Europe's major powers?

Adrian Hyde-Price

Introduction

In order to understand the strategic and political implications of the use of military force in international politics, it is helpful to begin by analysing the structural distribution of power at both the global and regional levels. Understanding the global and regional distribution of power is important because this establishes the parameters of expected state behaviour and identifies the systemic pressures that 'shape and shove' strategic interactions between key foreign policy actors.

In this respect, the demise of Cold War bipolarity is of decisive importance. It has significantly transformed the strategic context within which decisions concerning the use of military power are made. In place of the adversarial conflict between the US and its NATO allies on the one hand, and the Soviet Union and its Warsaw Pact affiliates on the other, a qualitatively different distribution of power has emerged. Globally, the United States has been left as the only superpower, with a dynamic economy, global military power projection capabilities and considerable soft power. The US, however, is not a global hegemon: it enjoys a hegemonic position in the Western hemisphere, and considerable influence in most other regions, but does not exercise hegemonic power in other regions of the globe.

In post-Cold War Europe, bipolarity faded following the unravelling of the Soviet Union and the precipitous decline of the rump Russian state. What replaced bipolarity was not American regional hegemony, but rather a more multipolar system. This multipolar system comprises five regional 'great powers': the US, Russia, Britain, France and Germany. The distinguishing feature of this multipolar system is that power differentials between the major regional actors are relatively balanced. In this context of balanced multipolarity, security competition between the great powers is relatively muted. Russia's weakness following the break-up of the Soviet Union allowed NATO and the EU to expand eastwards and shape new political and strategic relationships in much of Central and Eastern Europe. The process of NATO and EU expansion has been driven by the major powers involved, largely at the expense of Russia. Nonetheless, the emergence of balanced multi-polarity has provided the context for the emergence of more cooperative approaches to common security problems – as the example of the Contact Group illustrates.

One interesting aspect of the transformed post-Cold War strategic environment is the emergence of a potential new 'strategic triangle' involving the US, Russia and the EU. Despite the current crisis in the European integration process occasioned by the French and Dutch referenda on the proposed new European constitution, many commentators continue to suggest that the EU is evolving into a significant 'strategic actor'. This is certainly the aspiration of some influential EU member states – most notably, France and Germany, who together see themselves as providing the 'motor' of the European integration process. Indeed, the diplomatic tussles that preceded the 2003 Iraq War constitute a classic power political struggle, with Paris and Berlin seeking to project themselves as the leaders of a 'European' power bloc capable of challenging America's strategic pre-eminence. The Franco-German attempt to cement the EU as a counter-balancing force against the US failed amidst much rancour, primarily because of the opposition of Britain, Poland and other 'Atlanticist' states in what Donald Rumsfeld (with characteristic undiplomatic bluntness) termed 'new Europe'. Despite the fractures opened up between Europe 'old' and 'new', however, there is evidence that the EU may still serve as a collective vehicle for European aspirations to shape their 'near abroad' and project European power and values in the wider international system.

Operation Artemis

A prime example of this is the developing role of the EU in crisis management operations. Although none of the EU's major powers are willing to leave issues of vital national security to the vagaries of a Union of 25, there is broad consensus that the EU can and should tackle the three 'Petersberg tasks': peacekeeping, humanitarian missions and military crisis management. One example of this is Operation Artemis in the Democratic Republic of Congo (DRC). Operation Artemis was an 'autonomous' EU-led military operation conducted without recourse to NATO assets and capabilities. It was launched on 12 June 2003 in Bunia in the Ituri province in the DRC, in response to a request from the UN Secretary-General Kofi Annan. French President Jacques Chirac announced the willingness of France to mount an interventionary operation, and this was subsequently adopted as an EU operation. On the basis of the EU Framework Nation concept endorsed on 24 July 2002, France acted as the 'framework nation' for Operation Artemis, providing the bulk of the military assets and the command and control capabilities necessary for the planning, launch and management of the intervention. The EU Military Committee (EUMC) monitored the conduct of the operation, whilst the Political and Security Committee (PSC) was formally responsible for political control and strategic direction under the responsibility of the European Council. The Secretary-General/High Representative of the EU, Javier Solana, was responsible for cooperation with the UN, assisted by the EU Special Representative for the Great Lakes region.

Operation Artemis involved the deployment of a 1,850 strong French-led Interim Emergency Multinational Force (IEMF), consisting of contingents from nine countries. The objective was to protect civilians from ethnic conflict between militias based on the majority Lendu tribe and rivals from the Hema minority in the Ituri province. These conflicts were estimated to have cost some 50,000 lives and displaced 500,000 others since 1999. The IEMF was charged with a limited mission: to secure the regional capital, Bunia, and its immediate surroundings. This was successfully done, and involved securing the airport and establishing a weapons-free zone inside the town. IEMF demonstrated early on a willingness to use coercive military power to impose its will on the area, engaging in some fierce fire-fights and using overflights of Mirage jets based in neighbouring Entebbe airfield in Uganda to intimidate the combatants and to demonstrate resolve. The coercive powers of the French-led force were significantly enhanced by the use of special forces – 150 from France and 70–80 from Sweden – who gave IEMF a highly effective capability to engage and neutralize armed threats emanating from outside the area of operations. IEMF was replaced on 1 September 2003 by a 3,800-strong UN force, MONUC (UN Mission in the Congo), and completed its withdrawal on 7 September.[1]

Operation Artemis was an important test-case for the EU as a strategic actor, and illustrates some of the likely features of EU autonomous military crisis-management operations. First, it took place in an area of low strategic importance to the great powers. Second, it had a clear 'humanitarian' agenda, in keeping with the EU's self-image as an ethical actor and a 'force for good' in the world. Third, it was led by France acting as the 'framework nation', which ensured unity of command and the requisite political resolve. Fourth, it was limited in both space and time: IEMF operated only in Bunia and its immediate environs, and lasted only three months. Fifth, whilst Operation Artemis was primarily a French-led affair, its formal endorsement and adoption by the EU provided France with additional diplomatic leverage which was important in dealing with Rwanda and Uganda. Finally, IEMF was not afraid of using lethal military force in ensuring the success of its mission and the safety of its personnel. As such, Operation Artemis is a prime example of the peace support operations using coercive military power that have come to be such an important aspect of the military requirements of European armed forces since the collapse of the Soviet imperium.

Strategic coercion in the new strategic triangle

As Operation Artemis illustrates, the transformed strategic environment in post-Cold War Europe has significantly impacted upon European attitudes towards the use of military force. The Cold War emphasis on collective and territorial defence by mass conscript armies has given way to a growing concern with the calibrated use of military force as an instrument of statecraft. After four decades in which strategic thinking was primarily focused on nuclear deterrence and the prevention of war, Clausewitzean understandings of war as a continuation of politics by other means are back in vogue. Military coercion has become an integral aspect of milieu-shaping, in the form of peace support operations and humanitarian intervention. Since the end of the Cold War, therefore, military power has been used less as an instrument of 'brute force' to impose one's will on one's opponent, and more as an instrument of strategic coercion – in other words, as a means of influencing the behaviour of adversaries and shaping the international milieu.

The use of strategic coercion by major powers to shape their international milieu derives from the very nature of military force. The use of military force always has two dimensions, material and psychological. The purpose of using military force is to break the adversary's will to resist. This can be achieved either by crushing their material ability to resist, or by persuading them to concede in order to avoid significant damage and pain. Military force thus has both a material and a psychological impact, and one important aspect of military strategy is to maximize the psychological impact of using force whilst minimizing the material costs.[2] In most situations, the ideal outcome would be to achieve one's political goals without having to fight at all. When military force is used, the aim is to maximize its psychological impact on the adversary's will to resist. Strategic coercion thus involves using military force, or the threat of force, to break the enemy's will to resist.

The concept of 'strategic coercion' derives from the path-breaking work of Thomas Schelling and Alexander George in the 1960s–1970s. With the end of the Cold War, the concept has undergone something of a revival. At the same time, its meaning has become more contested. In his recent edited volume, Lawrence Freedman has defined strategic coercion as 'the deliberate and purposive use of overt threats to influence another's strategic choices' (p. 3). This definition is a broad one that includes deterrence as well as compellence. Mark Sullivan, on the other hand, uses the term 'strategic coercion' in a more limited sense as 'the act of inducing or compelling an adversary to do something to which he is not predisposed'. He sees this as synonymous with Schelling's term 'compellence', which involves 'a threat intended to make an adversary *do* something'.[3] Robert Pape also uses *coercion* in a similar way to Schelling's use of *compellence*, defining it as 'efforts to change the behaviour of a state by manipulating costs and benefits'.[4]

Here, strategic coercion is defined as the use of threats of force, or the limited use of force with the threat of further escalation, to change the decision-making calculus of the target actor. This chapter provides an overview and analysis of the concept of strategic coercion, focusing on its relevance for the EU and the problems of coalitional coercive diplomacy. It begins with a brief analysis of the changed strategic environment and the new European security agenda. It then goes on to examine the nature and meaning of strategic coercion, and to consider some of its implications and complications. It continues by examining the problems facing the EU if it is to evolve into a strategic actor capable of wielding coercive military power. The chapter concludes by suggesting that any effective 'European' use of strategic coercion will probably be led by either France or the UK, the two Western European powers with a significant power projection capability.

The European strategic environment

The end of Cold War bipolarity in Europe has been followed by the emergence of a multipolar structure of power in which five states play a key role: France, Germany, the UK, Russia and the USA. Regional power relations within Europe are roughly balanced resulting in a broad equilibrium of power, and there is no obvious candidate for hegemony against which a balancing coalition might be formed. Europe's strategic environment can thus be characterized as 'balanced multipolarity'. In the context of this balanced multipolarity, security competition has been relatively low-key, and a form of 'concert of Europe' has emerged which has developed more cooperative approaches to European security. This was evident from the role of the Contact Group in the Balkans, a region where none of the great powers had vital interests at stake.

Within continental Europe itself, there are four major powers: Britain, France, Germany and Russia. Throughout the Cold War, the US fulfilled Britain's traditional role as 'off-shore balancer' – a role which it continues to fulfil, albeit not without declining conviction. In addition to these major powers, there are six second-order powers: Italy, Spain, Sweden, Poland, Romania and Turkey. One distinctive feature of international politics in Europe is that patterns of interaction between states have been conducted within a dense and intricately woven network of overlapping and interlocking institutions, many of which are functionally differentiated and distinctive in terms of their membership. The two key institutions are the EU and NATO, both of which have had to develop new strategies for responding to the demands of a multipolar context.

One important development during the years of Cold War bipolarity was the emergence of a close strategic partnership between France and Germany. These two Western European great powers forged a highly institutionalized bond that was designed to provide the 'engine' or 'axis' of the European integration process. With the end of the Cold War, the EU has assumed the role of a collective hegemon, an *Ordnungsmacht*, seeking to shape the strategic environment in Europe's 'near abroad'. In the 1990s, the central focus of the EU as a collective actor was the post-communist lands of Central and Eastern Europe. At the same time, the EU has sought to shape developments in the Balkans, Eastern Mediterranean, Middle East and Maghreb (primarily through the Barcelona process, initiated in 1995).

For the next decade, however, the EU will not be able to deploy sufficient military force to carry out any but the simplest of the Petersberg tasks. It also continues to lack effective decision-making mechanisms to deal with crisis diplomacy. In this context, the task of strategic coercion on behalf of 'Europe' is likely to fall to the EU's major powers – more specifically, France and the UK. These two countries alone possess the military wherewithal and the political will to project military power into crisis situations in Europe's 'near abroad' or further afield. One clear trend in both is a process of military transformation that is giving them the capability for power projection and expeditionary warfare. This involves not only the acquisition of lighter and more mobile land forces, but also a switch from anti-submarine warfare to aircraft carriers and more multi-purpose surface vessels. The consequence of these changes is that both France and the UK are in a position to play the role of 'framework nation' in coalitional coercive diplomacy, acting 'in Europe's name'.

Europe's security agenda

Europe's contemporary international security agenda reflects the overall strategic context. First and foremost, security competition between the great powers is relatively low-key and restrained, with no major sources of interstate tension. Western and Central Europe enjoys a high level of stability, whilst relations with Russia are cordial and cooperative. Second, after a decade of recurrent crises and instabilities, the Balkans have been largely pacified, although the underlying sources of conflict have not been resolved. Third, the main international security concerns of EU member states are focused on a broad 'arc of instability' in its 'near abroad', which runs along the southern rim of the Mediterranean to the Middle East, extends up through the Eastern Mediterranean and the Balkans into the Caucasus and Central Asia, then curves around into Eastern Europe. This 'arc of instability' includes the region now known as the Greater Middle East, as well as the post-Soviet successor states around the peripheries of the former USSR. Fourth, whilst European security concerns are largely focused on the EU's 'near abroad', some security threats and challenges are more global in origin. These include the potential international fall-out from regional conflicts such as those in South Asia (Indio-Pakistan conflicts) and East Asia (Taiwan, North Korea); proliferation of weapons of mass destruction and ballistic missile technology; international terrorism; and the spill-over effect from weak or failing states in the global South.

Many of these security threats, risks and challenges are generated by structural economic and social problems associated with poverty, economic underdevelopment, social inequalities, injustice, political oppression and weak or failing states. Dealing with these underlying sources of insecurity and conflict will require non-military responses focused on aid, trade, developmental assistance and the application of 'soft power' resources. Defusing and resolving these security problems will require long-term and sustained engagement by NGOs and a raft of international organizations including the UN, EU, IMF, World Bank, the European Bank for Reconstruction and Development (EBRD), Council of Europe and OSCE. However, when crises of an acute and urgent nature occur, long-term strategies of conflict prevention and structural change are of limited relevance (in the long term, as Keynes noted, 'we are all dead'). The task then is crisis management: this can involve diplomacy backed up by economic carrots and sticks, but in some situations, soft power alone is not enough. As the experience of the 1990s underlined, crisis management can often entail the use of military threats to coerce the adversary into a change of behaviour.

Crisis management

Central to the contemporary European security agenda, therefore, is the issue of crisis management. Crisis management is one of the three 'Petersberg tasks' that now delineate the scope of the EU's security and defence policy, while non-Article V 'crisis response operations' are arguably now the core concern of NATO. Most European armed forces are being restructured away from mass conscript armies designed for national territorial defence towards leaner professional militaries capable of external power projection and expeditionary warfare – capabilities that are central to effective military crisis management.

Crisis management involves seeking to manage conflicts in order to avoid escalating to war, either through coercion or accommodation. Snyder and Diesing define a crisis as 'an intermediate zone between peace and war' and argue that it is 'a sort of hybrid condition, neither peace nor war, but containing elements of both and comprising the potential for transformation from peace to war'.[5] In managing the sorts of crises that could emerge in Europe's 'near abroad', therefore, EU member states need to develop their capabilities for operating in the 'grey zone' between war and peace. This involves rethinking some of the central pillars of Cold War strategy and developing new capabilities – political, diplomatic and military – for exercising strategic coercion and coercive diplomacy. One important consideration is that crisis management and coercive diplomacy now take place in a *multi-actor environment* – comprising governments, international organizations, NGOs, humanitarian organizations, non-state actors. As British General Sir Mike Jackson notes, 'The military have an essential part to play in bringing order out of chaos . . . But conflict resolution is by no means the preserve of soldiers: the military is but a single dimension, and not necessarily the dominant one. There has to be a coordinated approach in all dimensions – political, diplomatic, legal, economic, humanitarian, reconstruction, as well as military'.[6]

Strategic coercion and European crisis management

In the context of balanced multipolarity, European strategic thinking has focused increasingly on coercion and military crisis management rather than on the use of brute force. In any conflict situation, the strategic aim is to break the enemy's will to resist. 'It may be done in a number of ways', Colin McInnes notes, 'but the classic distinction is that of Thomas Schelling's between brute force and coercion.'[7] Brute force entails using military power to destroy the target's military assets in order to remove his power to resist. Coercion, on the other hand, involves the threat of force and, if that is insufficient, the actual use of limited force with the threat of more to come. It involves using what Schelling termed the 'diplomacy of violence' to influence the cost-benefit calculations of the adversary. The crucial point to note is that with coercion, the target retains an element of free choice.[8]

'The perfection of strategy', Liddell Hart argued, 'would be . . . to produce a decision without any serious fighting.'[9] The attraction of coercive strategies for

Western democracies is that they offer the prospect of achieving foreign policy goals without serious fighting. For this reason, they are particularly apposite to crisis diplomacy because they offer a means of addressing the political constraints facing Western democracies when contemplating the use of military force. Constraints on the use of force arise both from the structural features of institutional decision-making within pluralist political systems, and from the norms and values that infuse mature liberal-democracies. Democracies find it hard to undertake military operations in the teeth of significant domestic opposition, particularly if the operations are not concluded quickly and successfully. Second, where vital national interests are not at stake, public support for military operations becomes fragile when casualties are sustained or financial costs mount. Finally, public opinion is likely to grow critical if there are substantial casualties from 'collateral damage'.

Yet at the same time, although the institutions and norms of Western liberal-democracy can constrain policy-makers' options, they can also be a source of strength. They make it harder for democracies to act rashly or aggressively, and encourage them to try to exhaust all avenues for peaceful conflict resolution. Some commentators have made much of the 'bodybag syndrome' and the general aversion to war in Western societies. However, an examination of the available poll evidence suggests that public opinion can be mobilized behind coercive strategies aimed at reversing aggression or preventing oppression *if* the political leadership makes a strong enough case. Although democracies are sensitive to casualties, 'their impact is strongly mitigated by the real or perceived purposefulness of the action'.[10] In other words, if European democracies decide to use strategic coercion, either collectively or unilaterally, an essential political precondition is that the governments involved must make a credible and convincing case for using coercive threats, and explain the risks involved.

The institutions and values of European domestic politics have thus helped shape the way in which Western democracies use military power in pursuit of non-vital strategic interests. As General Rupert Smith has noted, there is now a general expectation that when the West uses military force, its destructive effects will be minimal and localized and that, wherever possible, political outcomes will be achieved directly without the prior passage through a major action that has produced technical military defeat in detail.[11] For this reason, coercion has assumed an ever more important place in the strategy of Western democracies since the end of the Cold War. Given the values and norms embodied in the political culture of mature democracies, the strategic culture of Western democracies emphasizes the use of coercion and discriminate force rather than brute force. Unless national survival is at stake (as in the Second World War), military power is used selectively and subject to strict political guidelines. Force is limited and targeted, and aimed not at the physical destruction of the enemy's society or even its armed forces, but rather at the leadership or regime. The aim is usually to influence the adversary's decision-making, not to eliminate his ability to resist. Coercive diplomacy is thus a continuation of politics by other – more limited – means, and embodies an aspiration to a more 'humane' form of warfare. Above all, strategic coercion is not about national territorial defence, but about power projection involving expeditionary forces to preserve or shape international politics.

Coercion and brute force

Coercion is usually counterposed to what Thomas Schelling termed 'brute force'. 'Brute force', he argued, 'succeeds when it is used, whereas the power to hurt is most successful when held in reserve. It is the threat of damage or of more damage to come, which can make someone yield or comply.'[12]

Coercive strategies are often associated with the use of air and naval assets (particularly airpower), whereas land warfare is seen as the realm of 'brute force'.[13] Yet the crucial distinction is not between the *instruments employed*, but the *intent*. Thomas Schelling explicitly argued that 'The difference between coercion and brute force is as often in the intent as in the instrument.'[14] In this respect, coercive strategies share much in common with 'limited war'. Indeed, in their book on coercion, Byman and Waxman explicitly state their intention 'to revive a once-active discussion about limited war'.[15] In his discussion of limited war, Henry Kissinger defines the concept in terms very similar to that of coercion. Brute force, or what Kissinger terms all-out war, 'represents an effort, perhaps subconscious, to transform foreign policy into an aspect of domestic policy, to bring about a situation abroad in which the will of other nations, or at least that of the enemy, is no longer a significant factor':[16]

> A limited war, by contrast, is fought for specific political objectives which, by their very existence, tend to establish a relationship between the force employed and the goal to be attained. It reflects an attempt to affect the opponent's will, not to crush it, to make the conditions to be imposed seem more attractive than continued resistance, to strive for specific goals and not for complete annihilation.
>
> (Kissinger 1979: 140)

One point of contestation in the literature on coercion is the degree of military force involved. Alexander George limited his concept of 'coercive diplomacy' to the threat of force or, at most, the 'exemplary' use of force. Successful coercive strategies, however, may involve more than simply the threat of force or exemplary force. The level of force applied to alter the adversary's cost-benefit calculation will vary from case to case, and cannot be arbitrarily defined in advance. Wesley Clark, for example, defined Operation Allied Force – NATO's operation in Kosovo in 1999 – as an exercise in 'coercive diplomacy', and distinguished between three levels of force in a coercive strategy: *diplomacy backed by threat* (threatening to bomb), *diplomacy backed by force* (the bombing campaign) and *force backed by diplomacy* (a ground invasion). In some cases, therefore, it might be difficult to distinguish coercion from brute force. As Byman and Waxman note, 'Distinguishing brute force from coercion is similar to the debate over what constitutes pornography or art: coercion is often in the eye of the beholder.'[17]

Strategic coercion is therefore not defined by the *degree of force used*, but by the *intent* governing its use. The important point is that coercion is not about establishing *control* over the target's behaviour, but about changing the way the adversary acts, whilst leaving him with the possibility of choosing other options. Coercion and brute force are not simple opposites, but end-points on a continuum of the use of force; both result from political calculations, and both involve military operations. In strategic coercion, the coercer's objective 'is usually not total destruction but the use of enough force to make the threat of future force credible to the adversary'.[18]

Cost-benefit analysis

At the heart of coercive diplomacy is a cost-benefit analysis. Alexander George noted that the central task of coercive diplomacy was 'to create in the opponent the expectation of costs of sufficient magnitude to erode his motivation to continue what he is doing'.[19] For George, coercive diplomacy is a strategy whereby threats are 'injected' into an enemy's calculations, persuading it to comply rather than resist. Similarly Robert Pape in his study of strategic bombing as an instrument of coercion has argued that 'Success or failure is decided by the target state's decision calculus with regard to costs and benefits. . . . When the benefits that would be lost by concessions and the probability of attaining these benefits by continued resistance are exceeded by the costs of resistance and the probability of suffering these costs, the target concedes.'[20]

The problem that this cost-benefit analysis raises is that it assumes a degree of rational calculation on the part of both actors.[21] Yet 'rationality' is not an unproblematic concept. Explaining foreign policy behaviour in terms of actors' rational calculation of their interests has been questioned by those who emphasize the importance of cultural, historical and societal factors. Rationality, it is often argued, is 'bounded'. Rather than following a rationalist 'logic of expected consequences', actors pursue a 'logic of appropriateness' deriving from political norms and shared understandings of what is or what is not appropriate.[22] In other words, political decisions are not simply ad hoc calculations of interest maximization, but are shaped by normative frames of reference that set the 'parameters of the possible'.

This has important implications for coercive diplomacy and suggests that 'many of the critical variables are psychological ones having to do with the perceptions and judgement of the target'.[23] Consequently, a cost-benefit analysis cannot be utilized with any hope of predictive accuracy without detailed knowledge of a policy-maker's goals and priorities. A key factor is the existence of very different cultural assumptions about conflict, war and acceptable costs. In the Cuban missile crisis, neither side wanted war and the issue was which side would back down first and at what cost. In the Kuwait crisis of 1990–1, on the other hand, neither side was willing to compromise. Coercive strategies are often premised on the assumption that the adversary shares a common rationality, and will recognize 'defeat' when they see it. However, Vietnam demonstrated that there is no automatic link between military and political victory: Tet was a US military victory but a strategic and political defeat. On the other hand, the 1973 Yom Kippur war was military defeat for Egypt but a political victory.[24] The important point to note here is that one cannot always assume that the coercer and the coerced share the same 'rationality': Al Qaeda, for example, has a fundamentally different world-view from Western governments. Hence, in coercive diplomacy and other forms of compellence and limited war, it is important to note that 'the rationality of the adversary is pertinent to the efficacy of a threat, and that madmen, like small children, can often not be controlled by threats.'[25] Richard Nixon consciously sought to manipulate his enemy's calculation of his strength of motivation by advocating what he described to Henry Kissinger as the 'crazy man approach' to deterrence: if the Soviets think I am crazy enough to do X then they'll believe that I might be crazy enough to do Y.[26]

A second problem inherent in any cost-benefit model of coercion is that the calculation of interests can be affected by the dynamics of institutional decision-making. Simply assuming that states function as unitary actors will not do. The institutional dynamics of policy-making within a state or non-state political actor is essential in order to identify the specific interests and concerns of its constituent elements. This was one of the principal findings of Graham Allison's seminal work on decision-making and the Cuban missile crisis. He proposed that the outputs of organizational processes and inter-organizational bargaining rather than the decisions of a monolithic government often explain important state behaviour.[27] Schelling recognized this in his path-breaking study, *Arms and Influence*: 'Collective decision depends on the internal politics and bureaucracy of government, on the chain of command and one the lines of communication, on party structures, on pressure groups, as well as one individual values and careers.'[28] Yet as Byman and Waxman note, this is an area that remains under-researched. 'Unfortunately', they argue, 'since Schelling's writing, analysts have made limited progress on learning how regime variations shape coercive diplomacy.'[29]

Carrots and sticks

Effective strategic coercion involves a mix of political, diplomatic, economic and military instruments, and the judicious combination of threats of military action with positive inducements for policy change. These 'carrots' can include economic sanctions or aid, preferential trade relations, improved political relations and membership of international organizations.'Carrots and sticks', as Byman and Waxman note, 'when combined, are often more effective than sticks alone':

> Traditionally, most coercive strategies focus on raising the costs to an adversary of continued provocations or on denying the benefits of defiance. Inducements, however, reverse this focus. Instead of raising the costs of defiance, inducements increase the value of concessions. In addition, inducements can decrease the political costs of capitulation

for an adversary, enabling leaders to claim victory even in defeat. When inducements are combined with more-traditional forms of coercion, resolution of a dispute is more likely.

(Byman and Waxman 2002: 9–10)

The problem here is of finding the right blend of carrots and sticks. Carrots can be seen as a sign of weakness or lack of resolve, and hence undermine the coercive strategy. Finding the right balance between carrots and sticks thus presents strategic actors with a series of apparently intractable dilemmas.

Strategies of punishment and denial

The distinction George draws between the exemplary use of force in coercive diplomacy and more traditional military strategies involving brute force is also problematic in situations in which coercion involves what are termed 'strategies of denial' rather than 'strategies of punishment'. A strategy of punishment involves using military instruments such as air power to impose civilian suffering, whereas a strategy of denial entails the targeting of the enemy's military capabilities and thus sense of vulnerability. Lawrence Freedman argues that the latter may be more effective and 'potentially more reliable than a strategy of punishment because its quality can be measured in more physical terms'.[30]

Robert Pape has argued that most effective coercive strategies will be directed against the benefit side of a cost-benefit analysis. His approach is very much rooted in conventional war and battlefield success, and he describes coercion as being 'to attain concessions without having to pay the full cost of military victory'.[31] He suggests that societies can cope with punishment, but that denial manipulates the opponent's military capability and thus sense of vulnerability, posing a direct challenge to his strategy. Sullivan in turn argues that a denial strategy resembles a brute-force strategy in that it targets an opponent's military capabilities. The advantage of denial is that if the opponent does not concede, 'military leaders are in a position to fully pursue a military victory'. The difference between brute force and denial, he argues, lies in 'attempts – which do not contribute directly to a military victory – to convince an adversary of the futility of his military strategy'.[32]

Coercive diplomacy as a dynamic process

At its most basic, the strategy of coercive diplomacy involves specifying objectives and determining the means to achieve them. This involves a series of steps: identifying the target's vulnerabilities and 'pressure points'; determining the mechanism through which change can be induced; and selecting the instruments to be employed. However, as Clausewitz notes, 'Everything in war is very simple, but even the simplest thing is very difficult.' This is certainly true of coercive diplomacy. The theory is relatively straightforward; its successful execution, however, is much more difficult.

A major complicating factor is that coercive diplomacy – like all strategy – is a highly *dynamic* process, where one action leads to response and to further actions, generating a non-linear logic with a high degree of inbuilt reflexivity. Coercive diplomacy is a form of strategic engagement, and strategy, by its very nature, is an interactive process involving the clash of two of more wills. As Edward Luttwak argues, 'there are of course at least two conscious, opposed wills in any strategic encounter of war or peace, and the action is only rarely accomplished instanta-neously, as in a pistol duel; usually there is a sequence of actions on both sides that evolve reciprocally over time.'[33] Thus he argues the realm of strategy is pervaded by a paradoxical, non-linear logic which tends to 'reward paradoxical conduct while defeating straightforwardly logical action, yielding results that are ironical or even lethally damaging'. Thus he argues, '*the entire realm of strategy is pervaded by a paradoxical logic* very different from the ordinary "linear" logic by which we live in all other spheres of life.'[34]

Escalation dominance

The dynamic nature of the coercion process means that 'a critical condition of successful coercion is *escalation dominance*: the ability to increase the threatened costs to the adversary while denying the adversary the opportunity to negate those costs or to counter-escalate'.[35] More precisely, it is the parties' *perception* of escalation dominance that is the key, rather than the actual military balance.

Escalation dominance is essential for successful coercive diplomacy because coercion involves the threat of force, or the limited use of force, *with the threat of more to come*. At the same time, the use of military force in a strategy of coercive diplomacy is always inherently risky. Threats which carry 'an explicit reference to possible military action if the target does not comply always risk events spinning wildly out of control. They are a gamble on big returns and big losses, which is why cautious democratic decision-makers are usually averse to them, while less restricted autocrats will at times be unable to resist the temptation.'[36]

The use of military force is sometimes viewed in terms of what Betts calls the 'chess model' – the cool, rational and deliberate use of military force in a strategy of graduated and finely tuned escalation. However, as Clausewitz reminds us, military conflict is also the realm of the irrational, of emotions and of chance. Schelling himself argued that a military threat is often one 'which leaves something to chance', and consequently what Betts terms the 'Russian roulette model' may be more apposite than the chess model.[37]

Coercive mechanisms

If coercion is to be effective, it is essential that it be applied in such a manner that it exerts maximum pressure upon the target. Given that coercive diplomacy involves the threat of force, or at the most the limited use of actual force, and that the target will continue to have the means to resist rather than being rendered defenceless, it is essential to identify what *mechanisms* can be used to make the target change its policy. Effective strategic coercion 'requires an understanding of coercive mechanisms – the processes by which the threat or infliction of costs generates adversary concessions. Mechanisms are the crucial middle link of the means-end chain of a coercive strategy'.[38]

The key problem facing coercive diplomacy is thus to determine what strategy will most effectively and economically alter the cost-benefit analysis of the target state. This is the key question, and yet the one that remains least understood. Coercive diplomacy involves a psychological strategy designed to affect the target's decision-making. The coercer must assess the threshold at which force will affect the target. 'But', as Colin McInnes notes, 'assessing this threshold is far from easy, and the mechanisms for successful coercion remain poorly understood.' Coercion is a highly dynamic process, a 'two-sided, iterative game in which the situation may change and with it calculations of costs and benefits. This uncertainty in turn makes it much more difficult to gauge an enemy's breaking point – the level of force that, with its implied escalation, will lead the enemy to give way.'[39]

Identifying the appropriate mechanisms involves opening up the 'black box' of decision-making in order to understand the political character of the target regime or actor. In particular, it involves identifying the most vulnerable *pressure points* of the target. Similarly, the target state will seek to counter-coerce by targeting the coercer's vulnerable points. These pressure points will vary from regime to regime. It is also evident that democracies have different pressure points from non-democracies. Whereas democracies will be vulnerable to casualties and to charges of arrogance and bullying, non-democracies may be vulnerable only when key elite groups underpinning the regime are attached. A coercive strategy thus involves identifying what the opponent values most and targeting it. 'To threaten effectively, a coercer must first understand what the adversary values. Then the coercer must determine what it can credibly put at risk without too much cost to itself. In other words, a coercer must seek out an adversary's pressure points: those points that are sensitive to the adversary and that the coercer can effectively threaten.'[40]

Problems with identifying effective coercive mechanisms

The problems inherent in identifying the appropriate coercive mechanisms can be illustrated from the example of Operation Allied Force. The Kosovo campaign, Edward Luttwak has argued, 'exposed the *strategic* limitations of fighting by remote bombardment alone'. A war

> fought by precision bombardment alone is necessarily a slow and tortuous process of identifying, selecting, and destroying single structures one by one. . . . Unless the entire purpose of the bombing is to deprive the enemy of some specific facilities or weapons, so that it can be achieved *physically* and unilaterally, the success of a bombing campaign must depend on the enemy's decision to accept defeat. That

97

decision can result only from a complex political process in which the impact of the bombing interacts with all sorts of other factors, including cultural determinants and historical memories, the inner politics of decision making, concurrent threats or reassurances from other powers if any, and more.

In the case of Kosovo, he notes, different coercive mechanisms were tried;

For example, when the 1999 Kosovo war started on March 24, initially the bombing was mostly symbolic and largely aimed at air defences, on the theory that the government of Slobodan Milosovic only needed to be convinced of NATO's determination to capitulate [before it became willing]. When that failed to happen, in April the bombing became distinctly heavier and focused on weapon factories, depots, bases, and barracks, on the theory that Serbian military leaders would pressure the government to accept the abandonment of Kosovo in order to save their remaining institutional assets. By May 1999, however, civilian infrastructures such as power stations and bridges were being destroyed to make everyday life as difficult as possible, on the different theory that the Milosevic government was not undemocratic after all, that it would respond to pressures for surrender from an increasingly uncomfortable public.

(Luttwak 2002: 77)

The EU and strategic coercion

Paradoxically perhaps, given the problems NATO faced in devising an effective coercive strategy in Operation Allied Force, it was the experience of Kosovo that provided the crucial catalyst for the ESDP. The ESDP is designed to give the EU a capability for military crisis management, both acting 'autonomously' and in conjunction with NATO (utilizing the 'Berlin Plus' arrangement); its significance is that it demonstrates that the Union has clearly moved beyond its former 'civilian power' identity. The ESDP is still in its embryonic stages and it will perhaps be a decade or more before the Union is in a position to undertake the full range of Petersberg tasks, including the most demanding. Within Europe, the EU has functioned as an instrument of collective regional hegemony, seeking to shape its external milieu through a mix of hard and soft power. With the lesson of the Balkans clearly in their minds, EU member states have recognized that if they are to act as a 'civilizing' power, they need to add coercive military power to their repertoire of foreign and security policy instruments. The development of the ESDP is further analysed by Arita Eriksson in Chapter 3 of this volume.

Before the EU can develop into an effective institutional forum through which its member states can collectively manage and resolve international crises, four shortcomings need to be addressed. The first is that the EU needs more streamlined procedures and mechanisms to ensure swift decision-making, whilst ensuring political accountability and control. In crisis diplomacy involving strategic coercion, it is essential to get inside the decision-making cycle of the adversary, in order to seize the initiative and set the agenda, rather than to be left responding to events. Speedy decision-making is thus essential. A complex 'wiring diagram' is now in place for the second pillar, and in the Nice Treaty the PSC was identified as the crucial body for crisis management. However, it is not clear how effectively this will work in practice, and there are still too many procedures involved. The Kosovo conflict demonstrated the problems NATO faced in trying to 'wage war by committee'. Formal procedures involving established institutions tend to lack flexibility, and much effective crisis management has involved the creation of ad hoc arrangements.

A further complicating factor is that effective EU action in a complex emergency may require 'horizontal links' between the different pillars, for example, the second and third pillars (CFSP and JHA), or the first and second pillars. It will also need to coordinate its activities with other international actors, including international organizations, states and NGOs. The central dilemma facing the EU is how to combine effective crisis management decision-making with political control and direction of crisis management operations. The problem here is that the EU consists of 25 member states, all with somewhat different geopolitical interests, political cultures and attitudes to the use of force. Differences in interest between large and small member states need to be taken into account, and all will want to have their say if the EU is acting in their name.

Second, EU member states need to identify the lacuna in their military capabilities and develop common approaches to defence procurement. At the same time, they will need to consider the implications of the RMA (Revolution in Military Affairs) for the sort of military forces they acquire. The problem facing EU member states is exemplified by the fact that only 3 per cent of the substantial numbers of men under arms were readily available in a crisis.[41] Not only has defence expenditure steadily fallen in the 1990s, Europe's armed forces have been largely trained and equipped for territorial defence, not expeditionary warfare or crisis management. EU member states are aware of this problem.

Given the strategic requirements of the Headline Goals, which have been defined by the Petersberg tasks, there is no need for member states to develop capabilities for the full spectrum of military operations. The EU is unlikely to want to conduct independent high-intensity operations at the tougher end of the Petersberg tasks for some time, so capabilities for long-range precision bombing or intense mechanized ground combat are not urgently required. However, EU member states will need to improve their capability to project military power and sustain operations in the field. The key to this is not simply increasing defence spending, but rather to adopt a more rational and synergistic approach to arms procurement.

Third, the finest armed forces in the world and the most effective decision-making procedures are useless if there is no agreement on *how* to use them. EU member states – or at the least, the serious players amongst them – must agree broad guidelines on how to use military force once the relevant political decision has been taken. This means that the EU must develop a common strategic culture and military doctrine covering the level and circumstance of the use of force, the general rules of engagement, military discipline (in the context of a variety of different legal frameworks) and the chain of command. Common rules of engagement are clearly important, but thought must also be given to shared understandings about how to work with other international agencies or NGOs who are likely to be present in complex emergencies; how to relate to the local authorities and population; and legal-technical questions of extra-territorial status and immunity. The EU strives to present an image as an 'ethical power', and therefore national contingents to EU military operations must share certain minimum standards regarding their operation in the field. This will require the elaboration of a common strategic doctrine, and shared training – neither of which are on the cards at the moment.

Finally, enlargement will have a major impact on the EU as an international actor. Enlargement has given the EU new geo-strategic interests in Eastern Europe, the Caucasus and the Balkans, along with the Mediterranean and the Maghreb. Further enlargement will extend the EU's 'near abroad' deeper into Eastern Europe and the Middle East. At the same time, enlargement has complicated decision-making within the second pillar, and brought more diverse interests into the policy-making process. This will further weaken the cohesion of the EU as an instrument of collective hegemony, and weaken its ability to shape its regional milieu. On the importance of enlargement for the actorness of the EU see also Chapter 2 in this volume.

In short, therefore, given the heterogeneity of political interests and values in an EU of 25 members, it will be very difficult to get political consensus for any operation that does not enjoy a clear and unambiguous mandate from the UN Security Council or the OSCE, or for one that involves a significant element of military coercion. For the foreseeable future, therefore, the EU is unlikely to be a viable instrument of coalitional strategic coercion. EU military operations are likely to focus on the low-risk end of the Petersberg tasks such as police missions, training, surveillance, blockades or protection of SLOC (sea lines of communication). Such missions include what has been termed 'coercive inducement' or 'coercive prevention',[42] and may involve taking over peace support operations from NATO. In Robert Kagan's terms, the EU will 'do the dishes', once NATO (or a coalition of the willing) has 'cooked the meal'.[43]

This has implications for the EU as a strategic actor. The EU as such is too diverse to act as a coherent actor in international politics where security issues of vital national importance are involved. In this regard, it remains less than the sum of its parts. Nonetheless, in some contexts, it can serve to amplify the power and influence of its largest and most capable member states acting in its name – as the example of Operation Artemis demonstrates. Such operations, however, are only possible in regions not caught up in the web of varying strategic interests and geopolitical concerns of its member states.

Conclusion: the limits of strategic coercion

Coercion is a very difficult strategy to implement, replete with risks and uncertainties. There is an ever-present risk of escalation in the context of a changing and dynamic environment. Once force or the threat of force is introduced into a crisis situation, the whole dynamics of the conflict change. Once a coercive threat has been issued, the coercer faces the prospect of backing down if it is rejected, with dire consequences for its future credibility as an international actor, or escalating to a more aggressive strategy based on brute force. The historical record is not reassuring: coercive strategies have failed more times than they have succeeded.

Strategic coercion is thus a high-risk approach that is difficult to implement effectively against a determined, crafty and unpredictable opponent.[44] It depends less on the precise balance of military capabilities between coercer and target, and much more on their relative motivation and political resolve. For this reason, strategic coercion is more of an art than a science, and depends on the ability to calibrate military operations to nuanced and effective diplomatic negotiation. As Freedman notes, therefore, '[t]here is no mechanical formula that can ensure success, even though we might be able to identify conditions that make success more likely'.[45] He thus concludes that

> Strategic coercion is not an easy option. Because the target remains a voluntary agent the objective must be to influence its decision-making and will therefore only be one of a number of influences. It is dependent on an appreciation of how the target constructs reality and its likely responsiveness to alternative forms of pressure. It lacks the legitimacy provided by consent or the certainty promised by control. Unsuccessful coercion may therefore necessitate a more aggressive approach based on control or else a more conciliatory approach geared to generating consent.
>
> (Freedman 1998: 17)

Despite the problems inherent in strategic coercion, it is likely to remain an attractive option for European policy-makers because it promises a way to achieve political and strategic objectives short of full-scale war. Strategies of military coercion employing the discriminate use of force that minimizes collateral damage are also attractive to Western democracies because they fit contemporary understandings of the 'just war' theory. In the 1990s, strategic coercion was used by NATO in Bosnia and Kosovo, with mixed results. As a result of the Kosovo campaign, the EU has moved to equip itself with the military and institutional capabilities to conduct military crisis management operations, 'including the most demanding'. Yet as we have seen, the EU's heterogeneous membership and cumbersome decision-making procedures mean that the Union is unlikely to engage in collective strategic coercion. Instead, this will be left to 'coalitions of the willing' led by one or more of the EU's major powers. In some contexts, this will be conducted with the US and NATO, utilizing the 'Berlin Plus' mechanism. At other times, non-EU OSCE states might be involved, most notably Russia, the Ukraine and Canada. Russia would make a suitable strategic partner given that it has military capabilities (for example, strategic airlift) that complement those of EU member states. Possible areas for joint EU-Russia military intervention include Moldova (Transdniestra) and Georgia (Abkhazia). Cooperation in addressing the long-running problem of Chechnya is unlikely given that Russia regards this as an area where vital national interests are at stake. The example of Chechnya illustrates the point made at the start of this chapter: collective strategic coercion is only possible in situations where none of the vital interests of Europe's great powers are involved.

Notes

1 For details see 'Operation Artemis: The Lessons of the Interim Emergency Multi-national Force', Peacekeeping Best Practices Unit, Military Division, United Nations, October 2004; C. Mace, 'Operation Artemis: Mission Impossible?', *ISIS Europe European Security Review*, Brussels, number 18 (July 2003); and Chronology of EU Operation Artemis in DR Congo, *http://www.eubusiness.com/afp/030816172714. a25inyv2/*

2 S. Bungay, *The Most Dangerous Enemy. A History of the Battle of Britain*, London: Aurum Press, 2000, p. 16.

3 This definition is from T. C. Schelling, *Arms and Influence*, New Haven, CT: Yale University Press, 1966. In his 1960 study, *The Strategy of Conflict*, he defined compellence as 'a threat intended to make an adversary do something (or cease doing something)'. Eric Herring argues that the category of 'cease doing' cannot be catego-rized clearly as either deterrence or compellence, and therefore his quiet modification of his definition of compellence in 1966 makes sense. Eric Herring, *Danger and Opportunity, Explaining International Crisis Outcomes*, Manchester: Manchester University Press, 1995, p. 17. See also A. L. George, D. K. Hall and W. E. Simons, *The Limits of Coercive Diplomacy*, Boston, MA: Little, Brown, 1971.

4 R. Pape, *Bombing to Win*, Ithaca, NY: Cornell University Press, 1996, p. 4.

5 G. Snyder and P. Diesing, *Conflict Among Nations: Bargaining, Decision Making, and System Structure in International Crises*, Princeton, NJ: Princeton University Press, 1977, p. 10.

6 General Sir Mike Jackson, 'Foreword', in G. Prins, *The Heart of War*, London: Routledge, 2002, p. xi.

7 C. McInnes, *Spectator-Sport War: The West and Contemporary Conflict*, Boulder, CO: Lynne Rienner, 2000, p. 100.

8 L. Freedman (ed.) *Strategic Coercion: Concepts and Cases*, Oxford: Oxford University Press, 1998, p. 36.

9 B. Liddell Hart, *Strategy: The Indirect Approach*, 4th edn, London: Faber & Faber, 1967, p. 338.

10 P. Everts, *Democracy and Military Force*, London: Palgrave, 2002, pp. 178, 200.

11 Quoted in G. Prins, *The Heart of War*, p. 218.

12 Schelling, op. cit., p. 3.

13 Stephen Biddle argues that maritime blockades, strategic bombing and guerrilla warfare are 'fundamentally coercive in nature: rather than seizing the stakes directly, aggressors seek to induce the opponent to give them their prize by threatening pain if the opponent refuses to comply. Each thus requires some degree of cooperation from the opponent to succeed; each also requires the ability to communicate a credible threat

of future consequences if the target state withholds concessions. Continentalist land warfare, by contrast, obtains objectives by seizing them directly – or by preventing an opponent from doing so. Continental strategy is thus an exercise in brute force in Thomas Schelling's terms: without the opponent's agreement or consent, resources are simply taken or kept by force of arms. Although the seizing of assets by brute force may itself be used coercively, brute force per se thus requires no cooperation from the opponent and is less dependent on credible communication of intent to the target state. As such, it has been the ultima ratio of modern strategy: where coercion fails, brute force on land has been the final arbiter of disputes.' S. Biddle, 'Land Warfare: Theory and Practice', in J. Baylis, J. Wirtz, E. Cohen and C. Gray (eds) *Strategy in the Contemporary World: An Introduction to Strategic Studies*, Oxford: Oxford University Press, 2002, pp. 91–112 (p. 92).

14 Schelling, *Arms and Influence*, p. 5.
15 D. Byman and M. Waxman, *The Dynamics of Coercion: American Foreign Policy and the Limits of Military Might*, Cambridge: Cambridge University Press, 2002, p. xiii.
16 H. Kissinger, *Nuclear Weapons and Foreign Policy*, New York: Doubleday, 1957, p. 140.
17 Byman and Waxman, *The Dynamics of Coercion*, p. 5.
18 Byman and Waxman, *The Dynamics of Coercion*, p. 5.
19 George, Hall and Simons, *Limits of Coercive Diplomacy*, p. 11. See also McInnes, *Spectator-Sport War*, p. 100.
20 R. Pape, *Bombing to Win*, pp. 15–16.
21 Schelling explicitly stated the three main assumptions underpinning this sort of cost-benefit analysis in a strategic confrontation: first, the presumption of common interest that is the basis of any bargain; second, rationality in the form of an optimizing or value-maximizing behaviour; and third, 'an explicit and mutually consistent value-system'. The bargain sought is not a 'mini-max' one, in which the victor achieves total gains and the loser total losses, but a 'gaining relative to one's own value system' through mutual accommodation and the avoidance of mutually damaging behaviour. Schelling, *The Strategy of Conflict*, pp. 4, 6. See also C. Reynolds, *The Politics of War: A Study in the Rationality of Violence in Inter-State Relations*, New York: St Martin's Press, 1989, pp. 104–5.
22 J. March and J. P. Olsen, 'The Institutional Dynamics of International Political Orders', *International Organization*, 1998, vol. 52, no. 4, pp. 948–52.
23 George, Hall and Simons, *Limits of Coercive Diplomacy*, pp. 14 and 81.
24 Philip Windsor, *Strategic Thinking, An Introduction and Farewell*, London: Lynne Rienner, 2002, p. 145.
25 Schelling, *Arms and Influence*, p. 6
26 Prins, *Heart of War*, p. 150.
27 G. T. Allison, *Essence of Decision*, Boston, MA: Little, Brown, 1971.
28 Schelling, *Arms and Influence*, p. 86.
29 Byman and Waxman, *The Dynamics of Coercion*, p. 14.
30 Freedman, *Strategic Coercion*, p. 27.
31 R. Pape, 'Coercion and Military Strategy: Why Denial Works and Punishment Doesn't', *Journal of Strategic Studies*, vol. 15, no. 4 (December 1992), pp. 423–75 (p. 425).
32 M. P. Sullivan, *Mechanisms for Strategic Coercion: Denial or Second Order Change?*, Maxwell AFB, AL: Air Force University, 1995, pp. 18–19.
33 E. Luttwak, *Strategy: The Logic of War and Peace*, Cambridge, MA: Harvard University Press, 2002, p. 16.
34 Luttwak, *Strategy*, p. 2.
35 Byman and Waxman, *The Dynamics of Coercion*, p. 38.
36 C. Hill, *The Changing Politics of Foreign Policy*, London: Palgrave, 2003, p. 143.

37 Quoted in Herring, p. 38.
38 Byman and Waxman, *The Dynamics of Coercion*, p. 48.
39 McInnes, *Spectator-Sport War*, p. 101.
40 Byman and Waxman, *The Dynamics of Coercion*, p. 44.
41 'Summary of the Meeting Held on 29 October 2002', Working Group VIII on Defence, the European Convention, Brussels, 12 November 2002, CONV399/02, p. 3.
42 D. Daniel and B. Hayes with C. de Jonge Oudraat, *Coercive Inducement and the Containment of International Crises*, Washington, DC: US Institute of Peace Press, 1999.
43 R. Kagan, 'Power and Weakness', *Policy Review*, 2002 (June).
44 This is one of Alexander George's main conclusions from his study of coercion diplomacy. See George, Hall and Simons, *Limits of Coercive Diplomacy*.
45 Freedman, *Strategic Coercion*, p. 14.

6

THE ALIEN AND THE TRADITIONAL

The EU facing a transforming Russia

Charlotte Wagnsson

Introduction

A most intriguing issue is why Russia–EU cooperation in the sphere of security has not evolved further, despite expected mutual gains and official declarations in support of closer collaboration. The aim of this chapter is to further explore both driving forces and obstacles to EU–Russia rapprochement in the sphere of security.[1] Is cooperation held back by diverging threat-conceptions, the two parties' differences in actorness, or perhaps by the shadow of the 'giant' on the other side of the Atlantic?

Security issues have been discussed at biannual EU–Russia summit meetings since 1999 and the cooperation has been described in terms of a 'strategic partnership'.[2] Representatives from both sides have paid generous tribute to the cause of rapprochement. The newly appointed High Representative of the EU's common foreign and security policy, Javier Solana, assessed relations with Russia as the Union's most important task, since a partnership with Russia 'offers the greatest opportunity to affect the cause of world affairs for the better and to begin the new century in a manner which will truly affect the course of history'.[3] Russian leaders interpret a strong EU as largely beneficial to Russia, since it contributes to spreading the power in the international system.[4] President Putin has described Europe as one of the most important poles in the emerging multi-polar world.[5]

The basic driving force for closer cooperation between EU and Russia is economics. Russia depends on the EU as its main trading partner. The Union accounted for 40 per cent of Russia's trade in the 1990 and answers for about 6 per cent of Russia's imports and export trade after the EU enlargement in 2004. European companies are the main foreign investors in Russia's expanding economy.[6] The EU counts on Russia above all as an exporter of energy. Russia provide 20 per cent of the EU's fuel.[7] (Economic relations between the EU and Russia are analysed in Chapter 9 in this book.) Despite many problems, the volume of trade will most probably increase in the future. Economic considerations spill over into the security area.[8] Russian leaders link security to the promotion of development goals. The overall most important political aim is to regenerate the economy by focusing on internal reform and establishing favourable external relations for its trade. The National Security Concept of 2000 states that 'Russia's national interests may be assured only on the basis of sustainable economic development.'[9] The Foreign Policy Concept of June 2000 also places security in relation to economic development as such and not only to traditional security goals.[10] President Putin displays an awareness of the link between a strong economy and international power and influence.[11] (The 'economization' of Russia's foreign policy is further explored in Chapter 7.)

Apart from economics, the pursuit of stability in the European sphere of security is a strong force for further rapprochement. A forceful EU motive for cooperation is the desire to promote stability along its borders. The EU's 'Common Strategy on Russia', adopted in Cologne in June 1999, states that lasting peace on the continent can only be achieved if Russia is democratic, stable and prosperous and firmly anchored in Europe. Russia's Middle Term Strategy for the Development of Relations between the Russian Federation and the EU (2000–10), published in October 1999, acknowledges the two parties' mutual interdependence and empha-sizes the advantages of cooperation for curbing common threats. It suggests that Russia could contribute to the solution of problems facing the EU, such as organized crime and local conflicts, and to the strengthening of Europe's common position in the world. The two parties already collaborate to reduce the risk of spillover. For example, a Co-operation Programme for Non-Proliferation and Disarmament in the Russian Federation was launched in 1999 in order to increase nuclear safety in Russia.[12] The EU also maintains an interest in boosting stability and prosperity in more distant regions where Russia plays a key role, most notably in the South Caucasus.[13]

Moreover, the two parties share some basic interests in global relations, most obviously a common will to strengthen the UN. At the summit in Rome in November 2003, the joint statement 'confirmed a high degree of mutual understanding with regard to a number of acute international issues and the central role of the UN in world affairs'.[14] Indeed, the rationales behind the promotion of the UN differ. Russia's seat in the Security Council is one of the few remaining signs of its status as a great power, which makes it quite focused on sustaining the importance of the Security Council. The EU, rather, sees in the UN a vehicle for advancing multi-lateralism and upholding the rule of law. Nevertheless, despite their differences the two parties share the same goal of retaining the UN's significance in world affairs.

If resources were pooled, Russia and the EU could indeed gain greater leverage in the international arena. The two parties already collaborate in the peace process in the Middle East and the EU has worked hard to convince Russia of the advantages of ratifying the international agreement that seeks to reduce the emissions of gases contributing to global warming, the Kyoto Protocol. The Russian ratification in October 2004 was vital for the implementation of the Protocol.[15] Also, Russia and the EU have taken a rather cohesive stance on North Korea, partially pursuing a different strategy from that of the US.[16] The two parties also share interests as regards to the struggle against international terrorism and organized crime and non-proliferation. In January 2005, Russia chose to join and thereby strengthen a European diplomatic imitative to persuade Iran to renounce any nuclear technology that could be used for military purposes.

The two parties could increase practical cooperation in many areas. In the field of conflict resolution and mediation, the EU can take advantage of Russian efforts; the latter is neither a member of NATO nor of the Union, and in the Balkans it also plays a particular role due to historical reasons.[17] There is also a considerable potential in the area of peacekeeping and peace-enforcement within the Commonwealth of Independent States (CIS). The Russian leaders could much more easily accept joint peacekeeping within the borders of the former Soviet Union together with the EU than they would consider launching such projects together with NATO. Closer cooperation in these areas would also provide the EU with valuable information on conditions within the CIS, e.g. augmenting transparency as regards to Russia's conduct in Chechnya.[18]

One possible way forward is to incorporate Russia into EU security structures, by seeing to that it plays an enhanced role in, or is integrated into, the ESDP.[19] However, so far Russia has only made a limited contribution, by participating in the EU Police Mission in Bosnia and Herzegovina which became operational on 1 January 2003.[20] Russia could also provide assets in support of an EU-led crisis management operation, such as heavy-lift transport aircraft and satellite reconnaissance. Military-technical cooperation has, however, not evolved very far.

This overview suggests that there are plenty of possibilities and some attempts to boost practical cooperation. However, tangible results are relatively poor.[21] Indeed, declarations of goodwill and formal agreements constitute achievements *per se* thanks to their strong symbolical value. This holds particularly true with regard to the Russian leadership, which has aimed at getting Russia accepted as a respected and prominent actor in the sphere of European security ever since the fall of the Soviet Union.[22] Still, why has so relatively little been achieved in practical terms? Three potential explanations to the relatively poor outcome are addressed below; differences in actorness, diverging threat-perceptions and the shadow of the US.

The first problem is about the quite different set-up and character of the two actors. The EU is a new and different kind of actor on the international scene. It is not primarily based upon the notion of sovereignty and cannot be equated with any other actor in the current international system.[23] (The special character of the EU as an international actor is also analysed in Chapter 2 of this volume.) Such a 'post-Westphalian entity' ought to encounter both advantages and difficulties when interacting with a traditional sovereign state like Russia. Most probably, difficulties are linked more to how the two actors perceive each other, rather than to factual differences. How do the EU's and Russia's interpretations of the 'existential barrier' impact on the prospects of further cooperation? This is the main question of the first section of analysis.

The second problem is that the *framing of threats* to security may diverge to an extent that causes difficulties for cooperation. There is a risk that Russia and the EU 'play different games' in the sphere of security, due to diverging definitions of threats and security. Russian leaders traditionally frame security in terms of high politics, state-to-state relations, power politics, spheres of influence and geopolitical balancing. This practice meets with a new actor in the international arena, which bestows the nation-state with a secondary position, and which places economics before power politics in the traditional military sense. This section of the analysis starts by capturing similarities and differences in the actors' subjective descriptions of reality; in other words, it asks how actors *frame* problems. A frame demonstrates how actors conceptualize political issues. The targets of analysis are official motivations used so as to describe and justify security policy; in Schön and Rhein's words, 'rhetorical frames'.[24] Politicians are obliged to communicate an acceptable basis for their politics to counterparts in both the domestic and international arena. Framing is essentially a power game; it affects the very essence of a debate, determining what issues are included and excluded in a communicative process, i.e. the boundaries of discourse.[25] The battle for control in a political debate is, in turn, a central battle in political reality. Competing framing is the result of frame conflicts, and ultimately, of *policy controversies* that have tangible political consequences.[26]

The third problem is that great international political transformations induce actors to adapt their strategies in the sphere of security. During the Cold War, the enmity between the two superpowers froze regional security dynamics, a phenomenon labelled 'overlay'.[27] After the end of the superpower confrontation, regional dynamics prospered all over the globe, resulting in both enhanced cooperation and unleashed conflicts. However, actors are still pressured to adjust their perspective on security to a new agenda and to a new distribution of international political power labelled unipolarity. This does not signify a renewed overlay on European security dynamics similar to the overlay of the Cold War, but it is still relevant to ask whether or not the looming shadow of the US serves as an obstacle to evolving relations between Russia and the EU.

The existential barrier: the alien and the traditional

Some scholars consider the EU to be more than an 'actor'. One way to conceptualize the EU is as being both a structure and an actor in the international arena. Its particular form of multi-level governance results in *structural processes*, such as long-term aid for development, or prevention of crises and the stabilizing of non-member states and regions. It also performs as a typical *actor* in international relations, carrying out tasks that have previously been handled only by states or alliances. When the EU on 4 July 2003 decided to send a joint peacekeeping force to the Democratic Republic of Congo to try to contain ethnic violence, it took a new step towards powerful actorness in the international arena. The 1,400-member force constituted the EU's first military operation outside Europe, and it was carried out without assistance from NATO. (See also the analysis in Chapter 5 in this volume.)

Moreover, the EU aims to develop a more multi-faceted capacity than traditional states present. The EU claims to possess exceptional qualities as an actor in the sphere of security. Larsen demonstrates that, since the St Malo summit, the EU has promoted a self-image as a power with access to both civilian and military means, thus constituting itself as a unique actor in international security.[28] The EU Security Strategy paper, which Javier Solana presented in June 2003, calls for more active policies to counter 'new, dynamic threats', stating that the EU has a particular value to add, particularly in operations involving both military and civilian capabilities.[29] In several ways, the EU is thus an 'alien' in the international system.

Russia has principally welcomed its new, peculiar, associate in the sphere of security, refraining from defining the Union's development towards increased actorness as a threat to its security.[30] Moscow still regards NATO and the US as threatening counterparts in the international arena – however only potentially – which presents challenges that can be conceptualized in terms of balance-of-power, polarity and geopolitical interests. Russia's intense protests against the enlargement of NATO testify to a die-hard tendency to view the alliance as a tangible danger to Russian interests which should be kept at a distance from its traditional sphere of influence in Eastern Europe and the former Soviet Union. The EU, by contrast, has most of all been interpreted as a rather weak body, governed by a wide range of different interests that are unlikely to generate any serious threat to Russian interests. In 2000, Moscow claimed that it did not feel threatened at all, but, rather, was positive to the EU's plans to form a European rapid reaction force.[31]

One source of concern, however, is the EU's relations to states in the perceived Russian sphere of interests, most notably the Ukraine. Russia's reluctance to cede influence in the Ukraine caused a major disagreement with the EU during the autumn of 2004, with the two parties holding starkly different views of the Ukrainian presidential election in November. The Russian president first received criticism for openly supporting the Kremlin-backed Viktor Yanukovich on the campaign trail. He then accepted Yanukovich's victory, while European observers considered that the elections had been rigged. Disagreements largely ruined the Russia–Europe summit on 25 November, since the EU did not accept the official outcome of the Ukrainian election, while the Russian side rejected what it termed as being 'outside interference in the affairs of a central-European sovereign state'.[32] (For more on the Ukrainian presidential elections see Chapter 7.)

Russian ambivalence towards the EU as an actor in the sphere of security is most of all linked to the fear of losing influence in the European security sphere, which could happen if Russian control of its perceived sphere of interests diminished. The fear of isolation has been a substantial theme in Russian rhetoric on security, most notably during the campaign against the NATO enlargement.[33] The Middle Term Strategy views the Union's enlargement in the light of the national interest, cautioning that the expansion will produce an 'ambivalent impact' on Russian interests. Recycling a customary catch phrase, the document warns that Europe has to be constructed 'without dividing lines'.[34]

The Russian sense of alienation *vis-à-vis* the EU is, however, not primarily linked to traditional threat perceptions. It is rather, the organization's quite different appearance that results in a sense of estrangement. Bureaucratic obstacles to cooperation have been abundant. Russians have had difficulties in learning to understand how to deal with the intricate structures in Brussels.[35] The Russian difficulties in dealing with EU bureaucracy and its ambivalence towards a totally new kind of international actor is reflected in deputy foreign minister Alexei Meshkov's description of Russia's relationship with Europe:

> Russia's relations with many European countries are several centuries old while the European institutions are comparatively young. It is important, therefore, to complement the multi-component and multi-level system of security and cooperation that is being formed with bilateral relations. They play the role of a 'safety net' when the situation grows too complicated.

(Meshkov 2002: 21)

The statement bears witness to a Russian view of some key European states – most notably Germany, France and Italy – as being more reliable and easy to deal with than the EU itself. Also, the EU's institutional complexity results in a multi-faceted, sometimes ill-synchronized, policy. The Commission shares a particular, long-term interest in Russia's economic and political reform, if only by virtue of having invested great sums for the sake of it. Russia received 2.281 billion euros in assistance between 1991 and 2000, most of which was intended to support institutional, legal and administrative reform, including the development of independent media and civil society, fiscal and banking sector reform and social reform.[36]

The durable, heavily organized engagement in the economic sphere contrasts with the more short-sighted process in the security sphere. Dempsey notes that EU diplomats blame the Union's passivity as regards Russia's conduct in Chechnya, and as regards its slowness in accepting the Kyoto Protocol, on institutional weaknesses. Above all, the EU lacks a foreign minister with tangible powers and the rotating presidency results in difficulties to verge a long-term, coherent foreign policy.[37] The EU officially conceded, in 2004, that its attempts at handling relations with Russia are ineffective and inconsistent, lacking an overall strategy. The Council – the representatives of the member states – and the Commission often pursue different, contradictory, strategies. The Union admitted that Russia is able to use differences among member states and EU institutions, for example by linking unrelated issues. The officially recommended remedy was to forge common EU positions on specific issues in the face of each summit, in order to make the member states and the Commission speak 'with one voice' on Russia.[38]

There is indeed a tension between the EU's diverse aims. For example, the Commission depends upon functional relations to the Russian leadership to be able to advance reforms in the economic sector, which may restrain EU criticism of human rights violations in Russia. Policy aims in one field may thus serve to hold back aims in another sphere. Also, the Union develops as a result of its complex set-up of self-interested member states, whose views of the Union's global role in the sphere of security differ substantially. The most obvious example is divisions over the US's intervention in Iraq in 2003. In such cases, Russia may choose to side with a few member states.

Then again, internal differences within the Union are not always to the disadvantage of EU–Russia relations. If Russia feels alienated by the Union's bureaucratic structure, or policies, member states can consciously intervene to comfort Russian leaders. Sometimes the Moscow leadership simply finds it easier to cooperate with leaders of particular member states, but this can still lead to a Russian rapprochement to European standards, interests or values that work to the advantage of the Union as a whole. During the crisis in Kosovo in 1999, France and Germany pursued such a path, exercising intense shuttle-diplomacy, going to Moscow on several occasions, to ensure that the Russians stayed 'on board' during the peace process Russia can also exploit such internal EU differences to its advantage, forming coalitions in a case-by-case pragmatic fashion. In November 2003, Putin remarked that Russia stands closer to individual European states on many important international issues than the EU states do in relation to one another, and stated that Russia is willing to pursue a dialogue both with all the individual states and the Union as a whole.[39]

While the EU has had some difficulties in 'explaining itself' to its eastern neighbour, Russian bureaucracy has also erected substantial hurdles in the way of cooperation.[40] The unreformed Russian military system is another factor that impedes practical cooperation.[41]

In sum, the EU and Russia have clashed to some extent in the 'borderland regions' between the two giants, most notably in the Ukraine. However, the two parties have not officially portrayed one another as 'threatening'. Still, the EU's set-up as a starkly different entity than its traditional neighbour has contributed to a rather slow development of collaboration. The Union's complexity, its sometimes contradictory policies and severe differences between member states have worked against the pursuit of long-term, strategic aims in its foreign policy towards Russia. However, individual member states may contribute to upholding good relations between Russia and the EU at times when the former disagrees with Brussels. Likewise, Russia can draw advantages from its traditional bilateral relations to key member states in order to improve relations with the EU. There are severe bureaucratic obstacles to cooperation on both sides, but the two actors seem to be gradually learning how to deal with one another. After all, it takes time to develop new ties and structures of cooperation. Just a little more than a decade has passed since the Cold War security order collapsed. It was only in the 1990s that the EU began to develop into a new type of international actor, presenting Russia with a wholly different kind of neighbourhood in the sphere of security. Simultaneously, Russia tried to find a new path forward in the field of security, exposing a new face to its European neighbours.

In conclusion, differences in actorness do not generate serious threat perceptions, but still contribute to explain the slow pace in the development of cooperation.

However, the existential barrier should not, in the long run, place any serious obstacles in the way of further rapprochement.

Diverging framing of threats

The second stumbling block to further cooperation is related to diverging stand-points on what constitute the most serious threats to security. Do the two parties' positions on 'the state-of-the-art' in the sphere of security differ to a substantial degree and what would be the political implications of such differences? The ensuing analysis asks to what degree and in what ways the actors' framing of threats differ, and discusses political consequences.

First, since the fall of the Soviet Union, Moscow has stubbornly proclaimed that it remains a great power in the international arena and should be treated accordingly. The leadership has called attention to the importance of traditional great power attributes such as a vast space of territory, geopolitical location, balance of power, large population and nuclear weapons.[42] The Russian culture of framing the world through the prism of geopolitics and the struggle for power clearly clashes with the EU's way of presenting itself as an actor in the sphere of security. The EU has emphasized the 'soft' edge of the security agenda in accordance with the WEU's Petersberg declaration of 1992 envisaging new, 'soft' threats.[43] The EU's Security Strategy adopted at the Brussels summit in December 2003 also frames security within a broader societal perspective. The document stresses the importance of promoting a ring of well-governed countries around the Union, adding that 'the best protection for our security is a world of well-governed democratic states'.[44]

Notably, the task of 'pre-emptive action', included in a previous draft of the treaty, was removed from the text, replaced by the milder term 'preventive engagement'. The latter is described as 'acting decisively before events get out of hand'; launching diplomatic initiatives and conducting civilian, police or military operations, before countries deteriorate, humanitarian emergencies arise, or when signs of proliferation of weapons of mass destruction are detected. The differences between the 'traditional' Russian framing of threats to security and of adequate methods of dealing with these threats, as well as the EU's 'new' way of framing these issues, should still not be exaggerated. The EU's capacity for acting in the sphere of security has increased. In 2003, the Union launched the European Union Police Mission in Bosnia and Herzegovina and launched its first military operation, taking over NATO's responsibility for establishing security in the former Yugoslav Republic of Macedonia. Its readiness to intervene beyond its borders was also manifested by the military operation in the Democratic Republic of Congo in the summer of 2003. Moreover, even though 'soft security' remains the Union's main focus, it has taken some tentative steps to 'sharpen' its security agenda; the Security Strategy adds some elements to the original Petersberg logic, describing new threats of which the major ones are terrorism, proliferation of weapons of mass destruction, regional conflicts, failed states and organized crime.[45]

Moreover, the EU's emphasis on organized crime, failed states and terrorism corresponds to what in the 1990s became Russia's normal practice of framing security, heavily drawing upon the threat of terrorism, leading the authorities, e.g. to combat organized crime and struggling to control unstable states such as Georgia and Afghanistan. Russia has long emphasized the seriousness of terrorist threats.[46] At least since the conflict in Kosovo in 1999, the leaders have asked other states for support in the struggle against separatism and international terrorism, describing it as a problem threatening 'the entire civilized world'.[47] The terrorist attacks of 11 September 2001 created a 'window of opportunity' to gain an ear for these claims. Putin concluded that 'we talked a lot about the threat of terrorism, but apparently we didn't find the words that would have persuaded the world community to create an effective defence against international terrorism'. He argued that the US had failed to anticipate the attack because of its unwillingness to recognize that the world had changed.[48]

Indeed, 11 September 2001 added a new dimension to Russia–EU relations. The altered outlook on international security in the US and Europe produced many practical consequences. Russia and the EU developed their cooperation against terrorism during the subsequent months. The Russian leaders increased contacts with the EU and President Putin called for a common security space in Europe.[49] According to a joint declaration of the EU–Russia summit of November 2003, 'the fight against terrorism and our commitment to prevent proliferation of weapons of mass destruction are cornerstones of our cooperation in the field of security.'[50]

Furthermore, the EU's process of strengthening its actorness in the sphere of 'not-so-soft security', albeit slow, evolves in tandem with Russia steadily pursuing a reverse path, from 'hard' to 'soft' security. Russia has experienced a far-reaching transformation of its security policy over the past decade, and is now focusing more on economics. The leaders have not abandoned the focus on 'high politics', they still largely frame the world using a global prism, are eager to maintain what is left of Russia's great power status, and fear US hegemony. A large, unreformed army that does not correspond to the new kind of international reality is still maintained. Yet, to these traditional standpoints the leadership has added an emphasis on economic power and 'new threats'. The 1990s can be characterized as a decade during which the Russian leadership has faced serious setbacks on the international arena, experiencing NATO enlargement, the rise of US predominance and the latter's attempts at infringing on Russia's sphere of interest in the former Soviet Union. Despite these trends, worrying in the eyes of the leaders, and despite the traditional collective threat perception based on the experience of being surrounded by potentially aggressive neighbours, the leadership adopted a 'modern' security agenda.[51]

Russia's search for a new orientation since the end of the Cold War corresponds rather well to the EU's emerging approach to 'low' and 'high' security politics as embodied in the ESDP/CFSP. In addition, both Russia and the EU have countered internal and trans-national threats using means other than military force, for example, employing the Russian Interior Ministry's forces and EU special police forces.[52] The will to collaborate against new threats was manifest at the EU–Russia summit of November 2003, when the two parties issued a joint declaration that stated, 'We are committed to intensified cooperation on new security threats and challenges.'[53] In his address to the Nation of 2003, Putin again stressed the severity of new threats, particularly mentioning international terrorism, the proliferation of weapons of mass destruction, regional and territorial conflicts and the narco threat.[54]

Even though Russia and the EU partly frame threats to security in different ways, the main differences between them do not primarily pertain to different definitions of threats, or even to different views of the use of force. The EU does not refrain from using force. It is, rather, the rationales behind the use of force and the concrete methods that differ. The main problem is not primarily that the two parties totally disagree on the list of threats, but that their priorities and their views on the roots of the problems and the relevant means to address them, diverge. The EU frames liberal values, stability and absence of threats as densely interlinked. The Union's policy of preventive engagement using non-military means stands in stark contrast to Russia's readiness to use extraordinary, military means in order to curb instability.

The discord essentially relates to the 'depth' of the security agenda – a referent object that ought to be in focus. Although Russian leaders ensure that security measures are designed to protect both the state and the individual, the integrity and security of the state is still the overriding concern. For example, in his Address to the Nation of 2003 Putin emphasized the necessity of maintaining Russia as a 'strong power', in order to preserve existing borders:[55]

> I would like to remind you that throughout our history Russia and its citizens committed and commit truly historic deeds for the sake of the country's integrity, for the sake of peace in it and stable life. Keeping the country together on vast expanses, preserving the unique community of peoples, with the strong positions of the country in the world, is not only a strenuous job but also tremendous sacrifices and deprivations of our people. Such is the thousand-year old history of Russia, such is the method of its reproduction as a strong country. And we have no right to forget this. We must take this into account as we assess present-day dangers and our main tasks.
>
> (Putin 2003)

The EU does not emphasize sovereignty to the same degree as Russia and the issue of intervention at the cost of sovereignty clearly divides the Union, which the Iraq war testified to. The Union proceeds towards upgrading the individual as a referent object in the sphere of security at the cost of the sovereign state. The EU Charter of Fundamental Rights of 1999 was an important step forward in the process towards providing individuals with increased opportunities to appeal to agencies with the power to compel national states to ensure human rights.[56]

Moreover, the altered discourse in Moscow towards emphasizing 'soft threats' has been explained partly as the result of a strategy of political correctness. Bobo

Lo even argues that practically no change has actually taken place, implying that it all boils down to Russian leaders paying lip service to Western world-views.[57] This is an exaggeration; the Putin regime does care about economic development and about new threats, at the very least those that are linked to terrorism. The campaign against terrorism essentially serves three main causes. First, it is waged to secure the territorial integrity of the Russian state. The Russian leaders equate separatism with terrorism and perceive this evil as a threat to the state's integrity. After 11 September 2001, they have gained better opportunities to legitimize their combat against separatists with reference to international terrorism. Second, the combat against terrorism provides the leaders with an internal enemy, a scapegoat to blame and rally against in order to win the electorate's support. Third, it is also plausible that the Russian anti-terror rhetoric partly arose from a will to improve the state's international reputation by conveying to the West that the intense combat against terrorism makes Russia a worthy, just actor that stands up for universal, democratic values, and by synchronizing threat perceptions. A united front against common enemies would increase identification and thereby the possibilities for cooperation with the West. When launching its new rhetoric, the leadership openly declared that the new threats were of concern for both Europe and Russia, thus uniting them.[58] In 2003, the Russian president explicitly placed value on the 'anti-terrorist community' and 'the fight against a common threat'.[59] In brief, the Russian stance should be interpreted as stemming from a mixture of political correctness intended to increase identification and collaboration with the West and to improve Russia's reputation, 'genuine' worries of new threats, and a die-hard tendency of adhering to the traditional view on security.[60]

The analysis suggests that Russia's and the EU's ways of framing threats differ to some degree, and their underlying principles and views on the methods to counter threats partly deviate. Diverging the framing of threats in some areas largely stems from different historical experiences; Russia retains the perspective of a traditional great power eager to remain influential in the international arena, while the EU depicts itself in other terms than being a traditional power and also sets up partly different goals.

The differences are partly counterbalanced by the shared emphasis on the need to combat international terrorism, the awareness of mutual interdependence and, to a rather large degree, converging global interests. Both parties promote the role of the UN and argue on behalf of multilateralism. Russia also shares a scepticism of US dominance in world affairs with a large number of EU states. Finally, the collaboration against terrorism bears witness of the fact that Russia is a contributor to European and global security. It wields experience and knowledge in areas where European states are relatively weak, such as the war against terrorism, organized crime and non-proliferation.

Differing underlying rationales for framing issues in certain ways, and diverging standpoints on humanitarian rights and methods to ensure stability, appear as the main differences between Russia's and the EU's view on security. The conflict in Chechnya captures this problem area very well. Moscow has tried to gain acceptance for its conduct in Chechnya, emphasizing the links between Chechen separatists, the attacks of 11 September 2001 and terrorists based in Afghanistan.[61] However, the EU is reluctant to accept Russia's justification of its actions in every instance with reference to the vital struggle against international terrorism. These differences were aggravated in the autumn of 2004. Russian authorities received criticism for their handling of the hostage-taking in the North-Ossetian town of Beslan, where hostage-takers seized an entire school and killed dozens of children. The Russian side reacted by linking the hostage-taking to the issue of international terrorism, arguing that the hostage-taking was supervised from abroad, and claiming that al-Qaeda operates on Russian territory.[62] The Russians complained of poor international coordination in the struggle against terrorism, e.g. criticizing the United Kingdom and the United States for granting political asylum to senior figures in the government of Chechen President Aslan Maskhadov. Putin stated that in order to fight terrorism effectively the international community must learn to find 'a common language'.[63] Putin's criticism should be seen against the background that the Parliamentary Assembly of the Council of Europe had recently rejected Moscow's definition of terrorism, considering it as being too broad.[64]

Hence, although Russia and the EU share a focus on 'soft' threats to security, definitions of threats – and in particular the root causes of threats and the means to deal with them – partly differ at a deeper level. Apart from the diverging standpoints on Chechnya, this has not placed any substantial hurdles in the way of further rapprochement, but the discrepancy contributes to explaining the slowness in boosting practical cooperation.

The shadow of the giant

The shadow of the US could indeed serve as an obstacle to further rapprochement between Russia and the EU. Russia's relations to Europe and the US have often been termed in an 'either–or' manner, according to the logic that a rapprochement to Europe entails a Russian strategy of rallying with the EU against the US. The formation of a 'troika' between Russia, Germany and France in October 1997 was commonly interpreted as directed against the US.[65] However, Russia's relations to the US have improved in the past years, and closer Russia–EU collaboration no longer unavoidably complicates relations to the US. In cases when Russia has joined in with European states against the US, as during the war in Iraq in 2003, the Moscow leadership has been careful to declare a determination to preserve good long-term relations to the US.[66]

The new Russian strategy of pursuing a 'strategic partnership' with both the EU and the US essentially began in 2001. Russia's relations to the US improved after the terrorist attacks of 11 September. Moscow gained increased acceptance for its conduct in Chechnya emphasizing the links between Chechen separatists, the attacks of 11 September 2001 and terrorists based in Afghanistan.[67] Fedorov notes that the upgrading of relations actually started a few months before the terrorist attacks, at the Ljubljana summit in Slovenia of Presidents Vladimir Putin and

George W. Bush in June 2001. The summit started a process during which Russia decided to withdraw its military bases from Cuba and Vietnam and implicitly accept the US exit from the ABM Treaty and the NATO enlargement.[68]

Foreign minister Igor Ivanov later described 2001 as the year when Russia returned to the international arena as a key player, and argued that the relationship to the US had radically improved.[69] Two years later, at the summit in Camp David of September 2003, Bush re-affirmed the value of a Russia–US cooperation in Afghanistan, Iraq, North Korea and Iran.[70] The two parties had declared a new strategic relationship already at the Moscow summit in May 2002, defining areas of cooperation including the struggle against terrorism and regional instability, non-proliferation of weapons of mass destruction and cooperation in order to solve the conflicts in southern Caucasus and between Israel and Palestine.[71] President Bush clarified that he valued the emerging cooperation with Russia within the sphere of security:

> Here in Russia, President Putin and I are putting the old rivalries of our nations firmly behind us, with a new treaty that reduces our nuclear arsenals to their lowest levels in decades and, for years, the planning for war. Russia and the United States are building a friendship based on shared interests — fighting terrorism and expanding our trade relationship.[72]
>
> (Bush 2002)

Remaining US–Russian differences include a negative Russian view of the US's tendency to act unilaterally. Moscow is also concerned with US advances in southern Caucasus and in the Ukraine, which is linked to the latter's interests in controlling energy resources and in curbing growing grounds for international terrorism in the Caucasus.[73] Washington's condemnations of anti-democratic tendencies in Russia in 2004 and 2005, such as Moscow's handling of the oil company Yukos and the continuing concentration of power in the Kremlin, also serve to strain relations.[74] Yet, overall, the US has expressed limited criticism of the Russian political system during the past years, and incentives for cooperation are probably stronger than are the differences in views. Among the key areas of cooperation, where Russia can make a contribution in line with the US's interests while also satisfying its own national interests, are the struggle against international terrorism and relations with North Korea. George Bush's personal judgement of Putin after the Ljubljana summit in Slovenia in 2001, as a 'man he can trust', also serves to ease relations between the two countries.

Relations with NATO, which infected the Russian perception of the US during the 1990s, have also improved. The Russian support for the US struggle against international terrorism has contributed to easing relations. NATO's Secretary-General, Lord George Robertson, named Russia 'NATO's first partner' in the struggle against international terrorism in December 2002.[75] The Russian foreign minister described the year 2001 as the year when Russia had returned to the international arena as a key player, and depicted relations to the US and NATO as radically improved.[76] More important than expressions of goodwill, the NATO–Russia Permanent Joint Council was created at the May summit of 2002. The Council provides Russia with opportunities of participating in NATO decisions, in particular with regard to the struggle against terrorism, to regional emergencies and to arms control. The fact that Tony Blair was a main initiator in creating the Council in turn indicates that if Russia maintains good relations with the EU, this may also serve to smooth relations to the US and NATO.[77] Closer relations to Europe may contribute to improving Russia's position as a reliable partner of the US, and vice versa.[78]

In conclusion, Russia's strategy of preserving good relations both with the US and the EU signifies that although 'the shadow of the giant' may disturb and sometimes complicate EU–Russia relations – above all since it is not always clear where the loyalties of Russia and the major EU states lie – it is not a substantial hindrance to further EU–Russia cooperation in the sphere of security.

Cooperation with impediments

Russia needs to cultivate functional relations to its major counterparts in the strategic triangle; the EU and the US. Notably, Russia is closer to the US than to the EU in the area of security. It traditionally shares with the US a global perspective on security politics, a very strong emphasis on the struggle against terrorism, and on regulating regional conflicts and combating the proliferation of weapons. Above all, Moscow is highly conscious of the US position as 'the sole superpower', and, as a consequence, of the necessity of pursuing close relations with Washington.

Still, in the long run, Russia will gain a lot in pursing a closer partnership with the EU, primarily due to the economic gains inherent in further cooperation, but also because of the need to co-manage 'soft' threats, and to preserve an influential partner in its efforts against unilateralism and in strengthening the powers of the UN. A range of motivating forces spur EU–Russia cooperation. The two parties experience converging global interests and a common stance against terrorism. They are interdependent both in the economic sphere and as regards 'soft threats' in Europe. Still, Russia–EU relations in the sphere of security have developed very gradually so far. A diverse set of impediments contributes to a rather slow pace of rapprochement.

One potential stumbling block addressed above is the shadow of the US. The review suggests that Russia shares with the US not only a firm focus on international terrorism, but also a generally strategic, global perspective on security politics. Moreover, Moscow leaders are accustomed to giving primacy to relations with the US. Russia is, however, also likely to value its relations to the EU, because of a common focus on 'low threats' to security in the broader area of Europe, a shared will to strengthen the UN, and most importantly, due to economic incentives. The likely conclusion is that the Russian leadership will continue to pursue its strategy of preserving functional relations to both the EU and the US.

A sense of alienation persists, based on differences in actorness. EU–Russian relations have been strained by the two actors' quite different, and quite complicated, bureaucratic set-ups. The EU's relatively weak foreign policy institutions, its internal differences and bureaucratic structure have contributed to a Russian sense of alienation. The latter's partly unreformed institutions have also hampered communication. These problems can partly be sidestepped by EU member states pursuing good relations with Russia when relations between the Union and Moscow become disconnected. Moreover, the actors ought to be able to improve their ability to communicate and adjust to one another with the passing of time. However, for the time being, differences between 'the alien' and 'the traditional' contribute to a slow pace of rapprochement.

Threat perceptions differ in some ways. The Russian leadership places considerably more emphasis on threats against territorial integrity, while the EU to a larger extent focuses on 'non-traditional' threats, such as hazards to the environment and the suppression of minority groups. Despite processes of changing threat perceptions on both sides, somewhat of a gap still remains between 'traditional' Russian threat conceptions focused on 'high politics' and the use of military means, and the EU's focus on 'soft threats' and the use of preventive diplomacy.

A key discrepancy is the Union's emphasis on the spreading of liberal values and protection of human rights, as compared to Russia's tendency to place territorial integrity and the struggle against terrorism above the protection of human rights and the cultivating of civil society. This point of divergence has caused severely strained relations, the most obvious example being the Union's criticism of Russia's conduct in Chechnya.[79]

Differing values may complicate further rapprochement in the sphere of security. To the EU, close cooperation with Russia must hinge on the latter's adherence to 'European values'. The Amsterdam Treaty declares that the EU is 'founded on the principles of liberty, democracy, respect for human rights and fundamental freedoms, and the rule of law, principles which are common to the Member States'.[80] Russia has been criticized in connection with each of these principles. The EU Commission's official homepage states that the EU aims at drawing Russia 'closer to European values, standards and capacities, including on issues such as the environment and combating organized crime and illegal immigration'.[81]

However, the parliamentary and presidential elections of 2003 and 2004 bred worries about the state of Russian democracy. In addition, Russia's tendency to stick a 'security label' on everything from farming to media politics, restricting activities of certain actors of civil society, threatens the development of democracy and civil society, which is clearly prioritized in the EU's policy. Moreover, two major sources of disagreement surfaced during the autumn of 2004. The EU and Russia disagreed on standards of democracy in relation to the Ukrainian presidential election in November, as recounted above. In addition, European and US leaders expressed concern about Putin's reform of the federal system, which according to his critics, would centralize power at the cost of democracy. Moreover, the sentence of one of the so-called Russian oligarchs Mikhail Khodorkovsky in May 2005 to nine years in prison for charges including tax evasion and fraud attracted wide attention in the US and Europe, causing some critics to suggest that the sentence was politically motivated.

Incompatible views on democratic values and civil society are thus a major source of discontent, impacting on relations between Russia and the US to some extent, but to a much larger extent on relations between Russia and the EU. A probable scenario is a sustained long-term EU strategy of pressuring and encouraging Russia to accommodate to European standards in both the economic and security sphere, coupled with an ad hoc, short-term foreign policy strategy, the results of which are difficult to predict. For its part, Russia is likely to remain largely positive towards the EU's evolving actorness in the sphere of security, and will attempt to take maximum advantage of mutual cooperation in the economic and security spheres.

In conclusion, the triangular relationship between Russia, the US and the EU is evolving to a large extent around the issues of international terrorism and values. EU–Russia relations depend much upon the continued evolution of Russian security policy, in particular with regard to what values are linked to perceptions of security, and to what means are used to counter threats. US–Russia relations on the other hand depend – not exclusively, but to a rather large degree – upon what alliances and agreements can be reached in the struggle against international terrorism. EU–Russia relations in the sphere of security will continue to evolve, but the hindrances described above make any major step forward in the nearest future unlikely. Complex bureaucracies restrain relations. However, the most severe obstacles to further integration are caused by diverging views on security, by differing values and, not least, on differences relating to what methods ought to be used to ensure stability. The EU views liberal values, stability and absence of threats as densely interlinked and largely follows a policy of preventive engagement using non-military means stands in stark contrast to Russia's readiness to use exceptional military means to curb instability. A key issue, maybe a decisive one, is to what extent the EU will allow intervention in sovereign states with reference to human rights, and, conversely, to what degree Russia will promote similar interventions with reference to the struggle against terrorism. If the EU follows the path of promoting or accepting military interventions for the sake of ensuring human rights, thus violating territorial integrity, this is likely to cause rifts in the relationship with Russia. Conversely, if Moscow joins the US in the event of future interventions in sovereign states under the pretext of curbing the growth of bases for terrorism, this may serve to distance Russia from the EU.

Notes

1 The chapter derives from the author's forthcoming study on the similarities and differences in their views on security between the EU and the traditional European great powers – Russia, France, Great Britain and Germany. The larger study makes use of James March's and Johan P. Olsen's new institutionalist theory on two logics of behaviour; 'the Logic of Consequentialism' and 'the Logic of Appropriateness'. It explores problems and possibilities for rapprochement by phrasing existing differences in terms of diverging *norms* and *interests* (J. March and J.P. Olsen,

Rediscovering Institutions. The Organizational Basis of Politics, New York: The Free Press, 1989).

2 E.g. 'EU Common Strategy on Russia (1999)', 4 June 1999; J. Solana, 'The EU–Russia Strategic Partnership', speech in Stockholm 13 October 1999; EU–Russia Summit, 'Joint Statement on strengthening dialogue and cooperation on political and security matters in Europe', Paris, 30 October 2000; Presidency of the Council of the European Union, 'Presidency Conclusions', EU Stockholm Summit, 23–24 March 2001.

3 Solana, 'The EU–Russia Strategic Partnership'.

4 *Diplomaticheskii Vestnik,* 2000, no. 12; and 2001, no. 1.

5 *Diplomaticheskii Vestnik,* 2000, no. 7.

6 K. Barysch and L. Kekic, 'Putin Should Tilt Toward the EU. Russia at a Crossroads', *International Herald Tribune,* 16 June 2003.

7 European Commission's delegation to Russia, official website.

8 For example, Lynch argues that Russia seeks to draw economic advantage from the ESDP, which could be achieved by offering strategic airlift to the EU (D. Lynch, 'Russia faces Europe', *Chaillot Paper,* no. 60, Paris: European Union Institute for Security Studies, May 2003). Moreover, Bobo Lo suggests that September 11 increased the Russian tendency to link economics and security issues; the leaders perceived a 'window of opportunity' to gain strategic benefits from the West in the new climate of partnership (B. Lo, *Vladimir Putin and the Evolution of Russian Foreign Policy.* Oxford: Blackwell Publishing, 2003, pp.121–2).

9 '2000 Russian National Security Concept', adopted 17 December 1999, paragraph 2.

10 B. Nygren, 'Russia and Europe, or Russia in Europe?, in Y. Fedorov and B. Nygren (eds) *Russia and Europe: Putin's Foreign Policy,* ACTA B23, Stockholm: Swedish National Defence College, Department of Security and Strategic Studies, 2002.

11 V. Putin, 'President Putin's Annual State of the Nation Address to the Federal Assembly', 18 April 2002; and V. Putin, 'Russian President Vladimir Putin's State of the Nation Address to the Federal Assembly', the Kremlin, Moscow, 16 May 2003b.

12 'Council Joint Action establishing a European Union Co-operation Programme for Non-proliferation and Disarmament in the Russian Federation (1999)', taken at the 2237th Council (Fisheries) on 17 December 1999 (1999/878/CFSP).

13 D. Lynch (ed.) 'The South Caucasus: A Challenge for the EU', *Chaillot Paper,* no. 65, Paris: European Union Institute for Security Studies, December 2003.

14 EU–Russia Summit, 'Joint Statement', Rome, 29 November 2003.

15 The Russian government approved of the Protocol on 30 September 2004. The Duma ratified it on 25 October and the Upper Chamber, the Federation Council, did so on 27 October.

16 Baranovsky notes that the EU sided with Russia when announcing a plan to establish diplomatic relations with North Korea at a point in time when the US had temporarily cancelled its active diplomacy (V. Baranovsky, 'Russian Views on NATO and the EU', in A. Lieven and D. Trenin (eds) *Ambivalent Neighbours. The EU, NATO and the Price of Membership,* Washington: Carnegie Endowment for International Peace, 2003, pp. 288–9).

17 C. Rontoyanni, 'So Far, So Good? Russia and the ESDP', *International Affairs,* 2002, vol. 78, no. 4, pp. 813–30; M. Webber, 'Third-Party Inclusion in European Security and Defence Policy: A Case Study of Russia', *European Foreign Affairs Review,* 2001, vol. 6, p. 425.

18 *Radio Free Europe/Radio Liberty Weekday Magazine,* 3 October 2003.

19 The conclusions of the EU's Helsinki summit in December 1999 suggest Russian participation in EU-led operations (Presidency of the Council of the European Union, 'Presidency Conclusions', EU Helsinki Summit, 10–11 December 1999).

20 European Union Police Mission in Bosnia Herzegovina, official website.

21 Both parties have expressed regret as to the relatively poor outcome. E.g. *Radio Free Europe/Radio Liberty Weekday Magazine*, 18 November 2003.
22 E.g. C. Wagnsson, *Russian Political Language and Public Opinion on the West, NATO and Chechnya*, Stockholm: Department of Political Science, Stockholm University, 2000, chapter 4.
23 Cf. B. White, *Understanding European Foreign Policy*, Basingstoke: Palgrave, 2001, pp. 22–3; I. Manners, 'Normative-power Europe: A Contradiction in Terms?', *Journal of Common Market Studies*, 2002, vol. 40, no. 2, pp. 240–1.
24 Schön and Rein distinguish between 'action frames' that inform policy practice and 'rhetorical frames' that underpin the use of argument in policy debate (D. Schön and M. Rein, *Frame Reflection Towards the Resolution of Intractable Policy Controversies*. New York: Basic Books, 1994, p. 32).
25 R. Entman, 'Framing: Towards Clarification of a Fractured Paradigm', *Journal of Communication*, 1993, vol. 43, no. 4, p. 55.
26 Schön and Rein, *Frame Reflection*, pp. 23, 29.
27 B. Buzan, *People, States, and Fear: An Agenda For International Security Studies in the Post-Cold War Era* (2nd edn), Hertfordshire: Harvester Wheatsheaf, 1991, pp. 219–21.
28 H. Larsen, 'Concepts of Security in the European Union After the Cold War', *Australian Journal of International Affairs*, 2000, vol. 54, no. 3, pp. 291–2; and H. Larsen, 'The EU: A Global Military Actor?', *Cooperation and Conflict*, 2002, vol. 37, no. 3.
29 'A Secure Europe in a Better World – The European Security Strategy', Brussels, 12 December 2003, Council of the European Union. Online.
30 Cf. Rontoyanni, 'So Far', p. 825.
31 *Diplomaticheskii Vestnik,* 2000, nos. 1, 12.
32 K. Bennhold, 'EU and Russians Split on Ukraine', *International Herald Tribune*, 26 November 2004.
33 Wagnsson, *Russian Political Language,* chapter 4.
34 'Russia's Middle Term Strategy Towards the EU (2000–2010)'.
35 J. Pinder and Y. Shishkov, *The EU and Russia: The Promise of Partnership*, London: The Federal Trust, 2002, p. 12; T. Forsberg, 'Forging the EU–Russia Security Partnership in the Crucible of Trans-Atlantic Relations', paper prepared for the joint International Convention of Central Eastern European International Studies Association & International Studies Association, Budapest, 26–28 June 2003, p. 15.
36 The greater part of the aid comes from the Tacis programme, which primarily aims at facilitating Russia's accession to the WTO and the implementation of the PAC. (European Commission, External Relations, 'EU Assistance to Russia'.)
37 J. Dempsey, 'Words of War: Europe's First Security Doctrine Backs Away from a Commitment to US-style Pre-emption', *Financial Times*, 5 December 2003.
38 J. Dempsey, 'Europe: EU Admits Flaws in Relationship with Russia', *Financial Times*, 23 February 2004.
39 V. Putin, 'Russian President Vladimir Putin Interview with the Italian News Agency ANSA, Newspaper Corriere della Sera and the Television Company RAI', the Kremlin, Moscow, 3 November, 2003a.
40 D. Trenin, 'A Russia-within-Europe: Working towards a New Security Arrangement', in F. Heisbourg *Russia's Security Policy and EU-Russian Relations*. ESF Working Paper, 2002, no. 6, p. 6.
41 Ibid., pp. 4–5.
42 Wagnsson, *Russian Political Language,* chapter 4.
43 Western European Union Council of Ministers, 'Petersberg Declaration Bonn', 19 June 1992.
44 'A Secure Europe in a Better World – The European Security Strategy'.

45 Ibid.
46 Wagnsson, *Russian Political Language*; Wagnsson, 'Expanding on the "Moral" Arguments'.
47 E.g. *Diplomaticheskii Vestnik*, 1999, nos. 11, 12; 2000, nos. 8, 10, 12; and 2001 no. 1.
48 *Radio Free Europe/Radio Liberty Newsline*, 17 September 2001.
49 *Radio Free Europe/Radio Liberty Newsline*, 3 October 2001.
50 EU–Russia Summit, 'Joint Statement', Rome, 29 November 2003.
51 Wagnsson, *Russian Political Language*.
52 D. Bigo, 'When Two become One: Internal and External Securitisations in Europe', in M. Kelstrup and M. Williams (eds) *International Relations Theory and the Politics of European Integration*, London: Routledge, 2000.
53 EU–Russia Summit, 'Joint Statement', Rome, 29 November 2003.
54 Putin, 'Russian President Vladimir Putin's State of the Nation Address to the Federal Assembly', 16 May 2003b.
55 Ibid.
56 J.H. Matlary, 'Human Rights', ARENA Working Papers, no. 19, 2003.
57 Lo, *Vladimir Putin*, p. 95.
58 *Diplomaticheskii Vestnik*, 1992, nos. 9,10, 15, 16, 23, 24.
59 Putin, 'Russian President Vladimir Putin's State of the Nation Address to the Federal Assembly', 16 May 2003b.
60 Fedorov phrases this tension in terms of two 'schools' of foreign policy thinking. The first one is named 'post-Soviet' since it reproduces the strategic concepts of Soviet times, viewing NATO and the West as key threats to Russian security. The second, 'realistic' school, discounts the West as a threat and focuses upon 'soft threats' (Y. Fedorov, 'Strategic Thinking in Putin's Russia', in Y. Fedorov and B. Nygren (eds) *Russian Military Reform and Russia's New Security Environment*. Swedish National Defence College, ACTA B28, 2003, pp. 158–9).
61 *Radio Free Europe/Radio Liberty Newsline*, 18 and 25 September 2001; 19 and 25 September 2003.
62 *Radio Free Europe/Radio Liberty Newsline*, 6 and 14 October 2004.
63 *Radio Free Europe/Radio Liberty Newsline*, 13 and 14 October 2004.
64 Delegates barred a clause on the 'misuse of the right to political asylum' and on the 'facilitation of extradition of individuals suspected of complicity to terrorism' from a Russia-backed resolution on international terrorism. The Russian and European delegates failed to agree on an acceptable definitions for 'terrorist' and 'accomplice to a terrorist' (*Radio Free Europe/Radio Liberty Newsline*, 7 October 2004).
65 Cf. H. Adomeit, 'Russia, Europe and "Euroatlanticism": Triangular Relationships in Transition', paper presented at the Moscow Carnegie Centre, 27 October 2003.
66 *Current Digest of the Post-Soviet Press*, 2 April 2003, vol. 55, no. 9; *Radio Free Europe/Radio Liberty Newsline*, 5, 17 and 31 March, 4 and 21 April, 26 September 2003.
67 *Radio Free Europe/Radio Liberty Newsline*, 18, 19 and 25 September 2001.
68 Fedorov, 'Strategic Thinking', p. 163.
69 *Radio Free Europe/Radio Liberty Newsline*, 3 January 2002.
70 G.W. Bush, 'Remarks by the President and Russian President Putin in Press Availability Camp David', Maryland, 27 September 2003.
71 'Text of US–Russia Joint Declaration', Moscow, 24 May 2002.
72 G.W. Bush, 'Radio Address by the President to the Nation', 25 May 2002, US Department of State, US–Russia relations.
73 P. Gowan, 'The EU and Eastern Europe: Diversity without Unity?', in M. Farrell, S. Fella and M. Newman, *European Integration in the 21st century*, 2002, vol. 42.
74 *Radio Free Europe/Radio Liberty Newsline*, 7 February 2005.
75 *Radio Free Europe/Radio Liberty Newsline*, 9 December 2002.

76 *Radio Free Europe/Radio Liberty Newsline*, 3 January 2002; cf. M. Skak, 'Russian Security Policy After 9/11', paper prepared for the Joint International Convention of Central Eastern European International Studies Association and International Studies Association, Budapest, 26–28 June 2003, pp. 6–7.
77 A. Lobjakas, 'NATO: Allies Await Russian Response to Cooperation Proposal', *RFE/RL Feature Articles*, 2002.
78 Rontoyanni, 'So Far', p. 818; Barysch and Kekic, 'Putin Should Tilt Toward the EU'.
79 Cf. Rontoyanni 'So Far', p. 826.
80 'Treaty of Amsterdam amending the treaty on European Union, the treaties establishing the European communities and related acts,' *Official Journal* C 340, 10 November 1997, article F, paragraph 1.
81 European Commission, 'The EU's relations with Russia, Introduction'.

7

THE IMPLICATIONS FOR PUTIN'S POLICY TOWARD UKRAINE AND BELARUS OF NATO AND EU EXPANSION

Bertil Nygren

Introduction

The New Strategic Triangle that includes the United States, the European Union and Russia has had a significant impact on other relationships as well, especially relations among states along the new borders. In recent years, this impact has been evident in the Caucasus (especially in Georgia) and in Central Asia (especially in Uzbekistan), but nowhere as evident as in Ukraine and Belarus. And as indicated in the introductory chapter of this volume nowhere has the clash of two (the US and the EU) with the third (Russia) been as evident as in the Ukrainian presidential elections in late 2004, where two political cultures and political norm systems clashed. The 'orange revolution' was in my view a showdown between the 'European' and the 'Asian' and the *normative* differences between the two, the importance of which goes far beyond Ukrainian domestic politics. Chapter 6 in this volume studies the way in which security issues are handled in the EU and Russia: different perceptions of security constitute an obstacle to further cooperation in the field. The analysis of the US–Russian relationship in Chapter 10 tells us how the NATO enlargement issue has affected – and not affected – the triangular relationship. In this chapter, we are concerned with the extent to which President Putin has attempted to surf on the enlargement debate and practice to regain control of the culturally, socially, politically, militarily and economically closest Russian neighbours – Ukraine and Belarus – by using geo-economic rather than geo-political means.

The purpose of this chapter is to give examples of the profound changes in Russian foreign policy attitudes towards Ukraine and Belarus that have taken place since the coming to power of President Vladimir Putin in 2000. The general argument is that Putin very consciously and from the very outset of his first presidential term distanced himself from the more traditional Russian (or 'Primakovian') geo-political thinking (despite the fact that Putin himself had been partly responsible for its formulation as Head of the Federal Security Service (FSB) and subsequently Prime Minister) and in favour of a more modern geo-economic thinking.

There are two ways of arguing this change. One is to point at instances where Putin has acted or argued contrary to the tenets of 'Primakovian' geo-political thinking in situations where geo-politically motivated actions or thinking have been directly applicable. Another is to point at situations where Putin has used geo-economic rather than geo-political actions or thinking to further Russian policies, languages and strategies that are more akin to modern European Union thinking than to 'Primakovian' foreign policy thinking. Putin has either dodged the implications of such 'Primakovian' thinking in confrontations with Ukraine – on border issues or her NATO application, and with Belarus – on the Union issue and on military cooperation, or he has used geo-economic thinking in promoting Russian energy and other industry interests – on issues like oil and gas prices, deliveries, transportation and transits.

My proposal is, then, that Putin argued for employing typical EU long-term strategies (to use economic interactions in political institution-building) in relations to the closest CIS neighbours. Putin had anticipated the EU and NATO enlargements to include former Soviet empire protegés and realized that Russia could do nothing whatsoever about these enlargements. Instead, Russia should take the opportunity to strengthen its grip over those countries that were not on the list of further enlargement plans. Putin has thus been using predicted consequences of the two enlargement processes, i.e. that Ukraine and Belarus would be left outside, in order to tie Ukraine and Belarus much closer to Russia and to do so with classical 'neo-imperialist' instruments for creating economic dependencies. Below, I use some examples to show this evidently 'modern' and 'neo-imperialist' Putin by pointing at his personal behaviour and involvement in some critical areas of contention in Russia's relations with Ukraine and Belarus.

In using these examples, we are focusing on leadership politics which follows from the idea that Putin has been the engine in the foreign policy changes that have taken place since Yeltsin's days, and often in a hostile (to Putin) decision-making environment.[1] Putin has shown a drastically new way for Russia in re-establishing herself as a regional great power, a way where both Tsarist-like, Soviet-like and general Great Power-like behaviour towards Russia's neighbours has been exchanged for a much more modern and 'EU-like' policy of economic reintegration for both economic and political purposes.[2]

Even in the most fundamental dimension of Russian foreign policy, i.e. 'what it is all about', Putin's foreign policy has been *very different* from that of the his predecessor Boris Yeltsin. Since this fundamental shift in orientation also colours Putin's policies vis-à-vis Ukraine and Belarus, we need to say a few words about these fundamental changes by the end of the Yeltsin period, when Russia's foreign policy was 'neither consistent, nor effective'.[3] It was heavily dominated by Yevgeny Primakov, probably the most 'geo-political' of all Russian foreign ministers ever, and by his balance of power thinking, his multi-polar world idea, and implicitly also power politics. Therefore, the most fundamental shift in the early Putin period concerns precisely the 'economization' of Russian foreign policy, i.e. a shift to a policy based on 'geo-economic' rather than 'geo-political' ideas, arguments and interests.

While this fundamental policy shift was only vaguely pronounced in the Foreign Policy Concept of the Russian Federation signed by Putin in June 2000, the ideological tenor of which was 'Primakovian', the Concept nevertheless suggested that 'more traditional security goals' were aimed at the well-being of the Russian economy.[4] By the time of his inauguration, Putin had already abandoned some of the ideas of the Concept and was instead pronouncing and stressing others. Judging from his behaviour in the two years that followed, Putin was the most dissatisfied with the Concept's presentation of Russian foreign policy towards the United States, Ukraine and Belarus. Within a short period of time, the United States was to be elevated to the highest rank in Russia's foreign relations, Ukraine seen as the most interesting object for economic 're-imperialization', and a political union with Belarus (on political and not on economic grounds) as the least attractive foreign policy goal, all of which was contrary to the goals expressed in the Concept. And after 11 September, Putin pursued 'a more single-minded' strategy of economic integration.[5] This is perhaps best seen in his addresses to the Federation Council in 2003 and 2004.[6] It must be realized, however, that although there generally is an unwillingness or inability among some Russian élites to forget altogether the Russian (and Soviet) imperialist past, based on political and military might (notably among some generals), such ideas are not necessarily the first that come to Putin's own mind in thinking about Russia's future.[7]

We know that, generally speaking, Russia has for almost a decade reacted positively to EU enlargement and negatively to NATO enlargement.[8] The two European enlargement processes have had different implications for Russia's Slavic neighbours, and the approaches of these countries to the processes have been very different; while the Ukraine under President Leonid Kuchma (and even more so under his successor Viktor Yushchenko) has been balanced between the EU and Russia in the economic sphere but has basically chosen NATO rather than Russia in the military sphere. President Aleksandr Lukashenka rejects both the NATO and EU options for Belarus, but at the same time resists being swallowed economically by Russia.

Before we dig deeper into Putin's handling of his two Slavic neighbours, we should briefly present the main features of Yeltsin's policies towards Ukraine and Belarus and to present the broader picture of Putin's policies towards the two Slavic neighbours.[9]

With respect to *Ukraine*, Yeltsin's foreign policy was hampered by several unresolved post-Soviet issues, which had delayed a normalization of relations. The signing of the Friendship Treaty and the final resolution of the Black Sea Fleet issue in the spring of 1999 did not yield the momentum expected for solving other long-delayed conflict issues, such as the delimitation of common borders, gas, oil, electricity and customs issues, since the new NATO strategic doctrine and the

Kosovo war in the spring of 1999 refuelled tension in the Russian–Ukrainian relationship because of Ukraine's open drive for NATO.

Putin immediately set out to restore good relations with Ukraine, and by February 2001, the two leaders had in their own words 'changed the quality of relations'.[10] Putin thus chose *not* to stick to the inherited Foreign Policy Concept in his policies towards Ukraine, and instead turned policies around 180 degrees. Already by Putin's first mid-term, Russia and Ukraine were jointly striving for closer relations with NATO and the EU and had become the closest of partners. In the political sphere, the strategic conflict over Ukrainian NATO membership had largely been defused, and in the military sphere, the former conflict over the Black Sea Fleet and its naval facilities have generated military and defence cooperation. In the economic sphere, the crucial gas and oil transportation issues, as well as joint production of military and civilian technologies, have become a natural element of satisfaction in the relationship.

Yeltsin's relations with *Belarus* were largely based on the notion of a future Union between the two Slavic countries. The appointment of Primakov as Prime Minister in the fall of 1998 strengthened the 'strategic partnership', and in December 1998, Yeltsin and Lukashenka signed an agreement that pointed towards a new Union of Russia and Belarus. Russia's conflict with NATO reinforced Yeltsin's drive for a Union, while the Belarusian President Lukashenka saw the Union as a way of increasing his own possibilities of entering a new power structure once Yeltsin was gone. Due to domestic élite opposition, Yeltsin could only sign a watered-down draft treaty on the Russia–Belarus Union in September 1999 and an even more thin, but new, Union Treaty in December 1999.[11]

From the start, Putin held an extremely low profile in his relations with Lukashenka on the Union issue. The 11 September volte-face with respect to Russia's US relations probably helped Putin take a definite stand on the Union issue in 2002, and the Russian–NATO rapprochement of May 2002 was a deadly blow to ideas of a 'political' Union. Putin's pragmatism has not left any room for pompous political declarations, and economic integration between the two is the name of the game for Putin.

Putin thus inherited Soviet-like or empire-like arm's-length policies with respect to Ukraine, and very intimate but equally Soviet-like or empire-like relations with Belarus. Policies towards Ukraine were immediately reversed by Putin in his first presidential year – 2000 – while he kept a low but chilly profile with respect to his Belarus policies, before he fundamentally reversed these policies in 2002. Not only were these policies towards Ukraine and Belarus the very opposite of Yeltsin's policies, they were also in total contradiction to the doctrinal formulations of Russian foreign policy in the Foreign Policy Concept adopted in June 2000. What happened next is the subject of this essay. The presentation that follows is structured on the division of geo-political and geo-economic standpoints and arguments, where Putin, it is argued, has resisted traditional Russian geo-political arguments and promoted more modern geo-economic arguments in his relations to Ukraine and Belarus, often in opposition to important Russian élite groups.

The geo-political dimension in Russian foreign policy towards Ukraine and Belarus

The general argument here is that Putin, although at times slipping back into old tracks of geo-political arguments, either involuntarily or voluntarily has been trying to change Russian thinking on international relations. Below, we will look at some of the main conflict issues in Russian–Ukrainian relations under Putin to show his reluctance to 'talk', to 'do', or to 'act' geo-politically, even in situations when such thinking would be the most 'natural' or easily available to a traditional Russian politician.

The NATO enlargement issue in Ukraine

The fundamental change caused by 11 September in Russian foreign policy, i.e. the band-wagoning with the US in its 'war against terrorism' and support of the Afghanistan operation, reinforced Putin's determination to continue on the road towards reintegration with the neighbouring countries. Since both Russia and Ukraine increasingly found themselves 'on the same side' with respect to the United States after 11 September and after the November 2001 Putin–Bush summit and then the establishment of the joint NATO–Russia Council in May 2002, the former cleavage between Russia and Ukraine with respect to the *NATO enlargement* issue by implication became less acute and dramatic. There was even an element of competition between Russia and Ukraine in improving their relations with NATO, especially in 2002.[12]

Nevertheless, the fundamental Russian problem with Ukraine's continued and outspoken desire to join NATO has remained. At the same time, the 'Russia first' policy pursued by the United States, NATO and the EU after 11 September and the 'NATO at 20' in November 2001 gave Ukraine an evident back seat in this competition for friendship with NATO. NATO has required structural military reforms, but Kuchma himself turned out to be the real problem. The Ukraine–NATO Action Plan adopted at the Prague summit in November 2002 basically left it to Ukraine to be 'worthy' of NATO membership.[13] In January 2003, the Ukraine NATO Action Plan entered into force; the plan talked of Ukraine's 'full integration into Euro-Atlantic security structures' and Kuchma set up a State Council for Issues of European and Euro-Atlantic Integration 'ensuring Ukraine's entry into the European political, economic, security, and legal area as well as creating preconditions for Ukraine's admission to the EU and NATO'.[14] The Iraq war helped Kuchma to improve his relations with George W. Bush. Later in 2003, Ukraine planned to bring its military structure more in line with NATO standards, and when Ukraine's military reforms were praised by NATO defence ministers in December 2003, Russia's listening ears were wide open.

Although Russia had no formal objections to these Ukrainian steps, the events at Tuzla in the Azovsk Sea in October–December 2003 (see next section) indicate a conflict in kind, since the Tuzla events were generally seen as intended to hamper

Ukraine's integration into NATO and since NATO is unlikely to easily digest an application where the applicant has unsolved border problems. One related problem with Ukraine's NATO membership has been the Russian Black Sea Fleet naval base in Sevastopol, which contradicts the NATO requirement that member countries should have no foreign military bases on their territory. Ukraine has so far abided by the agreement with Russia, and the twenty-year lease signed with Ukraine in 1997 remains in effect despite Russia's plans to build a new naval base in Novorossiysk. Russian sensitivity on the Ukraine-NATO issue has not disappeared, however, and the issue is likely to remain contentious under the Yushchenko regime.

This common Russian and Ukrainian interest in improving relations with NATO became overtly evident by May 2002, when the Russia–NATO accord was reached and the Russia–NATO Council was set up. When Putin met with Kuchma the same month, he noticed that 'the quality of relations . . . has recently improved' and assured that 'one would not like to change anything' in these relations. Kuchma was even more poetic in his declarations that 'there are no clouds over us, the air is clean and transparent, and the temperature is appropriate – neither too warm nor too cold, just normal'.[15] By the end of 2002, Kuchma hinted that relations were the warmest possible and on Putin's initiative, in January 2003, Kuchma was elected – as the first non-Russian – Head of the CIS. In May 2003, the Russian Foreign Minister Igor Ivanov concluded that relations between Russia and Ukraine 'have matured to such an extent that these two countries can set themselves more ambitious and long-term objectives'.[16] In June 2003, Ukraine was named Russia's 'strategic partner', a euphemism for the closest of friends.

The NATO Membership Action Plan did not foresee a speedy Ukrainian membership either, and the NATO membership issue had already by the summer of 2004 become directly tied to democratic values, which had hampered the Kuchma regime. After the 'orange revolution', the situation is altogether changed, and the Kuchma attempt to turn Ukraine's defence policy 180 degree around in late 2004 – with a new Ukrainian defence doctrine pointing to defence cooperation with Russia instead of NATO – may now be history.[17]

Nevertheless, the actual NATO enlargement and the clarification of Ukraine's (low) status did help Putin to tie Ukraine closer to Russia also in the geo-political dimension. However, the real point in this essay is, rather, that Putin has not allowed the NATO membership issue to interfere in other areas of cooperation or to poison the relationship. This kind of behaviour by Putin stands in sharp contrast to the behaviour of much of the Russian security establishment, as well as to the recommendations of the Foreign Policy Concept of the Russian Federation: Putin simply has not played the 'geo-political game'.

The Russia–Ukraine border delimitation issue

Another sour geo-political issue that has been on the Russian–Ukrainian agenda since 1992 is the question of *border delimitation*. While the delimitation of the 2,063-kilometre land frontier apparently did not involve severe problems –

the delimitation was, reportedly, more or less already finalized by November 2001 – only in January 2003 did Kuchma and Putin finally sign the border delimitation treaty, but left the division of the Azovsk Sea still to be agreed upon.[18]

The extent to which borders have remained sensitive in the relationship became evident in October 2003, when Ukrainian sabre-rattling over the *Tuzla islet* in the Kerch Strait developed into a major crisis with Russia. The Kerch Strait is a shallow channel that connects the Azovsk Sea with the Black Sea and separates the Crimea (Ukraine) in the west from the Taman Peninsula (Russia) in the east. Russian regional authorities had issued a plan to build a dam between Russia's Taman Peninsula and the Tuzla islet in order to protect the Russian coast from being washed away by the sea. The Ukrainian Foreign Ministry warned, at an early stage, Russia that such a dam might violate Ukraine's state border and territorial integrity.

The real crisis took off in mid-October when the Ukrainian Verkhovna Rada warned that all measures would be taken to 'protect the sovereignty of the [Ukrainian] state on its territory' should the dam construction continue. Several dozen Ukrainian border guards, bulldozers and excavators were sent to the Tuzla islet as well as a dredger and a sea-borne crane to mark a division line in the Kerch Strait with buoys. Kuchma called the construction of the dam an 'unfriendly' action and as a result the temperature increased further still. In a Ukrainian diplomatic note, Russia was warned that she would be held fully accountable for any potential border conflict.[19]

As the dam builders approached the Tuzla islet and the Verkhovna Rada held a hearing in which measures on how to meet the threat were discussed, Putin and Kuchma were eager not to let the issue get entirely out of hand. They agreed over the phone that their Prime Ministers should meet immediately. The Russian Foreign Minister, Igor Ivanov, reassured Ukraine that the dam project was dictated by economic and ecological considerations and was not at all connected to the border talks on the Azovsk Sea.[20]

As is often the case, conflicts tend to lead a life of their own, and crisis-related events developed rapidly. Kuchma cancelled a planned Latin American tour and instead visited the Tuzla islet. A couple of days later, seventeen Ukrainian jet fighters held an exercise, involving firing missiles into the water not far from Tuzla, and the Verkhovna Rada passed a resolution (by 369 to 5) calling for 'the removal of the threat to Ukraine's territorial integrity' and also recommended that the UN General Assembly discuss the dispute at its current session. The OSCE Parliamentary Assembly was asked to send international observers to the area. One leading Ukrainian politician said that we 'have never discussed so actively the possibility of an armed conflict even when we were dividing the Black Sea Fleet'.[21]

When the two premiers, Mikhail Kasyanov and Viktor Yanukovich, met to discuss the dispute, it was agreed that Russia should suspend the construction of the dam and that the Ukrainian side should withdraw its border guards from the island. This watered the fire, but Russian nationalists had by now picked up steam, and Kuchma pitied Putin's situation, of being 'forced to take into account neo-colonial sentiments in Russian society, in the Russian ruling class, and among the Russian generals'.[22]

On 30 October, the Russian and Ukrainian Foreign Ministers, Igor Ivanov and Kostyantyn Hryshchenko, agreed that the Tuzla issue should be resolved by working groups together with other issues related to the Azovsk Sea and the Kerch Strait. In December, the Ukrainian and Russian Presidents finally signed an agreement on the use of waters of the Kerch Strait and the Sea of Azovsk. The agreement provided for the delimitation of the state border on the bottom and the surface of the sea.[23]

The border agreement on the Kerch Straits and the Sea of Azovsk marked the end of the long drawn out border delimitation negotiations. The typical Ukrainian argument to this day is that the border issue has been used by Russia to slow down Ukraine's integration into Europe and NATO.[24] Putin, on the other hand, was eager to solve the issue of delimitation before Kuchma was to be replaced in November. The Tuzla issue indicates that Putin was not prepared to sacrifice Russia's successful 'economization' of the Russian–Ukrainian relationship, showing that geo-economic reasons prevailed over geo-political ones in his thinking. Putin's and Kuchma's personal relationship saved the situation from getting entirely out of hand.

The geo-political (and geo-economic) dimension: the Union issue in Russina–Belarusian relations – re-integration on Russian conditions

The Yeltsin heritage with respect to Russia's relations with Belarus was quite different from relations with Ukraine; the Yeltsin–Lukashenka attempt to create a *Russian–Belarusian Union* was inherited by Putin. As one of Yeltsin's very last deeds, he handed over the new Union Treaty to Putin. It soon became obvious, however, that Putin was less than eager to continue along the road envisaged by his predecessor.[25] When Putin visited Minsk within a couple of weeks of being elected, he firmly placed the economic aspects of the Union at the very centre, rather than the political or military issues. A year later, Lukashenka was already seriously disappointed and sharply criticized Russia for creating impediments to the development of the Union. After 11 September, the Union issue took a new turn when Putin simply refused to discuss an approval of the Union Constitutional Act.

By the summer of 2002, relations deteriorated further when Putin showed his open aversion to Lukashenka's integration scheme, i.e. the very scheme that had been endorsed by Yeltsin. In June, Putin formally offered Lukashenka to make Belarus a federation subject within the Russian Federation, i.e. to become part of Russia. Lukashenka was shocked at the proposal, as were Primakov and Yeltsin, but Putin insisted that the unification process must proceed 'unconditionally' and on the basis of a single state with a single parliament and a single government.[26] At a joint press conference after a summit between the two in August 2002, Putin openly insulted Lukashenka, again suggesting that Russia and Belarus should create a unified federal state, the institutions of which would be in accordance with the Russian and not the Belarusian constitution, 'because . . . the new country will . . . be a federation' (i.e. not a Union). This time, Putin also offered an alternative, an

'EU-like' proposal, which Lukashenka interpreted as part of a plan by 'rich people' in Russia 'to grab Belarus and criminalize its economy'.[27] A chilly period followed.

In the spring of 2003, Lukashenka warned that Belarus had other options than 'crawling into Russia' or 'remaining under Russia's foot'.[28] By September 2003 the idea of the Russia–Belarus Union was officially proclaimed dead by the Russian Premier Kasyanov, and the fact that the eight years of discussions had not produced any signed and ratified bilateral agreement indicated irresolvable differences. To date, nothing has come out of this attempt and to me it is evident that nothing short of a Belarusian adoption of market reforms and privatization of the economy will change Putin's principal standpoint that economic integration on Russian conditions is the more important goal.

The real test of Putin's attempt to make something out of the Russia–Belarus Union idea concerned the common *Union currency*. In April 2001, the formal decision to introduce the Russian rouble as the sole currency (on 1 January 2005) and a new union currency (on 1 January 2008) was made. The currency issue remained a major stumbling block and at a summit in January 2003, a formal rift over currency and monetary controls was obvious: Russia wanted full control while Belarus wanted to have a joint central bank.

In the summer of 2003, Lukashenka argued that a monetary union could go into effect only *after* all other Belarusian–Russian agreements on the union had been implemented.[29] In August 2003, Putin concluded that the time had come to make the final decisions on the proposed single Russian–Belarusian currency: 'We have come to the point at which we must decide to go one way or the other', he said.[30] Lukashenka continued his crusade, telling his home constituencies that 'we might be left without money, wages, and pensions' if Belarus signed the agreement. Another summit in mid-September brought no solution to the issue.[31] It seemed by now evident, as one source close to Putin put it, that the stalemate was really due to the fact that Lukashenka was first and foremost 'concerned with his own political role within the future union', and since no such role was foreseen, other activities on the union issue had been stalled.[32] In 2004, the discussions and later principal agreements on a Single Economic Space and a free-trade agreement (to be treated below) more or less superseded the discussions on the common currency of the Russia–Belarus Union.

The geo-political dimension: defence cooperation in Russia–Belarusian relations

Despite the failure of the unification efforts from the mid 1990s and the open Putin–Lukashenka conflict, *military and defence cooperation* had been fairly successful. In the field of military co-production, Russia and Belarus already in early 2000 merged two Belarusian and seventeen Russian weapons production companies producing air defence equipment. What is more, Lukashenka proposed a Russia–Belarusian joint defence force of some 300,000 troops, and in the spring of 2001, there were indeed some attempts to draft a military doctrine for the Russia–Belarus union, with a united or separate command.

Putin called the shots, however, and a conflict developed between Putin and the Russian defence forces on the issue. In April 2002, the Russian Defence Minister, Sergey Ivanov, complained that 'political decisions' were lacking and that 'we, the defence ministers pass relevant proposals all the time'. The general showdown between Putin and Lukashenka in the fall of 2002 killed all initiatives for some time, but when Sergey Ivanov suggested the creation of a joint Russian–Belarusian army a year later, Lukashenka backed down, believing that this might be used as a lever.[33] In October 2003, the strategic, long-range radar station Volga was put on combat-alert duty (a radar station that substituted the Skrunda radar base in Latvia abandoned by Russia in 1998), and there was also a large-scale military exercise (code-named Clear Skies 2003) in Belarus. In April and July 2004, however, it was announced that the establishment of a joint air defence had been delayed.

Obviously, although there have been some cooperation successes in the defence field, Putin does not want to be 'kidnapped' by Lukashenka's bad reputation in the West, and Lukashenka knows that Putin has an 'economized' agenda that spells problems for Lukashenka. Putin does not seem to think that the evidently good relations between the military structures of the two countries should be used at all; this, again, could be understood only if we accept that Putin has abandoned traditional Russian geo-political thinking. Otherwise, this stand is incomprehensible.

The geo-economic dimension in Russian foreign policy towards Ukraine and Belarus

To recapitulate the main thesis in this essay, Putin is increasingly changing the language and practice of Russian élites to think 'geo-economics' instead of 'geo-politics', which obviously is most evident on issues that more directly deal with trade and economic cooperation. But 'thinking geo-economics' does not necessarily mean that the final or end objective is geo-economic *per se*; very similar to the ideas on the European Union as a peace project, Putin might regard economics as a means to appease and to exert political power over his neighbours. In this section, we look at some examples of Putin's behaviour in the economic sphere.

Trade and economic cooperation with Ukraine

While national political interests dominated Russian–Ukrainian economic relations in the 1990s, and often resulted in conflicts, Putin broke this vicious circle in his first term. On the one hand, Russian–Ukrainian economic relations have probably saved Ukraine from recession, but on the other the Ukrainian dependency on Russia has become manifestly high: since 2000, Russian investments in Ukraine have concentrated on strategic branches like energy, aluminium, defence, telecom and banking. By 2002, almost 50 per cent of the Ukrainian industry was owned by Russian capital and the business élites of the two countries are closely connected.

This situation nourishes Ukrainian arguments about Russian 'economic imperialism'; during Ukraine's privatization process, the Ukrainian national security was supposedly threatened by Russian acquisitions of 'oil refineries, raw-aluminium production, communications, and many other strategic enterprises'.[34]

Economic cooperation boomed in the Russian–Ukrainian relationship. In November 2001, Putin and Kuchma agreed to sign a treaty on a 'free economic zone', and in December the two leaders took part in a breakthrough gathering of Ukrainian and Russian business executives and an agreement in principle was made on the signing of a 'free economic zone' treaty and on jointly striving for membership in the World Trade Organization (in December 2001).

One of the measuring rods of the Russian–Ukrainian relationship is, in my view, the issue of a *customs union*. In the early summer of 2002, Ukraine joined the Eurasian Economic Community (at the time composed of Russia, Belarus, Tajikistan, Kyrgyzstan and Kazakhstan), although with observer status only. There were even grander plans in the coming, which soon changed the perspective. By December 2002, no treaty on a bilateral free-trade zone had yet been designed, but instead a treaty on a *CIS free-trade zone* appeared as the more general trade issue.[35] Once this issue had been reborn, it developed quickly and the 'CIS Four' – Russia, Ukraine, Belarus and Kazakhstan – formally agreed to create a 'joint economic space' with the purpose of creating a new economic alliance in the autumn of 2003. Such a treaty would, in the words of the Prime Ministers, 'open a new phase in the development of trade relations within the CIS'. In January 2003, the new CIS head, Kuchma, said that such a zone would 'help us feel safe in the rough sea of globalization', and the Belarusian President Lukashenka prophesied that such a zone would liquidate other economic and semi-economic formations such as the Eurasian Economic Community or GUUAM.[36]

The idea acquired a more definite shape in late February 2003 when the Presidents of Russia, Ukraine, Belarus, and Kazakhstan, at an unexpected meeting in a Moscow suburb, reached an agreement in principle to create a 'joint economic space' (to be formalized in September after a period of co-ordinating economic policies). The ultimate goal was to create a regional integration organization in which economics would rule over politics, an idea similar to the EU project idea that Putin had floated with Lukashenka in August 2002. By April 2003, the main stumbling blocks had been detected, and by August, some of the stumbling blocks had already been lifted out of the negotiations: the four states were no longer considering either a common currency or a common customs union. The CIS summit in Yalta in September proved a success for the idea of a free-trade zone, and the CIS foreign ministers agreed on many draft documents on a CIS free-trade zone; most importantly, the Presidents of Russia, Ukraine, Belarus and Kazakhstan signed an accord on the creation of a single economic space – SES.

Putin reassured those who feared that the single economic space represented a step towards restoring the Soviet Union that this was pure nonsense. Kuchma suggested that the SES allowed for a switch to a 'subsequent, higher stage of mutual relations', and he added that 'when the European markets are closed for us . . . it is better to have a real bird in the hand than two in the bush'. President of Kazakhstan Nursultan Nazarbayev called the SES 'a very serious step toward real integration in the 12-year history (of the CIS)'. Lukashenka was much more cautious in his comments.[37]

The agreement on the SES was safely ashore, however, and the ratification of the SES treaty took place in April 2004 in all four countries. In May, Putin said that he was prepared to create a 'full-fledged free-trade zone' despite the likely Russian short-term losses. However, Putin had a hard time convincing the other leaders of adopting a single 'economic constitution', and, in the end, 61 separate agreements were adopted instead. There was no longer any desire to try to join the WTO as a single unit and the creation of a customs union was opposed by Ukraine.[38] The new Ukrainian President Yushchenko's interest in the SES has been lukewarm, especially since his prime goal is for Ukraine to join the European Union. The SES is of interest to Ukraine today only to the extent that it does not dim the prospects for EU membership.

Obviously, the issue of a SES ties Ukraine and Belarus closer to Russia and is seen as an alternative to EU association. Ukraine had openly expressed its intentions of joining the EU as a high priority goal already in 1998 (and Kuchma had paved the way already in 1995 and 1996). In 1999, Kuchma decreed integration into the EU by 2007, the first steps of which would be to join the WTO and to be followed by a free-trade agreement with the EU as an associated member, and subsequently to conduct talks between 2004 and 2007 on full membership. The EU remained cool, however. In 2002, the refusal to grant Ukraine the status of a market economy, which Russia had been granted a couple of months earlier, crushed Ukrainian hopes. At the EU–Ukraine summit in October 2003, Kuchma already accused the EU of a lack of interest in Ukraine and of forcing integration within the CIS.[39] Kuchma himself thus argued that the increased Russian influence in the CIS could at least partly be blamed on the EU. In May 2004, there was another setback when Ukraine and Belarus were seen to be part of the 'ring of friends' for Europe (stretching from the Baltic Sea through the Middle East to North Africa).

Yushchenko has made it abundantly clear that EU membership is the main objective under his reign and that Ukraine will not accept anything less than membership, but it is also evident that Ukraine has a long way to go before it could become a member. In the meantime, there are no signs of SES being dissolved. To Ukraine, the SES means much less than EU membership, but there is an iron dynamic in economic dependencies, too, that Yushchenko will have to acknowledge. For Putin, the SES is nothing but a borrowed success idea which, if it succeeds, will reintegrate the neighbouring economies into the Russian one, whether the neighbours like it or not.

Energy issues in Russian–Ukrainian relations

Ukraine's *energy dependence* on Russia and the Russian transit dependency on Ukraine have been constant features of Russian–Ukrainian relations. Putin's policy has been consistent with the more general foreign policy parameter of transforming Soviet-type relations (based on subsidized prices) into normal market economy relations (based on international market prices). In this effort, there has been an evident element of 'economic imperialism', i.e. an attempt to increase Ukrainian dependency on Russian energy deliveries, and diminish Russia's dependency on transit through Ukraine by buying energy installations and controlling pipelines.

Oil, gas and pipelines were issues that Putin could not avoid and already in the spring and summer of 2000, the Ukrainian *gas debt* to Russia had become a major conflict issue. The debt issue was defused only in late autumn and both Putin and Kuchma hailed the agreement. The related issue of *gas thefts* had not in any way made agreements easier to reach, but this issue was also tuned down immediately after the Russian presidential elections in the spring of 2000.[40]

Gas deliveries have also been locked to the issue of *transit gas pipelines* in Ukraine. Russia had repeatedly threatened to bypass Ukraine in its gas exports to Europe despite the high costs involved, and Russia's Gazprom and Germany's Ruhrgas continued to discuss the construction of such additional pipelines. The fact that Poland had a stake in the alternative pipeline did not make the issue any easier. In June 2002, the gas pipeline issue took a giant leap forward when Putin and Kuchma, together with the German Chancellor Gerhard Schröder, decided to create a joint gas transport consortium for the joint development and exploitation of the existing pipeline infrastructure for both oil and gas through Ukraine to Western Europe. This was for all practical purposes an end to alternative plans to build a bypass pipeline. In August 2002, the tripartite consortium was set up and in April 2003, the consortium was registered. The prospecting work is in progress.

Another energy issue developed in the summer of 2003 and was related to *oil pipelines* and it involved the same type of reciprocal dependency as in the case of gas; the Odessa–Brody pipeline was built to pump Caspian oil to Europe, but had been idle since 2002. The pipeline had great symbolic value to Ukraine since it signified a 'return to Europe'. The Odessa–Brody pipeline had been connected to the Druzhba pipeline in 2001 (the pipeline that provided Central Europe with oil from the former USSR), but since Ukraine was unable to find exporters in the Caspian region to use the pipeline, it looked more like a failure.

In the summer of 2003, Russian appeals to employ the pipeline in a 'reverse mode', i.e. to pump oil in the opposite direction, immediately touched a 'nationalistic' chord in Ukraine; the pipeline was used as a lever in negotiations both with Russia and the European Union. When Ukraine and Russia signed a draft 15-year agreement on oil transit through Ukraine, it explicitly excluded the Odessa–Brody project. In November, Ukraine and Poland signed an agreement, with EU participation, on the development of the Odessa–Brody–Plock pipeline for Caspian oil, i.e. an attempt to link the Polish and Ukrainian oil-transport systems by reloading oil in Brody and transporting it by rail to Plock in northern Poland, awaiting plans to build a Brody–Plock oil pipeline link.

The issue of integrating the Druzhba and Adria oil pipelines were solved in an agreement by Russia, Ukraine, Belarus, Hungary, Slovakia and Croatia to transport an additional 15 million tons of oil annually via these pipeline systems to the world markets, with reloading to tankers at the Croatian port of Omisalj. The general Ukrainian argument was to diminish Ukrainian dependency on Russian oil by also tapping Caspian oil on route to Europe. In July 2004, a decision was made to actually build the link from Ukrainian Brody to Polish Plock.[41]

This will be a story to be continued in Putin's second term and under the new Ukrainian leadership. Once the Ukrainian strategic assets are in Russian (although semi-private) hands, Russian political influence on Ukraine's political developments is bound to increase. More important, however, Putin has learned from the history of the European Union that economic integration also locks states together politically, which is a positive side-effect, or prime goal to Putin with respect to his Slavic neighbour.

Energy issues in Russia–Belarus relations

Belarusian energy dependence on Russia has been even greater than that of Ukraine, and has also been blatantly used by Russia. After the Putin–Lukashenka showdown on the Union issue in August 2002, Russian *oil and gas deliveries* soon became a major irritant in the relationship. In November 2002, Gazprom had fulfilled its export contracted for 2002, and, in order to deliver extra gas, Gazprom wanted a higher price, which in Belarus was seen as a way of exerting economic pressure. In the end, Belarus gave in to necessities.

The problem with respect to gas deliveries continued in 2003, with some new spices being added. One had to do with the transit of Russian gas through Belarus to Western Europe, another involved the privatization of Belarusian petrochemical enterprises. By the summer of 2003, Lukashenka backed down on a previous promise and proclaimed that Belarus would not sell the Belarus gas-pipeline operator Beltranshaz to Russia's Gazprom 'for nothing', that the stakes in Beltranshaz would be sold only at 'the market price set by Belarusian experts'. The arguments were that if Belarus sold control of Beltranshaz, she 'would sell control of the country'.[42] Yet a third energy issue was the Russian *oil companies* in Belarus, and in September 2003, Belarusian authorities decided to freeze some of Slavneft's and Transneftprodukt's assets in Belarus: Russia was certain to defend its ownership rights of the Transnefteprodukt company's pipelines located in Belarus.

Russia's *pricing of gas deliveries* to Belarus continued to be a problem, and in September 2003, Gazprom announced that it intended to stop selling natural gas to Belarus at the subsidized price. The issue was directly linked to the deadlocked issue of selling shares in the Belarusian gas transit company Beltranshaz. In Belarus, the question of raising gas prices was interpreted as part of Putin's personal strategy vis-à-vis Belarus and seen as evidence of a 'hardening of Russia's foreign-policy course in relation to Belarus'. Russia's supply of natural gas to Belarus at subsidized prices was to end by 1 January 2004.[43] The linkage between the issues of the union common currency, the selling of shares in Beltranshaz, and the pricing of gas became evident at a Putin–Lukashenka summit later in September, when the two leaders agreed in principle on market-based pricing and on creating a joint pipeline company. In October, Belarus agreed to sell a non-controlling share of Beltranshaz to Gazprom in exchange for a quota of cheap Russian gas under a 2002 agreement.

The pricing issue soon took on an ugly character in what could be called the 'gas war'. On 1 January 2004, Gazprom ceased gas supplies to Belarus because of the failure to reach an agreement on the creation of a joint company to run Beltranshaz. Gazprom explained that it did not want to be a milk cow any longer, Gazprom had 'subsidized the Belarusian economy and budget for several years, supplying gas at a loss and having nothing in return'. Instead, other Russian gas companies (Itera and Transnafta) entered the scene, but these companies too halted deliveries after Belarus had consumed the contractual volume of gas already by mid-January. New contracts on temporary gas deliveries were signed with Itera and Transnafta to give Belarus sufficient amounts of natural gas until the end of January. Lukashenka phoned Putin to discuss the issue, but while Belarusian official comments noted that 'an understanding was reached that natural gas would be delivered continuously and in the full amount that our country needs', Putin's comments did not confirm this. New negotiations with Gazprom also failed, and the Gazprom head, Aleksei Miller, noted that 'the "romantic" period is over'. Both Lukashenka and the Russian Foreign Minister Ivanov tried for a while to downgrade the issue, all in vain.[44]

On 12 February, Itera and Transnafta halted the supply of Russian gas for several hours. The next day, Lukashenka threatened to demand higher transit fees on natural gas bound for Europe in exchange for the same price as that Ukraine pays for Russian gas. Itera and Transnafta gas deliveries were again halted a week later due to 'the lack of a contract between economic entities'. On the same day, Gazprom also halted gas transit completely as a response to the siphoning off of Russian gas flowing in transit to third countries. The next day, Belarus recalled its Ambassador to Russia for consultations, and the Belarusian government issued a statement saying 'such an unprecedented step as the disconnection of gas from people in winter with the temperature nearly 20 degrees below zero has not taken place since the Great Patriotic War 1941–45'. Later the same day, however, Lukashenka accepted the Russian terms. This was not the end, though, because later in the day, the very Belarusian company that Russian Gazprom wanted to have a controlling stake in (i.e. Beltranzhaz) cut off natural gas supplies to the Russian enclave Kaliningrad. The Kaliningrad Governor Vladimir Yegorov appealed the same evening for immediate assistance from Putin and Kasyanov, after which a gas pipeline between Latvia and Lithuania that had not been in use for the past 14 years was reactivated. The next afternoon, the gas supply was normalized again. Lukashenka severely criticized Gazprom for the halt, calling it 'an act of terrorism at the highest level', taking natural gas away 'from people half of whom have Russian blood in their veins, when it's minus 20 degrees outside'. The same day, the Belarusian government unilaterally raised its gas transit fee.[45]

In response to this, the Russian Foreign Ministry accused Lukashenka of 'trying to divert criticism from himself and shift responsibility for his own mistakes to Russia'. The Belarusian Foreign Ministry, in turn, called the Russian statement 'an apparent attempt to reverse the blame and mislead the public', adding, 'the price [of gas] that Gazprom was thrusting on us directly contravened (all Russian–Belarusian interstate) agreements.'[46]

Lukashenka yielded to the pressure and warned against politicizing the recent row which he called 'solely economic', and an agreement on a loan that would allow gas deliveries to Belarus to continue was signed. Ambiguities were not entirely gone, however, since a Lukashenka spokesman noted that the decision to cut off natural-gas supplies could only be taken by Putin himself. Putin's spokesman commented that Lukashenka was 'grossly mistaken', adding that 'it's very clear who is freezing the Belarusian people'. In March through May 2004, the extremely short-term purchases of Russian gas continued, and only in June, an agreement for the rest of 2004 was finally signed.[47] There was no 'repeat war' in the winter of 2005, even though Lukashenka has kept on grumbling about the high prices: an agreements was signed with Fradkov in December 2004 to avoid a repetition.[48]

The 'gas war' shows the discrepancies of views on the part of Putin and Lukashenka, the former arguing along market lines and the latter along 'Soviet' lines. The bottom line is a fight over the economic system that is to prevail, and Russia is not likely to give in on this fundamental issue. Russian capital is to buy up Belarusian industries of interest, and Lukashenka fears a complete sell-out of the one lever he has, i.e. gas transit.

Summary and conclusions: Russian imperialism – the highest stage of Russian capitalism, and Putinism – the highest stage of Russian imperialism?

In conclusion, Putin's foreign policies towards Ukraine and Belarus have increasingly been pointing in the same general direction, and actual policies pursued reinforce the main argument of this essay: Putin has exchanged Yeltsin's geo-political focus for a geo-economic focus and from this derived policies vis-à-vis Ukraine and Belarus, policies that aim at drawing Ukraine and Belarus closer to Russia and at forcing Ukraine and Belarus into an inescapable and firm economic embrace, which will also give Russia stronger political leverage. Traditional Russian geo-political objectives have mutated with these neo-economic objectives. This specific mutation can be termed 'Putinism' – the highest stage of Russian imperialism. The two EU and NATO enlargements have *reinforced* this trend precisely because Putin very early on decided that resisting the two enlargements would be utterly futile and would continue to alienate Russia from Europe.

In summary, Russia–Belarus relations have seen a downward spin under Putin, and the grand designs for political integration inherited from the Yeltsin era have been effectively stopped by Putin's 'economization' of Russian foreign policy. The Union issue has been drastically transformed and today, the question is whether or not Belarus should give in to Putin's demand for economic integration on Russian conditions. A privatization in Belarus with Russian capital ready to buy the most interesting Belarusian objects would yield a similar outcome as in Ukraine and a political neutralization of Lukashenka and his Soviet-type regime. Despite the negative relationship between Putin and Lukashenka, however, military and defence cooperation at the grass-roots level has rather flourished. Only at the highest strategic level has Putin hesitated, and a two-level game in Russia has been evident. The post-11 September sentiments might have played some role here, since a closer relationship with the United States is difficult to reconcile with good relations to Lukashenka's Belarus. The international isolation of Lukashenka has increased with the two European enlargement processes and in the end, Putin might have to choose between support for US 'democratization' goals (with respect to Belarus) and/or engulfing Belarus economically (at high costs), or simply waiting for the economic and political collapse of Belarus. The big question mark is Lukashenka himself: he is rather an obstacle to any positive developments and his present attempts to hang on to a third presidential period after 2006 will, if successful, only cement the present stalemate in Belarus' relations to Russia, the EU and NATO.

The Russian–Ukrainian relationship has up to 2005 been an example of pragmatic foreign policies based more on immediate geo-economic than geo-political interests. The economic and infra-structural cooperation on energy issues that has been initiated under Putin's first term is far from running smoothly, but it seems to me that the joint efforts of Putin and Kuchma for integration with the West *in tandem* indeed were partly the result of closer economic integration also *between* the two Slavic states. To the extent that Putin has been acting like an 'imperialist', he is thus a rather modern one, also involving domestic élites in the interstate relationship. Putin has also used Kuchma's bad standing in the West to force Ukraine into the Russian embrace. While Kuchma accepted this situation, there has also been strong opposition in Ukraine, and it remains to be seen whether Yushchenko will continue to walk hand in hand with Putin. Yushchenko's firm commitment to join the European Union as soon as possible – and also NATO – cannot but be seen as a major setback to Putin's 're-imperialization' strategies.

There is much more to be said on this issue, but the presidential elections in Ukraine in late 2004 indicate future problems, since the elections posed Russia in clear opposition to both the European Union and the United States. In some respects, the elections looked like a contest between Russia and the West over Ukraine in the shape of the two main contestants, Viktor Yanukovich and Viktor Yushchenko. Putin's flagrant support of the former on the eve of the elections indicated a 'free but not fair' election round. Since no candidate received the necessary 50 per cent of the votes, a second round was necessary. Before long, Yushchenko supporters and youth organizations took to the streets to protest against the obviously incorrect vote count, and the campaign in the second round took on an ugly character. Putin again visited Kiev and offered support for Yanukovich, while the US warned of the consequences of not adhering to the values of the Euro-Atlantic community.

In the second election round, Yanukovich was first given the victory over Yushchenko. Putin made the mistake of prematurely congratulating Yanukovich on his victory. Yushchenko called on his supporters to peaceful demonstrations against the vote count, and large-scale and persistent demonstrations followed in Kiev and elsewhere. Putin severely criticized the European Union, the OSCE and the United States for their rejection of the election results and the stand-off between Russia and the West on the issue was open for everyone to see. Attempts at a compromise were made with EU assistance, but only after the German Chancellor Gerhard Schröder and the EU leader Jan Peter Balkenende had had telephone conversations with Putin, a second run-off election was agreed upon to solve the situation. A new election round was set to take place on 26 December. By now, permanent mass protests in front of parliamentary and government buildings in Kiev threatened this third election round – the 'orange revolution' was in full swing. Putin continued to heavily criticize US and European leaders for their support of Yushchenko.

The third election round gave Yushchenko a clear majority. Yanukovich stepped down as Prime Minister, and in early January 2005, a new government was formed. The new Ukrainian President set off for Moscow in an attempt to remedy the damage done to the Russian–Ukrainian relationship without compromising his main foreign policy goal – to enter the European Union. The future of the 'Slavic triangular relationship' will to a considerable extent now depend on policies in the EU, NATO and the United States, and not only because the double enlarge-ments have placed all three Slavic countries on the border to the EU and NATO. Russia is not likely to give up on 're-imperializing' Ukraine and Belarus by economic means.

In the final analysis, the two European enlargement processes have not brought about the closeness of the three Slavic states in any direct way; Putin foresaw the futility of resistance and tried to adapt to enlargements already in 2000. The two European enlargements have, however, served as catalysts for substantial changes in Russian thinking on international relations, changes from a 'geo-political' to a 'geo-economic' thinking, which (if it is not hampered) might lead Russia into the post-modern world. Whether or not this new thinking will also be successful with respect to the economic and political integration of Russia, Ukraine and Belarus is too early to tell, but as we all know, it takes two to tango, and Yushchenko will not be as willing a dancing partner as Kuchma has been. The stage for new games in the New Strategic Triangle is set.

Notes

1 For a description of this environment, see B. Lo, *Vladimir Putin and the Evolution of Russian Foreign Policy*, London: Blackwell, 2003. Lo argues that Russian foreign policy became more personalized and 'presidential' after September 11; see p. 121.

2 The two terms used to denote such thinking here, geo-politics and geo-economics, are not really meant as analytical concepts but rather used to denote an inherent inclination present in expressed ideas, standpoints or arguments. In suggesting that Russian foreign policy has changed from a geo-political to a geo-economic character under Putin does not suggest that economic goals are the more final or over-arching goals, or that geo-economic goals may not be used for purposes of political dominance. It simply suggests that geo-economic ideas, standpoints and arguments seem to be more important for Putin, *for whatever purpose or reason.*

3 D. R. Herspring and P. Rutland, 'Putin and Russian Foreign Policy', in D. R. Herspring (ed.) *Putin's Russia. Past Imperfect, Future Uncertain*, Lanham, MD: Rowman & Littlefield, 2003.

4 See *Diplomatichesky Vestnik*, August 2000, no. 8.

5 See B. Lo, *Vladimir Putin and the Evolution of Russian Foreign Policy*, p. 121.

6 For Putin's addresses to the Federation Council in 2003 and 2004, see President Putin's address to the Federation Council 16 May 2003; and President Putin's address to the Federation Council 26 May 2004. For an analysis of these speeches along the lines of my argument here, see Y. E. Fedorov, 'Putin's Russia: Foreign Policy and the Nature of the Regime', in Y. E. Fedorov and B. Nygren (eds) *Putin I and Putin II. Results of the First Term and Prospects for the Second*, Stockholm: Swedish National Defence College, 2004. For a more thorough analysis of the Foreign Policy Concept, see B. Nygren, 'Russia and Europe, or Russia in Europe?', in Y. E. Fedorov and B. Nygren (eds) *Russia and Europe: Putin's Foreign Policy*, Stockholm: Swedish National Defence College, 2002.

7 This might seem all the more strange, since Putin himself has been molded and formed by the security ideology of the KGB and FSB, which clearly makes its imprints in his handling of some domestic political problems.

8 For an account of Russia's sometimes hysterical relations with NATO after the Cold War, see J. L. Black, *Russia Faces NATO Expansion. Bearing Gifts or Bearing Arms?* Lanham, MD: Rowman & Littlefield Publishers, Inc., 2000. For an account of Russia's relations to Germany, see C. A. Wallander, *Mortal Friends, Best Enemies. German-Russian Cooperation After the Cold War*, Ithaca, NY and London: Cornell University Press, 1999.

9 I will not make an attempt to summarize Yeltsin's general foreign policy or his foreign policy towards the West: the literature abounds with such descriptions. Among the best of those dealing with Russia's foreign policy generally are (chronologically): N. Malcolm et al., *Internal Factors in Russian Foreign Policy*. Oxford: Clarendon Press, 1996; C. A. Wallander (ed.), *The Sources of Russian Foreign Policy After the Cold War*, Boulder, CO: Westview Press, 1998; H. Trofimenko, *Russian National Interests and the Current Crisis in Russia*, Aldershot: Ashgate, 1999; D. Trenin, *The End of Eurasia: Russia on the Border between Geopolitics and Globalization*, Washington, DC and Moscow: Carnegie Endowment for International Peace, 2002; G. Gorodetsky (ed.) *Russia Between East and West. Russian Foreign Policy on the Threshold to the Twenty-first Century*, London: Frank Cass, 2003; J. L. Black, *Vladimir Putin and the New World Order. Looking East, Looking West?*, London, Boulder, CO, New York, Toronto, Oxford: Rowman & Littlefield Publishers, 2004.

10 *RFE/RL Newsline*, 8 February 2001.

11 The full text of the treaty was published in *Nezavisimaya Gazeta*, 9 December 1999

12 See M. Kalashnikova, 'NATO budet tam, gde nado', in *Nezavisimyia Gazeta*, 11 June 2002, p. 6.

13 See J. Hedenskog, *The Ukrainian Dilemma. Relations with Russia and the West in the Context of the 2004 Presidential Elections*, Stockholm: Swedish Defence Agency (FOI-R-1199-SE), March 2004, pp. 38–39.

14 For the plan, see online Ukraine–NATO action plan, and for the Council, see *RFE/RL Newsline*, 31 January 2003.

15 A. Khanbabian, 'NATO, gaz i khorozhaia pogoda', *Nezavisimaia Gazeta*, 20 May 2002, p. 6.

16 *Diplomatichesky Vestnik*, 2003, no. 6, p. 78.

17 See T. Ivshenko, 'Kiev ne bolshe mechtaet o vstuplenie v NATO i Evrosojuz', *Nezavisimaya Gazeta*, 28 July 2004, p. 5.

18 While Ukraine wanted the Azovsk Sea to be divided both by the bottom and the surface, Russia wanted to treat the sea as internal waters of the two countries, the bottom to be

divided and the surface to be available for joint use by both countries. The possibility of oil and gas reserves on the shelf did not facilitate a solution to the different approaches.

19 For the development of the crisis in the first days, see *RFE/RL Newsline*, 3, 14, 15, 17, 20 and 21 October 2003. Ukraine was also aggravated by a formal Russian request to provide 'copies of documents, including cartographic ones, on which the Ukrainian side is basing its suppositions regarding its ownership of the island of Tuzla', a rather typical backbone reaction of the Russian Foreign Ministry. See *RFE/RL Newsline*, 21 October 2003.

20 The headlines talked of war; see *Nezavisimaya Gazeta*, 22 October 2003, pp. 1, 5. For Ivanov's judgement, see *Nezavisimaya Gazeta*, 23 October 2003, p. 5.

21 The then leader of 'Our Ukraine' and new President of Ukraine Viktor Yushchenko, see *RFE/RL Newsline*, 23 and 24 October 2003.

22 The Yabloko Duma Deputy, Aleksei Arbatov (and deputy chairman of the Duma's Defence Committee) commented that he could not rule out the possibility of 'armed contacts of a limited character' between the two sides in the disputed area. See *RFE/RL Newsline*, 27 and 29 October 2003 for the statements. See also C. Schreck, 'Rogozhin Rallies Cossaks for Tuzla', *Moscow Times*, 27 October 2003, p. 1.

23 For the sequence of events, see *RFE/RL Newsline*, 31 October, 6, 7, 13 and 20 November 2003. The Ukrainian Foreign Minister implied that Ukraine might ask the International Court of Justice in The Hague to resolve the Tuzla Island dispute should Ukraine and Russia themselves not be able to do so. In early December, the new Ukrainian border post on Tuzla Island was inaugurated. For the agreement, see *Diplomatichesky Vestnik*, 2004, no. 1, pp. 66ff.

24 For analyses, see T. Vickery, 'Ukraine Broke Tuzla Pledge, Says Kazyanov', *Moscow Times*, 29 October 2003, p. 3, *RFE/RL Poland, Belarus and Ukraine Report*, 29 October 2003, vol. 5, no. 4; ibid., 20 January 2004, vol. 6, no. 2, and P. Felgenhauer, 'From Tuzla to Great Russia', *Moscow Times*, 30 October 2003, p. 9.

25 The revival of pan-slavist and 'Slavic unification' ideas is a post-imperial syndrome; see V. Karbalevich, 'The Prospects of Slavic Unity. Belarus' Relations with Russia and Ukraine', in A. Moshes and B. Nygren (eds) *A Slavic Triangle? Present and Future Relations between Russia, Ukraine and Belarus*, Stockholm: FHS, (Acta B25) 2002, pp. 95–106. At least three reasons for this revival stand out: the interconnectedness of the economies of the former Soviet republics (especially the Russian, Ukrainian and Belarusian economies), the (Soviet) culture of the political elites, and the ethnic-linguistic factor (see O. Haran and S. Tolstov, 'The Slavic Triangle. Ukraine's Relations with Russia and Belarus: A Ukrainian View', in A. Moshes and B. Nygren (eds) *A Slavic Triangle?*, pp. 75–94.) For the reasons of the Russian policy, see B. Nygren, 'The History of the "Slavic Union" Idea', in A. Moshes and B. Nygren (eds) *A Slavic Triangle?*, pp.107–128.

26 For Lukashenka, see *RFE/RL Newsline*, 19 and 20 June 2002. For Yeltsin, see ibid., 25 June 2002. For Primakov, see ibid., 27 June 2002. Both Yeltsin and Primakov criticized Putin for his handling of the issue. See Borodin, *Nezavisimaya Gazeta*, 11 June 2002, p. 5. For an analysis see also *Izvestiya*, 19 June 2002, p. 4. Analysts in *Nezavisimaya Gazeta* said that Putin had offered Lukashenka a 'backdoor entrance', *Nezavisimaya Gazeta*, 20 June 2002, p. 5. For later analyses of the situation, see Jan Maksymiuk, 'A Union Fractured', End Note, *RFE/RL Newsline*, 16 June 2002; Taras Kuzio, 'Will Lukashenko Survive as Putin Loses Interest in Union with Belarus?', End Note, *RFE/RL Newsline*, 16 July 2002; *RFE/RL Poland, Belarus and Ukraine Report*, 18 June 2002, vol. 4, no. 24.

27 See *RFE/RL Newsline*, 14, 15, 19 and 20 August 2002. See also *Nezavisimaya Gazeta*, 14 August 2002, pp.1 and 5, and *RFE/RL Poland, Belarus and Ukraine Report*, 20 August 2002, vol. 4, no. 31. For an analysis, see J. Maksymiuk, 'Lukashenko Trades

Insults with Putin over Integration', *RFE/RL Newsline,* End Note, 29 August 2002. For an analysis of the unification issue by the end of the year, see J. Maksymiuk, 'Lukashenko Subdued' *RFE/RL Newsline,* End Note, 17 December 2002.

28 See *RFE/RL Newsline,* 12 March 2003.

29 *RFE/RL Newsline,* 19 June 2003. See also *Nezavisimaya Gazeta,* 20 June 2003, p. 5.

30 *RFE/RL Newsline,* 12 and 28 August 2003.

31 *RFE/RL Newsline,* 2 September 2003. For a report, see *Moscow Times,* 15 September 2003, p. 5.

32 *RFE/RL Newsline,* 15 October 2003.

33 For Ivanov's comment, see *RFE/RL Newsline,* 17 April 2002. For Lukashenka's hesitation, see *Nezavisimaya Gazeta,* 29 April 2003, p. 5.

34 See J. Hedenskog, *The Ukrainian Dilemma,* pp. 15, 16; and *RFE/RL Newsline,* 28 February 2003.

35 The idea of a free-trade zone within the Commonwealth of Independent States was a long-standing one. In 1994, the CIS presidents had pledged to create a CIS free-trade zone, and the CIS Executive Secretary Boris Berezovski, resurrected the idea in 1998.

36 See *RFE/RL Newsline,* 10 December 2002, and 30 January 2003.

37 *RFE/RL Newsline,* 15 and 19 September 2003. For Lukashenka's comments, see ibid., 22 September 2003.

38 One analyst (Delyagin) suggested that the Russian interest in the Single Economic Space was to buy out the 'most valuable and profitable enterprises (functioning) in the economies of the former Soviet Union', but that Russia also had a responsibility for those countries that are not admitted to the EU. See *RFE/RL Newsline,* 26 May 2004.

39 In December 1999, the EU adopted a Common Strategy on Ukraine that did not foresee membership as a goal. The reason for this rather cool EU interest in Ukraine was to be found in the stagnation of the Ukrainian reform process and lack of political transparency. See J. Hedenskog, *The Ukrainian Dilemma,* pp. 43–44, and Y. Tymchuk, 'Krim prinimaet Evropy', *Nezavisimaya Gazeta,* 8 October 2003, p. 5.

40 See A. Moshes, 'The Evolution of Relations within the Slavic Triangle: A View from Russia', in A. Moshes and B. Nygren (eds) *A Slavic Triangle?,* p. 61.

41 *RFE/RL Belarus and Ukraine Report* 20 July 2004, vol. 6, no. 26.

42 See *RFE/RL Newsline,* 25 June and 31 July 2003, respectively.

43 See *RFE/RL Poland, Belarus, and Ukraine Report,* 2 September 2003, vol. 5, no. 32; and the *Moscow Times,* 8 September 2003.

44 See *RFE/RL Newsline,* 12, 23, 26, 27 and 30 January and 3 February 2004. See also *RFE/RL Poland, Belarus and Ukraine Report,* 13 January 2004, vol. 6, no. 1 and ibid., 27 January 2004, vol. 6, no. 3.

45 For the sequence of events, see *RFE/RL Newsline,* 11, 13 17, 18, 19 and 20 February 2004. See also Valeria Korchagina, 'Furious Belarus Bows to Gazprom', *Moscow Times,* 20 February 2004, p. 1; *RFE/RL Belarus and Ukraine Report* 18 February 2004, vol. 6, no. 6, and ibid., 2 March 2004, vol. 6, no. 7.

46 The Russian Deputy Prime Minister, Viktor Khristenko, then warned that there could be more disruptions in gas deliveries to Belarus if Minsk fails to sign a 'full-scale contract' with Gazprom on gas supplies: '[I]f you want to drink, do you go to the store or just lie in the bed crying that you want to drink?', *RFE/RL Newsline,* 23 February 2004. For an analysis, see V. Korchagina, 'Furious Belarus bows to Gazprom', *Moscow Times,* 20 February 2004, p. 1.

47 For the sequence of buys, see *RFE/RL Newsline,* 24, 25 and 26 February and 3, 11, 24 and 31 March and 18 May and 9 June 2004. See also *RFE/RL Belarus and Ukraine Report,* 15 June 2004, vol. 6, no. 22.

48 See *RFE/RL Belarus and Ukraine Report,* 23 December 2004, vol. 6, no. 47.

8

THE 'NEW STRATEGIC TRIANGLE' AND THE US GRAND STRATEGY DEBATE*

Peter Dombrowski and Andrew L. Ross

Introduction

During the Cold War, policymakers and strategic thinkers had it relatively easy. Most strategic choices were defined by a central, apparently enduring cleavage. Led by the Soviet Union and the United States, two camps – East and West – were locked into what was thought to be a perpetual confrontation. This bipolar relationship provided the framework that informed analysis and strategy. International politics and national strategies revolved around this bipolar juxtaposition. What mattered and what did not was largely defined by it. Regardless of issue area, it was the United States vs. the Soviet Union; NATO vs. the Warsaw Pact, West vs. East, liberal democracy vs. communism, free markets vs. central planning. Even the international economic order, a Western order from which the Soviet Union and its clients were largely excluded, was largely defined by the Cold War divide.

With the Cold War's end and the Soviet Union's demise, what was a given gave way. The seemingly futile search for a new security construct to replace the bipolar framework of old continues. Candidates have included unipolarity (or, at the least, a unipolar moment); a return to multipolarity; the end of history; growing anarchy; and a clash of civilizations, particularly between the West and Islam. Yet, none of these ordering devices match bipolarity's parsimonious power or is accompanied by a strategic concept with containment's clarity.

That the concept of a strategic triangle has been resurrected is not surprising. The analytical attraction of the metaphor is readily apparent. After all, the US–Soviet–PRC strategic triangle figured prominently during the second half of the Cold War after the United States under Nixon and Kissinger belatedly exploited a long-evident Sino–Soviet rift. That Cold War strategic triangle is a near classic example of how three powers, in shifting calculations of converging and diverging interests, each might attempt to play one of its two 'partners' off against the other. The logic underlying the new US–EU–Russia strategic triangle envisioned by this volume's editors is not as classically geopolitical. Instead, ideational factors as well as strictly objective material interests are thought to inform the relationships among

146

and interactions of the United States, EU, and Russia. Essentially, the parties to the new strategic triangle are thought to have been brought together less by the traditional geopolitical calculations that motivated the United States, Soviet Union and China during the Cold War than by the prospect of a partnership that will yield common benefits. The endurance of this new strategic triangle is predicated on a common set of shared societal values and, better yet, domestic and international institutions that are roughly compatible. In the absence of shared values and compatible institutions, the triangle is likely to be weak and prone to disintegrate in times of crisis or extreme stress.

Despite the intuitive significance of the US–EU–Russia strategic triangle, particularly for committed Atlanticists, a different strategic triangle captured America's attention after March 2003. Centred on Baghdad, Ramadi, and Tikrit, it was the Sunni triangle, the locus of Sunni opposition to the US occupation of Iraq that then topped the US list of strategic triangles of concern. Another Iraqi triangle, that among Sunnis, Shiites, and Kurds, was high on the list as well. Other potential strategic triangles also compete for the attention of American strategists. Among the broadest is the North American, European, East Asian 'triad', which incorporates the world's greatest concentrations of power and wealth. Another significant state-centric triangle spans not only Eurasia but the northern hemisphere of the globe: the US–Russia–China triangle. An alternative conception of a 'new strategic triangle' features the United States and the EU in a relationship not with Russia but with China.[1] Within Europe, there is the EU's 'Big Three' – Britain, France, and Germany – as well as the French, German, Polish and French, German, Russian triangles. For those who would have us believe that Asia is the future and Europe is history, the focus is on Pacific Rim triangles. In East Asia, both the US–PRC–Japan and the US–PRC–Taiwan triangles command attention. Other Asia-centric strategic triangles of note include that consisting of Russia, China, and India and that comprised of China, India, and Pakistan. A triangle focused on South Asia links the United States, India, and Pakistan.

As this small sampling of potential 'triangles' reveals, there is considerable diversity. First, the complexity of strategic triangles varies; some are essentially unidimensional, others multidimensional. Second, some consist exclusively of states; others of an admixture of states and multilateral institutions. Yet others are domestic manifestations of transnational religious and/or ethnic groupings. Third, their significance varies across issue areas. Fourth, their relative importance, for the world as a whole, for particular regions, and for the United States, varies tremendously. Despite all this variation, however, there exists a striking commonality: the US–centric character of contemporary strategic triangles. Even when the United States is not a party, it figures prominently. This shared feature of today's strategic triangles reflects the reality of contemporary geopolitics. Like it or not, America's pre-eminence often defines reality for others. As a senior advisor to President Bush reportedly observed, 'We're an empire now, and when we act, we create our own reality . . . . And while you're studying that reality . . . we'll act again, creating other new realities . . . . We're history's actors . . . .'[2]

147

The US–EU–Russia strategic triangle: premise(s)

The central premise underlying the US–EU–Russia 'new strategic triangle' is that the poles of this triangle are, in the words of our volume's editors, 'the three most important actors in the greater transatlantic region'.[3] In the long term, that may well turn out to be the case. At present, however, the premise is open to question, at least from the perspective of Washington, DC. The events of the Bush administration's first four years suggest that the United States is focused less on further developing its relationships with Europe and Russia than on challenges in the Middle East, Central Asia, and elsewhere. Europe and Russia have often opposed American initiatives in these regions and sometimes collaborated only reluctantly. Many aspects of the multidimensional relationships among the United States, the EU, and Russia have been neglected. Miscommunication, confrontation, and sometimes outright hostility have plagued relations among the poles of this strategic triangle.

As the project editors have acknowledged, this strategic triangle is not an equilateral triangle. Its members include a United States that is the world's sole full-service superpower with global political, economic, and military reach. Both America's hard power and soft power are unrivalled. Across the entire spectrum of power, the United States is without peer in this or any other strategic triangle to which it is party. That said, one dimension of American power outstrips the others: its large, globally capable military. In both political and economic terms the relationship, especially with Europe, is less unequal.[4] Russia lags along all three dimensions, although the vestiges of Soviet nuclear systems give it weight disproportionate to its conventional military, political, and economic capacities. It is tempting to conclude that from America's perspective, the triangular relationship among the United States, the EU, and Russia is a relationship among actors in possession of, respectively, hard power, soft power, and no power.[5]

In Washington, the EU is rarely viewed as a worthy geopolitical partner on security and diplomatic issues. The European Union's combined economies may be more than the equal of America's, but its political-military potential remains unrealized. While the EU is often able to speak and act as a unitary actor on economic issues, it cannot yet do so in the political-military realm, despite the European Security and Defence Policy (ESDP). Washington's Eurosceptics doubt that the ESDP will amount to much; they believe that EU is quite unlikely to emerge as a geopolitical counterweight to the United States.[6]

Washington's preferred multilateral instrumentality in Europe remains NATO. The United States did not create NATO, but it became a US creature. While Washington does not have a seat at the EU table; it is *primus inter pares* in NATO. Even as NATO's strategic significance continues to diminish with the demise of the Soviet threat and the rise of the EU, the United States continues to invest in NATO by attempting to modify its roles and missions. Schemes ranging from the creation of a Rapid Reaction Force to the Defense Capabilities Initiative share the common goal of making NATO a useful partner for 'out-of-area' military actions.

148

On a tactical level, Washington generally prefers bilateral dealings with the EU's member states to a bilateral relationship with the EU in Brussels. Dealing with individual states enables the United States to take advantage of its geopolitical weight. Salami-slicing tactics can be more effectively employed against weaker members than against the combined strength of the whole. Further, historically, the United States and Britain have long enjoyed a 'special relationship'. During the Cold War, Britain and (West) Germany were Washington's favourites. That continued to be the case through the immediate post-Cold War period. More recently, Washington has returned to a focus on a Britain that has proved to be more pliable than continental powers. A preference has also emerged for what Secretary of Defense Donald Rumsfeld has termed the 'new Europe': former subjects of the Soviet empire so eager to be in the good graces of the United States that they have proved even more cooperative than Tony Blair's Britain.

Russia is in an inferior position in this triangle. Its presence is due largely to both the inertia of history and the weight accorded a country possessing nuclear weapons, a pivotal position on the Eurasian landmass, and vast reserves of natural resources. Politically, militarily, and economically Russia is outclassed by the other parties to the triangle. Russia's influence today is only a fraction of that once wielded by the Soviet Union. It inherited the Soviet Union's formidable nuclear arsenal, but its conventional forces are a now a hollow shell. Its economy is barely on a par with those of the EU's middle powers. In many respects, Russia is of interest to the United States and the EU today more because of its weakness than its strength, its oil than any residual military might, its fragile political and economic institutions than its ideological appeal, and its apparent latent interest in rebuilding the Soviet empire than its current reach. As a political partner on the world stage it has proven unreliable for both the American and European poles of the strategic triangle.

Although it has become commonplace to assert that 11 September changed everything, its implications for the US–EU–Russia strategic triangle should not be overstated. 11 September did not fundamentally alter the foundations of the relationships among the United States, EU, and Russia. It did have an impact on the security issues atop the agenda. Terrorism and the proliferation of weapons of mass destruction (re)emerged front and centre, insofar as Russia and the European states have been willing to share Washington's obsession, the strategic relationship has taken a turn for the better. Russia in particular, has tried to use this to its advantage by equating its war against Chechen terrorists with America's war against al Qaeda.

In the long term, however, America's handling of the Iraq war may well have a greater impact than 11 September on relationships within the new strategic triangle. The close strategic relationship that 9/11 appeared, however briefly, to revive has faltered. Aside from Great Britain, Spain, Italy and several central European states, few bought into the Bush administration's assertion that Iraq is a central front in the war on terror. With the possible exception of Great Britain, even the states that supported the American decision to invade Iraq did so in the hopes of other political, economic, and military benefits. The insurgency that followed the overthrow of

Saddam Hussein did not bring European states around to America's view of Iraq's centrality in the global war on terror or make them any more eager to share with America the burden of rebuilding Iraq.

The US grand strategy debate and the new strategic triangle

Despite a September 2002 White House document with the grand title of *The National Security Strategy of the United States*, a post-Cold War US grand strategy vision that can command widespread support has yet to emerge. Instead we have contending visions of America's role in the world. As a result, the relative significance of any one geopolitical construct, particularly one as multifaceted and complex as the US–EU–Russia strategic triangle, is open to interpretation and debate.

Our assessment of the import of the triangular relationships among the United States, the European Union, and Russia revisits and builds upon the earlier analysis of US grand strategy by Posen and Ross.[7] They identified four contending grand strategy visions: neo-isolationism, selective engagement, cooperative security (which we re-label 'liberal internationalism'[8]), and primacy. We add 'empire' to the original menu of choices. For each alternative we summarize the political-military (or security) and economic components of the strategic vision and assess, in notional terms, the significance of the US–EU–Russia strategic triangle. The importance of this triangle varies considerably across the alternative visions of America's role in the world.

We employ this approach because the post-Cold War US grand strategy debate is far from settled. In 2004, for the first time since the end of Cold War – indeed for the first time since the Vietnam era – national security and foreign policy emerged as a defining, and extremely divisive, issue in a US presidential election. An emphasis on American primacy that verges on the imperial will no doubt continue to be evident in a second Bush administration. Despite, or perhaps because of, the 're-election' of George W. Bush, the US grand strategy debate will continue. That debate has concrete implications for the US–EU–Russia strategic triangle.

Neo-isolationism

America's new isolationists have little interest in a US–EU–Russia strategic triangle or any other sustained strategic relationship. They would have the United States take advantage of the predominance it has enjoyed since the end of the Cold War by pulling back from the world. In the absence of a major power threat akin to that posed by the former Soviet Union, there is no justification for continued US internationalism. This neo-isolationist alternative is built upon a distinctly narrow interpretation of US national interests. The central vital US interest is defence of the homeland. Fortunately, according to this school of thought, there are few if any conventional threats to the homeland; the United States is remarkably secure.

The maintenance of a balance of power in Eurasia no longer requires active US involvement. The United States can safely assume the more passive posture of an offshore balancer.[9] Its military presence around the world is no longer necessary. Indeed, as 11 September demonstrated, that presence can be counterproductive and 'a magnet for trouble'.[10] As one long-time advocate of US disengagement observed in the aftermath of 11 September, 'terrorism must be understood as an inevitable consequence of global [US] intervention'.[11] Islamist terrorists strike the United States because it mucks around in their backyard. Homeland security would be best served if the United States were to withdraw from foreign entanglements and jealously guard its strategic independence – and its values.

In the economic, as in the political-military, realm, the United States needs Europe, Russia, and the rest of the world far less than the world might need or desire relations with the United States. The unmatched size, strength, and resilience of its economy sets the United States apart from the rest of the world. It is significantly less dependent on imports and exports of goods and services than other countries. Economically, the United States, to a greater extent than others, can go it alone.

Whatever international economic engagement is necessary is best left to the private sector. It is up to the challenge of ensuring American prosperity. Markets, whether domestic or international, function best in the absence of intrusive government involvement according to the libertarians and paleoconservatives who are among the most prominent proponents of the new isolationism. Globalization would be left to its own devices.

Multilateralism and economic institutions alike are suspect. Both are thought to constrict US freedom of action. Neo-isolationists do not necessarily advocate the abandonment of international economic institutions, but their support for them is tepid. The cost of supporting institutions such as the WTO, World Bank, and IMF and exercising leadership in them is perceived as greater than the benefits they provide.

Neo-isolationism and the new strategic triangle

America's new isolationists do not privilege a US–EU–Russia strategic triangle. Even the intimate, prized relationship with the Western European Cold War allies responsible for founding and leading the EU is not exempt from their pronounced emphasis on strategic independence. The recent escape from strategic nuclear interdependence with the Soviet Union is simply to be welcomed, not replaced with an unnecessarily close strategic relationship with its successor state. For the neo-isolationists, there is no new strategic triangle and no need to construct, or imagine, one. The United States is now able to distance itself from the EU and its members as well as NATO. There is little reason to either support or oppose the ESDP. Whether collectively under the auspices of the EU or a Europeanized NATO or individually, the states of Europe have the resources to provide for their own security. Precisely how that is done is their business. The burden of European security should not be shared; it should be shed. American forces would be redeployed, but homeward rather than eastward. Only the Soviet threat necessitated an American military presence in Europe after World War II. In the absence of a comparable threat, there is no reason for the United States to remain entangled in the affairs of Europe.

Russia's future and its relationship with the EU should be left to the Russians and EU members. A politically, economically, and militarily weak Russia is of little concern to the United States. The United States is under no obligation to provide material support for Russian political and economic reforms. Neither is it obliged to ensure the security of the Russian nuclear stockpile; that is Russia's responsibility. If the EU feels the need to invest in Russia's future, so be it.

Selective engagement

The members of the European Union (at least its leading members) and Russia are accorded a significantly higher priority by the realist proponents of selective engagement. National interests are more broadly framed than by neo-isolationism but not as broadly as by either liberal internationalism, primacy, or empire. For selective engagement, the greatest threat to US security and international order is conflict among the world's major powers. The purpose of US engagement abroad is to (1) ensure peace among the major powers and (2) prevent the emergence of a great power capable of challenging US predominance. It should focus on those parts of the world in which the major powers reside – the two ends of Eurasia – or compete – essentially, today, the Greater Middle East/Southwest Asia. Under this construct, the leading powers of the EU and Russia matter. Always mindful that resources are scarce, the advocates of selective engagement reject what they portray as the indiscriminate engagement of liberal internationalism and the demands of preserving, indefinitely, US primacy. America cannot afford to be either the world's policeman or the 'indispensable nation'.

Selective engagement's discretionary approach carries over into the economic realm, where it exhibits a realist fix on 'large concentrations of power'.[12] Outside of North America, large concentrations of economic power are located only at the two ends of Eurasia. Managing relationships, whether cooperative or uncooperative, with the principal economic powers such as Japan, the leading members of the European Union (rather than the EU as such), and China would be assigned the highest priority. Next on the list of priorities are economic relationships with other members of the core, or peak, economic associations. On both counts, the leading members of the EU require attention.

Selective engagement would have the United States remain both economically engaged with the rest of the world and committed to, as Robert Art put it, 'international economic openness'.[13] There are distinct limits to international economic engagement and the commitment to an open international economic order, however. For Art, international economic openness is a 'desirable' rather than a 'vital' interest. In his view, the demise of an open global economic order would not pose 'severe' or 'catastrophic' costs for the United States.[14]

Economic globalization, multilateralism, and institutions should be subjected to a scrutiny of benefits and costs informed by the dictates of great power politics.

Realist sceptics demand that the alleged virtues of this liberal triad be balanced against their costs. To the extent that globalization, multilateralism, and institutionalism erode state, particularly US, power and influence, they should be resisted; to the extent they help set the global agenda in ways favourable to the United States and allow for more efficient systems management they should be encouraged. The outcome of such a calculation is likely to be a distinctly measured commitment to globalization, multilateralism, and institutions.

Selective engagement and the new strategic triangle

This major power, state-centric approach suggests that selective engagers would be inclined to prize individual relationships with the EU's leading members more than any relationship with the EU itself. But an increasingly effective EU would come to command the attention of even the advocates of selective engagement. They would have little choice but to engage with a collective that represents the concentration of power evident in the EU, especially if the EU increases its ability to control outcomes, whether economic or political-military. Among its members, however, Britain, Germany, and France would count as major political-military and economic powers. Russia too, despite the loss of the Soviet Union's superpower status, counts, if more because of its potential than anything else. Moreover, given uncertainties in global energy markets Russia's growing role as a producer state and the possibility that still greater oil reserves remain to be tapped ensure this Soviet successor state a place among those regarded as major powers.

Since the United States remains the leading member of NATO and is not a member of the EU, NATO would continue to be America's preferred multilateral instrumentality in Europe; as such the United States might seek to 'securitize' economic and political issues in order to influence outcomes it might otherwise not have a say in. For example, dual-use export and technology controls would remain a province of security specialists rather than those primarily interesting in expanding trade, saving on defence procurement, or preserving industrial sectors or individual firms. The proponents of selective engagement would have been loath, however, to rush into what they see as the ill-advised and unnecessary post-Cold War expansion of NATO, a project that needlessly alarmed and, even worse, antagonized nationalist elements in a still smarting Russia. In the absence of the threat it was established to deter and if necessary fight and defeat, NATO's significance is expected to decline. The decline of NATO need not imply an automatic, corresponding rise in the EU's political-military significance, however.

In the security realm, selective engagement's stance on the EU might be best characterized as 'studied ambiguity'. Ever mindful of the need to husband scarce resources, the proponents of selective engagement are inclined to share with European partners the burdens of ensuring order and stability, even if that means sharing leadership on occasion. Therefore they are receptive to the EU's ESDP even while remaining unconvinced of its ultimate success. But the acceptance of the ESDP would be contingent. Those interested in selective engagement have an interest in promoting a favourable division of labour in the military and defence realms. If the EU and the European contributions to NATO could be focused on military tasks that the United States is either unable or unwilling to take on, so much the better. As former Secretary of State Madeline Albright put it, the ESPD and similar efforts are fine if there is no decoupling, duplication, or discrimination.[15]

On the economic front, even the realist advocates of selective engagement recognize that the European Union is a force to be reckoned with. Despite the preference for bilateral dealings, a US–EU economic relationship is a necessary inconvenience that even can benefit the United States if managed correctly. Consensus between the United States and the EU on international economic issues such as trade, finance, and development could make it more difficult for others to resist continued liberalization.

Whatever the issue area – Russian political and economic reforms, loose nukes, access to Russia's energy resources, Chechnya, or latent Russian revanchism – selective engagement's proponents are inclined to prefer a direct, bilateral US–Russia strategic relationship to a triangular US–EU–Russia relationship. That preference would likely be modified if a *de facto* division of labour is developed in US and EU dealings with a struggling Russia. There is little reason that selective engagers, always acutely aware of the need to safeguard scarce resources, would object to a more active EU role in, for instance, Russian political and economic liberalization. The new strategic triangle need not be a merely nominal relationship under selective engagement.

Liberal internationalism[16]

It is the liberal internationalist alternative that most prominently features an emerging US–EU–Russia strategic triangle. Informed by contemporary liberalism rather than realism, its starting point is strategic interdependence: 'peace is effectively indivisible.'[17] Conflict of any kind is thought to threaten world order. National security requires security for all. Consequently, US interests must be broadly conceived. Neither traditional nor, especially, non-traditional, transnational threats to peace can be countered unilaterally. Security requires an approach that is collective, preventive, and comprehensive. 'Multilateralism,' it is asserted, 'matters.'[18] Dramatic evidence of the potential of multilateral, institutionally based cooperation is provided by the history of the European Union and the other institutions that comprise Europe's highly developed security architecture.

Security communities and the democratic peace are central to liberal internationalism's cooperative security project. Democratic security communities are, essentially, security regimes, complete with sets of principles, norms, rules, conventions, and procedures that constrain, even govern, the behaviour of members. Advocates call for the development and broadening and deepening of webs of 'overlapping, mutually reinforcing arrangements'.[19] The model, admittedly imperfect and incomplete, is the transatlantic security community encompassing North America and much of Europe. The European Union, along with NATO and the OSCE, is a central component of that democratic security community. Significantly, the web of overlapping arrangements evident in this model has long featured not only security but also economic arrangements, particularly those involving the EU.

The US pursuit of a liberal world order is not, of course, a post-Cold War phenomenon. As Ikenberry has pointed out, it dates to the 1940s. It was then that the foundation of a 'liberal democratic order', featuring 'economic openness, political reciprocity, and multilateral management of an American-led liberal political system', was put in place.[20] The task for liberal internationalism is not to create a new order but to 'reclaim and renew'[21] the existing order that was collaboratively constructed by the United States and key European allies such as Britain and France.

The economic counterpart of, and historical predecessor to, Carter, Perry, and Steinbruner's webs of 'overlapping, mutually reinforcing arrangements' in the security arena is Ikenberry's 'dense web of multilateral institutions, intergovernmental relations, and joint management of the Western and world political economies'[22] constructed in the aftermath of the Great Depression and World War II. For liberal internationalism, prosperity, and peace, require the broadening and deepening of today's open economic order. Open markets, transparency, free trade, non-discrimination, shared economic and social welfare – collaboratively arrived at – ensure prosperity in this order. At the heart of the liberal internationalist economic program is the multilateral and institutional management and continued broadening of globalization so that prosperity, and peace, can be extended to all. If prosperity is to be preserved for the haves, it must be shared with the have-nots.

Liberal internationalism and the new strategic triangle

Liberal internationalists are much more inclined than the realist advocates of selective engagement and primacy to embrace enthusiastically the new, emerging strategic triangle. America's relationship with Europe's leading institutions, the EU and NATO, would be more evenly balanced. The liberal internationalist enterprise has long highlighted the continued broadening and deepening of the binding security and economic relationships between the North American and European components of the transatlantic democratic security community, a community that is envisioned as a model for the rest of the world. The EU's ESDP, no less than NATO initiatives such as Partnership for Peace (PfP), is a welcome addition to the increasingly thick web of overlapping and reinforcing institutional relationships. There is little reason for the United States to object to the development of military capabilities that will enable the EU to be a genuine strategic partner.

The continued success of the transatlantic security community may require the capabilities and leadership of a pre-eminent America. But the preservation of that pre-eminence is not the objective. Nor is ensuring that the United States will always sit at the head of every table the objective. The goal, rather, is the construction of a liberal order, a project, clearly, that is most advanced in the democratic security community that spans the North Atlantic. This showcase community and its myriad benefits must be tended, not taken for granted.

Successfully integrating the components of the former Soviet empire, particularly Russia, into this community is critical. That cannot be accomplished by the United States alone. The continued political and economic liberalization of Russia and other successor states and their integration into an enlarging security community necessitates extensive political, economic, and security collaboration between the United States and the European Union. EU, and NATO, expansion serve the cause of political and economic liberalization. From this perspective the new strategic triangle is still under construction; it is likely, however, to be a prominent feature of Europe's security architecture.

Primacy

The advocates of US primacy have little interest in constructing strategic triangles or any other multilateral arrangements that empower others and constrain the United States. Informed by the maximal realism of hegemonic stability theory, primacy's proponents emphasize the virtues of a unipolar world. While liberal internationalists would have the United States squander the 'unipolar moment' in a misguided, resource-depleting attempt to construct a liberal world order that risks dethroning the United States from its lofty perch, the proponents of primacy seek to perpetuate indefinitely the unipolar moment. In their view, the interests of both security and world order require that the United States maintain its primacy. America's national interests must be broadly conceived – though not quite so broadly and all-encompassing as by liberal internationalists. The central objective of the United States must be to preserve its sole-superpower status by preventing the emergence of peer, or even near-peer, competitors. An across-the-board predominance must be maintained. Even a one-dimensional challenge, such as may be posed by a regional power or grouping such as the EU, must be met. Assurances about the limits of US hegemonic designs, appropriately leavened with an at least minimal commitment to multilateralism and institutions, should serve to persuade others that US hegemony is relatively harmless.

Primacy's advocates emphasize maintaining US economic hegemony and preventing the emergence of an economic rival. American economic hegemony means American leadership. It is that leadership that is responsible for the relatively open, even liberal, global economic order that exists today. Leadership can be exercised, as it has been, in a multilateral and institutional context. But the advocates of this realist primacy are suspicious of institutions, such as the EU, in which the United States does not have a seat, much less a seat at the head of the table. It is not genuine collaboration with the EU and others that is critical, but rather the maintenance of US economic hegemony. The US attitude towards multilateralism should be instrumental; it should seek solutions that favour its own interests even at the expensive of the collective. In the economic as in the political-military realm, the resort to unilateralism cannot be ruled out.

The advocates of primacy would have the United States remain on top by 'outdistancing any global challenger'.[23] Most likely to emerge in the near-to mid-term is not a political-military rival on the order of the former Soviet Union but an economic rival. Concerns about the early emergence of such an economic challenger have even led some to a near-mercantilist fixation on the 'large concentrations of power' from which an economic challenger may emerge. In the early 1990s, the concern was Japan. Today China and/or the EU worry advocates of primacy. Economic relationships with China and the EU that disproportionately benefit them are to be regarded with suspicion. Russia, with the possible exception of its natural resource endowments, is largely irrelevant as a global economic actor.

Primacy and the new strategic triangle

Primacy's advocates have little interest in a new strategic triangle that would only foster the illusion that the European Union and Russia are America's equals. In their view there is little reason to encourage European or Russian delusions of grandeur.

Under primacy, European security and economic institutions such as NATO and the EU are of interest only to the extent they can be used by the United States to maintain its hegemony or by Europe to challenge US hegemony. NATO, as opposed to an eternally 'becoming' EU, remains the preferred instrumentality of the United States. Its role is no longer to keep the United States in Europe, Germany down, and Russia out; instead, NATO's role is to provide institutional cover for the exercise of US hegemony in Europe. NATO expansion is a means of incorporating elements of the former Soviet Union and its empire into the American sphere. Russia's protestations are to no avail; it has little choice but to resign itself to NATO's (i.e. America's) continuing encroachments, just as it resigned itself to America's unilateral abrogation of the ABM Treaty. To the extent that the EU, and particularly the EU's ESDP, is intended to provide a potential counterweight to US hegemony and a European alternative to a US-led NATO, it will be opposed by the United States. However, an ESDP that leads to a beneficial military division of labour between the United States and Europe will be looked upon more favourably.

In the military realm, if not in the economic realm, the Soviet Union was a superpower during the Cold War. Russia, the proponents of primacy need hardly remind us, is not. It is a mere rump of the former Soviet Union. It has displayed little potential since the break up of the Soviet empire. It has far less weight in Eurasian and international affairs than its vast expanse might imply. In return, however, for Russia's cooperation in the global war on terror and in stemming proliferation, and perhaps for greater access to its energy resources, primacy's advocates are prepared to sacrifice liberal internationalists' emphasis on Russia's political and economic liberalization. These continuing interests in dealings with Russia do not require the cumbersome workings of a trilateral relationship. The imagined US–EU–Russia strategic triangle will little affect the calculations of a hegemonic America. There is no compelling strategic logic for investing resources in its construction.

Empire

The supposed new strategic triangle would affect the calculations of an imperial America no more than those of a hegemonic America. Once employed in critiques of America's Cold War foreign policy by revisionist historians and their fellow travellers, 'empire' has been resurrected, and rehabilitated, by assertive nationalists and neo-conservatives out to remake the world in America's image. For its advocates, 'American empire' is no longer a term of opprobrium or censure but a term, and a reality, to be embraced, even celebrated. After all, America's is an exceptional, liberal, and benevolent empire.

Whether intentionally or not, the United States emerged from the twentieth century atop an empire. In the view of one prominent neo-conservative, 'The Unipolar moment has become the unipolar era'; history has bequeathed America an empire that cannot but be kept.[24] A coalition of neo-conservatives and often strident nationalists, the new imperialists intend for America to save the world. Of course, saving the world requires ruling it. That imperial responsibility can be escaped only at great peril to the world and the United States. America's is the indispensable empire.

For the proponents of empire, mere primacy is insufficient. They offer, instead, primacy on steroids. While primacy emphasizes the simplicity of a unipolar world, empire emphasizes the great virtue of an even simpler world. The new world order is an American order. No distinction between US interests and the interests of others need be admitted. What is good for America is good for the world (including the EU and Russia).

For America's liberal imperialists, making the world safe for democracy and free markets requires that the United State act forcefully. If necessary, it can and will act alone. Pre-emptive, even preventive, war is its prerogative. Europe, Russia and others are welcome to join the cause, but America will forge ahead with or without their support. The United States will not be prevented by others from doing what is right and necessary. The array of principles, norms, rules, conventions, and procedures beloved by liberal internationalists do not apply to the United States. Empires make the rules; they follow them only when it is convenient. International institutions provide little more than a convenient rallying ground for others to bandwagon behind the United States. The United States does not require multilateral approval to act. 'Old Europe' and 'rogues' alike must recognize that if they are not with the United States, they are against it.

While the advocates of empire often tout the virtues of an open, liberal international economic system, the international economic order is viewed as an American order. American leadership means American rules. While others will be accorded the privilege of sitting at the US economic table, they will be there in a distinctly subordinate position. Despite the institutional, multilateral veneer provided by organizations such as the World Bank, IMF, and WTO, for empire's advocates it is to be the US that makes the rules and deals the cards. Globalization is Americanization. The institutional and organizational accoutrements of globalization are merely tools, however unwieldy at times, for maintaining imperial order.

International economic liberalism need not be considered sacrosanct. Economic organizations such as the EU to which the United States is not party are by definition peripheral. For American imperialists, international economic cooperation entails the rest of the world following America's lead.

Empire and the new strategic triangle

Empire does not bode well for a new US–EU–Russia strategic triangle. The notion of a strategic triangle that amounts to anything more than another way to ensure that EU members and Russia do America's bidding with a minimal amount of obstruction is not acceptable to proponents of empire. If pursuing empire represents the strategy of choice for America's leaders, neither the EU nor Russia should labour under the illusion that they are even the nominal equals of the United States.

Trilateral discussion and consultation will mean listening to the United States. Trilateral negotiation will mean agreeing with the United States. Trilateral collaboration will mean doing it America's way. Trilateral action will mean following America's lead. Burden-sharing will mean bearing the costs of American adventures (empires, of course, need not shed or share burdens; they impose them on others). Costs can and will be imposed; tribute will be exacted. The EU's members should remember that the Iraq war demonstrated that the EU is not monolithic. Its divisions can and will be exploited. In the view of America's new imperialists, in time the EU's members and Russia will recognize, if not accept, their place in the American geopolitical universe. America is the hub; they are the spokes. There is no strategic triangle.

The new strategic triangle under the Bush administration

Behind a veil of liberal internationalist rhetoric, the Bush administration has pursued a primacy that borders on the imperial. The administration's imperious, if not explicitly imperial, stance has not privileged the new strategic triangle. Neither the trilateral relationship nor bilateral relations with either the European Union or Russia have been accorded any status of note. Indeed, US relations with both Europe and Russia began on a negative tack with the ascendance of George W. Bush to the presidency. His administration acted quickly to reject a number of multilateral agreements, including the Kyoto Protocol and later the International Criminal Court. In some ways, the rejection of the specific agreements was less important than the implicit denigration of the multilateral process by which they had been concluded. Even if the Kyoto Protocol was deeply flawed and the Bush administration had good reasons to be unhappy with it, the cavalier manner in which it was rejected demonstrated a lack of appreciation for the complexity of the negotiations, the preferences of America's international partners, and the difficulty of restarting discussions from ground zero.

If the unilateralist bent of the new Bush administration set an early tone for its international relationships, the aftermath of the 11 September attacks defined and dominated relations among the United States, Europe, and Russia during the administration's first term. Initially both Russia and Europe (both institutionally through NATO and the EU and individually as states) expressed tremendous solidarity with the United States. The Bush administration fielded numerous offers of help including intelligence-sharing, policing, and offers of troops and equipment in the event of military action. Although the administration expressed its gratitude, it soon became clear that, with some exceptions, it preferred to undertake the Afghan campaign nearly alone save for a few trusted allies. The United States did ask Russia for a free hand to negotiate deals with Central Asian states that had been a part of the Soviet Union, potentially station troops in the region, and conduct over-flights in airspace near Russian borders.

With the collapse of the Taliban regime and the rout (it was believed) of al Qaeda the United States turned its attention to Iraq.[25] At least initially, the main selling point for the focus on Iraq was the supposed connection between Saddam Hussein and al Qaeda *and* the assumption that Saddam Hussein possessed weapons of mass destruction (WMD) that he might be willing to share. Although most European intelligence agencies and their governments believed at that point that Iraq possessed WMD capabilities, few were convinced that a direct connection existed between the perpetrators of 11 September and the Baathist regime. At the same time it pressed the case for war, the United States showcased in its new national security strategy[26] and other documents a new approach to the use of military force – the so-called Bush Doctrine which with breathtaking imprecision reserved the right for the US to undertake pre-emptive strikes and even preventive war. The American position directly contradicted an emerging European consensus on the use of force that had arisen in the aftermath of the Cold War.[27] What followed was a long and acrimonious debate carried out publicly within the UN and other international venues that served largely to poison relations between the US and its long-standing European allies.[28]

In the weeks, months, and years following the quick collapse of Saddam Hussein's regime, the United States once again found it necessary to turn to Europe and Russia for help. Given the high costs of Iraqi stabilization and reconstruction, the United States sought to persuade Europe, Russia, and other members of the international community to contribute more. Former Secretary of State and Bush family factotum James Baker was sent across the globe to ask friends and allies to forgive Iraqi debts. Nearly simultaneously, the United States attempted to punish, in a rather heavy-handed fashion, those countries that had not supported it within the UN or joined the so-called coalition of the willing in a meaningful way. Uncooperative countries were excluded from bidding for lucrative contracts for post-war reconstruction. Later it would turn again and again to Europe and others to contribute more troops as it became clear that the number of available US and British troops would be insufficient to re-establish order and defeat the growing insurgency in Iraq.

From the beginning, Iraq was a major irritant between the governments of those countries opposed to America's actions and a United States stuck in a quagmire of its own making. The rift widened further as it became clear that the European publics were vehemently anti-war, even in those countries like Great Britain, Italy, and Spain that had followed the US lead.[29]

The US and Europe

It is important to remember that many of the disagreements between the United States and the European Union, the United States and European members of NATO, and the United States and various individual states are simply part of the give and take of partners operating within a close and long-standing relationship under stress. In and of themselves they should not lead anyone on either side of the Atlantic to ponder the ultimate fate of the Western alliance. Yet the accumulation of petty grievances and the breach that developed over Iraq resulted in the most significant crisis in transatlantic affairs since the end of the Cold War. The chronic unwillingness of senior leaders in the Bush administration to acknowledge their mistakes and treat allies with respect and dignity drove a wedge between the United States and Europe. That then-national security advisor, and now Secretary of State, Condoleezza Rice could in April 2003 remark that the way to deal with three prominent recalcitrants was to 'Forgive Russia. Ignore Germany. Punish France' reveals the depths to which US relations with its European and Russian partners had sunk.[30]

Efforts to repair the relationship have not been especially successful. Even as French, German, and American leaders pay ritual homage to the importance of transatlantic relations, there has been little give on outstanding issues. Although European states assumed a leading role in the Balkans, a much greater role in Afghanistan, and had begun during 2005 to contemplate a larger role in Iraq, their contributions were much less than members of the Bush administration foreign policy team had hoped for. Part of this is an artefact of lesser European capabilities, but part also stems from the reluctance to join what is perceived to be a losing battle. Relations were less contentious on the economic front, although outstanding trade and financial issues remained to be dealt with.

The US and Russia

Since unilaterally withdrawing from the ABM Treaty in June 2002, the Bush administration has treated Russia with benign neglect. It refused to be drawn into moral and ethical arguments over the Russian approach to the Chechnya insurgency. Nor did it comment at great length and with any relish on President Putin's various campaigns to centralize power in Moscow. The campaign against the remaining media 'independents', administrative machinations to weaken provincial governments, and the progressive emasculation of opposition parties all passed largely unremarked until early in the administration's second term. Even Russia's refusal to acquiesce to American efforts to force action on Iraq within the UN Security Council did not invoke the Bush administration's anger as much as did the refusal of France and Germany to follow America's lead into Iraq.

The Bush administration regards Russia as a key partner in the war on terror and, no less importantly, as an alternative source of oil. Increased Russian production, in some cases with the active participation of American firms, could take some pressure off global energy markets and thus help contain energy prices and sustain economic growth (however modest) in the United States. More significant, however, is the Bush administration's conscious effort to downgrade Russia's international status and its place in US foreign and security policies. In the view of some experts within (and outside) the administration, Russia is no longer worthy of peer status. It does not have the conventional military strength, political and diplomatic credibility, and economic base to be a global player. By this thinking, if Russia is to be part of a new strategic triangle it will be because of its vast territory, dominant geographic position on the Eurasian landmass, and economic potential. It will not be because Russia brings much that is of strategic consequence for the United States.

In our introductory observations, we noted that the new strategic triangle is thought to be built on material interests, shared values and common institutions. As indicated here, the prospects for a new strategic triangle have been endangered by divergence on at least two of the three prerequisites. Although it seems straight-forward to note that all three parties share material interests in both the security and economic realms, we must recognize that values have and are shifting in the three regions. The United States has embraced wholeheartedly a willingness to use force pre-emptively, and even preventively if necessary, to combat terrorists and rogue states. Europe has been much less willing to do so, either in theory or in practice. In principle it does not view military force as the all-purpose solution that Washington sometimes does; in practice it does not have the capability to contribute on a global scale.

Triangular relations in the future

Prospects for a cooperative and productive triangular relationship have been undermined by the actions and attitudes of the Bush administration. Despite the enormous good will toward the United States generated by 9/11, the push to war with Iraq quickly and, some fear, perhaps permanently altered American relations with Europe.[31] Although Russia joined France and Germany in outright opposition to the war, the US–Russia relationship did not suffer as much as that between Europe and the United States. For America, this is largely a function of need. To prosecute the Afghan campaign the US needed Russian support for constructing relationships and ultimately bases in Uzbekistan and elsewhere in the 'near abroad'. It also needed Russian support to continue preventing Russian nuclear materials and expertise from falling into the hands of terrorists or states that might pass them along to terrorists. In return for Russia's support, President Putin desired American acquiescence if not silence in the case of his own brutal war in Chechnya and his aggressive campaign to centralize power in Moscow. The customer–supplier relationship in global oil markets also helped both countries overcome political and diplomatic tensions.

Not unexpectedly, the Bush administration's high-handed treatment (both real and perceived) of Europe and, to a lesser extent, Russia in the aftermath of 9/11 have provoked soul-searching in Europe and Russia alike. The results have been the most dramatic in the case of the European Union. At the request of EU member states, Javier Solana, High Representative of the Common Foreign and Security Policy (CFSP), developed a strategic vision for the European Union. Solana's efforts resulted in the emergence of the first ever European Security Strategy, which was approved by the European Council in December 2003.[32] The five key threats identified in the document – terrorism; the proliferation of weapons of mass destruction; regional conflict; state failure; and organized crime – closely track those featured in American strategic and planning documents. Any convergence in European and US strategic thinking may be more apparent than real, however. The ESS features a strong focus on multilateralism and conflict prevention rather than the pre-emptive or even preventive military action favoured by the United States.[33]

For a time after 9/11 it appeared that Russia hoped to ally itself more closely with the United States, despite its objections to the Iraq war. President Putin appeared to share the Bush administration's interest in fighting terrorism; some Russian strategists hoped cooperation in the global war on terror would help win US support or at least acquiescence in Russian policies in Chechnya. The limits of the alliance of convenience are suggested by the Bush administration's early second-term expressions of impatience with President Putin's version of democratic governance and Russian concerns about the US and European roles in Ukraine's 'Orange Revolution' and the continued expansion of both the EU and NATO into the realms of the former Soviet Union.

Both European Union members and Russia have expanded their options for responding to American primacy and potential American challenges in the future. The EU has strengthened the institutional framework for cooperating on foreign policy and defence policies outside NATO.[34] Much depends on how the policies and organizations outlined in the new European Security Strategy are implemented. Much also depends on the nature and timing of future crises. A crisis in central Europe or renewed hostilities in the Balkans might expose once again rifts in the transatlantic relationship and push Europe toward greater autonomy.

For Russia, the options are less clear, especially given its resource constraints and the numerous security challenges it faces internally and in the 'near abroad'. It confronts more immediate threats than does Western Europe, and even perhaps the United States, with far fewer economic, political and military assets at its disposal. Russia may choose, or be forced to seek, alternative partners and security frameworks if neither the United States nor NATO nor the emerging EU defence apparatus appears sufficiently compatible with Russian interests. Some have proposed that Russia might seek to tighten security ties with China, for example.

For both Russia and the EU, though, the wild card is the US position. A unilateralist America bent on maintaining its primacy and not expending political and military capital on crises and concerns lying outside its narrowly construed self-interest might push the other two poles of the strategic triangle away from the

United States. Early returns since the 2004 presidential election are more promising but still not entirely comforting for those interested in closer triangular relations.

Presidential candidate John Kerry pledged to restore multilateralism to the vocabulary of American diplomacy; there is little reason to doubt that he would have done so. The US–European relationship could have been the biggest beneficiary of a renewed and revitalized US commitment to multilateralism and institutionalism. Even though the post-presidential election effort to enlist Europe in America's Iraqi (mis)adventure may have been no more successful under a President Kerry than it has been under President Bush, the prospects for a transatlantic reconciliation would have been greater.

In a high-minded, idealistic second inaugural address, President Bush declared that advancing freedom and liberty around the world is to be America's mission. Unmentioned was the role of partnerships – with members of the European Union (whether collectively or otherwise) or anyone else – in the pursuit of this mission. That strategic partnerships might actually be useful again went unremarked when the president returned to this theme in his February 2005 state of the union address. Shortly thereafter, during the course of his remarks with EU leaders in Brussels, President Bush did acknowledge that it was in US interests for the European Union to become a 'viable, strong partner' and that the United States and the EU share common values and an interest in spreading those values; he also expressed a desire for a 'constructive relationship' with Russia.[35] A meaningful trilateral partnership, however, requires that the United States more consistently recognize and give voice to its value and that US behaviour be aligned with its high-minded rhetoric.

The extent to which the United States might more fully embrace a new strategic triangle during the Bush administration's second four years remains to be seen. The experience of the administration's first four years provides grounds for concern. There is some evidence that the president and his advisors recognize, if somewhat belatedly, that the United States is not strong enough to stand alone as an empire and is barely capable of maintaining its primacy in the face of multiple and multi-faceted security challenges arising as a result of the ongoing military campaigns, North Korean and Iranian nuclear ambitions, and China's emergence as a regional power and a potential near-peer competitor. Yet the Bush administration puts great stock in 'staying the course' even in the face of unremittingly negative developments. The ability to acknowledge mistakes and shift course does not seem to be in its repertoire. Staying the course may well serve both to embolden those who would have the EU emerge as a counterweight to the United States and to drive the EU and Russia into a genuine strategic partnership. The resulting trilateral relationship between the United States, the EU, and Russia will then resemble the geopolitical strategic triangles of old rather than the envisioned new trilateral partnership.

Notes

*The authors thank Jan Hallenberg, Håkan Karlsson, and the other participants in the Swedish National Defence College's November 2004 conference on 'The New Strategic Triangle: The US, EU, and Russia in an Evolving Security Environment' for their valuable comments and suggestions. The views expressed here are those of the authors alone; they do not necessarily reflect those of the Naval War College, the United States Navy, the Department of Defense or any other US government organization (and apparently won't any time soon).

1　D. Shambaugh, 'The New Strategic Triangle: U.S. and European Reactions to China's Rise', *The Washington Quarterly*, 2005, vol. 28, no. 3, pp. 7–25.

2　As quoted in R. Suskind, 'Without a Doubt', *The New York Times Magazine*, 17 October 2004, p. 51.

3　See Chapter 1 of this book.

4　For a discussion of the gap in economic performance between the United States and Europe, see R.C. Pozen, 'Mind the Gap: Can the New Europe Overtake the U.S. Economy?', *Foreign Affairs*, 2005, vol. 84, no. 2, pp. 8–12.

5　Giegerich and Wallace argue that the EU possesses more than soft power (B. Giegerich and W. Wallace, 'Not Such a Soft Power: The External Deployment of European Forces', *Survival*, 2004, vol. 46, no. 2).

6　On the ESDP in transatlantic relations, see I. Peters, 'ESDP as a Transatlantic Issue', *International Studies Review*, 2004, vol. 6, issue 3.

7　B. R. Posen and A. L. Ross, 'Competing Visions for U.S. Grand Strategy', *International Security*, 1996/1997, vol. 21, no. 3.

8　'Cooperative security' is the political-military component of a broader liberal internationalist strategy.

9　C. Layne, 'From Preponderance to Offshore Balancing', *International Security*, 1997, vol. 22, no. 1, pp. 86–124.

10　Posen and Ross, 'Competing Visions for U.S. Grand Strategy', p. 13.

11　D. Bandow, 'Price of Global Interventionism?', *The Washington Times*, 18 October 2001, p. 19.

12　Posen and Ross, 'Competing Visions for U.S. Grand Strategy', p. 17.

13　R. J. Art, 'Geopolitics Updated: The Strategy of Selective Engagement', *International Security*, 1998/1999, vol. 23, no. 3, pp. 95–7. See also R. J. Art, *A Grand Strategy for America*, Ithaca, NY: Cornell University Press, 2003.

14　Art, 'Geopolitics Updated', p. 83.

15　M. Albright, 'The Right Balance Will Secure NATO's Future', *The Financial Times*, 7 December 1998.

16　In the interests of full disclosure: Ross is a card-carrying liberal internationalist. Dombrowski has yet to come out of the closet.

17　Posen and Ross, 'Competing Visions for U.S. Grand Strategy', p. 23.

18　J. G. Ruggie (ed.) *Multilateralism Matters: The Theory and Praxis of an Institutional Form*, New York: Columbia University Press, 1993.

19　A. B. Carter, W. J. Perry and J. D. Steinbruner, *A New Concept of Cooperative Security*, Brookings Occasional Paper, Washington, DC: The Brookings Institution, 1992, p. 8.

20　G. J. Ikenberry, 'The Myth of Post-Cold War Chaos', *Foreign Affairs*, 1996, vol. 75, no. 3, p. 81.

21　Ikenberry, 'The Myth of Post-Cold War Chaos', p. 79.

22　Ikenberry, 'The Myth of Post-Cold War Chaos', p. 80.

23　Posen and Ross, 'Competing Visions for U.S. Grand Strategy', p. 32.

24　C. Krauthammer, 'The Unipolar Moment Revisited', *The National Interest*, 2002/03, no. 70, p. 17.

25 B. Woodward, *Plan of Attack*, New York: Simon & Schuster, 2004. Some in the administration argued for focusing on Iraq immediately after the attacks of 9/11. See R. A. Clarke, *Against All Enemies: Inside America's War on Terror*, New York: Free Press, 2004.

26 *The National Security Strategy of the United States of America*, Washington, DC: The White House, September 2002.

27 I. H. Daalder, 'The Use of Force in a Changing World: U.S. and European Perspectives', November 2002.

28 P. J. Dombrowski and R. Payne, 'Global Debate and the Limits of the Bush Doctrine', *International Studies Perspectives*, November 2003, vol. 4, issue 4, pp. 395–408.

29 P. Norris, '*Le Divorce*: Who Is to Blame for the Transatlantic Rift?', *Compass: A Journal of Leadership,* Fall 2003, pp. 22–5.

30 Rice's remark was widely reported, especially at the outset of the second term of the Bush administration. See, for example, E. Sciolino, 'French Struggle Now With How to Coexist With Bush', *The New York Times*, 8 February 2005.

31 For a more optimistic assessment, see M. Dassù and R. Menotti, 'Europe and America in the Age of Bush', *Survival*, Spring 2005, vol. 47, no. 1, pp. 105–22.

32 'A Secure Europe in a Better World – The European Security Strategy', Brussels, 12 December 2003, Council of the European Union. Online.

33 P. van Ham, 'Europe Gets Real: The New Security Strategy Shows the EU's Geopolitical Maturity', *AICGS Advisor*, 9 January 2004.

34 On the alleged threat posed by EU institutional developments, see J. L. Cimbala, 'Saving NATO From Europe', *Foreign Affairs*, November/December 2004, vol. 83, no. 6, pp. 111–20.

35 'President Meets with E.U. Leaders', 22 February 2005.

9

THE TIES THAT BIND?

Economic relations among the United States, the EU, and Russia

Jan Hallenberg

Introduction

This chapter focuses on economic relations among the United States, the EU and Russia, present and future, as well as on the question of the actorness of the EU. Washington has clearly been the most influential actor – the initiator – of the three under study here in this policy arena.[1]

The overriding question here is what influence does economic relations have on the strategic triangle as a whole? Do they contribute to stronger relations among the three actors, or do they tend to be counter-productive for the strategic triangle? In addition, the chapter covers the strength of each of the three dyads – US–EU, EU–Russia and Russia–US – which, together, make up the strategic triangle. How strong are the economic linkages in each of the dyads, and do these economic ties have any influence on security relations, traditionally defined? Finally, the chapter takes up the strains put on relations among the transatlantic three as a result of the Iraq War. What influence, if any, did these sometimes profound political disagreements have on the economic ties among the three parties?

Before analysing the crucial dimensions of current economic relations among the three actors, the chapter covers three essential starting points. First, it briefly characterizes how the United States after the Second World War constructed an international economic system in which ties between itself and Western Europe were crucial. To quote Lars S. Skålnes: 'The interdependence existing between the United States and Western Europe was in part the result of an American strategy consciously designed to make the American and European economies more interdependent, to reflect and to bolster a strategy determined not by domestic interests but by policymakers' strategic assessment.'[2] The analysis here is generally in line with that of Skålnes in starting out from the assumption that 'foreign economic policies are used to promote international political objectives and as such are instruments of high politics'.[3]

Second, while the strategies pursued by the United States laid the foundation for the institutionalized global economic-political system in general, as well as the more specific ties between the US and Western Europe in the economic arena, the position taken here is that the economic strategies pursued by the European Union, particularly since the Community became the Union in 1993, are in many respects similar to those pursued by the United States in creating the system for global economic cooperation after 1945. The geographical reach of the Union is much more limited than has been that of the US. From the perspective of an eagle soaring high above the petty details of everyday politics, there are, however, important similarities in the overarching economic strategy pursued by the two economic giants in their respective times and geographical arenas. Consequently, a brief analysis of the broad lines of the economic strategies pursued by the Union towards the United States and Russia during the period from 1993 up to the time of writing (2005) is necessary as a background to the analysis of the current state of economic relations among the three actors.

Third, after the collapse of the Soviet Union in 1991, the Russian government has also pursued economic strategies towards the other two actors in our presumptive triangle. A short analysis of the main aspects of these strategies is also necessary as a backdrop to the assessment of current relations among the three actors.

Setting the stage: the economic grand strategies of the three actors

The United States was the driving force behind the construction of the international economic system whose inception was the conference at Bretton Woods in 1944. In addition, US support for the continuation of this system of cooperation – which originally encompassed a fairly small group of Western and westernized countries but which has gradually spread around the globe – has been almost as crucial as its role for the inception of the system.

> US leaders . . . were determined to avoid the 'mistakes' of post-World War I political and economic isolationism . . . For them, a reconstructed, integrated Europe was central to US security and future economic growth. They mobilized to pump US money into Western Europe to finance its reconstruction, counter the spread of communism and anchor West Germany into a larger European framework.
>
> (Pollack and Shaffer 2001b: 8)

It is a matter of some contention in the literature to what an extent this strategy was mainly self-serving or altruistic. The position taken here is that in this strategy, as in many other cases in US foreign and security policy during the last 100 years, policymakers in Washington fashioned and pursued strategies that ingeniously served both what has traditionally been called the national interest of the home country, and the interests of the governments in the countries of Western Europe after the Second World War. Washington thus supported the creation of political cooperation in Europe, a cooperation that had some supranational traits. While doing so, the leaders in the Superpower were always clear that this new cooperative venture would continue to be linked to the United States in a fashion that meant that the two parties would continue to cooperate. There was never any doubt in the minds of the highest leadership in Washington that this cooperation would continue to be led by the United States.[4] In other words, the system would be in the interest of the Western Europeans, but it would also certainly be in the continued interest of the United States.

Another building-block in this chapter's analysis of the economic ties among the transatlantic three concerns the beliefs held by first decision-makers in Washington, and subsequently by those in Brussels, concerning the links between economic strategies, primarily those serving free trade on the one hand and peaceful relations among nations on the other. The assumption guiding this study of the economic linkages among the three actors is that such linkages serve to tie countries together. In a paper written for the Heritage Foundation, Ariel Cohen expresses well this line of thinking:

> Economists and political thinkers have long recognized that free trade and the spirit of commerce promote international understanding and reduce hostility and mistrust among nations. The reality of the global economy today reinforces that priority . . . . Free trade is a U.S. foreign policy priority: an effective way to promote and protect America's economic interests. Given Russia's new role as a strategic partner in the U.S.–led campaign to end terrorism, expanding trade with Russia and helping it to become a full member of the community of developed democratic states is in America's best interests.
>
> (Cohen 2002)

To some extent, the strategies pursued by Washington towards Russia after the collapse of the Soviet Union in 1991 have resembled those pursued towards Western Europe after the start of the Cold War. As pointed out by Michael Mastanduno, however, 'US statecraft became less integrated as foreign economic policy and national security policy proceeded on separate diplomatic and institutional tracks'[5] from around 1980. This certainly does not mean that there is no relationship between US foreign economic policy and national security policy after 1980, but it does mean that the two policies are, after that point in time, to some extent pursued along separate tracks and not always with one of these broad strands controlling the other, as was the case with the security strategy controlling the economic one during the Cold War.

If the economic strategies of the United States towards Russia thus to some extent resemble those pursued toward Western Europe more than fifty years ago, there have, in Western Europe itself, been crucial changes. As analysed further in other chapters of this book assessing the actorness of the European Union is a complex matter (see in particular Chapter 2, as well as Chapters 3 and 4). It cannot be denied, however, that the economic strategies pursued by the modern Union in several ways resemble those practiced by the United States as the Second World War ended and as the global economic system of cooperation was being constructed.

The EU has, from the beginning, been an economic-political construct in which the ties between first six member states, and, gradually, ever more candidates, many of whom have successively been converted into members, have become increasingly tighter. If there ever was a case in modern international relations where an actor used economic-political strategies to reach political goals, that actor is the European Union. The quote above from Ariel Cohen about the positive effects of increasing trade relations for the creation of peace between trading nations is thus very applicable to the strategies of the Union as well.

In terms of the relationship with the United States, the Union has since 1990 had an institutional framework in which to pursue its strategies. The first step in this development was the issuance of the Transatlantic Declaration between the George H. W. Bush Administration and the European Commission in November 1990. Five years later, the Clinton Administration signed a new declaration on the importance of US–EU relations called the New Transatlantic Agenda, which had even more far-reaching goals than the earlier declaration. Together, these documents initiated a period in which US decision-makers regularly meet EU decision-makers for broad-ranging discussions.[6]

In its relations with Russia, it is a sign of the importance the Union attached to relations with that country that the first example of a new policy instrument that the Union decided upon in the late 1990s – common strategies – was one regarding Russia, decided upon in 1999.[7] Informed Western European observers have had conflicting assessments about the success of this first EU common strategy during its first five years in operation, while Russian specialists have issued assessments that include both positive evaluations and clear statements of the limitations that, in their view, still characterize EU–Russian relations.[8] At a summit in Moscow in May 2005, the two parties signed a new agreement on a 'Road Map for the Common Economic Space' and a 'Building Block for Sustained Economic Growth'[9] (relations between Russia and the EU are also analysed in Chapter 6 of this volume). It seems clear that both have made an effort to create an institutional framework within which better economic relations may be constructed.

Russian economic strategies after the collapse of the Soviet Union in 1991 can broadly be characterized as going through the same stages as most other transition economies. The former Russian Prime Minister Yegor Gaidar, one of the most important actors in the creation of the new Russian economy, characterized in a book the three first stages of economic development as 'post-socialist recession', 'post-socialist reconstruction', and 'investment growth'.[10] A part of this economic strategy, a part that seems to have received increased attention after President Vladimir Putin succeeded Boris Yeltsin in 2000, has been to increase Russia's role as an international economic actor, particularly in global trade. Russia applied for membership in the World Trade Organization (WTO) as early as in 1993, but only during the last few years has the pace of negotiations for Russian membership increased.[11]

The other side of the Russian application for membership in the WTO, as seen from the perspective of the strategic triangle, is of course what strategies the United States and the EU, respectively, have conducted in response to the Russian application for accession. For Washington and Brussels, Russian membership may serve their political strategies of getting Moscow more integrated in this economic system, which Brussels as well as Washington also believe would, if anything, serve as a positive influence for the strengthening of democracy in Russia.[12] A brief analysis of the development of Russian negotiations for membership in the WTO is thus included in this chapter.

Economic ties among international actors

In the modern era, states and other international actors operate in a global economic arena that contains several distinct issue-areas. This assessment of the economic ties among Washington and the two other actors in the transatlantic strategic triangle focuses on three such issue-areas.[13] The first is trade relations, where international cooperation is supported by beliefs among statesmen as well as among economists that countries that trade with each other do not go to war with each other. In addition, cooperation in international trade is supported by a general belief among both categories that liberal trade rules aid economic growth in all states that participate in the trading system.[14]

The second economic issue-area covered here is monetary relations. The role of currencies has a potential influence that is so great that it can hardly be overlooked in any deeper assessment of the economic ties among the United States, the EU and Russia. This is despite the fact that the effects of various arrangements regarding currencies are ambiguous, in contrast to trade relations where the starting-point here is that strong such relations, at least in principle, have positive effects for relations between actors.

Third, this analysis covers direct investment. We believe that a large amount of mutual private investments between two actors in the international system serves to tie these actors closer together, in a way that induces their governments to pursue security policies that are more considerate to the policies of the other party than they would have been without the existence of such ties.[15]

One problem in studying political economy has to do with the concept of actor. Who are the actors in international political economy? To what extent do states, as well as the EU in this case, regulate and control political and economic processes in the three issue-areas presented here? The conception in this chapter is that the problem is relatively small when it comes to trade and monetary issues. In both these fields the US government, the EU and Russia regulate economic activities to such an extent that it is legitimate to assume that they are actors in both issues.

The problem is larger when it comes to Foreign Direct Investment (FDI). In principle, decisions in this third field are taken by private actors. There are different views among scholars as to which roles are played by Multinational Companies (MNCs) and the role these play in the world economy more generally, and in FDI more precisely. The position taken here is, first, that 'the nation-state is still the principal actor in international economic affairs . . . and that multinational corporations are simply national firms with foreign operations and that, with few exceptions, these firms remain deeply embedded in their national societies'.[16] Second, I agree with Hamilton and Quinlan that 'While trade is the benchmark typically used to gauge global economic engagement, international production by Multinational Enterprises through FDI has superceded international trade as the most important mechanism for international integration.'[17]

Assessing the importance of economic ties

One starting-point in attempting to analyse economic relations among the United States, Russia and the European Union is that these are three very different beasts in the economic field. The United States is a traditional nation-state, a state in which the immense domestic market still means that this country is less dependent on the outside world than is either of the other two actors. To use one common measure in this respect, the ratio of US total trade to GDP was 11.7 per cent in 2002. For the EU the equivalent figure was 48.1 per cent.[18] It is difficult to compare Russia to the other two actors in this respect, as the country is neither a member of the OECD, the club for the most developed market economies, nor of the WTO. Russia has, however, been a member of the World Bank and the International Monetary Fund (IMF) since 1992. Data from Eurostat, the EU statistical office, indicate that Russia is much closer to the EU than to the US when it comes to trade dependence.[19] This means that the United States is much less dependent on international trade for the health of its domestic economy than is either of the two other actors.

This book is concerned with the power of three important international actors, and with various dimensions of their relationships. Taking the step from considering their respective dependence on international trade for the health of their economy to the assessment of the economic ties among the three actors is very difficult indeed, as so many aspects enter into the picture. There is, however, one pair of analytic concepts which may aid us in the assessment of the strength of the ties between each of the three pairs in the relationship. These concepts are *sensitivity* and *vulnerability* from *Power and Interdependence* by Robert Keohane and Joseph Nye.[20]

Keohane's and Nye's reasoning starts from the assertion that modern global politics are not only concerned with power politics but also with interdependence. They define the latter term in this way: '*Interdependence*, most simply defined, means *mutual dependence*. Interdependence in world politics refers to situations characterized by reciprocal effects among countries or among actors in different countries.'[21] The analysis is this chapter is based on the premise of the simultaneous existence of power and interdependence. States, and other important actors such as the European Union, possess power, but they are also interdependent. The question then arises what the role is of power in a situation where there is interdependence.

Sensitivity and *vulnerability* are introduced in this next step of Keohane's and Nye's analysis.[22] Sensitivity measures how quickly outside events influence processes within a polity, as well as how large that influence is, before the influenced state has been able to undertake any policy response. Vulnerability measures the costs for an actor of outside events even after that actor has undertaken policy changes to alleviate the effects of the external event in question.

Sensitivity and vulnerability are not applicable in assessing whether or not an economic triangle exists among between the three actors. The two concepts are, however, applied in this chapter to an overall assessment of the importance of the dyadic economic ties between: the United States and the EU, the EU and Russia, and Russia and the United States. It is of course possible, even likely, that the interdependence is asymmetric, that is that one party is more dependent on the second than the second is on the first. The overriding question is the role of economic relations for the strategic triangle broadly seen, and the secondary question concerns the strength of the economic ties in the three dyads that are formed by bilateral relations among the three actors.

These economic ties are important in themselves. They are also, particularly if they are very strong, potentially of such importance that they matter for other issue-areas. The conception here is that very strong economic ties serve to stabilize relations in other issue-areas, such as security policy more strictly seen. In other words, if two parties disagree on an issue of security policy and they simultaneously have very strong economic ties, there is a strong tendency for the economic ties to influence the two parties' courses of action in security policy so as not to threaten the commercial ties. This chapter assesses to what extent the three dyads mentioned above contain such strong economic links that either one, or perhaps both parties, feel that these links serve as a strong influence to manage disagreements in other policy fields.

Trade relations among the United States, the EU and Russia

The economic relations between the United States and the EU are arguably the strongest between any two economies in the current global system. The only conceivable exception, when seen from the vantage-point of the United States, is the trade relationship between Washington and Canada.[23] In gross figures – including trade in goods as well as in services – the two-way trade between the United States and EU-25 was over €590 billion in 2003.[24] The equivalent figure for Canadian trade with the United States was €390 during the same year.[25] The comparable trade between Washington and Russia for 2004 was somewhat more than €12 billion for merchandise trade.[26] While precise comparisons are impossible, the trade relationship between the EU of 25 and the United States was thus many times larger than the similar figure for United States trade with Russia. There is thus a strong trade link between the United States and the EU, with both parties having the other as the most important, or second most important, trade partner concerning both exports and imports in 2003 as well as 2004.

The equivalent figure for EU trade with Russia was for the same year €145 billion.[27] For Russia, the EU was by far the most important trading partner, both in terms of its exports and for its imports, with the EU accounting for roughly 50 per cent of total Russian external trade.[28] For Brussels, Russia was much less important, representing somewhat more than 6 per cent of total external trade.[29] It is thus obvious that the trade link between Russia and the EU is very asymmetrical – when seen in overall terms – with the Russians being much more dependent on trade links with the EU than the reverse. The fact that an important part of EU imports from Russia – nearly 60 per cent according to Eurostat data – are 'mineral fuels etc.' to some extent makes the trade relationship less asymmetrical. It is difficult to estimate whether likely Russian efforts to increase the exports of these products to the EU may over the medium-term make the trade relationship between the parties less asymmetrical. Indications are that Russian oil will not be available for export for a very long time in the future, whereas Russian exports of natural gas may gradually take over some of the role of oil in Russian trade relations with the EU.

Monetary relations among the United States, the EU and Russia

In the monetary area the US dollar has reigned nearly supreme since the end of the Second World War, at least until the gradual entry of the euro as an international currency, beginning in 1999.[30] In the first years of the twenty-first century the US dollar was still the world's most important currency. To take one example, in 2001 the dollar was one of two currencies in 90 per cent of all currency transactions. The equivalent figure for the euro was 38 per cent.[31] However, the very fact that the euro became a currency in all respects in 2002 meant that the United States and the EU became more equal powers in the monetary arena than they had been previously.[32] One illustration of this fact is that a tool that Washington used to attempt to influence France and the United Kingdom in 1956 in their disagreement over the Suez invasion, i.e. putting pressure on the currencies of the two countries, was unavailable to the United States in the disagreement leading up to the Iraq War.[33] With the introduction of the euro, the US dollar was no longer the unique reserve currency for it to be used as a tool to put pressure downwards on the euro.[34]

In the monetary arena, the United States is still the world's most important actor. However, with the entry into force of the euro, the EU – in this case in the form of the Euro-zone – represents a challenger that is not the equal of the United States, but that, nevertheless, possesses much more monetary power than it did prior to the existence of the euro.[35] The fact that the Russian currency, the rouble, is still not fully convertible, means that Russia can be neglected as an actor in this field. Russia, in broad terms, possesses no monetary power in its relations to the other two actors.

Foreign Direct Investment (FDI) among the parties

Partly due to the fact that Russia is a fairly new member of the global market economy, there are comparatively few direct investments either going into the Russian market, or emanating from Russia. In the case of the relationship between Russia and the EU, estimates by the latter indicate that the book value of EU investments in Russia increased from about €9 billion in 2002 to about €17 billion in 2003. The book value of Russian FDI in the EU was somewhat more than €4 billion in both years. When it comes to the flow of new FDI funds, EU investments into the Russian market increased markedly from only slightly more than €1 billion in 2002, to about €8 billion in 2003.[36] The flow from Russia into the EU decreased from €1 billion to €500 million between 2002 and 2003. While the increased flows of funds from the EU into Russia may indicate a growing interest on the part of EU-based companies in the Russian market, still the volumes are so small that they have so far not created any strong interdependence between the two parties.[37]

The FDI figures for the EU–Russian dyad are dwarfed by those of the US–EU dyad. In the latter case, companies based in the EU-15-owned assets in US companies worth more than €700 billion in 2002, a value that increased to more than €750 billion in 2003. This represented more than 62 per cent of the book value of foreign FDI-owned stock in the US in 2003. The corresponding figures for US FDI in the EU-15 were €590 billion in 2002, and €640 billion in 2003, which represented slightly less than 50 per cent of total US holdings outside that country in 2003. While such immense investments, in terms of stock as well as flow, as those between the US and the EU fluctuate from year to year, still the enormous values they represent are vastly greater than for any other dyad in the global economy.[38]

Russian efforts to become a member of the WTO

In 1993, the Russian Government applied for membership in the WTO.[39] Formal negotiations started in 1995. The Working Party on Russia's accession to the WTO held its twenty-fifth official meeting in November 2004. Both the United States and the EU are in principle positive towards Russian membership in the global trade organization. The EU and Russia concluded a bilateral agreement on Russian accession to the WTO at the Moscow Summit in May 2004.[40] The United States and Russia issued a Joint Statement on Russia's accession to WTO in connection with the meeting between Presidents Bush and Putin in February 2005.[41] In the statement, the two parties stated that they were committed to working together to complete their bilateral negotiations for Russian membership of the WTO in 2005. In a statement by Secretary of State Condoleezza Rice in April 2005, the Secretary indicates worries about Russian progress up to that time in terms of intellectual property rights issues, as well as on some alleged protectionism in agriculture. In addition, the Secretary mentions 'some inconsistency about how foreign investments will or will not play' concerning Russian energy resources.[42] The obvious reference here is to the treatment of the Russian 'oligarch' Mikhail Khodorkovsky and to the uncertainty that the treatment of him and his company Yukos has created among current and potential foreign investors in Russia, particularly in the energy sector.

While all three parties in the strategic triangle have thus in principle expressed their positive view of Russian membership in the WTO, it appears that as of this writing in mid-2005 there are still some hurdles for Russia to clear before it becomes a member of the global trade organization. The United States has still not come to any full agreement with Russia on this matter, while the EU has done so. It is probably not an exaggeration to state that there is a difference in strategies between the United States and the EU regarding an issue that is crucial to Russia. For the US, Russia is one of several large powers that has to be handled, a power that to some extent creates problems on important issues. For the EU, Russia is a constantly important actor, with which it is easier to attempt to conduct positive relations, for the alternative is difficult to contemplate.

The state of economic relations among the three actors

There are several reasons why an economic triangle is only just developing among the three actors under study in this book. Most of those have to do with Russia. First, Russia is not sufficiently integrated into the global economic network to create conditions for it to have strong ties to the other two actors simultaneously. Second, linked to the first point, Russia is a very small economic actor compared to the other two, with a GDP representing roughly €380 billion in 2003, compared to around €9,700 billion for both EU-25 and the US.[43]

If the conclusion is now that there is a nascent economic triangle under construction among the three parties, it seems that if this triangle is to be developed into something more solid, much depends on Russia. An economically stronger Russia would generally be a more attractive partner with which to deepen relations for the United States and the EU. A Russia that treats its large companies in a fashion that is less arbitrary than has been the case during the last few years would work towards enticing more companies to invest in Russia, thus creating stronger economic ties in the triangle.[44]

At the same time, the United States still has political restrictions that may make it more difficult to create stronger economic ties with Russia. The most important problem here is the Jackson-Vanik Amendment to the 1974 Trade Act, which 'effectively denies unconditional normal trade relations to certain countries, including Russia, that had non-market economies and that restricted emigration rights'.[45] Even if the US President can waive the restrictions on trade with Russia on a temporary basis each year, and has been doing so starting in 1992 and more completely from 1994, still the fact that Congress has not repealed the Jackson-Vanik Amendment is an irritant in US–Russian trade relations that at the very least does not serve as an encouragement for the further increase of trade between the two parties.[46]

The three dyads that collectively form the nascent economic triangle among the United States, Russia and the EU thus differ a lot in the strengths of their economic ties. The least important economic dyad, in these terms, is that between the United States and Russia. There is some trade, a trade which has been fluctuating somewhat since the early 1990s, but with an upward trend.[47] As seen from the perspective of total United States international trade, the exchange of goods and services with Russia is still insignificant. For the United States – if the EU is excluded as a trade partner in favour of the member states – Russia was in 2003 in 30th place among its trade partners, counting total imports and exports.[48] For a country that is comparatively little trade-dependent to begin with, total trade with Russia represented less than 1 per cent of total trade in 2003–4. Russia is more dependent on trade with Washington than the other way round, with exports plus imports representing nearly 5 per cent of total Russian trade in 2003.[49] In the terms utilized by Keohane and Nye, it is probably most correct to say that Russia is gradually becoming sensitive to the maintenance of a healthy trade relationship with the United States, whereas the latter has not yet developed any such dependence on trade relations with Moscow.

The second dyad in terms of importance when it comes to the economic links between the two actors is that between the EU and Russia. For the EU, Russia was in 2004 the fourth of the major trading partners, while for Russia the EU was by far the most important in total trade in merchandise, representing nearly 50 per cent of Russian trade in such items.[50] For the EU, trade with Russia represented more than 6 per cent of its two-way trade in merchandise. In the other two dimensions of economic affairs – monetary issues and the flow and stock of FDI – relations between the two parties are much less important. Still, it is probably fair to state that both actors have already developed some sensitivity in terms of the continuation of trade in merchandise. A severe downfall in the trade exchange with the EU would potentially be disastrous for the Russian economy, while it would be more of a nuisance for the EU. Perhaps it can be stated that while there is at least some sensitivity on the part of both parties facing the prospect of a strong fall in trade exchanges, it is only on the Russian side where such a prospect will raise the possibility that the situation could also be characterized as vulnerability in the terms used by Keohane and Nye. In other words, if for some reason there was an important break-off in trade relations between the EU and Russia, the latter would find it very difficult indeed, even after taking counteraction, to mitigate the negative consequences that such an event would have on the Russian economy.

If there are thus moderately strong economic ties between the EU and Russia, these ties are infinitely stronger between the United States and the EU. In terms of total trade – merchandise as well as service trade – the two are each other's major trading partner, representing about 20 per cent of the total trade of each.[51] When it comes to FDI, the overwhelming importance to each of the other party is even clearer. Of the total book value of FDI in the United States 62 per cent was held by companies from EU-15, while the equivalent figure for US Foreign Direct Investment abroad was that 47 per cent of the book value of all companies owned by US interests abroad was located in the EU-15 countries.[52] While one may debate particularly the extent to which either the nation-states, or even the EU as an organization, can really control the activities of private companies, the linkages between the United States and the EU in trade and FDI are still so very strong that it must be obvious that these two actors are very sensitive to the effects of strong disturbances in the economic relations between them. Indeed, so strong and deep are the economic relations between the two that both would be very vulnerable to serious disturbances in their economic relations, even after taking counter-measures. Or, to put it the other way around, disagreements in other policy areas are over time bound to be positively influenced by the immense strength of the economic ties between the two parties.

The Iraq War as a strain on the transatlantic relationship

It is well known that the run-up to the war in Iraq in March and April of 2003, as well as the war itself and its aftermath, created important strains among the three transatlantic actors.[53] These strains did not have the character of falling exactly between the three actors as they are conceived in this volume. Instead, the United States was strongly supported by several members of the EU, most prominently by the United Kingdom, Spain and Italy, while France and Germany, in particular, opposed US policies. Indeed, the opposition of the latter two to what was widely perceived as a US-led political strategy was so strong that it created strains among some of the transatlantic partners that were as severe as perhaps any such transatlantic strains after the start of the Cold War. Russia also opposed the United States and to a very great extent allied itself with France and Germany in opposition to the strategy followed by US President George W. Bush.

This is not the place to analyse the details of this complicated political process, nor to state precisely which actors supported which during these tumultuous events. What is crucial for this chapter is, instead, to uncover to what extent, if any, the disagreements over the Iraq War had negative consequences for the economic relations among the three parties.

The fundamental one-word response to this question has to be 'no'. It is true that some US citizens and pundits advocated a boycott of French products, such as wine, after the outbreak of the Iraq War. From a larger perspective, however, these actions were but superficial movements on a vast river of economic linkage that continued to flow strongly and majestically in the relationship between the United States and the EU. Economic data show that in several respects the flow of trade and FDI funds between the parties broke records in several ways in 2003. The total transatlantic trade in goods was higher than ever at $395 billion (€296 billion). US imports from several of the largest EU countries were also higher than ever, as were profits for US companies in Europe. In addition, Europeans bought United States corporate bonds to a greater value than ever before.[54] In other words, there appears to be no indication whatsoever that economic ties between the United States and the EU suffered because of the diplomatic spats between Washington and France and Germany in particular. Indeed, there is also hardly any evidence that bilateral economic relations among the latter three countries were negatively influenced.

The economic relationship between the United States and Russia, as stated above, is the weakest link among the three legs of the economic triangle. It is thus hard to believe that these ties were important enough to be really consequential for relations in traditional security policy between the two parties. Still, from what can be seen from the data, there was no real impact on the relationship between Moscow and Washington as a result of the Iraq War. According to information from the US Census Bureau, trade with Russia increased every year from 2002 through 2004 without any slowdown whatever that can be attributed to disagreements over Iraq.[55]

Conclusions

This chapter has shown that in the economic field there exists a very weak, but slowly strengthening, triangle among the United States, Russia and the EU in the first decade of the twenty-first century. The respective strengths of the ties within the three dyads that are formed by the three pairs of actors differ importantly. The economic links between the United States and the EU are here seen as the strongest and most multi-faceted among any two actors in the world. The strength of this economic link means that whatever strains may exist between the US and the EU in other policy areas, the very strength of the economic ties are apt to be a positive influence for the proper handling, if not resolution, of such strains. In this view the improvements in ties in early 2005 between the United States and some important members of the EU, as well as between Washington and Brussels more broadly after the enormous strains caused by the Iraq conflict particularly in 2003–4, depend at least partly on the enormous strength of economic ties between the parties.

Economic relations between the EU and Russia are not nearly so strong. They are, however, becoming increasingly stronger in the trade field. When seen from the Russian side, they are now so developed that the Russian economy would be very sensitive to any severe disturbances in this economic relationship. The importance for the EU of economic links with Russia is harder to determine. They are less crucial, when seen in terms of overall trade. In addition, the fact that these linkages are comparatively small in the stock and flow of FDI do not serve to increase EU economic dependence on Russia. The fact that some 60 per cent of Russian exports to the EU are made up of energy products may, however, if they continue and increase, perhaps mean that the EU also develops sensitivity to any disturbances in its economic ties with Russia.

The third leg of the triangle – the relationship between Russia and the United States – contains by far the weakest economic links among the three. For the United States, Russia is still a negligible actor, when judged on the basis of the three dimensions of economic relations considered here. For Russia, however, economic ties with Washington are gradually becoming more important.

To conclude, if we attempt to depict this most quantifiable of relationships in international politics in terms of a triangle, we must draw three lines of very different character between the three actors. Between the United States and the EU, the line will be very thick indeed, so strong that it appears almost impossible to break for

179

any reason. Between the Union and Moscow, the line is considerably thinner, but it still indicates a relationship that benefits both parties, and where Russia, first, and the EU, second, will be sensitive to any important strains in this relationship. It is the line between Moscow and Washington that is the weakest and the most problematic to characterize in these terms. The most apt way of depicting this relationship in terms of a line would be in terms of a dotted line. The line is not non-existent, but is as yet fairly weak.

As this chapter is being completed in mid-2005, there are strong indications that Russia will become a member of the WTO either in late 2005 or in early 2006. If indeed this turns out to be true, there will be greater opportunities for Russia to increase its trade with both the United States and the EU. If this happens, there are clear chances that the dyadic economic links between Moscow and Washington, and Moscow and Brussels will gradually strengthen over the coming years. As this chapter has shown, the EU–Russia relationship has already become so strong that both parties have some dependence on continued trade, even if that dependence is asymmetrical to the detriment of Russia. The United States–Russia economic relationship is much less developed, and there will have to be a substantial increase in bilateral trade for the United States to develop any real dependence upon Russia. For Russia, such dependence will occur earlier.

An analysis of the consequences of the Iraq War indicated that this did not have much influence on economic relations among the parties. In particular, the economic relationship between Washington and Brussels now seems so strong that it supports the thesis made here, i.e. that very strong economic relations between two parties in international relations would work to mend strains in other parts of the mutual relationship. What we know about the relationship between Brussels, and to some extent Paris and Berlin on the one hand, and Washington on the other, seems to lend some credence to such a view. Even if many disagreements remain, the visit by the US President to Europe and Brussels in February of 2005 indicates to us at the very least that many of the tensions that flared up in 2003 have been if not completely mended, then at least substantially ameliorated.

A final aspect of economic relations in the strategic triangle has to do with the balance of power between the two economic giants that form two corners of the triangle, the United States and EU. In the trade arena, the EU is a strong actor, in some respects as strong as the United States. Still, the problems of the actorness of the Union (see the analysis in Chapter 2 in this book) means that Brussels is less able to take initiatives and lead global negotiations in the WTO than is the traditional actor, the United States. As stated in this chapter, the birth of the euro means that the two parties are now more equal in monetary affairs as well. For more than fifty years after the Second World War the US dollar reigned supreme. It is still the world's most important currency, but the euro represents the first serious alternative for decades. None of this indicates that the US–EU economic dyad is negatively affected by the fact that the EU, in some respects, is becoming more of an equal to the United States in terms of political economy than has been the case before.

Notes

1 The approach to studying foreign economic policy in this chapter is the 'state-centred' one, to use the terms chosen by G.J. Ikenberry, D.A. Lake and M. Mastanduno ('Introduction: Approaches to Explaining American Foreign Economic Policy', *International Organization*, 1988, vol. 42, no. 2). In other words, the analysis in this chapter 'conceives the state as an actor, and focuses directly on politicians and administrators in the executive as independent participants in the policy process' (ibid., p. 10). The other two main alternative analytic approaches to the study of US foreign economic policy, according to the authors, are 'system-centred' and 'society-centred' approaches.

2 L.I. Skålnes, *Politics, Markets, and Grand Strategy: Foreign Economic Policies as Strategic Instruments*, Ann Arbor, MI: The University of Michigan Press, 2000, p. 13.

3 Skålnes, *Politics*, p. 3.

4 The perspective taken here is thus the same as that taken by Geir Lundestad in *'Empire' by Integration: The United States and European Integration, 1945–1997*, Oxford/New York: Oxford University Press, 1998, see particularly pp. 3–4.

5 M. Mastanduno, 'Economics and Security in Statecraft and Scholarship', *International Organization*, 1998, vol. 52, no. 4, p. 843.

6 Lundestad, *'Empire'*, pp. 108–25.

7 S. De Spiegeleire, 'Recoupling Russia to Europe: Staying the Course', *The International Spectator*, 2003, pp. 79–97. See also H. Haukkala, 'The Making of the European Union's Common Strategy on Russia', in H. Haukkala and S. Medvedev (eds) *The EU Common Strategy on Russia: Learning the Grammar of the CFSP*, Helsinki: The Finnish Institute of International Affairs/Berlin: Institut für Europäische Politik, 2001, pp. 22–80.

8 De Spiegeleire, 'Recoupling Russia to Europe: Staying the Course'. See also S. De Spiegeleire, 'The Implementation of the EU's Common Strategy on Russia', in H. Haukkala and S. Medvedev (eds) *The EU Common Strategy on Russia: Learning the Grammar of the CFSP*, Helsinki: The Finnish Institute of International Affairs/Berlin: Institut für Europäische Politik, 2001, pp. 81–116. Cf. H. Haukkala, 'What went right with the EU's Common Strategy on Russia?', in A. Moshes (ed.) *Rethinking the Respective Strategies of Russia and the European Union*, Moscow: Carnegie Moscow Center/Helsinki: The Finnish Institute of International Affairs, 2003, pp. 62–96. For two Russian views, see K. Khudolev, 'Russia and the European Union: New Opportunities, New Challenges,' in A. Moshes (ed.) *Rethinking the Respective Strategies of Russia and the European Union*, Moscow: Carnegie Moscow Center/Helsinki: Finnish Institute of International Affairs, 2003, pp. 8–30; and T.V. Bordachev, 'Strategy and Strategies', in A. Moshes, (ed.) *Rethinking the Respective Strategies of Russia and the European Union*, Moscow: Carnegie Moscow Center/Helsinki: Finnish Institute of International Affairs, 2003, pp. 31–61.

9 See Council of the European Union, '15th EU–Russia Summit, Moscow, 10 May 2005, Road Maps: Road Map for the Common Economic Space, Building Blocks for Sustained Economic Growth', 2005.

10 Y. Gaidar, *The Russian Economy in 2002. Tendencies and Perspectives,* Moscow: Institute of Transition Economy, 2003, pp. 9–13 (in Russian) as quoted in B.Y. Frumkin, 'Russia's Economic Development: Summing up the First Presidential Term of Vladimir Putin and Prospects for the Future,' in Y. Fedorov and B. Nygren (eds) *Putin I and Putin II: Results of the First Term and Prospects for the Second*, Stockholm: Swedish National Defence College, 2004, p. 105.

11 Frumkin, 'Russia's Economic Development', pp. 122–6.

12 See, for example, A. Aslund, 'WTO Entry: No Time to Lose', *The Moscow Times*, 3 February 2003.

13 In its analysis of economic issues, this chapter is to a large extent modelled on the analysis in Robert Gilpin's magisterial *Global Political Economy: Understanding the International Economic Order*, Princeton, NJ: Princeton University Press, 2001.

14 See Gilpin, *Global Political Economy,* pp. 196–233. See also J. Grieco and G.J. Ikenberry, *State Power and World Markets: The International Political Economy*, New York and London: W.W. Norton, 2003, pp. 29–43.

15 Gilpin covers these issues in a slightly different way. See Gilpin, *Global Political Economy,* pp. 278–304. This means that macroeconomic coordination is excluded mainly for reasons of space.

16 Gilpin, *Global Political Economy*, p. 299.

17 D.S. Hamilton and J.P. Quinlan, *Partners in Prosperity: The Changing Geography of the Transatlantic Economy*, Washington, DC: Center for Transatlantic Relations, Paul H. Nitze School of Advanced International Studies, Johns Hopkins University, 2004, pp. 5–6.

18 Data from *OECD Factbook 2005*.

19 Eurostat data state that the exports to GPD ratio for Russia in 2003 was 30.2 per cent. Given the fact that the same source states that Russian imports were less than half as large as exports indicates that an estimated figure for Russian total trade to GDP would have been about 45 per cent in 2003. See the European Commission's Centre for External Trade, 'Bilateral Trade Relations with Russia', online.

20 R.O. Keohane and J.S. Nye, *Power and Interdependence*, 2nd edn, Glenview, IL: Scott, Foresman. 1989.

21 Keohane and Nye, *Power and Interdependence*, p. 8. Emphasis in original.

22 This and the following paragraphs are based on Keohane and Nye, *Power and Interdependence*, pp. 11–16.

23 The North Atlantic Free Trade Agreement (NAFTA), which includes the United States, Canada and Mexico, is also important economically, but NAFTA totally lacks the political ties that exist in the EU.

24 Figures from Eurostat. The data for merchandise trade include all 25 EU members, whereas the data for trade in services only include EU-15. See the European Commission's External Trade Issues, 'Bilateral Trade Relations' with USA, online. In all measurements of EU trade dependence, trade among the EU members is excluded.

25 Figures computed from Eurostat for merchandise trade, see ibid. For service trade the figures are from the Department of Commerce, Bureau of Economic Analysis, *Survey of Current Business*, October 2004, pp. 46–7. The data for service trade have been converted from US dollars to euros by use of OzForex Foreign Exchange online.

26 US Department of Commerce, 'TradeStats Express Home' online, with tables for Russia analogous to those for NAFTA and the EU. Figures for service trade were unavailable, but cannot amount to more than a couple of billion euros since Russia is nowhere to be found among the most important US trade partners in service trade.

27 From Eurostat, including data for both merchandise and service trade. See the European Commission's External Trade Issues, 'Bilateral Trade Relations' with Russia, online.

28 'Russian Federation', online.

29 'European Union', online.

30 R. Cohen discusses the roles of the most important currencies in the current global economy in Chapter 3 'Life at the Peak', in *The Future of Money* (Princeton, NJ: Princeton University Press, 2004) pp. 07–58. Gilpin, *Global Political Economy,* covers some of the same territory on pp. 236–8, 255–7.

31 Both figures from Cohen, *The Future of Money*, p. 12.

32 Cf. F. Bergsten, 'America and Europe: Clash of the Titans?', *Foreign Affairs*, 1999, vol. 78, no. 2, pp. 20–34.

33 See J. Kirshner, *Currency and Coercion: The Political Economy of International Monetary Power,* Princeton, NJ: Princeton University Press, 1995, pp. 67–70.

34 See S.S. Cohen, 'Euro Shield', *Wall Street Journal*, 29 April 2003.
35 On this point, see J. Van Oudenaren, 'Europe as Partner', in D.C. Gompert and F.S. Larrabee (eds) *America and Europe: A Partnership for a New Era*, Cambridge/New York: Cambridge University Press, 1997, p. 124. On the coming role of the euro, see also M.O. Hosli, 'The EMU and International Monetary Relations: What to Expect for International Actors?', in C. Rhodes (ed.) *The European Union in the World Community*, Boulder, CO/London: Lynne Rienner, 1998, pp. 165–91.
36 All data in this paragraph are from Eurostat. See note 27 above.
37 OECD data indicate that the FDI inflow into Russia from 1999 through 2003 was low even compared to other developing economies such as Argentina, Brazil, Chile, India and, of course, China. See OECD, 'International Investment Perspectives: 2004 Edition', p. 6.
38 The role of Multinational Corporations for the global economy and for international relations is another contested issue within social science. The position taken here is the 'state-centric position' according to which 'multinational corporations are simply national firms with foreign operations . . . that . . . with few exceptions . . . remain deeply embedded in their national societies' (Gilpin, *Global Political Economy,* p. 299). Gilpin, one of the pioneers in political science studying political economy, assesses 'The State and the Multinationals' in Chapter 11 of his important work.
39 For WTO documentation on Russia's WTO Accession Negotiations see Russia and World Trade Organization: 'Current state of accession negotiations'; 'Main stages of negotiations', and 'Aims and objectives of accession', online.
40 See the European Commission's External Relations, 'The EU's relations with Russia', online.
41 See 'Joint Statement by President Bush and President Putin on Russia's Accession to WTO', online.
42 Secretary of State Condoleezza Rice, 'Briefing En Route to Moscow', 19 April 2005.
43 Data for Russia from Eurostat, see note 27. Data for the US from the European Commission's delegation to the USA, official website. Cf. also data from the World Bank, *World Development Indicators 2005*, table 4.2 'Structure of Output'.
44 See N. Buckley, 'Aftershocks will keep foreign investors on edge,' *Financial Times*, 17 May 2005.
45 The White House, 'Jackson-Vanik and Russia Fact Sheet', 13 November 2001. For a broader assessment of the Jackson-Vanik Amendment in the context of US–Russian trade relations see W.H. Cooper, 'Permanent Normal Trade Relations (PNTR) Status for Russia and US–Russian Economic Ties', Washington, DC: Congressional Research Service, CRS Reports for Congress, 28 January 2002.
46 Cf. Cooper, 'Permanent Normal Trade Relations'.
47 See data from the US Census Bureau online. Cf. Cooper 'Permanent Normal Trade Relations'.
48 See statistics from the International Trade Administration online.
49 Data from Eurostat. See note 27 above.
50 Data from Eurostat. See note 27 above.
51 Data from Eurostat. See note 24 above.
52 Data from the European Commission's delegation to the USA, official website.
53 This process is well analysed in P.H. Gordon and J. Shapiro, *Allies at War: America: Europe and the Crisis over Iraq*, New York: McGraw-Hill, 2004; and in E. Pond. *Friendly Fire: The Near-Death of the Transatlantic Alliance*, Pittsburgh, PA: European Union Studies Association/Washington, DC: Brookings, 2004.
54 See Hamilton and Quinlan, *Partners in Prosperity*, p. 14.
55 US Census Bureau online.

10

THE UNITED STATES AND RUSSIA

A clash of strategic visions

Håkan Karlsson

Introduction

During the Cold War, the power structure of the international system was basically bipolar. Two superpowers, the United States and the Soviet Union, represented the poles in the system. With the demise of the Soviet Union, the bipolar structure vanished and the United States emerged as the sole remaining superpower. Many analysts have therefore characterized the current system structure as unipolar.[1] More than a decade ago, they recognized that America's 'unipolar moment' had arrived.[2] The economic and military might of the United States is preponderant and unprecedented. Thus, the claim that the post-Cold War world has only one predominant pole seems reasonable. 'If today's American primacy does not constitute unipolarity, then nothing ever will', William C. Wohlforth and Stephen G. Brooks conclude.[3]

The United States clearly has an interest in preserving its dominant position in the international system. US efforts to prolong the unipolar moment, the period in which the United States is substantially more powerful than other states, are to be expected. Logically, the United States should strive to prevent new great powers from emerging and balancing against it.[4] It is the contention of this author that US grand strategy after the end of the Cold War has indeed been aimed at perpetuating unipolarity. The pursuit of this objective is evident in the specific policies of the United States with respect to four national security issues: enlargement of the North Atlantic Treaty Organization (NATO), strategic nuclear force planning, strategic arms control, and missile defence. The present study examines these US policies and explains how they can serve the strategic purpose of preserving America's dominant global position.

Analysts who grant that the structure of the international system has become unipolar differ over the stability and durability of unipolarity. Some adherents of the theory of international politics called structural realism believe that unipolarity is an inherently unstable structure that will not endure. For these theorists, America's unipolar moment is just that, a relatively short interlude in world history. According to their view, a structural shift from unipolarity to multipolarity is inevitable. New great powers will inevitably emerge and balance against the United States. When this happens, the present unipolar system will give way to a structure comprising several powerful poles.[5]

The experience with unipolarity after the Cold War calls into question the theoretical claim that this structure is unstable and cannot last. Predictions of a rapid collapse of unipolarity have failed to come true. The structure has already lasted for more than a decade. This fact has prompted some analysts to suggest that unipolarity is stable and durable. In their view, it is no longer appropriate to talk about a unipolar moment.[6] 'The unipolar moment has become the unipolar era', as Charles Krauthammer puts it.[7] The principal basis for the argument that unipolarity can be sustained is the observation that great power balancing against the United States has not occurred since the disappearance of the Soviet Union.[8]

In explaining the perceived absence of counterbalancing, scholars have pointed out that the power of the United States grew more overwhelming in the 1990s. The result is increased American dominance. In other words, the world has become even more unipolar than it was a decade ago. It has been argued that the enormous concentration of American power should dissuade all other states from balancing against the United States. According to William Wohlforth, the United States is simply too powerful to be balanced. Wohlforth and others also point out that it will be decades before any single state can match the United States in terms of either military or economic power.[9]

Does this mean that counterbalancing is avoidable? Kenneth N. Waltz, a leading structural realist, insists that it cannot be prevented. In fact, he disputes the observation that balancing against the United States has not taken place during the last decade. Actually, counterbalancing has already begun, but haltingly so, he claims. Full-scale counterbalancing is not yet manifest, but Waltz argues that one does observe 'balancing tendencies'.[10]

If Waltz is right, what states have sought to balance against the United States and what counterbalancing steps have they taken? Arguably, the most important counterbalancers include Russia and China. This study focuses on Russia as prime challenger in the greater transatlantic region. Russian grand strategy has developed in accordance with a counterbalancing imperative. Russia is determined to regain true great power status and promotes the emergence of multipolarity. From Russia's perspective, unipolarity is not a desirable state of affairs. Russian leaders resent America's dominance in international politics. They feel threatened by what they see as American attempts to achieve global hegemony. Specifically, they view NATO's expansion and the US acquisition of a ballistic missile defence system as threats to Russian security.

This study explores ways in which Russia is attempting to counterbalance the United States. Russian balancing against America can be pursued both internally and externally.[11] Internal counterbalancing is what Russia does when it tries to increase its own capabilities. Unfortunately for Russia, this form of counterbalancing is both costly and time-consuming. It depends on sustaining rapid economic growth over many years. A potentially cheaper and quicker route to multipolarity is external counterbalancing. The most obvious way to counterbalance externally is to aggregate capabilities by forming alliances with other states. It is, however, difficult to organize and coordinate effective alliances. Moreover, alliance commitments mean sacrificing national autonomy, and Russia has shown little inclination to make that kind of sacrifice.

Another, less conspicuous, way for Russia to counterbalance by external means is to restrain the United States within international regimes.[12] In Russian grand strategy, international regimes have become balancing mechanisms. Russia supports the United Nations (UN) as an overarching instrument for providing a system of norms and rules of behaviour in international affairs. It has also defended the US–Russian strategic arms control regime created during the Cold War, a complex system of treaties on the limitation and reduction of offensive and defensive strategic weapons. The purpose of such efforts, perfectly logical from a counterbalancing perspective, is to constrain American power. This chapter investigates the results so far of Russia's attempts to tie down the United States with institutional restraints. Finally, the study deals with Washington's reaction to Russia's pursuit of a multipolar world and the implications of this reaction for what in this book is called a new strategic triangle consisting of the United States, Russia, and the European Union (EU).

The US post-Cold War grand strategy

First evidence of an ambition to preserve the dominant global position of the United States after the Cold War came in March 1992, when a government document was leaked to the press. This was a draft of the Defense Planning Guidance (DPG) for fiscal years 1994–9, a classified planning document prepared by the US Department of Defense under the supervision of Under Secretary of Defense for Policy Paul D. Wolfowitz. In the draft, the Pentagon's strategic planners maintained that America's post-Cold War grand strategy should seek to perpetuate unipolarity by preventing new global competitors from emerging: 'Our strategy must now refocus on precluding the emergence of any potential future global competitor.' To implement the strategy, the United States, according to the draft, 'must maintain the mechanisms for deterring potential competitors from even aspiring to a larger regional or global role.' Russia was identified in the document as a possible candidate for becoming a competitor, although the authors recognized that a global Russian challenge to US security was unlikely to emerge in the near future.[13]

In the final version of the planning document the controversial language referring to the goal of preventing the emergence of a global rival was eliminated. Nevertheless, the earlier version had a lasting impact. Its logic and guiding principles have in fact decisively shaped US security policy for the post-Cold War era.

Despite some ambiguities, the public rhetoric and the actions of the Clinton administration suggest that its grand strategy had at least strong tendencies towards maintaining the US-dominated unipolar international system. In Michael Mastanduno's opinion, the United States under President William J. Clinton actually pursued a consistent grand strategy of preserving primacy.[14] Similarly, Christopher Layne argues that the country followed a grand strategy of preponderance.[15] Barry R. Posen and Andrew L. Ross characterize the grand strategy of the Clinton administration as an uneasy amalgam consisting of several strategic visions. They conclude that the strategy was basically cooperative in line with a liberal internationalist tradition and constrained by principles of selective engagement but evolved to a point where it had many of the trappings of primacy.[16]

To be sure, the Clinton administration in its foreign policy pronouncements eschewed the blunt language of the 1992 Pentagon planning document, but it readily acknowledged that the United States occupied a position of pre-eminence in the international system. The 1995 version of the administration's National Security Strategy report stated it explicitly: 'We stand as the world's preeminent power.'[17] Central to the Clinton strategy was US leadership and engagement in world affairs. The United States was seen as indispensable to the forging of stable international relations. 'America truly is the world's indispensable nation', Clinton declared.[18] Administration officials did not advertise as a strategic objective the preservation of American geopolitical dominance, speaking instead of perpetuating America's role as world leader. Clinton himself announced this goal in a speech: 'We must continue to bear the responsibility of the world's leadership.'[19]

The insistence by the Clinton administration on the continued need for American leadership abroad indirectly betrayed an intention to secure the geopolitical status quo. Implicit in the official statements was the belief that the United States must remain in a position of primacy in order to lead the world.[20]

While the Clinton administration was careful not to depict Russia as an adversary, its rhetorical record and actual practice of policy revealed that it viewed Russia as a potential threat. The administration maintained a substantial nuclear arsenal directed primarily against Russia. US nuclear war planning continued to target the Russian nuclear forces because they remained capable of destroying the United States. A principal result of the Clinton administration's 1993–4 Nuclear Posture Review was the adoption of a 'hedge' policy for the configuration of the US nuclear force structure. The review concluded that the United States would retain strategic nuclear forces of sufficient size and capability to hedge against the possibility that Russia could become a strategic rival at some time in the future.[21]

NATO enlargement became a cornerstone of Clinton's foreign policy. His firm commitment to the enlargement process was consistent with a US grand strategy of primacy. By expanding eastward, NATO established a renewed containment of Russia in Europe.[22] The Clinton administration never spoke of a new policy of containment, but its case for extending NATO to Eastern Europe did incorporate containment considerations. In laying out the various rationales for NATO's eastward expansion, US officials made clear that the expansion would function as a hedge against a potential Russian threat.[23]

The Russian reaction

Russia's quest for multipolarity is largely a response to the US grand strategy of primacy laid out in the early 1990s, but the Russian reaction emerged through a gradual process. Only by the mid-1990s did Russian leaders begin to speak seriously of building a multipolar world in which the United States would not be the only major centre of power. Initially, the leadership pursued a radically Western-oriented foreign policy seeking extensive economic and political integration with the West. The period of Russian deference to the West proved short-lived, however. Since 1993, Russia gradually abandoned its accommodating orientation and moved towards a more assertive and realist stance.[24]

The shift away from a pro-Western foreign policy solidified following the appointment of Evgenii Primakov as foreign minister in 1996. Primakov perceived Russia's national interests in terms that conflicted with the grand strategy of the United States. Securing for Russia the appearance of great power status constituted a fundamental part of his definition of its state interests. At the very centre of Primakov's long-term foreign policy vision was his view that 'Russia was and remains a great power.'[25] Primakov also maintained that Russia had an interest in counterbalancing the United States and in fostering a multipolar international system. He firmly established the idea of multipolarity, grounded in realist theory's conception of power balancing, as an official doctrine, arguing persistently that Russia should play the role of a counterweight to US hegemonic aspirations.[26]

The multipolarity doctrine was formally proclaimed in a Russian–Chinese joint declaration of April 1997, which stated that the two countries as partners would make efforts to further the development of a multipolar world.[27] It was also enshrined in the National Security Concept of the Russian Federation. The concept, approved by President Boris Yeltsin in December 1997, indicated that the Russian national interests in the international sphere boiled down to 'the consolidation of Russia's position as a great power, one of the influential centres of the emergent multipolar world'.[28]

Missile defence in focus

In 1999, national missile defence (NMD) broke cover as a contentious issue in US–Russian relations. It was apparent that the United States would develop and deploy a limited NMD system designed to defend its territory against small numbers of attacking long-range ballistic missiles. Conceding to pressure from the US Congress, the Clinton administration in January 1999 decided to move ahead more vigorously in developing NMD technology. In announcing its decision to press on with a focused NMD programme, the administration acknowledged that the 1972 Anti-Ballistic Missile (ABM) Treaty with Russia prohibited the deployment of any ballistic missile defence covering the entire United States. Since the administration believed in the value of international arms control regimes and therefore wanted to preserve the ABM Treaty, it stated that it would seek Russian agreement on amending the treaty to permit deployment of its modest NMD system.[29]

Russian leaders flatly rejected the idea of changing the severe restrictions of the ABM Treaty. They looked askance at the US missile defence programme and saw the treaty as a means of preventing the United States from proceeding with NMD deployment. Despite US assurances that the NMD system under development was intended to meet a potential threat from 'rogue states', the Russians feared that the United States was in fact attempting to secure a strategic advantage over Russia. There were concerns in Moscow that even a limited American NMD system, especially in combination with the US strategic offensive forces, might threaten Russia by neutralizing its strategic nuclear arsenal.[30]

Russian grand strategy under President Putin

Russia's foreign policy under President Vladimir Putin has rightly been described as a continuation of the main line followed by Primakov.[31] One of Putin's first moves in coming to power was to espouse the Russian great power ambitions. He echoed Primakov's motto in a programmatic statement released just before he was appointed Acting President: 'Russia was and will remain a great power.'[32] At a meeting of the Russian Security Council held on the day of his appointment, Putin said: 'I want to emphasize at once that the Russian Federation's foreign policy line will not be changed.' Promoting multipolarity was a central theme of Putin's foreign policy agenda, as part of the continuity he promised. 'Russia will strive for the construction of a multipolar world', he told the Security Council.[33]

Early in his presidency, Putin approved two grand strategy documents. The primary document, approved in January 2000, was a revised version of the National Security Concept. In June 2000, Putin approved a secondary strategic document, the Foreign Policy Concept of the Russian Federation. Both documents endorsed the political strategy set by Primakov. The new National Security Concept repeated that Russia's national interests in the international sphere lay in strengthening its position as a great power and as one of the influential centres of a multipolar world.[34]

According to the 1997 version of the National Security Concept, the international situation was characterized first of all by the strengthening of a trend towards multipolarity. The 2000 version was more pessimistic but by no means defeatist. It stated that 'two mutually exclusive tendencies' predominated, one towards multipolarity and the other towards US–led unipolarity.[35]

In describing two opposed tendencies in the world, decrying one of them and supporting the other, the National Security Concept presented a strategic vision that implied US–Russian rivalry, but it avoided confrontational language. Russian officials, however, did not hesitate to discuss the striving for multipolarity in terms of an ideological struggle. Foreign Minister Igor Ivanov stated: 'Two fundamentally different attitudes to the creation of a new world order have clashed.'[36]

The Foreign Policy Concept mirrored the strategic perspective outlined in the National Security Concept. It noted that 'negative tendencies' posing new challenges and threats to the national interests of Russia had arisen in the international sphere. In particular, the threat of unipolarity was emphasized. As a counter, the concept advocated multipolarity. 'Russia will seek to achieve the formation of a multipolar system of international relations', the document pledged.[37]

In what has been termed Soviet-like threat assessments, the grand strategy documents portrayed the United States and NATO as the sources of Russia's greatest external security problems.[38] The National Security Concept asserted that NATO's eastward expansion produced one of the main threats to Russian security in the international sphere.[39] According to the Foreign Policy Concept, implementation of the plans of the United States to build an NMD system could compel Russia to take countermeasures. However, the Russian leadership was determined to block the US missile defence plans. The Foreign Policy Concept proclaimed that Russia would seek to preserve the ABM Treaty.[40]

Russian leaders were explicit in subsuming NATO's enlargement and the US NMD effort under the perceived unipolarity menace. They considered both phenomena as reflections of a desire to create a unipolar world based on US global dominance. Foreign Minister Ivanov maintained that the expansion of NATO revealed the tendency towards unipolarity in Europe in that it promoted 'NATO-centrism', a scheme for building the future system of European security around the US-dominated alliance. Furthermore, he alleged that a unipolar logic manifested itself in policies undermining strategic stability. In the first place, this referred to the plans for an American NMD system.[41] When asked about the connection between Russia's opposition against US NMD deployment and the Russian position in favour of multipolarity, Ivanov replied: 'It is quite obvious that the deployment by the USA of a national ABM system is a road to the creation of a unipolar world.'[42] A recurring theme in the Russian military's approach to the US NMD programme was the assumption that the real purpose of the programme was to ensure America's strategic supremacy over the rest of the world. Just as significant, Russian military officers repeatedly insisted that a US NMD system would be primarily directed against Russia.[43]

Putin's anti-NMD campaign

In the first years of the new millennium, NATO enlargement and US missile defence were both major contentious issues between the United States and Russia. Russian leaders spoke out strongly against further NATO expansion to the east.[44]

In addition to opposing NATO's second round of enlargement, Putin staged a campaign to keep the United States from deploying an NMD system. This campaign involved a vigorous drive on behalf of the existing treaty-regulated US–Russian strategic arms control regime. Putin's opening move was to obtain leverage over the NMD issue by linking implementation of the 1993 strategic arms reduction treaty (START II) to preservation of the ABM Treaty. He used the START II ratification process to establish a direct linkage. In April 2000, the Federal Assembly of the Russian Federation at long last approved START II, making Russia's future adherence to the treaty contingent on strict compliance with the ABM Treaty. Putin had been pushing vigorously for this decision as a vehicle for strengthening Russia's hand when it came to maintaining the ABM Treaty intact and thereby preventing US NMD deployment. Addressing the Russian State Duma before its vote, he stressed that if the United States proceeded to 'destroy' the ABM Treaty, Russia would actually withdraw from the START II Treaty.[45] Putin's gambit relied on the understanding that the Clinton administration wanted START II ratified. As a matter of fact, START II ratification was one of the administration's priorities.

Putin also took advantage of the Clinton administration's commitment to the ABM Treaty itself. He steadfastly refused to accept any modifications of the treaty that would allow the United States to deploy a limited NMD system, confident that the Clinton administration would not violate or abandon the treaty even if Russia stonewalled on amending it. The administration's statements clearly signalled its unwillingness to act unilaterally without Russian consent to treaty amendments. As early as March 1999, Clinton said that he had no intention of abrogating the ABM Treaty.[46]

Russia successfully mobilized other nations in the campaign against a US NMD system. As Russia's principal 'strategic partner' in opposition to US-centred unipolarity, China supported the Russian anti-NMD position, and so did the member states of the Commonwealth of Independent States (CIS).

Putin was less successful in his attempts at persuading the European allies of the United States to share in Russia's struggle to constrain US freedom of action on missile defence. Although several European states were apprehensive about NMD, with France standing out in voicing concern and criticism, most US allies in Europe would not fall out with the United States over the issue.[47] Russian leaders were interested in forming a strategic partnership with the EU, particularly against American unipolar designs.[48] They regarded a strong, independent Europe as a natural pole in the emerging multipolar world.[49] Support from the EU for the Russian stance would have given a distinctly triangular aspect to the transatlantic dispute over amending the ABM Treaty. There was no single European position on the treaty issue, however. Russia's appeal for strict compliance with the ABM Treaty was inserted in a joint statement issued at the conclusion of the May 2000 EU–Russia summit meeting but was not endorsed by the EU leaders.[50] Following the next EU–Russia summit in October 2000, French President Jacques Chirac, also EU President at the time, claimed that the EU had made common cause with Russia. 'The European Union and Russia have an identical viewpoint because, as you know, we have condemned any questioning of the ABM Treaty', he said.[51] Chirac's assertion had a hollow ring in view of the fact that the official declarations issued after the meeting contained no such denunciation. Because of the differences among the attitudes of the member states, Putin could not count on the EU to support his policy. Accordingly, he campaigned against the US NMD plans at meetings with individual European governments, urging them to come out in favour of preserving the ABM Treaty.[52] The Europeans proved receptive to such calls, but Putin's efforts to win European support for Russia's policy of stonewalling on US amendment proposals essentially failed.

Invigorating the US grand strategy

By 2001, the United States and Russia were poised for confrontation. The grand strategies of the two countries were antithetical. Russian leaders reaffirmed their pursuit of multipolarity. 'We come out for the creation of a multipolar world', Putin declared.[53]

The election of George W. Bush as President of the United States brought into US foreign policy a renewed emphasis on America's superior military strength and great political influence. The Bush administration came into office enunciating a grand strategy vision that was fundamentally opposed to Russia's multipolar vision. Words like 'hegemony', 'dominance', 'primacy', and 'empire' have been used by analysts to describe the administration's grand strategy. Ivo H. Daalder and James M. Lindsay see Bush's foreign policy as springing from a strain of realist political thinking best labelled hegemonist.[54] Peter Dombrowski and Andrew L. Ross (in Chapter 8 of this volume) argue that the Bush administration has pursued a primacy that verges on the imperial.

The unipolarist philosophy of the new leadership in Washington was expressed in Bush's statements in 1999–2000 and in the pre-election writings and remarks of the people he chose to serve in his administration. While denying that his aims were imperial, candidate Bush argued for using America's preponderant military capabilities 'to extend our peaceful influence, not just across the world, but across the years'.[55] The Bush team clearly aimed at preserving US global dominance for the foreseeable future through discouraging the emergence of rival great powers. Paul Wolfowitz, later appointed Deputy Secretary of Defense, wrote an article implying that the conceptual thrust of the draft DPG paper prepared by his Pentagon office in 1992 was right and 'crucially relevant to our immediate future'.[56]

Before the terrorist attacks of 11 September 2001 refocused America's attention, Bush and his aides showed relatively little interest in international terrorism. Instead, they concentrated on the threat of great power competition. This is the typical behaviour of advocates of unipolarity. Condoleezza Rice, Bush's closest campaign adviser on foreign policy and then assistant to the president for national security affairs, insisted that the crucial and most daunting task for the United States was to focus on relations with other powerful states, notably Russia and China. 'These states', she argued, 'are capable of disruption on a grand scale.'[57] Bush and Rice had a sharply negative view of Russia. According to Rice, there was a Russian threat. 'I sincerely believe that Russia constitutes a threat to the West in general and to our European allies in particular', she told a French journal.[58]

Bush proposed maintaining a policy of 'tough realism' in dealing with Russia.[59] His initial hard line is termed 'neocontainment' by James Goldgeier and Michael McFaul.[60] Their characterization seems appropriate, since the incoming Bush administration was disposed to keep Russia in check and hedge against its rise to great power status. The neocontainment policy could be seen clearly in the new administration's approach to the issue of NATO expansion. Even before the election, the Bush team made clear that it would push for further enlargement of

NATO without consideration for Russia's objections against it. The Republican Party platform said: 'Russia must never be given a veto over enlargement.'[61]

Unlike his predecessor, Bush was deeply committed to the deployment of a missile defence system. Moreover, Bush rejected the limited system envisaged by the Clinton administration. He favoured building a more extensive system to protect the entire American homeland.[62] To make this possible, he planned to withdraw from the ABM Treaty if Russia refused to accept the necessary major changes to the treaty.[63]

Partnership and strife

In 2001, Russian officials continued their campaigns against US NMD deployment and further NATO enlargement.[64] There was, however, no real prospect that Russian efforts would be successful in either case. Bush's determination was unshakable. In early May, Bush outlined ambitious plans to build a robust, layered NMD system that could eventually include sea-, air-, and even space-based components, all prohibited by the ABM Treaty. On the treaty, Bush's position had actually hardened since the election campaign. He proposed that the United States and Russia 'move beyond' the ABM Treaty rather than seek to amend it.[65]

Meanwhile, Bush energetically pressed forward with the plans for NATO expansion. In June 2001, he announced US backing for a continued enlargement process. 'We strongly stand on the side of expansion of NATO', he said.[66] In advancing the enlargement, Bush opted for a 'big bang' approach. He called for NATO to admit all applicant countries 'from the Baltic to the Black Sea', clearly including the three Baltic states.[67]

The Russian campaign against further NATO enlargement tapered off after the first meeting between Bush and Putin in June 2001, when Bush, according to Rice, bluntly told Putin that Russia would have no veto over the admission of new members to NATO.[68] Russia's anti-NMD campaign, in contrast, continued unabated. Putin led the way, asserting that if the United States were to abrogate the ABM Treaty, then Russia would 'automatically' renounce the START II Treaty.[69]

Following the terrorist attacks on the United States in September 2001, the Bush administration was compelled to reorient its foreign policy. The administration's focus on potential great power rivals shifted abruptly to the pressing danger posed by terrorist groups and their governmental patrons, and the global struggle against terrorism became its highest priority. In Russia, too, the September terrorist strikes produced a foreign policy reorientation.[70] Putin aligned Russia with the United States in combating terrorism, which the Russians perceived as a serious threat to their own security. This alignment, confirmed by a series of US–Russian statements issued at Bush–Putin meetings in 2001–2, represented a major shift in Russia's strategic priorities, since it came at the expense of the attention paid to the task of combating unipolarity.

Cooperation on the issue of terrorism did not fundamentally change the strategic relationship between the United States and Russia. The security issues that divided the two countries were still on the bilateral agenda essentially unaffected by the new spirit of partnership. With respect to the controversy over NMD, no compromise could be reached. The Bush administration did not offer any proposals for amendments to the ABM Treaty because it wanted to get rid of all constraints on its NMD programme. What the administration offered was a joint withdrawal from the treaty. Putin rejected that proposal but presented no counteroffer to break the impasse.[71] After months of negotiations, the Bush administration gave up on convincing Russia to join the United States in withdrawing from the ABM Treaty. In December 2001, Bush announced that he had given Russia formal notice that the United States would unilaterally withdraw from the treaty in six months.[72]

Bush's withdrawal announcement reflected the central reality of US unipolar dominance in contemporary world politics. The Russians had to recognize that their attempt to use the ABM Treaty to prevent the US NMD system had failed dismally. Putin said that Russia did everything it could to preserve the treaty.[73] Indeed, Russian officials fought for the treaty to the bitter end, working hard to galvanize international support. Together with China and Belarus, Russia introduced a resolution in support of the treaty at the UN General Assembly. Of course, the assembly's adoption of the resolution in late November 2001 was disregarded by Washington.[74] The elaborate Russian manoeuvre of political extortion conditioning the START II Treaty's entry into force on the preservation of the ABM Treaty also backfired as it turned out that Bush did not care about START II. In short, the outcome of the NMD controversy ultimately proved the futility of attempts at constraining America's freedom of action through international regimes.

Russia in June 2002 renounced START II, but Putin did not follow through on his implicit threat, issued in November 2000, to abandon strategic offensive arms control if the United States abrogated the ABM Treaty. On the contrary, he was eager to negotiate an agreement with the United States on substantial mutual force reductions to levels that Russia could sustain economically. Moreover, he wanted to constrain the US NMD programme within a new conditional treaty regime linking offensive and defensive capabilities.[75]

The Bush administration's preferred approach to the issue of strategic arms reductions was for the United States to go it alone, without entering any legally binding agreement with Russia. Putin, however, insisted on a formal treaty, and Bush eventually agreed to sign one. In the Strategic Offensive Reductions Treaty (SORT), signed in Moscow on 24 May 2002, the United States gave up nothing. The treaty committed the United States and Russia to reduce their strategic offensive forces so that by the end of 2012 the number of deployed nuclear warheads on each side would not exceed 1,700–2,200, precisely the level that the Bush administration had decided unilaterally to reach within ten years, but did not require either country to destroy any warheads. Nor did it contain any language on defensive capabilities.[76] Thus, the Russians once again failed to restrain America. SORT provided the Bush administration with the flexibility it desired.

Formalizing the US grand strategy

Although the Bush administration remained preoccupied with the war on terrorism, its strategic documents indicated that the inclination of the members during their first months in office was not a passing attitude. A review of the US nuclear force posture, completed in December 2001, gave clear evidence that the administration, while seeking a new US–Russian relationship based on mutual interests and cooperation, considered Russia as a potential threat. The Defense Department's classified report on the 2001 Nuclear Posture Review acknowledged that the United States would continue to include a Russian threat among the contingencies for which it had to be prepared. According to the Bush administration's public comments, US nuclear force sizing was not driven by an 'immediate contingency' involving Russia.[77] In other words, Russia was not seen as a current danger. However, the Nuclear Posture Review report assumed that Russia could be involved in a 'potential contingency', meaning that a threat from Russia, while neither immediate nor expected, was still considered plausible.[78]

The need to be on guard against possible great power rivals was also a theme of the 2001 Nuclear Posture Review. It was recognized in the study that a 'hostile peer competitor' could emerge in the future. The Bush administration viewed the rise of such a powerful challenger as a potential contingency the United States might have to address when developing its nuclear force posture.[79]

The Bush administration's Nuclear Posture Review continued the policy of hedging established by Clinton. In the case of the Bush plans for the US strategic offensive forces, the hedge aspect was the decision to maintain a large reserve force of nuclear warheads called the 'responsive force'. This force was intended to provide a capability to augment the deployed strategic forces to meet emerging threats.[80] In addition, the responsive force was justified in terms of the administration's strategic goal of dissuading potential competitors from initiating a military competition. The force was described as an important dissuasion factor in the field of nuclear weapons.[81]

Perhaps the most striking element of the 2001 Nuclear Posture Review was its acknowledgement of the possible contribution of the NMD programme to the maintenance of America's military superiority over potential competitors such as Russia and China. In the words of the Defense Department report: 'The demonstration of a range of technologies and systems for missile defense can have a dissuasive effect on potential adversaries.' Defensive systems, the report pointed out, would make it more arduous and costly for rival powers to compete militarily with the United States.[82]

The 2001 Nuclear Posture Review anticipated the thrust of the Bush administration's National Security Strategy report, issued in September 2002. In the latter document, a grand strategy that centred on the assumption of American primacy was laid out openly by the administration. 'The United States possesses unprecedented – and unequaled – strength and influence in the world', the report asserted.[83] At its core, the Bush strategy called for the United States to keep the world unipolar. Its fundamental tenet, expressed in appealing language, was that America should preserve the international disparity in overall power: 'The great strength of this nation must be used to promote a balance of power that favors freedom.'[84]

The National Security Strategy report confirmed that the US grand strategy mainly consisted of maintaining military dominance. The United States, the report promised, would build and maintain military forces 'beyond challenge'. Dissuading military competition was a priority: 'Our forces will be strong enough to dissuade potential adversaries from pursuing a military build-up in hopes of surpassing, or equaling, the power of the United States.'[85] All of this echoed the Pentagon draft plan drawn up under Wolfowitz in 1992.

Although terrorism tended to distract attention from the threat of great power competition, the Bush administration was aware of the danger. 'We are attentive to the possible renewal of old patterns of great power competition', the strategy report stated, referring directly to the potential great powers Russia and China. 'Tough realism' towards Russia persisted despite the recent rapprochement. According to the report, the administration was 'realistic about the differences that still divide us from Russia'.[86]

The Iraq War and the US–Russian polarity debate

Putin's initial fervour espousing multipolarity cooled after 11 September 2001. For more than a year, he hardly even mentioned the concept in public. The preoccupation with terrorism and the new US–Russian partnership evidently distracted him from the vision of a multipolar world.

Some Western analysts concluded, rashly as it turned out, that Putin had abandoned the multipolarity doctrine.[87] However, these premature hopes were dashed by the statements of Putin's minister of foreign affairs. Whereas Putin largely eschewed the rhetoric of multipolarity, Ivanov showed no such discretion.

Multipolarity was a major theme in Ivanov's book *The New Russian Diplomacy*. In the book, Ivanov saw the world as an ideological battleground where 'two fundamentally opposed approaches to a new international system have come into competition in recent years'.[88] He stated that the struggle between the trend towards a unipolar world dominated by the United States and the opposite trend towards a multipolar world order had intensified. The fundamental question for the world community, according to Ivanov, was which of the rivalling trends would finally triumph.[89] Ivanov explained that the multipolar world system proposed by Russia relied on multilateral mechanisms for maintaining international peace and security. The UN was regarded as an indispensable means of establishing this system.[90] Critical to the role of the UN in the process was the principle of unanimity of the permanent members of the Security Council. 'It is this principle that has the potential to form a multipolar world', Ivanov asserted.[91] It was, of course, no accident that Ivanov insisted on the centrality of the UN as the 'linchpin of a multipolar world system'. Russia's staunch support for the global organization was determined above all by the country's permanent seat in the UN Security Council and the veto power it carried.[92]

196

In the run-up to the US–led invasion of Iraq in March 2003, Russian foreign policy was decisively reframed within the context of the quest for a multipolar world. Charlotte Wagnsson relates why this happened: 'The Iraq crisis presented Vladimir Putin with an opportunity to put the idea of multipolarity into practice.'[93] Russia's main strategic objective during the crisis was to constrain the United States through the multilateral UN mechanism. The Russians realized that the United States could bypass the UN, as it did during the Kosovo crisis in 1999, but this time it seemed to be more difficult for Washington to do so.[94] One of the important circumstances that distinguished the crisis over Iraq from the Kosovo crisis was the open breach in the Western camp. Vigorous French and German opposition to US military action against Iraq created an exceptional opportunity for Russia to join with two major West European powers in seeking to use the UN mechanism as a constraint on the United States. Putin, who had virtually stopped using the term multipolarity, now once again publicly promoted the multipolar vision. During a visit to France in February 2003, he said that 'the future edifice of global security must be based on a multipolar world'.[95]

The determined Russian–French–German diplomatic effort to forestall the Iraq War culminated in a joint statement of 5 March announcing that Russia and France in the UN Security Council would veto a US-sponsored draft resolution authorizing the use of force against Iraq. Russian Foreign Minister Ivanov on 10 March reaffirmed that Russia would definitely vote against the resolution. Ultimately, of course, Russia and France failed to constrain the United States. Operation Iraqi Freedom began on 19 March after the Bush administration had decided not to call for a vote on its war-authorizing resolution.

The Iraq crisis served as a wake-up call for the Bush administration. The fact that Russia not only refused to support one of the administration's most significant foreign policy initiatives but actively opposed it brought to light the fundamental difference between US and Russian grand strategies that was concealed by the partnership in the war against terrorism. Administration officials, especially Condoleezza Rice, grasped the conceptual essence of Russia's strategy and started attacking it.

Responding to Putin's clamour for multipolarity, Rice recognized the term and rejected its logic. 'Multipolarity', she said, 'is a theory of rivalry, of competing interests – and at its worst – competing values.' Washington's criticism of the multipolarity concept was based on the belief that because American power was linked to the values of freedom and democracy there was no reasonable need to constrain or counterbalance the United States. In an implicit advocacy of continued US global dominance, Rice asked: 'Why would anyone who shares the values of freedom seek to put a check on those values?'[96]

The US rejection of multipolarity was answered by Russian Foreign Minister Ivanov. He defended the Russian vision of a multipolar world, stressing that multi-polarity, as understood in Russia, had nothing to do with confrontation or rivalry. To Russia, he protested, multipolarity meant in the first place close cooperation among the world's major power centres 'on the basis of equality'.[97] The US leadership, however, remained suspicious of Russia's multipolar strategy. In Washington's understanding, multipolarity inevitably involved conflict and competition. 'Poles mean opposite positions', Secretary of State Colin L. Powell noted.[98]

Undaunted by the US criticism, Putin indulged in the rhetoric of multipolarity. He did not hide the fact that Russia's grand strategy was designed to contain US power. On the contrary, he discussed multipolarity in balance of power terms. 'The world', he said, 'must be balanced and multipolar.'[99] Putin was at pains to point out that by multipolarity Russia did not mean confrontation. The Russian conception of the term encompassed no thesis of rivalry or hostility, he claimed. At the same time, however, he called for containment of US global power. Although Putin did not refer specifically to the American power position, his remark 'we will be able to build a system of checks and balances and create a balanced world' obviously implied balancing against the United States.[100]

While the Iraq crisis did not rupture the relationship between the United States and Russia, it was clear that the relationship had changed. Both Bush and Putin at their meetings in 2003 expressed a determination to continue the partnership in the war on international terrorism, but the serious discord in US–Russian relations had become apparent. Distrust and dispute crept back into the bilateral dialogue. By the end of the year, the war of words over multipolarity escalated. 'I think we need to work against multi-polarity', Bush said in a November interview.[101]

After a year-long hiatus, Putin in October 2004 resumed his rhetorical push for multipolarity. Interviewed for Chinese newspapers, he repeated that the world must be multipolar.[102] As Bush and Putin at a time of renewed US–Russian tension[103] prepared for their meeting in Bratislava in February 2005, multipolarity re-emerged as a controversial topic. Bush spoke again about his displeasure with the idea that America should be counterbalanced.[104] Putin, for his part, restated what had become an ideological mantra. 'This world must be balanced', he declared. 'It must be multipolar, as we say.'[105]

Conclusion

Primakov, in a book published in 2002, makes the concluding statement that Russia can be a true partner of the United States if the United States adjusts to the 'real prospects' of a multipolar world.[106] For a Russian to suggest that the United States should accept multipolarity is quixotic to say the least. The Bush administration is totally against it and works instead towards maintaining a unipolar world structure in which the United States remains the paramount power. There is little that the United States can do to prevent changes in the distribution of economic strength in the world, but the Bush administration, in its exposition of US grand strategy, has strongly committed itself to preserving the US dominant global position in the military realm. As shown in this study, policies to uphold American military dominance are pursued in the areas of NATO enlargement, strategic nuclear force planning, strategic arms control, and missile defence. This emphasis on America's military might will no doubt continue.

Because of the conscious US efforts to perpetuate unipolarity, a structural shift to a multipolar world is not likely to come about in the near term. Instead, unipolarity has the potential to last for many decades. Militarily, the United States has established firmly its overwhelming superiority over other powers, and this superiority will probably endure well into the century.

America's preponderance makes attempting to counterbalance US power and achieve multipolarity a daunting affair. While deliberately refraining from counterbalancing alliances with other powers, Russia has tried to use international regimes and institutions as balancing mechanisms. The Russian attempts to constrain the United States, described in some detail here, have not been successful, however. Russia has invariably failed to check US policy through arms control regimes and the UN system. Thus, the external routes to multipolarity are essentially blocked. In the absence of real allies and strong international regimes and institutions, Russia's only effective means to build the preferred multipolar world is to balance against the United States via increased internal mobilization of power. However, Russia still has a long way to go before it can become a great power and global challenger. It is unlikely to regain its great power status over the next several decades and will do so only if it prospers economically.

Washington is apt to view negatively anything that smacks of multipolarity. This basically negative attitude has profound implications for the development of the new strategic triangle, which is supposed to include the United States, Russia, and the EU. In so far as this triangle is conceived as a subsection of a future multipolar world structure, the proponents of US primacy will resist it.

Russian politicians who support the official line about the need for a multipolar world order have broached the idea of an equal triangular relationship between the United States, Russia, and Europe.[107] According to the deputy chairman of the State Duma's foreign affairs committee, an 'equilateral triangle' comprising these three 'centers of force' is an 'indispensable element' of a new geopolitical arrangement.[108] Such propositions are probably intriguing to Russian leaders. For them, Europe is still an important potential partner in the struggle for multipolarity. Ivanov's successor as Russian Foreign Minister, Sergei Lavrov, has argued that the existence of the EU confirms that the world can only be multipolar.[109] Within the EU itself, the French have long pleaded for a common pursuit of a multipolar world.[110] The British, however, reject the multipolarity concept. It would be going too far to say that the common European Security Strategy adopted by the EU leaders in December 2003 is even close to the long-term Russian strategy aimed at eliminating unipolarity and establishing a multipolar world order, but Russia and the EU evidently share a joint interest in promoting a world order based on multilateralism.[111]

A United States pursuing a grand strategy of primacy quite naturally will not encourage the establishment of an equilateral transatlantic triangle. It would mean a step away from unipolarity. As Dombrowski and Ross point out (in Chapter 8 of this volume), primacy's advocates have little interest in fostering a triangular relationship based on equality that would constrain the United States. In fact, the strategy of primacy leaves little ground for any relationships with the United States on an equal basis. Its proponents clearly prefer arrangements in which the United States plays the leading role and other states play only supporting roles.

America's enormous economic and military strength, Russia's continuing weakness, and the active US opposition to multipolarity are not likely to steer Russian leaders away from their vision of a multipolar world. It is the very fact of American unchecked power that sustains Russia's enduring quest for multipolarity. Russia's dissatisfaction with America's high-handed attempts to lead the world also explains in large measure why Russian leaders continue to promote multipolarity. Russia does not want to be a junior partner of the United States. Hence, the Russian grand strategy directed at forming a multipolar world order will probably persist for many years ahead.

The inescapable finding of this study is that the United States and Russia have diametrically opposite approaches to the shaping of the future world order. Behind the US–Russian partnership in combating terrorism lies a fundamental divergence and clash between two strategic visions. The US vision of a durable unipolar order is straightforward and understandable, given the obvious power asymmetries in America's favour, while Russia's multipolar vision has a complex and even contradictory character. On the one hand, Russia is willing to cooperate with the United States on many security issues and seeks to integrate with the US-dominated world economy. On the other hand, Russia attempts to balance against the United States, primarily by pursuing policies to strengthen multilateral mechanisms that might limit America's freedom of action. In combining the dual elements of cooperation and balancing in their foreign policy, Russian leaders are playing a delicate double game. They appear to be determined to continue to play it for years to come.

Notes

1 M. Mastanduno and E. B. Kapstein, 'Realism and State Strategies After the Cold War', in E. B. Kapstein and M. Mastanduno (eds) *Unipolar Politics: Realism and State Strategies After the Cold War*, New York: Columbia University Press, 1999, p. 14
2 The term was introduced in C. Krauthammer, 'The Unipolar Moment', *Foreign Affairs*, 1991, vol. 70, no. 1, p. 24.
3 S. G. Brooks and W. C. Wohlforth, 'American Primacy in Perspective', *Foreign Affairs*, 2002, vol. 81, no. 4, p. 21.
4 M. Mastanduno, 'Preserving the Unipolar Moment: Realist Theories and U.S. Grand Strategy after the Cold War', *International Security*, 1997, vol. 21, no. 4, pp. 60, 63, 86; J. Joffe, 'Defying History and Theory: The United States as the 'Last Remaining Superpower'', in G. J. Ikenberry (ed.) *America Unrivaled: The Future of the Balance of Power*, Ithaca, NY: Cornell University Press, 2002, p. 158.
5 C. Layne, 'The Unipolar Illusion. Why New Great Powers Will Rise' *International Security*, 1993, vol. 17, no. 4, pp. 5, 7–8, 11; K. N. Waltz, 'Structural Realism after the Cold War', in Ikenberry (ed.) *America Unrivaled*, pp. 51–6, 65; C. A. Kupchan, 'Hollow Hegemony or Stable Multipolarity?' in Ikenberry (ed.) *America Unrivaled*, pp. 68–9, 96; C. A. Kupchan, *The End of the American Era: U.S. Foreign Policy and the Geopolitics of the Twenty-first Century*, New York: Vintage Books, 2003, pp. 28–9, 57, 61–2.

6 W. C. Wohlforth, 'The Stability of a Unipolar World', *International Security*, 1999, vol. 24, no. 1, pp. 8–9, 28, 37; W. C. Wohlforth, 'U.S. Strategy in a Unipolar World', in Ikenberry (ed.) *America Unrivaled* pp. 98, 114, 118; C. Dueck, 'New Perspectives on American Grand Strategy: A Review Essay', *International Security*, 2004, vol. 28, no. 4, pp. 199, 204–5, 210–11, 216.

7 C. Krauthammer, 'The Unipolar Moment Revisited', *The National Interest*, 2002–3, no. 70, p. 17.

8 Ibid., p. 8; Wohlforth, 'U.S. Strategy in a Unipolar World', pp. 100, 116; Dueck, 'New Perspectives on American Grand Strategy', p. 198.

9 Wohlforth, 'The Stability of a Unipolar World', p. 8; Wohlforth, 'U.S. Strategy in a Unipolar World', p. 117; Brooks and Wohlforth, 'American Primacy in Perspective', pp. 27, 30; Krauthammer, 'The Unipolar Moment Revisited', pp. 6–7.

10 K. N. Waltz, 'The Emerging Structure of International Politics', *International Security*, 1993, vol. 18, no. 2, p. 77; Waltz, 'Structural Realism after the Cold War', pp. 52, 62.

11 Wohlforth, 'The Stability of a Unipolar World', p. 35; Wohlforth, 'U.S. Strategy in a Unipolar World', p. 100.

12 Joffe, 'Defying History and Theory', pp. 175–6; Krauthammer, 'The Unipolar Moment Revisited', pp. 12–13.

13 'Excerpts from Pentagon's Plan: "Prevent the Re-emergence of a New Rival"', *The New York Times*, 8 March 1992, p. 14.

14 Mastanduno, 'Preserving the Unipolar Moment', pp. 51–2.

15 C. Layne, 'Rethinking American Grand Strategy: Hegemony or Balance of Power in the Twenty-First Century?' *World Policy Journal*, 1998, vol. 15, no. 2, p. 8.

16 B. R. Posen and A. L. Ross, 'Competing Visions for U.S. Grand Strategy', *International Security*, 1996–7, vol. 21, no. 3, pp. 5, 9, 44, 50.

17 *A National Security Strategy of Engagement and Enlargement*, Washington, DC: The White House, 1995, p. 1.

18 W. J. Clinton, 'Remarks . . . to the People of Detroit', 22 October 1996, online.

19 W. J. Clinton, 'Remarks . . . in Freedom House Speech', 6 October 1995, online.

20 J. Joffe, 'Clinton's World: Purpose, Policy, and Weltanschauung', *The Washington Quarterly*, 2001, vol. 24, no. 1, pp. 144, 151.

21 J. E. Nolan, *An Elusive Consensus: Nuclear Weapons and American Security after the Cold War*, Washington, DC: Brookings Institution Press, 1999, pp. 58–9; A. F. Woolf, *U.S. Nuclear Weapons: Changes in Policy and Force Structure*, CRS Report RL 31623, Washington, DC: The Library of Congress, Congressional Research Service, 2004, pp. 1, 4, 13, 18.

22 Poland, Hungary, and the Czech Republic were admitted as NATO members in March 1999.

23 R. D. Asmus, *Opening NATO's Door: How the Alliance Remade Itself for a New Era*, New York: Columbia University Press, 2002, pp. 269–70, 273; J. M. Goldgeier, *Not Whether But When: The U.S. Decision to Enlarge NATO*, Washington, DC: Brookings Institution Press, 1999, pp. 93–4, 173–4.

24 A. C. Lynch, 'The Realism of Russia's Foreign Policy', *Europe-Asia Studies*, 2001, vol. 53, no. 1, pp. 7–8, 20, 23, 25.

25 J. L. Black (ed.) *Russia & Eurasia Documents Annual 1996*, vol. 1: *The Russian Federation*, Gulf Breeze, FL: Academic International Press, 1997, p. 182.

26 T. Ambrosio, 'Russia's Quest for Multipolarity: A Response to US Foreign Policy in the Post-Cold War Era', *European Security*, 2001, vol. 10, no. 1, pp. 53–4; C. Wagnsson, *Russian Political Language and Public Opinion on the West, NATO and Chechnya: Securitisation Theory Reconsidered*, Stockholm: University of Stockholm, Department of Political Science, 2000, pp. 121–2, 131.

27 J. L. Black (ed.) *Russia & Eurasia Documents Annual 1997*, vol. 1: *The Russian Federation*, Gulf Breeze, FL: Academic International Press, 1998, p. 165.

28 'Kontseptsiia natsional'noi bezopasnosti Rossiiskoi Federatsii', 17 December 1997, *Diplomaticheskii vestnik*, 1998, no. 1, online.

29 J. M. Goldgeier and M. McFaul, *Power and Purpose: U.S. Policy toward Russia after the Cold War*, Washington, DC: Brookings Institution Press, 2003, pp. 289, 291, 294–5; M. T. Clark, 'The Clinton Legacy on Ballistic Missile Defense', *Comparative Strategy*, 2000, vol. 19, no. 3, pp. 201, 212–14; S. Kile, 'Nuclear arms control and non-proliferation', in *SIPRI Yearbook 2000: Armaments, Disarmament and International Security*, Oxford: Oxford University Press, 2000, pp. 443–9.

30 A. Shoumikhin, 'Current Russian Perspectives on Arms Control and Ballistic Missile Defense', *Comparative Strategy*, 1999, vol. 18, no. 1, p. 50; Kile, 'Nuclear arms control and non-proliferation', pp. 444, 449–50.

31 R. H. Donaldson and J. L. Nogee, *The Foreign Policy of Russia: Changing Systems, Enduring Interests*, 2nd edn, Amonk, NY: M. E. Sharpe, 2002, pp. 330–1; J. L. Black, *Vladimir Putin and the New World Order: Looking East, Looking West?* Lanham, MD: Rowman & Littlefield Publishers, 2004, p. 69.

32 V. V. Putin, 'Rossiia na rubezhe tysiacheletii', *Nezavisimaia gazeta*, 30 December 1999, online.

33 V. V. Putin, 'Vystuplenie na zasedanii Soveta Bezopasnosti', 31 December 1999, online.

34 'Kontseptsiia natsional'noi bezopasnosti Rossiiskoi Federatsii', 10 January 2000, online.

35 Ibid.

36 J. L. Black (ed.) *Russia & Eurasia Documents Annual 2000*, vol. 1: *The Russian Federation*, Gulf Breeze, FL: Academic International Press, 2001, p. 191.

37 'Kontseptsiia vneshnei politiki Rossiiskoi Federatsii', 28 June 2000, online.

38 S. J. Blank, *Threats to Russian Security: The View from Moscow*, Carlisle, PA: U.S. Army War College, Strategic Studies Institute, 2000, pp. 1, 12–13, 19.

39 'Kontseptsiia natsional'noi bezopasnosti Rossiiskoi Federatsii' (2000 version).

40 'Kontseptsiia vneshnei politiki Rossiiskoi Federatsii.'

41 I. S. Ivanov, 'Stat'ia . . . opublikovana v zhurnale "Internationale Politik". . .', *Informatsionnyi biulleten'*, 24 October 2000, online.

42 I. S. Ivanov, 'Stenogramma press-konferentsii. . .', 10 July 2000, *Informatsionnyi biulleten'*, 11 July 2000, online.

43 A. F. Woolf, *National Missile Defense: Russia's Reaction*, CRS Report RL30967, Washington, DC: The Library of Congress, Congressional Research Service, 2002, pp. 7, 9; A. Shoumikhin, 'Evolving Russian Perspectives on Missile Defense: The Emerging Accommodation', *Comparative Strategy*, 2002, vol. 21, no. 4, p. 317; Black, *Vladimir Putin and the New World Order*, pp. 32, 50, 66, 70, 193.

44 Black, *Vladimir Putin and the New World Order*, pp. 33–4, 58, 64, 68–9, 94, 96, 101.

45 V. V. Putin, 'Vystuplenie na zasedanii Gosudarstvennoi Dumy. . .', 14 April 2000, online.

46 B. Graham, *Hit to Kill: The New Battle Over Shielding America From Missile Attack*, New York: Public Affairs, 2001, pp. 115–20.

47 On the European scepticism towards the US NMD plans, see C. S. Gray, 'European Perspectives on U.S. Ballistic Missile Defense', *Comparative Strategy*, 2002, vol. 21, no. 4, pp. 279–310; W. Q. Bowen, 'Missile Defence and the Transatlantic Security Relationship', *International Affairs*, 2002, vol. 77, no. 3, pp. 485–507.

48 D. Lynch, 'Russia's Strategic Partnership with Europe', *The Washington Quarterly*, 2004, vol. 27, no. 2, p. 103.

49 B. Nygren, 'Russia and Europe, or Russia in Europe?' in Y. Fedorov and B. Nygren (eds) *Russia and Europe: Putin's Foreign Policy*, Acta B23, Stockholm: Swedish National Defence College, Department of Security and Strategic Studies, 2002, pp. 25–6.

50 'Joint Statement, EU–Russia Summit', 29 May 2000, online.
51 J. Chirac, 'Conférence de presse. . .', 30 October 2000, online.
52 V. V. Putin, 'Interv'iu . . . gazete "Vel't am Zonntag" (FRG)', *Informatsionnyi biulleten'*, 14 June 2000, online.
53 V. V. Putin, 'Interv'iu kanadskim telekompaniiam. . .', 14 December 2000, online.
54 I. H. Daalder and J. M. Lindsay, *America Unbound: The Bush Revolution in Foreign Policy*, Washington, DC: Brookings Institution Press, 2003, p. 40. See also R. Jervis, 'Understanding the Bush Doctrine', *Political Science Quarterly*, 2002, vol. 117, no. 3, pp. 365–88; S. R. Schwenninger, 'Revamping American Grand Strategy', *World Policy Journal*, 2003, vol. 20, no. 3, pp. 25–44.
55 G. W. Bush, 'A Distinctly American Internationalism', 19 November 1999, online.
56 P. Wolfowitz, 'Remembering the Future', *The National Interest*, 2000, no. 59, p. 36.
57 C. Rice, 'Promoting the National Interest', *Foreign Affairs*, 2000, vol. 79, no. 1, pp. 47, 49, 54, 55.
58 'Entretien avec Condoleezza Rice', *Politique internationale*, 2000–1, no. 90, p. 30.
59 G. W. Bush, 'A Period of Consequences', 23 September 1999, online.
60 Goldgeier and McFaul, *Power and Purpose*, p. 306.
61 'Republican Party Platform 2000', online.
62 G. W. Bush, 'New Leadership on National Security', 23 May 2000, online.
63 'Presidential Election Forum: The Candidates on Arms Control', *Arms Control Today*, 2000, vol. 30, no. 7, p. 3.
64 Black, *Vladimir Putin and the New World Order*, pp. 109–10, 114–15, 131, 140–1, 206, 211–12; Shoumikhin, 'Evolving Russian Perspectives on Missile Defense', pp. 321–4.
65 G. W. Bush, 'Remarks . . . to Students and Faculty at National Defense University', 1 May 2001, online.
66 G. W. Bush, 'Press Conference. . .', 15 June 2001, online.
67 G. W. Bush, 'Remarks . . . in Address to Faculty and Students of Warsaw University', 15 June 2001, online. At NATO's Prague summit meeting in November 2002, seven countries were invited to apply for NATO membership (they became members in March 2004).
68 C. Rice, 'Press Briefing. . .', 16 June 2001, online.
69 V. V. Putin, 'Beseda s rukovoditeliami predstavitel'stv vedushchikh amerikanskikh SMI', 18 June 2001, online.
70 B. Nygren, 'Continuity and Change in Russia's Foreign Policy in Putin's First Presidential Term', in P. Forsström and E. Mikkola (eds) *Russian Military Policy and Strategy*, series 2, no. 27, Helsinki: National Defence College, Department of Strategic and Defence Studies, 2004, pp. 30–2.
71 A. F. Woolf, *Nuclear Arms Control: The US–Russian Agenda*, CRS Issue Brief IB98030, Washington, DC: The Library of Congress, Congressional Research Service, 2002, pp. 15–16; D. E. Sanger and P. E. Tyler, 'Officials Recount Road to Deadlock Over Missile Talks', *The New York Times*, 13 December 2001, pp. A1, A18.
72 G. W. Bush, 'President Discusses National Missile Defense', 13 December 2001, online.
73 V. V. Putin, 'Zaiavlenie. . .', 13 December 2001, online.
74 UN General Assembly resolution no. 56/24A, 29 November 2001, online.
75 C. A. Wallander, 'Russia's Strategic Priorities', *Arms Control Today*, 2002, vol. 32, no. 1, p. 4; P. C. Bleek, 'U.S. and Russia at Odds Over Strategic Reductions Agreement', *Arms Control Today*, 2002, vol. 32, no. 4, p. 22.
76 'Text of Strategic Offensive Reductions Treaty', 24 May 2002, online.
77 J. D. Crouch, 'Special Briefing on the Nuclear Posture Review', 9 January 2002, online.
78 'Nuclear Posture Review [Excerpts]', 31 December 2001, online.
79 D. H. Rumsfeld, *Annual Report to the President and the Congress*, Washington, DC: US Department of Defense, 2002, p. 89.

80 'Nuclear Posture Review [Excerpts].'
81 Rumsfeld, *Annual Report to the President and the Congress*, pp. 17–18, 90.
82 'Nuclear Posture Review [Excerpts].'
83 *The National Security Strategy of the United States of America*, Washington, DC: The White House, 2002, p. 1.
84 Ibid.
85 Ibid., pp. 29–30.
86 Ibid., pp. 26–7.
87 D. Lynch, 'Russia Faces Europe', *Chaillot Papers*, no. 60, Paris: European Union, Institute for Security Studies, 2003, p. 9; B. Lo, *Vladimir Putin and the Evolution of Russian Foreign Policy*, Oxford: Blackwell Publishing, 2003, p. 116.
88 I. S. Ivanov, *The New Russian Diplomacy*, Washington, DC: The Nixon Center and Brookings Institution Press, 2002, p. 43.
89 Ibid., pp. 39, 41–2.
90 Ibid., pp. 45, 47, 79.
91 Ibid., p. 78.
92 Ibid., pp. 48, 71.
93 C. Wagnsson, 'Russia's Choice: Preserve the Status Quo', in J. Hallenberg and H. Karlsson (eds) *The Iraq War: European Perspectives on Politics, Strategy and Operations*, London and New York: Routledge, 2005, p. 71. See also M. M. Katz, 'Playing the Angles: Russian Diplomacy Before and During the War in Iraq', *Middle East Policy*, 2003, vol. 10, no. 3, pp. 43–4.
94 On the failure of Russia's attempt to restrain the United States in the Kosovo conflict, see I. H. Daalder and M. E. O'Hanlon, *Winning Ugly: NATO's War to Save Kosovo*, Washington, DC: Brookings Institution Press, 2000, pp. 36, 44, 102, 218.
95 V. V. Putin, 'Interv'iu frantsuzskoi telekompanii "Frans-3"', 9 February 2003, online.
96 C. Rice, 'Remarks. . .', 26 June 2003, online.
97 I. S. Ivanov, 'Vystuplenie . . . v MGIMO(U). . .', 1 September 2003, *Informatsionnyi biulleten'*, 1 September 2003, online; I. S. Ivanov, 'Stat'ia . . . opublikovannaia v zhurnale "Mezhdunarodnaia zhizn". . .', *Informatsionnyi biulleten'*, 22 October 2003, online.
98 C. L. Powell, 'Interview on The Charlie Rose Show', 22 September 2003, online.
99 V. V. Putin, 'Interv'iu telekanalu "Al'-Dzhazira"', 16 October 2003, online.
100 V. V. Putin, 'Otvety na voprosy uchastnikov Delovogo sammita ATES', 19 October 2003, online.
101 G. W. Bush, 'Interview of the President by Trevor Kavanagh of "The Sun"', 14 November 2003, online.
102 V. V. Putin, 'Interv'iu kitaiskim gazetam. . .', 13 October 2004, online.
103 See Bertil Nygren's account of the Ukrainian election crisis in Chapter 7 of this volume.
104 G. W. Bush, 'Roundtable Interview of the President with European Print Media', 18 February 2005, online.
105 V. V. Putin, 'Interv'iu "Radio Slovensko" i slovatskoi telekompanii STV', 22 February 2005, online.
106 E. M. Primakov, *Mir posle 11 sentiabria*, Moscow: Izdatel'stvo 'Mysl', 2002, p. 189.
107 M. A. Smith, *The Russia–USA Relationship*, Russian Series 04/12, Camberley, Surrey: Defence Academy of the United Kingdom, Conflict Studies Research Centre, 2004, pp. 4–5.
108 N. A. Narochnitskaia, 'Russia in the New Geopolitical Context (Part II)', 10 May 2004, online.
109 S. V. Lavrov, 'Stenogramma interv'iu . . . nemetskoi gazete "Khandel'sblatt"', 28 December 2004, online.
110 See P. H. Gordon, 'The French Position', *The National Interest*, 2000, no. 61, pp. 57–65.
111 *A Secure Europe in a Better World: European Security Strategy*, Paris: The European Union Institute for Security Studies, 2003, p. 14.

11

CONCLUSIONS

Jan Hallenberg and Håkan Karlsson

Introduction

In this concluding chapter, we take stock of factors that further and inhibit the formation of what we have termed a new strategic triangle in the greater transatlantic region. Recent developments make it appropriate to start with circumstances pertaining to the European Union. As this book project is being concluded, the EU is undergoing what is conventionally termed a crisis because the proposed Treaty on a European Constitution, designed – among other things – to enhance the ability of the Union to act coherently in international affairs, has been rejected in referenda in France and the Netherlands. It is the assumption in this chapter that even though the constitutional treaty has been at least temporarily rejected, this does not prevent the EU from continuing to be an important actor in the greater transatlantic region. We regard the extent to which the rejection of the constitutional treaty will stop or slow the building of what we in this book call the actorness of the EU as an empirical question.

The actorness of the European Union

It is a premise in this book that if the conditions for the existence of the strategic triangle are to be met, then there has to exist an EU that has both external and internal legitimacy. There can be no triangle if the other two parties – Russian and the United States – do not accept the Union as an actor. Nor can there be any triangle if the Union itself is unable to act. This section deals with the issue of internal legitimacy, covering the efforts within the EU to achieve actorness.

In Chapter 2 of this book Magnus Ekengren and Kjell Engelbrekt analyse the internal aspects of EU actorness after the expansion of the Union to include 25 members in 2004. In their analysis they employ capacity and cohesiveness as central concepts signifying actorness. By the first, they mean an aggregate of the resources that an actor can bring to bear in a given situation. The term capacity is deliberately chosen instead of capability, since the former implies a measure of aggregate ability that the latter lacks. The authors conclude that a Union with 25 members has a greater capacity than does a Union with only 15 members. By definition, this means greater actorness.

There are, to be sure, also complications concerning actorness that may be greater for a Union if it consists of 25 members rather than 15. Some of these complications are, in the analysis in Chapter 2, related to the concept of cohesiveness. This concept has to do with similarities of perceptions in terms of values, threats, identities and interests. It also includes the tendency for an actor to 'stick together' in threatening situations in global politics, a tendency that has to be there at least to some extent if an entity is to be regarded as an international actor. With regard to the EU's cohesiveness, the authors find two complications arising from the entry of 10 new members in 2004. The first is that the number of countries entering the Union at the same time is greater than has ever been the case in the past. To put it simply, if it was difficult to take decisions at 15, it must be even more difficult to take decisions at 25. The second complication for EU cohesiveness is that the Union of 25 contains a group of member states that are vastly more diverse than has ever been the case before. This is also bound to make it more difficult to come to decisions on the security issues that mainly interest us here.

While the effects on EU actorness of the latest enlargement of the Union thus are complex, there is – as Arita Eriksson shows in Chapter 3 – another development going on in the Union which is bound to affect its actorness in a decidedly positive way. This is the build-up of a more or less independent military capability in the EU. This process started in 1999, after the new Labour Government in Great Britain in 1997 had dropped its insistence that all common European defence capabilities that could be employed in an alliance context had to be kept within NATO. There are strongly conflicting assessments of what this development means for the transatlantic security system. One interpretation, which is the one supported by Arita Eriksson, is that what has been started is a process – the Europeanization of national defence policies – that over time is bound to lead to a greater role for the EU in military matters in Europe, to the detriment of NATO. Another interpretation, often expressed by long-time experts on transatlantic security issues, is that whatever the EU is up to in matters of security and defence, it is insignificant in comparison to NATO. One common expression of this view is that as long as the EU has 100 military planning officers, while NATO has 15,000, there is no question where the anchor of transatlantic security will continue to be, at least for the medium-term future. Moreover, several EU members, most notably Great Britain, still insist that the EU's defence policy institutions should be closely tied to NATO and thus complement the US-led alliance, not compete with it.

Fredrik Bynander in Chapter 4 focuses on one fascinating aspect of the uncertainty regarding what organization will be the anchor of European security in the future. He studies how two new members of both NATO and the EU – Poland and the Czech Republic handle the inevitable cross-pressures that are bound to exist for a new member state in two organizations with at least some competing pretences to be the fulcrum of European security. As Bynander shows, Poland in particular has a strong affection for the United States, coupled with a deep mistrust towards the ability of some European powers to honour their commitments when the security of Poland is threatened. Warsaw must thus be said to have entered both organizations with a very strong preference for NATO when it comes to security and defence policies. Bynander's analysis shows that for this commitment to NATO to change, Poland would have to be exposed to both an American disengagement from European security affairs that goes much further than has been the case after 11 September, as well as the development of a more cohesive EU in military affairs. The conclusion is roughly the same for the Czech Republic, even though the attachment of that country to NATO and the US appears somewhat weaker than in the case of Poland.

In the final chapter of our section on the EU, Adrian Hyde-Price covers the circumstances under which France and Great Britain might consider using the military forces in what in the literature has been called strategic coercion in an EU context, rather than in a purely national one, or a NATO context. He finds it very unlikely that France and Great Britain may use this military power in a strictly EU context at least during the next decade. It is much more likely, however, that these two countries may play a leading role in constructing 'coalitions of the willing' where like-minded countries might intervene militarily in security situations deemed threatening. Such 'coalitions of the willing' may sometimes be formed under the auspices of NATO, sometimes perhaps in an EU setting, as has already happened with the mission led by France into the Democratic Republic of Congo in 2003.

The picture that thus emerges from the analyses in this book that bear upon the actorness of the EU is a complex one. On the positive side there are at least three factors indicating an important and growing role for the Union in the strategic triangle. First is the very fact of enlargement itself from 15 to 25 members. There can be no doubt that this increases the capacity of the Union to undertake external action, whether in the context of the strategic triangle or more broadly. Second, the slow growth in military capabilities that the EU is able to mobilize also serves to strengthen the Union as an international actor. Third, as analysed in Chapter 9, the very fact that 12 members of the EU now have the same currency increases both the potential capacity – at the very least of the eurozone – to act, and it nullifies the previous ability of the United States to use the strength of the US dollar to pressure the members of the eurozone to change their policies.

On the negative side, enlargement makes the cohesiveness of the Union more problematic. To this can be added – at least temporarily – the uncertainties created by the fact that France and the Netherlands voted to reject the Treaty on a European Constitution in successive referenda. Thirdly, it is shown in Chapter 4 that at least one of the new members of the EU, a member with potential ability to make its voice heard, Poland, is at least over the medium term very likely to anchor its security and defence in NATO rather than in the EU. Fourthly, the fact that France and Great Britain are very unlikely to let the EU dispose of their respective military forces for strategic coercion any time soon means that there will be clear limits to the military power of EU at least over the medium term.

Still, the analysis in this book has also shown, as is detailed later in this chapter, that on some issues and under some circumstances the EU has already played the role of a legitimate actor in the strategic triangle. There can, in our estimation, be no question that the EU sometimes is a strong actor in transatlantic security affairs.

The EU is already, as shown in Chapter 9, a very strong actor in some economic issues. The question is whether this economic actor capability will spread into ever more issues with relevance for transatlantic security. It seems to us that some of the most important developments in this field, such as the creation of the European Defence Agency (EDA) are bound to increase the actorness of the Union. Even if developments in the fields where the EDA is active, such as the development of defence capabilities and weapons acquisition, are slow, it seems to us that there is only one direction in which this development is likely to go: the creation of ever more cooperation among members of the EU on these issues. Barring the extremely unlikely development that the Union falters fundamentally as a result of disagreements over the proposed constitution, or over the next steps in the enlargement of the EU, it seems to us that an analysis of the greater transatlantic region in 2015 will find an EU that is at least as important an actor as it is in 2005.

Russia in the strategic triangle

The analysis in this book has shown that there are some similarities between Russia and the EU with respect to the roles that they want to play in the new strategic triangle. In developing their security strategies, Russia and the EU are in fact gradually becoming more alike, even though major differences persist in the framing of threats and the use of force. As Charlotte Wagnsson puts it in Chapter 6, 'the EU's process of strengthening its actorness in the sphere of "not-so-soft security", albeit slow, evolves in tandem with Russia steadily pursuing a reverse path, from "hard" to "soft" security'. In other words, both actors are undergoing similar processes of broadening their approaches, albeit starting from opposite sides of the 'hard-to-soft' security continuum.

Russia, Charlotte Wagnsson's analysis brings out, also clearly manifests ambivalence in conducting its relations with the EU. As indicated in the quote from Deputy Russian Foreign Minister Alexei Meshkov there appears to be a strong Russian tendency to view nation-states as still the most important actors in the greater transatlantic region. This tendency creates a constant problem in a region where a non-state actor – the European Union – has been playing an ever more important role in security policy for many years. There are – as highlighted in Chapters 6 and 9 in this volume – several examples of strategies on the part of each of these actors towards the other, and of important agreements directly between the two. At the same time, the uncertainty created by the ambivalence in the Russian approach to the EU seems to create obstacles in the way of the development of ever closer ties between the two in the strategic triangle. As studied in Chapter 9, economic relations are to some extent an exception to this rule, as the EU is by far Russia's most important international trading partner. Still, even in this area, Moscow takes care to conclude bilateral deals with individual members of the Union that it regards as crucial, such as Germany.

Russian relations with the United States can also be characterized by the term ambivalence. On the one hand, after the terrorist attacks on New York and

Washington on 11 September 2001, Russian President Vladimir Putin clearly showed his solidarity with his US counterpart George W. Bush and made obvious that Russia saw the two countries as being allies in the war on terror. On the other hand, as shown by Håkan Karlsson in Chapter 10, there is a 'clash of strategic visions' between the two countries. To quote Chapter 10, 'the United States and Russia have diametrically opposite approaches to the shaping of the future world order.' It is thus apparent that the future relations between Moscow and Washington at least over the medium term will continue to be at least two-sided. Cooperation in the 'war on terror' is very likely to continue but Russia is at the same time determined to try to shape an international order not dominated by the United States, a world order that is multipolar rather than unipolar.

There is a clear contrast in the economic sphere between EU–Russian relations, on the one hand, and US–Russian relations, on the other. In the case of the EU and Russia, economic relations have developed so much that the two parties are clearly mutually dependent – even if Russia is more dependent on the EU than the other way around. No such economic interdependence exists in the case of the United States and Russia. At the risk of overstating the importance of economic ties for broader security relations, we believe that the economic ties between Moscow and Brussels are so strong that they are bound to influence positively the solution, or at least the handling, of disagreements on other issues in the security sphere. There is no such anchor in relations between Moscow and Washington. It is thus possible to imagine a future development in US–Russian relations in which the solidarity in the war on terror subsides, whereas the rivalry inherent in what Håkan Karlsson calls clashing strategic visions comes to the fore. It is very difficult, to put it mildly, to envisage a future in which the United States and the EU can similarly enter a situation of strife between the two, for many reasons, not least the immensely strong and broad economic ties between them that are detailed in Chapter 9 in this volume.

The United States in the strategic triangle

One of the starting-points of this book is that the United States is the only actor of the three that we have chosen to study that has the choice of whether it wants to be an actor in Europe or not. Peter Dombrowski and Andrew L. Ross in Chapter 8 in this volume point out that the focus of US security policy during the past four years has not been on Europe, but rather on the Middle East and Central Asia. This change of focus indicates that the EU and Russia have become less important to the United States. Whether the United States still takes the other two into account when planning and pursuing security policy depends to a great extent on what grand strategy US policy makers choose to follow. A debate about various grand strategy options is going on in the United States This debate has been presented and discussed previously in several articles and books. It has been common to distinguish between a neo-isolationist option, an option called selective engagement, a third option called liberal internationalism and a fourth option called primacy. The distinctions between these options are spelt out in Chapter 8. Dombrowski and Ross are of the opinion, however, that what has happened in both the debate on US global policy in the past few years, as well as to some extent in its practice, means that it is now necessary to add a fifth vision of America's role in the world: that of empire. The term empire in this context is not used in terms of some type of leftist critique against 'imperialist' US policies, but is rather an affirmation of a role that the United States, in the eyes of some, ought to be happy to play.

In the perceptive analysis of Dombrowski and Ross it is really only when Washington pursues policies that correspond to the grand strategy of liberal internationalism that a strategic triangle in the greater transatlantic region is a realistic prospect, if not yet currently a reality. In so far as the triangle presupposes shared societal values, it would be in jeopardy even under liberal internationalism. The current Russian leadership does not seem to share the standard values of American society fully. From the US point of view, the Russia of today is not a state that is sufficiently liberal, in the economic as well as the political sense of the term, to be really integrated with the other two actors in the emerging triangle to the extent necessary for there to be a strategic triangle in the full sense of that conception. A President with a political vision corresponding to liberal internationalism would, however, in the view of Dombrowski and Ross, be strongly inclined to pursue a strategy in cooperation with the EU that made it a common goal to induce Russia to change in a liberal direction, thus creating circumstances under which a truly functioning strategic triangle might emerge in the greater transatlantic region in the foreseeable future.

We now turn to the possible implications for the new strategic triangle of the grand strategy adopted by the Bush Administration. To what extent has the United States under President George W. Bush pursued policies taking the triangular context highlighted in this book into serious consideration? As noted in Chapters 8 and 10, the Bush Administration has chosen to follow a grand strategy of primacy. A logical corollary of this choice is a reluctance to promote the creation of a transatlantic strategic triangle. According to Dombrowski and Ross, there is little incentive in primacy to construct triangles or any other multilateral arrangements that constrain the United States. As they make clear, during his first term President Bush cannot be said to have pursued policies that to any great extent took triangular relations into consideration. Instead, the President explicitly played upon divergences among EU member states regarding the Iraq War, thus effectively working to deny the EU any role in this conflict. The fact that Russia explicitly sided with two large members of the EU – that is France and Germany – against the US in the run-up to the Iraq War also served to make any efforts by the EU to pursue a consistent policy more difficult. After his re-election, President Bush has, however, shown some signs that he is willing to take the EU into greater consideration when pursuing policies regarding the greater transatlantic region. This wish was notably manifested during the President's visit to Brussels and the EU in February 2005.

The question is whether the visit by President Bush to Brussels in early 2005 is just a straw in the wind, or an indication of a more substantial shift of US policy regarding the EU. Another question, a more long-term one, is what policy a Democratic President taking office in January 2009 would pursue in relation to the two other actors in the strategic triangle. Dombrowski and Ross regard it as probable that John Kerry, had he won in 2004, would have pursued a more multilateralist foreign policy than will President Bush. If a Democrat takes the oath of office on 20 January 2009, it appears likely that he or she would also be more inclined towards multilateralism than President Bush has been. A larger element of multilateralism in US policy is one precondition for a more strongly functioning strategic triangle.

The strategic triangle in the greater transatlantic region and beyond

This book is to a large extent centred on the question of to what extent, and under what circumstances, the EU can be regarded as an independent actor in transatlantic security policy. As already mentioned, there are two aspects to this question. The first has to do with the domestic prerequisite of EU actorness – internal legitimacy –and the second with the international precondition – external legitimacy.

Concerning internal legitimacy we strongly believe that despite the fact that the proposed Treaty on a European Constitution has been rejected in two member states in the spring of 2005, the EU is apt to continue to be regarded by the citizens of the 25 member states as a legitimate actor on their behalf on at least some issues of relevance for security policy. Most clearly, we believe that this will continue to be the case concerning economic issues, as analysed in Chapter 9 in this volume. There is no reason to believe that the events of 2005 have made the EU a less potent actor in terms of trade and monetary policy than it was before those events. This very fact alone means to us that the Union does have relevance for security affairs in the greater transatlantic region currently, and that it will continue to have such relevance at the very least over the medium-term future.

Indeed, we believe that the Union is not only internally legitimate in economic affairs in the greater transatlantic region, the other two actors in the strategic triangle also grant it external legitimacy on many economic issues by accepting it as an independent actor. Perhaps one can detect some Russian strategies to play member states off against the Union – such as in terms of the delivery of oil and natural gas to some important EU members – but this cannot stop the fact that Moscow on many economic issues simply has to deal directly with Brussels.

In many economic issues, all three actors thus acknowledge each other already. Still, the fact that Russia is such a marginal player in most economic fields – particularly if we compare it to the other two actors in the strategic triangle who are genuine giants in this arena – means that in economic issues there are only some intimations of what we would regard as a strategic triangle in action, where all three parties take each other into account when formulating economic policies for the greater transatlantic region. The one issue where such interaction has already occurred to some extent concerns the process regarding the Russian application for membership in the World Trade Organization (WTO). It seems logical to infer that one of the strategies that both the United States and the EU pursue in their actions on this important issue of political economy is that Russian membership of the WTO would be likely to serve at least two purposes of interest for both Washington and Brussels. The first is that Russian membership would simplify trade among the parties, which would be very likely to lead to increased trade among them, particularly over time. The second is that if trade does increase, then this – in the calculations of both Washington and Brussels – is apt to improve Russia's adherence to Western principles of the respect for law and for contracts. This in turn may, following the same logic, spill over into domestic politics in Russia and serve to strengthen democratic rights that have in some respects been curtailed during the years after President Putin came to power in 2000.

If there is thus a nascent strategic triangle in the economic realm, there have been a few other occasions in recent years when the relations among the three actors under study here seem to have been at least partly governed by what we might call triangular logic. The most recent case of triangular politics, and also one of the most illustrative, is the complex political and diplomatic process in which the EU and the United States cooperated in support of the eventually winning candidate Viktor Yushchenko in the presidential elections in the Ukraine in late 2004, jointly opposing Russian preferences for the other candidate, Viktor Yanukovich. This process, analysed by Bertil Nygren in Chapter 7, has several interesting aspects relevant to this book. First, the leadership in Washington on an issue with clear implications for European security explicitly chose to cooperate with the EU, thus rendering the latter external legitimacy on an issue that may be important for other events in that part of Europe in the future. Second, on this issue Washington and Brussels acted on ideational grounds, in protesting against a political process that they initially believed to be a perversion of democracy, where candidate Yanukovich, on very dubious grounds, was first declared the winner of the election. In this they united against a Russian leadership whose actions were based on a combination of geopolitical and economic considerations.

As pointed out in Chapter 8 in this volume, the new strategic triangle in the greater transatlantic region is conceived in a different manner than the old US–Soviet–Chinese triangle in the 1970s and 1980s. The relationships in the previous triangle were informed by traditional geopolitical considerations, in which a balance of power, measured primarily in terms of strategic nuclear arms, was the overriding element. The logic underlying the new strategic triangle is, as Dombrowski and Ross write, not as classically geopolitical. This is not to deny that geopolitical concerns may play a significant role in the new triangle as well. It is, rather, to suggest that the relations among the three parties depend at least as much on ideational and material (i.e. economic) factors. The actions of the United States, the EU and Russia during the Ukrainian election crisis tend to support this proposition.

At the same time, the case of the tug of war over the Ukraine also reminds us that interaction in the new strategic triangle is not necessarily only about partnerships and common interests among all three actors. It may involve temporary alignments of two against one faintly reminiscent of old-time great power games. On the

Ukrainian election issue, Russia to its surprise faced a united front of the United States and the EU. Only a few years earlier, Russia tried to align itself with the EU against the United States on the issue of preserving the ABM Treaty. Although EU–Russian relations are currently under strain for several reasons, Russian leaders continue to view the EU as contributing to their pursuit of a multipolar world without US domination.

In a second case of what is here termed triangular politics, the United States has also at least nominally acknowledged the role of the other two parties in the Middle East, another area bordering the greater transatlantic region. Since 2002, the peace process in that region has at least to some extent been undertaken under the umbrella of the Road Map, a plan for peace in steps underwritten by the 'quartet' of the United States, Russia, the EU and the UN. The very fact that the United States has accepted the inclusion of the other two parties in the strategic triangle in this process must be regarded as an acknowledgment that both Moscow and Brussels are regarded as legitimate interlocutors to Washington on the issue of peace between Israelis and Palestinians.

The two clearest examples of triangular politics on security issues with relevance for the greater transatlantic region have thus occurred under a President – George W. Bush – whose policies have been widely characterized, including by Dombrowski and Ross in this volume, as containing a large dose of unilateralism, as well as corresponding to the grand strategy of preserving US primacy in the world. The policies of the US President in office since 2001 have, on this analysis, not been conducive to the type of multilateral considerations that are necessary for the strategic triangle to exist in practical politics, at least if, by the new strategic triangle, we intend to denote only a relationship among the three parties that are based on 'shared values and compatible institutions', as Dombrowski and Ross put it in Chapter 8 in this volume. Nevertheless, there have been at least two clear examples where what we term triangular politics has clearly taken place in recent years.

There are two important questions that should be posed and tentatively answered here regarding the future of the United States as an actor in our putative new strategic triangle. The most immediate question concerns whether or not the second Bush Administration after the President's re-election in 2004 is more prone to multilateralism, perhaps even willing to follow a slightly modified grand strategy containing more elements of what Dombrowski and Ross term liberal internationalism than was the case during the President's first four years in office. In the summer of 2005, it is not possible to draw any definite conclusions on this point. If one wants to believe in some of the rhetoric, as well as some of the actions, emanating from Washington after January 2005, then there is some room for hope for those who wish for a more multilaterally inclined United States administration pursuing policies that are more liberally internationalist than before. The President's second inauguration speech paid homage to the role of ideational forces in today's world in supporting the spread of democracy, a process that the President stated should be based on internal developments and that could and should not be imposed from outside.

A second hopeful development from this perspective was the President's visit to Brussels in February 2005, in which he hailed the role of the EU as an important partner of the United States. It remains to be seen how much of that statement was mere rhetoric, and how much of it may translate into policies that take the EU's interests into account. A third positive development from this perspective is that the new Secretary of State – Condoleezza Rice – has taken control of US diplomacy after succeeding Colin Powell. While Powell in office represented a more multi-lateralist outlook, Secretary Rice clearly has the President's ear and thus has much greater leeway in conducting diplomacy, as well as more direct influence on the President, than her predecessor had. There has been at least one concrete change of position as a result of this that indicates a greater US acceptance of multilateralism during the second Bush Administration than during the first. This concerns the fact that before 2005, the United States consistently vetoed all attempts to use the International Criminal Court (ICC) in cases where crimes against human rights are suspected, in addition to pursuing bilateral deals with many states in which the other party acknowledged that US citizens would not be party to trials by the ICC. The US change of position came in the first half of 2005 on the issue of the possible prosecution of some suspected perpetrators of crimes against human rights by people in the region of Darfur in Sudan. Whereas before the United States had consistently resisted involving the ICC in international conflicts, on this occasion the US representative on the UN Security Council abstained, thus permitting a majority on the Council to decide to involve the international court. The role of the ICC has been one prominent bone of contention between the United States and the EU in recent years, and the US abstention on the Security Council vote at the very least indicates that Secretary Rice is prepared to listen more to the concerns of the EU, among others, on questions of multilateralism.

The more long-range question regarding the role of the United States in the future in the new strategic triangle is of course what happens when a new President succeeds George W. Bush in January 2009. In a world of terrorism and war in Iraq and Afghanistan, it is not easy to try to look into the future of international politics, and it is not any easier to reflect upon how such changes may influence the notoriously difficult to predict US electorate. Still, it is reasonable to assume that barring any major terror attacks on the US homeland, and surmising that developments in Iraq are at best likely to continue to be very unstable and thus problematic for the Bush Administration, a strong Democratic candidate for President would have a very good chance of getting elected. As also stated in Chapter 8, it is much more likely that such a candidate would pursue multilateralist policies that could be classified as at least resembling liberal internationalism than would be the case if another Republican were elected. If a Democrat is thus elected President in 2009, we believe that this would increase the chances that relations among the three parties in the new strategic triangle would be more characterized by triangular considerations than has been the case during recent years.

For the strategic triangle to become even more apt as a concept by which to understand relations among the United States, Russia and the EU, Russia would also need to develop in a direction in which democracy to a greater extent permeates the Russian polity than has been the case in recent years. As this book has shown, there are developments that point in this positive direction in Russian politics, as well as other developments that point in the opposing direction.

In conclusion, we believe that we have shown in this book that the metaphor of the new strategic triangle has helped us better understand relations in security policy among the United States, Russia and the EU. It is not the case that all three parties in recent years have consistently taken each other into account when formulating their security policies on issues that are pertinent to this area of the world. Still, we have been able to document some cases on which this has indeed occurred. If we return to study changing transatlantic security relations in 2015, the strategic triangle may perhaps prove to be an even more apt device for understanding relations among the three actors that we have chosen to highlight here. For this to be true to any more developed extent, however, each of the three actors will need to change. The United States will need to pursue a global strategy that is more clearly multilateralist and contains more elements of liberal internationalism than has been the case in recent years. Russia will need to become a member of the WTO, continue to develop its market economy as well as to develop into a more true liberal democracy. As for the EU, it will need to develop more internal legitimacy, including a stronger ability to take and implement decisions in security policy, as well as to become more legitimate in the views of the other two parties in the triangle. The likelihood that each of these three broad developments will indeed occur over the coming ten years is not something that can be determined by the scholars who wrote this book at the present time. It is our hope, however, that we have given our readers a better basis on which they can come to their own conclusions regarding the ways in which security relations in the greater transatlantic region will develop in the future.

REFERENCES

Adomeit, H., 'Russia, Europe and "Euroatlanticism": Triangular Relationships in Transition', paper presented at Moscow Carnegie Centre, 27 October 2003.

Agrell, W., *Fred och Fruktan Sveriges säkerhetspolitiska historia 1918–2000*, Lund: Historiska Media, 2000.

Albert, M., Jacobson, D., Lapid, Y. (eds), *Identities, Borders, Orders – Rethinking International Relations Theory*, Minneapolis, MN: University of Minnesota Press, 2001.

Albright, M., 'The Right Balance Will Secure NATO's Future', *Financial Times*, 7 December 1998.

Allison, G.T., *Essence of Decision*, Boston, MA: Little, Brown, 1971.

Ambrosio, T., 'Russia's Quest for Multipolarity: A Response to US Foreign Policy in the Post-Cold War Era', *European Security*, 2001, vol. 10, no. 2, 45–67.

Andrews, D. M., 'The United States and Its Atlantic Partners: The Evolution of American Grand Strategy', *Cambridge Review of International Affairs*, October 2004, vol. 17 no. 3, 421–36.

Art, R.J., 'Geopolitics Updated: The Strategy of Selective Engagement', *International Security*, 1998/1999, vol. 23, no. 3, 79–113.

—— *A Grand Strategy for America*, Ithaca, NY and London: Cornell University Press, 2003.

Asiedu, D., 'Spidla: Czech Republic Will Not Support NATO Engagement in Iraq', *Radio Prague*, 25 May 2004.

Aslund, A., 'WTO Entry: No Time to Lose', *The Moscow Times*, 3 February 2003. Online. Available HTTP: http://www.carnegieendowment.org/publications/index.cfm?fa=print &id=1173 (accessed 3 May 2005).

Asmus, R.D., *Opening NATO's Door: How the Alliance Remade Itself for a New Era*, New York: Columbia University Press, 2002.

Authors' interview with an anonymous, top-level national civil servant and member of the EU's Political and Security Committee, 21 September 2004 (Chapter 2).

Aznar, J.M. et al., 'Europe and America Must Stand United', *The Wall Street Journal*, 30 January 2003.

Bacevich, A.J., *American Empire: The Realities and Consequences of U.S. Diplomacy*, Cambridge, MA: Harvard University Press, 2002.

Baldwin, D., 'Power and International Relations', in W. Carlsnaes, T. Risse, and B.A. Simmons (eds), *Handbook of International Relations*, London/Thousand Oaks, CA/New Delhi: Sage, 2002, 177–91.

Bandow, D., 'Price of Global Interventionism?', *Washington Times*, 18 October 2001.

Banusiewicz, J.D., 'Rumsfeld: Reagan Legacy Present in Iraq Today,' *American Forces Press Service*, 10 October 2003.

Baranovsky, V., 'Russian Views on NATO and the EU', in A. Lieven and D. Trenin (eds), *Ambivalent Neighbours. The EU, NATO and the Price of Membership*, Washington, DC: Carnegie Endowment for International Peace, 2003.

Barysch, K. and Kekic, L., 'Putin Should Tilt Toward the EU. Russia at a Crossorads', *International Herald Tribune*, 16 June 2003.

Bennhold, K., 'EU and Russians Split on Ukraine', *International Herald Tribune*, 26 November 2004.

Benoit, B. and Thorhill, J., 'Fear that Gas Supply Gives Russia Too Much Power over Europe', *Financial Times*, 12 January 2005.

Bereuter, D. and Lis, J., 'Broadening the Transatlantic Relationship,' *Washington Quarterly*, 2003, vol. 27, no. 1, 147–62.

Bergsten, F., 'America and Europe: Clash of the Titans?', *Foreign Affairs*, 1999, vol. 78, no. 2, 20–34.

'Beyond Enlargement: Commission Shifts European Neighbourhood Policy into Higher Gear', IP/04/632, Brussels, 12 May 2004.

Biddle, S. 'Land Warfare: Theory and Practice', in J. Baylis, J. Wirtz, E. Cohen and C. Gray (eds), *Strategy in the Contemporary World: An Introduction to Strategic Studies*, Oxford: Oxford University Press, 2002.

Biernat, J., Cieslik, J. and Kochanowicz, M., 'Polish Management of the Yanayev Coup Crisis in the USSR 1991', in F. Bynander and P. Chmielewski (eds), *The Politics of Crisis Management in Transitional Poland*, Stockholm: Crismart/Swedish National Defence College, forthcoming.

Bigo, D., 'The Möbius Ribbon of Internal and External Security(ies)', in M. Albert, D. Jacobson, Y. Lapid (eds), *Identities, Borders, Orders – Rethinking International Relations Theory*, Minneapolis: University of Minnesota Press, 2001, 91–136.

—— 'When Two Become One – Internal and External Securitisations in Europe', in M. Kelstrup and M.C. Williams (eds), *International Relations and the Politics of European Integration – Power, Security and Community*, London: Routledge, 2000, 171–204.

Black, J.L., *Russia Faces NATO Expansion. Bearing Gifts or Bearing Arms?*, Lanham, MD: Rowman & Littlefield Publishers, Inc., 2000.

—— *Vladimir Putin and the New World Order. Looking East, Looking West?* Lanham, MD: Rowman & Littlefield Publishers, 2004.

Black, J.L. (ed.), *Russia & Eurasia Documents Annual 1996*, vol. 1: *The Russian Federation*, Gulf Breeze, FL: Academic International Press, 1997.

—— *Russia & Eurasia Documents Annual 1997*, vol. 1: *The Russian Federation*, Gulf Breeze, FL: Academic International Press, 1998.

—— *Russia & Eurasia Documents Annual 2000*, vol. 1: *The Russian Federation*, Gulf Breeze, FL: Academic International Press, 2001.

Blair, T., 'Speech at the Lord Mayor's Banquet', 15 November 2004. Online. Available HTTP: http://www.pm.gov.uk./output/Page6583.asp (accessed 23 November 2004).

Blank, S.J., *Threats to Russian Security: The View from Moscow*, Carlisle, PA: U.S. Army War College, Strategic Studies Institute, 2000.

Bleek, P.C., 'U.S. and Russia at Odds Over Strategic Reductions Agreement', *Arms Control Today*, 2002, vol. 32, no. 4, 22.

Bleichelt, T., 'The Impact of the Eastern Enlargement on the Common Foreign and Security Policy of the Union', paper presented at the Annual Convention of the International Studies Association, Honolulu, USA, 1–5 March 2005.

Bordachev, T.V., 'Strategy and Strategies', in A. Moshes, (ed.), *Rethinking the Respective Strategies of Russia and the European Union*, Moscow: Carnegie Moscow Center/ Helsinki: Finnish Institute of International Affairs, 2003, 31–61.

Bowen, W.Q., 'Missile Defence and the Transatlantic Security Relationship', *International Affairs*, 2001, vol. 77, no. 3, 485–507.

Bretherton, C. and Vogler, J., *The European Union as a Global Actor*, London: Routledge, 1999.

Britz, M., *The Europeanization of Defence Industry Policy*, Ph.D. Thesis, Stockholm: Department of Political Science, Stockholm University, 2004.

Britz, M. and Eriksson, A., 'The European Security and Defence Policy: A Fourth System of European Foreign Policy', *Politique européenne*, no. 17, 35–62.

Brooks, S.G. and Wohlforth, W.C., 'American Primacy in Perspective', *Foreign Affairs*, 2002, vol. 81, no. 4, 20–33.

Brzezinski, Z., *The Choice: Global Domination or Global Leadership*, New York: Basic Books, 2004.

Buckley, N., 'Aftershocks Will Keep Foreign Investors on Edge', *Financial Times*, 17 May 2005.

Bungay, S., *The Most Dangerous Enemy. A History of the Battle of Britain*, London: Aurum Press, 2000.

Bush, G.W., 'A Period of Consequences', 23 September 1999. Online. Available HTTP: http://citadel.edu/r3/pao/addresses/pres_bush.html (accessed 16 June 2004).

Bush, G.W., 'A Distinctly American Internationalism', 19 November 1999. Online. Available HTTP: http://www.mtholyoke.edu/acad/intrel/bush/wspeech.htm (accessed 14 June 2004).

Bush, G.W., 'New Leadership on National Security', 23 May 2000. Online. Available HTTP: http://www.brookings.edu/fp/research/areas/nmd/bush1.htm (accessed 22 May 2004).

Bush, G.W., 'Radio Address to the Nation', 25 May 2002, US Department of State, US–Russian relations.

'Bush Plans to Cut Forces in Europe, Asia', *Fox News Online*, 15 August 2004. Online. Available HTTP: http://www.foxnews.com/story/0,2933,129024,00.html (accessed 17 June 2005).

Buzan, B., *People, States, and Fear: An Agenda For International Security Studies in the Post-Cold War Era* (2nd edn), Hertfordshire: Harvester Wheatsheaf, 1991.

Byman, D. and Waxman, M., *The Dynamics of Coercion: American Foreign Policy and the Limits of Military Might*. Cambridge: Cambridge University Press, 2002.

Bynander, F., 'Conclusions,' in F. Bynander and P. Chmielewski (eds), *The Politics of Crisis Management in Transitional Poland,* Stockholm: Crismart/Swedish National Defence College, 2005 (forthcoming).

Bynander, F., Chmielewski, P. and Simons, G. (eds), *The Politics of Crisis Management in Transitional Poland.* Stockholm: Crismart/Swedish National Defence College, forthcoming.

Cambone, S., *The Debate in the US Senate on NATO Enlargement*, Brussels: NATO Academic Forum, 1997.

Cameron, R. and Asiedu, D., 'EU Summit: No More Cash for Candidate Countries', *Radio Prague*, 13 December 2002.

Carlsnaes, W., 'Introduction', in W. Carlsnaes, H. Sjursen and B. White (eds), *Contemporary European Foreign Policy*, London: Sage, 2004.

Carlsnaes, W., Sjursen, H. and White, B. (eds), *Contemporary European Foreign Policy*, London: Sage, 2004.

Carter, A.B., Perry, W.J., and Steinbruner, J.D., *A New Concept of Cooperative Security*, Brookings Occasional Paper, Washington, DC: The Brookings Institution, 1992.

Chirac, J., 'Conférence de presse . . .', 30 October 2000. Online. Available HTTP: http://www.elysee.fr/elysee/francais/interventions/conferences_et_points_de_presse/2 000/octobre/sommaire_octobre.13012.html (accessed 3 March 2005).

—— Speech given at the International Institute for Strategic Studies (IISS), London, 18 November 2004. Online. Available HTTP: http://www.elysee.fr/cgi-bin/auracom /aurweb/search/file?aurfile=discourse/2004/041 . . . (accessed 23 November 2004).

Chronology of EU Operation Artemis in DR Congo. Online. Available HTTP http://www. eubusiness.com/afp/030816172714.a25inyv2/ (accessed 10 July 2005).

CIA World Factbook: 'The Czech Republic'. Online. Available HTTP: http://www.cia. gov/cia/publications/factbook/geos/ez.html (accessed 23 November 2004).

Cimbala, J.L., 'Saving NATO From Europe', *Foreign Affairs*, November/December 2004, vol. 83, no. 6, 111–20.

Clark, M.T., 'The Clinton Legacy on Ballistic Missile Defense', *Comparative Strategy*, 2000, vol. 19, no. 3, 201–19.

Clarke, R.A., *Against All Enemies: Inside America's War on Terror*, New York: Free Press, 2004.

Clinton, W.J., 'Remarks . . . in Freedom House Speech', 6 October 1995. Online. Available HTTP: http://www.clintonfoundation.org/legacy/100695-speech-by-president-in-freedom-house-speech.htm (accessed 14 February 2005).

—— 'Remarks . . . to the People of Detroit', 22 October 1996. Online. Available HTTP: http://www.clintonfoundation.org/legacy/102296-speech-by-president-on-foreign-policy.htm (accessed 14 February 2005).

Cohen, A., 'Why Russia's Accession to the WTO is in America's Economic and Strategic Interests', *Backgrounder*, no. 1551, Washington, DC. The Heritage Foundation, 2002. Online. Available HTTP: http://www.heritage.org/Research/RussiaandEurasia/ BG1551.cfm (accessed 11 May 2005).

Cohen, R., *The Future of Money*, Princeton, NJ: Princeton University Press, 2004.

Cohen, S.S., 'Euro Shield', *Wall Street Journal*, 29 April 2003.

Conference on EU Capability Improvement, Brussels, 19 November 2001 – Statement on Improving European Military Capabilities, reproduced in M. Rutten, 'From Nice to Laeken European Defence: Core Documents, Volume II', *Chaillot Paper*, no. 51, Paris: European Union Institute for Security Studies, April 2002.

Cooper, R., *The Breaking of Nations: Order and Chaos in the Twenty-First Century*, London: Atlantic, 2003.

Cooper, W. H., 'Permanent Normal Trade Relations (PNTR) Status for Russia and U.S.-Russian Economic Ties', Washington, DC: Congressional Research Service, CRS Reports for Congress, 28 January 2002.

Council on Foreign Relations, 'Transcript: France, Germany and the US: Putting the Pieces Back Together, a Debate between Jean-David Levitte, Richard Holbrooke and Wolfgang Ischinger', CIAO Working Papers, March 2003. Online. Available http: //www.ciaonet.org/ (accessed 23 November 2004).

Crouch, J. D., 'Special Briefing on the Nuclear Posture Review', 9 January 2002. Online.

Available HTTP: http://www.defenselink.mil/news/Jan2002/t01092002_t0109npr.html (accessed 3 December 2003).

Current Digest of the Post-Soviet Press, 2 April 2003, vol. 55, no. 9. Online. Available HTTP: http://www.currentdigest.org/ (accessed 17 September 2003).

Czech Embassy to the United States, 'Statement by H.E. Mr. Cyril Svoboda at the General Debate of the Fifty-Ninth Session of the United Nations General Assembly, New York, 29 September 2004'. Online. Available HTTP: http://www.czechembassy.org (accessed 23 November 2004).

'Czech Republic: Rough Patches on Way to the EU', *Deutsche Welle,* 12 October 2002.

Daalder, I. H., 'The Use of Force in a Changing World: U.S. and European Perspectives', November 2002. Online. Available HTTP: http://www.brookings.edu/views/articles/daalder/20021101.htm (accessed 4 April 2005).

Daalder, I. H. and Lindsay, J. M., *America Unbound: The Bush Revolution in Foreign Policy*, Washington, DC: Brookings, 2003.

Daalder, I. H. and O'Hanlon, M., *Winning Ugly: NATO's War to Save Kosovo*, Washington, DC: Brookings Institution Press, 2000.

Dalgaard-Nielsen, A. and Søby Kristensen, K., *Catalogue of Ideas. Homeland Security – Bridging the Transatlantic Gap*, Report of the Conference, 19–21 September 2003, Copenhagen, Danish Institute for International Studies (DIIS).

Daniel, D. and Hayes, B. with C. de Jonge Oudraat, *Coercive Inducement and the Containment of International Crises*, Washington: US Institute of Peace Press, 1999.

Dassù, M. and Menotti, R., 'Europe and America in the Age of Bush', *Survival*, Spring 2005, vol. 47, no. 1, 105–22.

Delors, J., 'A la recherche du miracle', speech at L'Académie des sciences morales et politiques, Paris, 7 January 2004. Online. Excerpts available HTTP: http://www.notre-europe.asso.fr/article.php3?id_article=345 (accessed 25 April 2005).

Dempsey, J., 'Europe: EU Admits Flaws in Relationship with Russia', *Financial Times*, 23 February 2004.

—— 'Words of War: Europe's First Security Doctrine Backs Away from a Commitment to US-style Pre-emption', *Financial Times*, 5 December 2003.

—— 'Poland Sets Pullout in Iraq for 2005', *International Herald Tribune,* 10 April 2004.

De Spiegeleire, S., 'The Implementation of the EU's Common Strategy on Russia,' in H. Haukkala and S. Medvedev (eds), *The EU Common Strategy on Russia: Learning the Grammar of the CFSP*, Helsinki: The Finnish Institute of International Affairs/ Berlin: Institut für Europäische Politik, 2001, 81–116.

—— 'Recoupling Russia to Europe: Staying the Course', *The International Spectator*, 2003, 79–97.

Deutsch, K. et al., *Political Community and the North Atlantic Area*, Princeton, NJ: Princeton University Press, 1957.

Diedrichs, U. and Wessels, W., 'Die erweiterte EU als internationaler Akteur', *Internationale Politik*, 2003, vol. 58, no. 1, 11–18.

Diez, T., *The European Union and the Cyprus Conflict – Modern Conflict, Postmodern Union*, Manchester: Manchester University Press, 2002.

Diplomaticheskii Vestnik, 1992, nos. 9, 10, 15, 16, 23, 24; 1999, nos. 11, 12; 2000, nos. 1, 7, 8, 10, 12; and 2001, no. 1.

—— August 2000, no. 8; June 2003, no. 6, January 2004, no. 1, Moscow: MID RF.

Dombrowski, P.J. and Payne, R., 'Global Debate and the Limits of the Bush Doctrine', *International Studies Perspectives*, November 2003, vol. 4, issue 4, 395–408.

Donaldson, R.H. and Nogee, J.L., *The Foreign Policy of Russia: Changing Systems, Enduring Interests*, 2nd edn, Amonk, NY: M.E. Sharpe, 2002.

Dueck, C., 'New Perspectives on American Grand Strategy: A Review Essay', *International Security*, 2004, vol. 28, no. 4, 197–216.

Economist, The, 'Europe in a Spin', *Economist*, 10 January 2004.

—— 'France and Farming', 29 May 2004.

Ekengren, M., 'National Foreign Policy Vo-ordination: The Swedish EU Presidency', in H. Sjursen, W. Carlsnaes and B. White (eds), *Contemporary European Foreign Policy*, London: Sage, 2004.

—— 'The Interface of External and Internal Security in the EU and in the Nordic Policies', in A. Bailes (ed.), *ESDP and the Nordic States*, Oxford: Oxford University Press, 2005.

Engelbrekt, K., 'Multiple Asymmetries: The European Union's Neo-Byzantine Approach to Eastern Enlargement', *International Politics*, 2002, vol. 39, 37–52.

Entman, R., 'Framing: Towards Clarification of a Fractured Paradigm', *Journal of Communication*, Autumn, 1993, vol. 43, no. 4.

Ehrhart, H.-G., 'What Model for CFSP?', *Chaillot Paper,* no. 55, Paris: European Union Institute for Security Studies, 2002.

'Entretien avec Condoleezza Rice', *Politique internationale*, 2000–1, no. 90, 29–40.

Eriksson, A., 'Sweden and the Europeanisation of Security and Defence Policy', in B. Huldt, T. Ries, J. Mörtberg, and E. Davidson (eds), *The New Northern Security Agenda – Perspectives from Finland and Sweden*, Strategic Yearbook 2004, Stockholm: Swedish National Defence College, 2003.

—— 'The Europeanization of Swedish Defence Policy', Ph.D. Dissertation at Department of Political Science, Stockholm University, forthcoming.

European Commission, EU Common Strategy on Russia (1999)', 4 June 1999. Online. Available HTTP: http://www.eur.ru/en/p_244.htm (accessed 20 January 2004).

European Commission, 'The EU's Relations with Russia, Introduction'. Online. Available HTTP: http://europa.eu.int/comm/external_relations/russia/intro/ (accessed 28 October 2003).

European Commission, External Relations, 'EU Assistance to Russia'. Online. Available HTTP: http://europa.eu.int/comm/external_relations/russia/intro/ass.htm (accessed 23 December 2003).

European Commission, Delegation to Russia, official website. Online. Available HTTP: http://www.delrus.cec.eu.int/en/p_216.htm (accessed 1 December 2004).

European Commission. 'Joint Statement, EU-Russia Summit', 29 May 2000. Online. Available HTTP: http://europa.eu.int/comm/external_relations/russia/summit_29_05_00/joint_final_statement.htm (accessed 3 March 2005).

European Commission, *Communication from the Commission – Paving the way for a New Neighbourhood Instrument*, Brussels, 1 July 2003, COM (2003) 393 final.

European Commission, Centre for External Trade, 'Bilateral Trade Relations with Russia'. Online. Available HTTP: http://trade-info.cec.eu.int/doclib/cfm/doclib_section.cfm?sec=138&lev=2&order=date (accessed 15 April 2005).

European Commission, Delegation to the USA, official website. Online. Available HTTP: http://www.eurunion.org/profile/EUUSStats.htm (accessed 17 April 2005).

European Commission, External Trade Issues, 'Bilateral Trade Relations' with USA. Online. Available HTTP: http://europa.eu.int/comm/trade/issues/bilateral/countries/usa/index_en.htm (accessed 15 April 2005).

European Commission, External Trade Issues, 'Bilateral Trade Relations' with Russia.

Online. Available HTTP: http://europa.eu.int/comm/trade/issues/bilateral/countries/russia/index_en.htm (accessed 3 March 2005).

European Commission, External Relations, 'The EU's Relations with Russia'. Online. Available HTTP: http://europa.eu.int/comm/external_relations/russia/intro/index.htm (accessed 3 May 2005).

European Council, Presidency of the Council of the European Union, 'Presidency Conclusions', EU Helsinki Summit, 10–11 December 1999. Online. Available HTTP: http://ue.eu.int/sv/Info/eurocouncil/index.htm (accessed 30 December 2003).

European Council, 'Council Joint Action establishing a European Union Co-operation Programme for Non-proliferation and Disarmament in the Russian Federation (1999)', taken at the 2237th Council (Fisheries) on 17 December 1999, (1999/878/CFSP). Available HTTP: http://www.eur.ru/en/p_256.htm (accessed 19 January 2004).

European Council, General Affairs/Defence, 'Military Capabilities Commitment Declaration', press release, no. 13427/2/00, Brussels, 20 November 2000.

European Council, Presidency of the Council of the European Union, 'Presidency Conclusions', EU Stockholm Summit, 23–24 March 2001. Online. Available HTTP: http://ue.eu.int/en/info/eurocouncil/ (accessed 19 January 2004).

European Council, 'The Way Forward on the European Capabilities Action Plan', paper, spring 2003a.

European Council, 2509th Council meeting (External Relations), 'Declaration on EU Military Capabilites', press release, no. 9379/03 (Presse 138), Brussels, 19–20 May 2003b.

European Council 'A Secure Europe in a Better World – The European Security Strategy', Brussels, 12 December 2003, Online. Available HTTP: http://ue.eu.int/cms3_fo/showPage.asp?id=266&lang=en&mode=g (accessed 12 July 2005).

European Council, 'European Defence: NATO/EU Consultation, Planning and Operations', press release, 15 December 2003, reproduced in A. Missiroli, 'From Copenhagen to Brussels. European defence: core documents, Volume IV', *Chaillot Paper*, no. 67, Paris: European Union Institute for Security Studies, December 2003c.

European Council, 'Headline Goal 2010', as finalised by PSC, Brussels, 4 May 2004a, 6309/6/04.

European Council, 'The European Union launches a police mission to Kinshasa in the Democratic Republic of Congo (DRC) (EUPOL KINSHASA)', press release, no. 15855/04 (Presse 349), Brussels, 9 December 2004b.

European Council, 'ESDP Presidency Report', endorsed by the European Council of 17 December 2004c.

European Council, 'Council Establishes Mission to Provide Advice and Assistance for Security Sector Reform in the DRC', press release, no. 8644/05 (Presse 105), Brussels, 2 May 2005.

European Council, '15th EU-Russia Summit, Moscow, 10 May 2005, Road Maps: Road Map for the Common Economic Space, Building Blocks for Sustained Economic Growth', 2005. Online. Available HTTP: http://ue.eu.int/ueDocs/cms_Data/docs/pressdata/en/er/84815.pdf (accessed 18 May 2005).

European Convention, 'Summary of the Meeting Held on 29 October 2002', Working Group VIII on Defence, Brussels, 12 November 2002, CONV 399/02, p.3

European Defence Agency, 'Second Meeting of the European Defence Agency's Steering Board', press release, Brussels, 22 November 2004.

European Parliament/Directorate General for Research. 'Information Note on the Economic and Political Situation of the Czech Republic and Its Relations with the EU. 2003'. Online. Available HTTP: http://www.europarl.eu.int/meetdocs/delegations/czec/20030518/494995EN.pdf (accessed 23 November 2004).

European Union, Background Paper, 'Breaking the Barriers', Ministerial Conference, Dublin, 23–24 February 2004.

European Union, 'Treaty of Amsterdam aAmending the Treaty on European Union, the Treaties Establishing the European Communities and Related Acts', *Official Journal*, C 340, 10 November 1997. Online. Available HTTP: http://europa.eu.int/eur-lex/en/treaties/dat/amsterdam.htm. 040120.l (accessed 28 January 2004).

European Union. Military Capability Commitment Conference, Brussels, 22 November 2004

European Union, 'Nice Treaty', *Official Journal of the European Union*, C 325/1, 24 December 2002.

European Union, 'Treaty Establishing a Constitution for Europe', *Official Journal of the European Union*, C 310, 16 December 2004.

European Union Police Mission in Bosnia Herzegovina, official website. Online. Available HTTP: http://www.eupm.org/ (accessed 30 December 2003).

EU–Russia Summit, 'Joint Statement on Strengthening Dialogue and Co-operation on Political and Security Matters in Europe', Paris, 30 October 2000. Online. Available HTTP: http://www.eur.ru/en/images/pText_pict/228/sum22.doc (accessed 19 January 2004).

EU–Russia Summit, 'Joint Statement', Rome, 29 November 2003. Online. Available HTTP: http://www.russiaeu.org/sum-rom031106.htm (accessed 19 January 2004).

Everts, P., *Democracy and Military Force*. London: Palgrave, 2002.

Everts, S. and Keohane, D., 'Introduction', in L. Freedman, F. Heisbourg and M. O'Hanlon, *A European Way of War*, Centre for European Reform, 2004.

'Excerpts from Pentagon's Plan: "Prevent the Re-emergence of a New Rival"', *The New York Times*, 8 March 1992, 14.

Featherstone, K. 'Introduction: In the Name of Europe', in K. Featherstone and C. Radaelli (eds), *The Politics of Europeanization*, Oxford: Oxford University Press, 2003.

Fedorov, Y.E., 'Strategic Thinking in Putin's Russia', in Y. Fedorov and B. Nygren (eds), *Russian Military Reform and Russia's New Security Environment*, Swedish National Defence College – ACTA B28, 2003.

—— 'Putin's Russia: Foreign Policy and the Nature of the Regime', in Y.E. Fedorov and B. Nygren (eds), *Putin I and Putin II Results of the First Term and Prospects for the Second*, Stockholm: Swedish National Defence College, 2004.

Ferguson, N., *Colossus: The Price of America's Empire*, New York: Penguin, 2004.

Filtenborg, M.S., Gänzle, S. and Johansson, E., 'An Alternative Theoretical Approach to EU Foreign Policy – Network Governance and the Case of the Northern Dimension Initiative', *Cooperation and Conflict*, 2002, vol. 37, 387–407.

Forsberg, T., 'Forging the EU-Russia Security Partnership in the Crucible of Trans-Atlantic Relations', paper prepared for the joint International Convention of Central Eastern European International Studies Association & International Studies Association, Budapest, 26–28 June 2003.

Försvarsmakten, HKV/PLANS INT PM 2004–03–31 L-O Roos, Stockholm: 2004a.

—— Försvarsmaktens Budgetunderlag för år 2005 med särskilda redovisningar, HKV beteckning 23 383:62995, 27 February, Stockholm: 2004b.

Freedman, L. (ed.), *Strategic Coercion: Concepts and Cases*, Oxford: Oxford University Press, 1998.

—— 'Can the EU Develop an Effective Military Doctrine?', in L. Freedman, F. Heisbourg and M. O´Hanlon, *A European Way of War*, London: Centre for European Reform, 2004.

Friedman, G., America's Secret War: Inside the Hidden Worldwide Struggle Between America and Its Enemies, New York: Doubleday, 2004.

Friis, L. and Murphy, A., 'The European Union and Central and Eastern Europe: Governance and Boundaries', *Journal of Common Market Studies*, 1999, vol. 37, issue 2, 211–32.

Frowein, J., Bernitz, U. and Lord Kingsland, 'Legal Opinion on the Benes-Decrees and the Accession of the Czech Republic to the European Union', European Parliament/ Directorate-General for Research, 2002. Online. Available HTTP: http://www. europarl.eu.int/studies/benesdecrees/pdf/opinions_en.pdf (accessed 12 November 2004).

Frumkin, B.Y., 'Russia's Economic Development: Summing up the First Presidential Term of Vladimir Putin and Prospects for the Future,' in Y. Fedorov and B. Nygren (eds), *Putin I and Putin II: Results of the First Term and Prospects for the Second*, Stockholm: Swedish National Defence College, 2004.

Gaddis, J.L., *Surprise, Security, and the American Experience*, Cambridge, MA and London: Harvard University Press, 2003.

Gaidar, Y., *The Russian Economy in 2002. Tendencies and Perspectives*, Moscow: Institute of Transition Economy, 2003, 9–13, (in Russian) as quoted in B.Y. Frumkin, 'Russia's Economic Development: Summing up the First Presidential Term of Vladimir Putin and Prospects for the Future,' in Y. Fedorov and B. Nygren (eds), *Putin I and Putin II: Results of the First Term and Prospects for the Second*, Stockholm: Swedish National Defence College, 2004.

Garamone, J., 'Jones Discusses Changing Troops' "Footprint" in Europe', *American Forces Press Service*, 10 October 2003.

Garver, J.W., 'The China-India-U.S. Triangle: Strategic Relations in the Post-Cold War Era', *NBR Analysis*, 2002, vol. 13, no. 5, The National Bureau of Asian Research, October.

George, A., Hall, D. and Simons, W., *The Limits of Coercive Diplomacy: Laos, Cambodia, Vietnam*, Boston: Little, Brown, 1971.

Giegerich, B. and Wallace, W., 'Not Such a Soft Power: The External Deployment of European Forces', *Survival*, 2004, vol. 46, 163–82.

Gilpin, R., *Global Political Economy – Understanding the International Economic Order*, Princeton and Oxford: Princeton University Press, 2001.

Ginsberg, R., 'The EU's CFSP: The Politics of Procedure', in M. Holland (ed.), *Common Foreign and Security Policy. The Records and Reforms*, London: Pinter, 1997.

—— The European Union in International Politics: Baptism by Fire, Lanham, MD: Rowman & Littlefield, 2001.

Gnesotto, N. (ed.), *EU Security and Defence Policy: The First Five Years (1999–2004)* Paris: EU Institute for Security Studies, 2004.

Goldgeier, J. M., *Not Whether But When: The U.S. Decision to Enlarge NATO*, Washington, DC: Brookings Institution Press, 1999.

Goldgeier, J. M. and McFaul, M., *Power and Purpose: U.S. Policy toward Russia after the Cold War*, Washington, DC: Brookings Institution Press, 2003.

Goldmann, K., 'The Swedish Model of Security Policy', in J-E. Lane (ed.), *Understanding the Swedish* Mode, London: Frank Cass, 1991.

Goldmann, K. and Sjöstedt, G. (eds), *Power, Capabilities, Interdependence: Problems in the Study of International Influence*, London: Sage, 1979.

Goldstein, J., Kahler, M., Keohane, R.O. and Slaughter, A.-M., 'Introduction', in J. Goldstein, M. Kahler, R.O. Keohane and A.-M. Slaughter (eds), *Legalization and World Politics*, Cambridge, MA and London: MIT Press, 2001, 1–15.

Gordon, P. H., 'The French Position', *The National Interest*, 2000, no. 61, 57–65.

Gordon, P. H. and Shapiro, J., *Allies at War: America: Europe and the Crisis over Iraq*, New York: McGraw-Hill, 2004.

Gorodetsky, G. (ed.), *Russia Between East and West. Russian Foreign Policy on the Threshold to the Twenty-first Century,* London: Frank Cass, 2003.

Gowan, P., 'The EU and Eastern Europe: Diversity without Unity?', in M. Farrell, S. Fella and M. Newman, *European Integration in the 21st Century*, London: Sage, 2002..

Grabbe, H., 'Europeanization Goes East: Power and Uncertainty in the EU Accession Process', in K. Featherstone and C. Radaelli (eds),*The Politics of Europeanization*, Oxford: Oxford University Press, 2003.

Graham, B., *Hit to Kill: The New Battle Over Shielding America From Missile Attack*, New York: Public Affairs, 2001.

Grant, C., 'Conclusion: The Significance of European Defence', in L. Freedman, F. Heisbourg and M. O´Hanlon, *A European Way of War*, London: Centre for European Reform, 2004.

Gray, C. S., 'European Perspectives on U.S. Ballistic Missile Defense', *Comparative Strategy*, 2002, vol. 21, no. 4, 279–310.

Grieco, J. and Ikenberry, G. J., *State Power and World Markets: The International Political Economy*, New York and London: W.W. Norton, 2003.

Gromadzki, G. and Osica, O., *An Overview of European (In)Security*, Policy Papers, no. 7, Warsaw: Stefan Batory Foundation, 2002.

Gustavsson, J., *The Politics of Foreign Policy Change*, Lund: Lund University Press, 1998.

Haftendorn, H. and Kolkmann, M., 'Germany in a Strategic Triangle: Berlin, Paris, Washington . . . and What about London?', *Cambridge Review of International Affairs*, 2004, vol. 17, no. 3, 467–80.

Hamilton, D. S. and Quinlan, J. P., *Partners in Prosperity: The Changing Geography of the Transatlantic Economy*, Washington, DC: Center for Transatlantic Relations, Paul H. Nitze School of Advanced International Studies, Johns Hopkins University, 2004.

Hanley, S , 'The Political Context of EU Accession in the Czech Republic', Royal Institute of International Affairs Briefing Paper, 2002.

Haran O. and Tolstov S., 'The Slavic Triangle. Ukraine's Relations with Russia and Belarus: A Ukrainian View', in A. Moshes and B. Nygren (eds), *A Slavic Triangle? Present and Future Relations between Russia, Ukraine and Belarus,* Stockholm: Swedish National Defence College, 2002.

Hart, B. H. L., *Strategy: The Indirect Approach*, 4th edn, London: Faber & Faber, 1967.

Harvey, F., 'Now That Putin Has Accepted Kyoto, the Real Work Can Start', *Financial Times*, 29 December 2004.

Haukkala, H., 'The Making of the European Union's Common Strategy on Russia', in H. Haukkala and S. Medvedev (eds), *The EU Common Strategy on Russia: Learning the Grammar of the CFSP*, Helsinki: The Finnish Institute of International Affairs/ Berlin: Institut für Europäische Politik, 2001, 22–80.

—— 'What Went Right with the EU's Common Strategy on Russia?', in Moshes, A. (ed.), *Rethinking the Respective Strategies of Russia and the European Union*, Moscow: Carnegie Moscow Center/Helsinki: The Finnish Institute of International Affairs, 2003, 62–96.

Hedenskog J., *The Ukrainian Dilemma. Relations with Russia and the West in the Context of the 2004 Presidential Elections*, Stockholm: Swedish Defence Agency (FOI-R-1199-SE), 2004.

Hederstedt, General J., former Supreme Commander, Swedish Armed Forces, Interview, 13 February 2004.

Hermann, C., Kegley, C. and Rosenau, J. (eds), *New Directions in the Study of Foreign Policy*, Boston: Allen & Unwin, 1987.

Herring, E., *Danger and Opportunity. Explaining International Crisis Outcomes*, Manchester: Manchester University Press, 1995)

Herspring, D.R. and Rutland, P., 'Putin and Russian Foreign Policy', in D.R. Herspring (ed.), *Putin's Russia. Past Imperfect, Future Uncertain*, Lanham, MD: Rowman & Littlefield, 2003.

Hettne, B., Inotai, A. and Sunkel, O., *Comparing Regionalisms: Implications for Global Development*, Basingstoke, Palgrave/Macmillan, 2001.

Heusgen, C., Dr. Director, Policy Planning Unit, Secretariat General of the Council of the European Union, Brussels at the Young Faces Conference, 'The New Security Challenges and Europe's International Role', Berlin, 20–22 January 2005.

Hill, C., 'The Capability-Expectations Gap, or Conceptualising Europe's International Role', *Journal of Common Market Studies*, 1993, vol. 31, 305–28.

—— 'Closing the Capabilities-expectations Gap?', in J. Peterson and H. Sjursen (eds), *A Common Foreign Policy for Europe? Competing Visions of the CFSP*, London, Routledge, 1998.

—— *The Changing Politics of Foreign Policy*, London: Palgrave, 2003.

—— 'Renationalizing or Regrouping? EU Foreign Policy Since 11 September 2001', *Journal of Common Market Studies*, 2004, vol. 42, 143–63.

Höltschi, R., 'Die EU-Erweiterung weckt russische Sorgen', *Neue Zürcher Zeitung*, 6 February 2004.

Horakova, P., 'Czech Republic Hoping to Get a Better Deal at Copenhagen Summit', *Radio Prague*, 12 November 2002.

—— 'Czech Republic Reaches Agreement at Copenhagen Summit', *Radio Prague*, 17 December 2002.

Hosli, M.O., 'The EMU and International Monetary Relations: What to Expect for International Actors?', in C. Rhodes (ed.), *The European Union in the World Community*, Boulder, CO/London: Lynne Rienner, 1998, 165–91.

Hrobsky, M., 'Support among Czech Public for War in Iraq Running Thin', *Radio Prague*, 14 March 2003.

Hughes, K., 'European Foreign Policy under Pressure', *The Brown Journal of World Affairs*, 2003, vol. IX, issue 2, 125–33.

Hyde-Price, A., *The International Politics of East Central Europe*. Manchester: Manchester University Press, 1996.

—— '"Burning a Path to Peace?" International Society, Europe and Coercive Military Power', paper presented at the British International Studies Association (BISA) Annual Conference, December 2002.

Ikenberry, G.J., 'The Myth of Post-Cold War Chaos', *Foreign Affairs*, 1996, vol. 75, no. 3, 79–91.

Ikenberry, G.J., Lake, D.A. and Mastanduno, M., 'Introduction: Approaches to Explaining American Foreign Economic Policy', *International Organization*, 1988, vol. 42, no. 2, 1–14.

International Affairs, Special Issue, 2003, vol. 79, no. 5.

International Organization for Migration (IOM), 'EU Enlargement Will Pose Migration Challenge in Accession States', news release, 30 April 2004, no. 868.

Ivanov, I.S., *The New Russian Diplomacy*, Washington, DC: The Nixon Center and Brookings Institution Press, 2002.

Izvestiya, 19 June 2002.

Jackson, General Sir M., 'Foreword', in G. Prins, *The Heart of War*, London: Routledge, 2002.

Jacobsson, B., 'Europeiseringen och statens omvandling', *SCORE Rapportserie* 1999, no. 2.

Jakobsen, P.V., *Western Use of Coercive Diplomacy after the Cold War: A Challenge for Theory and Practice*, New York: St Martin's Press, 1998.

Jervis, R., 'Understanding the Bush Doctrine', *Political Science Quarterly*, 2003, vol. 118, no. 3, 365–88.

Joffe, J., 'Clinton's World: Purpose, Policy, and Weltanschauung', *The Washington Quarterly*, 2001, vol. 24, no. 1, 141–54.

—— 'Defying History and Theory: The United States as the "Last Remaining Superpower"', in G.J. Ikenberry (ed.) *America Unrivaled: The Future of the Balance of Power*, Ithaca, NY: Cornell University Press, 2002.

Judis, J.B., *The Folly of Empire: What George Bush Could Learn from Theodore Roosevelt and Woodrow Wilson*, New York: Scribner, 2004.

Juncker, J.-C., 'Nous agissons comme si nous réformions le code de la route alors que nous devons inventer un nouvel atlas', *Les Echos*, 19 September 2000.

Kaczorowska, M., 'Commenting on Copenhagen', *Polish Voice,* 31 January 2003.

Kagan, R., 'Power and Weakness,' *Policy Review,* 2002, vol. 113, 3–28.

—— 'Embraceable EU', *Washington Post*, 5 December 2004, B07.

Kalniete, S., 'Latvia's Foreign Policy at the Crossroads', speech by Latvia's Minister of Foreign Affairs, Sandra Kalniete, at the 62nd Scientific Conference, University of Latvia, 27 January 2004.

Kaminski, A., 'Poland: Compatibility of External and Internal Democratic Designs' in J. Zielonka and A. Pravda (eds), *Democratic Consolidation in Eastern Europe,* 2001, vol. 2, Oxford: Oxford University Press.

Karbalevich V., 'The Prospects of Slavic Unity. Belarus' Relations with Russia and Ukraine', in A. Moshes and B. Nygren (eds), *A Slavic Triangle? Present and Future Relations between Russia, Ukraine and Belarus,* Stockholm: Swedish National Defence College, 2002.

Katz, M. M., 'Playing the Angles: Russian Diplomacy Before and During the War in Iraq', *Middle East Policy*, 2003, vol. 10, no. 3, 43–55.

Katzenstein, P. J., 'Same War – Different Views: Germany, Japan, and Counterterrorism', *International Organization*, 2003, vol. 57, no. 4, 731–60.

Kaye, D., 'Bound to Cooperate? Transatlantic Policy in the Middle East,' *The Washington Quarterly*, 2003, vol. 27, no. 1, 179–95.

Kelley, D., *Politics in Russia and the Successor States*, Fort Worth, TX: Harcourt Brace, 1999.

Keohane, R. and Nye, J.S., *Power and Interdependence*, 2nd edn, Glenview, IL: Scott, Foresman, 1989.

Khudolev, K., 'Russia and the European Union: New Opportunities, New Challenges', in A. Moshes (ed.) *Rethinking the Respective Strategies of Russia and the European Union*, Moscow: Carnegie Moscow Center/Helsinki: Finnish Institute of International Affairs, 2003, 8–30.

Kihl, General J., Chief of Joint Strategic Plans and Policy, Swedish Armed Forces, Interview, 4 February 2004.

Kile, S., 'Nuclear Arms Control and Non-proliferation', in *SIPRI Yearbook 2000: Armaments, Disarmament and International Security*, Oxford: Oxford University Press, 2000.

Kirshner, J., *Currency and Coercion: The Political Economy of International Monetary Power*, Princeton, NJ: Princeton University Press, 1995.

Kissinger, H., *Nuclear Weapons and Foreign Policy*. New York: Doubleday, 1957.

—— *White House Years*, Boston/Toronto: Little, Brown, 1979.

Klaus, V., 'The Importance of NATO Enlargement to the Czech Republic', speech to The Heritage Foundation, 21 October 1997. Online. Available HTTP: http://www.heritage. org/research/europe/hl602.cfm (accessed 12 November 2004).

Kopeck, P. and Mudde, C., *Uncivil Society? Contentious Politics in Post-Communist Europe*, London: Routledge, 2003.

Král, D., *The Czech Republic and the Iraq Crisis: Oscillating between the Two Sides of the Atlantic*, Prague: Europeum Institute for European Policy, 2003.

Krauthammer, C., 'The Unipolar Moment', *Foreign Affairs*, 1991, vol. 70, no. 1, 23–33.

—— 'The Unipolar Moment Revisited', *The National Interest*, 2002–3, no. 70, 5–17.

Kreyenbühl, T., 'Die osterweiterung ist ein voller erfolg', *Neue Zürcher Zeitung*, 8 March 2005.

—— 'Ostmitteleuropas bauern in erwartung des EU-shocks', *Neue Zürcher Zeitung*, 7/8 February 2004.

Kupchan, C., 'Hollow Hegemony or Stable Multipolarity?', in G.J. Ikenberry (ed.) *America Unrivaled: The Future of the Balance of Power*, Ithaca, NY and London: Cornell University Press, 2002, 68–97.

—— *The End of the American Era: U.S. Foreign Policy and the Geopolitics of the Twenty-First Century*, New York: Knopf, 2002.

Kyoto Protocol. Online. Available HTTP: http://www.kyotoprotocol.com/ (accessed 12 July 2005).

Larsen, H., 'Concepts of Security in the European Union After the Cold War', *Australian Journal of International Affairs*, 2000, vol. 54, no. 3.

—— 'The EU: A Global Military Actor?', *Cooperation and Conflict*, 2002, vol. 37, no. 3, 283–302.

Lavrov, S.V. 'Stenogramma interv'iu … nemetskoi gazete "Khandel'sblatt"', 28 December 2004. Online. Available HTTP: http://www.ln.mid.ru/brp_4.nsf/spsvy (accessed 18 April 2005).

Layne, C., 'The Unipolar Illusion: Why New Great Powers Will Rise', *International Security*, 1993, vol. 17, no. 4, 5–51.

—— 'From Preponderance to Offshore Balancing', *International Security*, 1997, vol. 22, no. 1, 86–124.

—— 'Rethinking American Grand Strategy: Hegemony or Balance of Power in the Twenty-First Century', *World Policy Journal*, 1998, vol. 15, no. 2, 8–28.

Livingston, K., 'EU Bars Czechs from Iraq Summit', *Prague Post*, 19 February 2003.

Lo, B., *Vladimir Putin and the Evolution of Russian Foreign Policy,* Oxford: Blackwell Publishing, 2003.

Lobjakas, A., 'NATO: Allies Await Russian Response to Cooperation Proposal', *RFE/RL Feature Articles*, 2002. Online. Available HTTP: http://www.rferl.org/features/2002/02/27022002085719.asp (accessed 23 February 2004).

Longhurst, K., 'From Security Consumer to Security Provider – Poland and Transatlantic Security in the Twenty-First Century', *Defence Studies,* 2002, vol. 2, no. 2, 50–63.

Luif, P., 'EU Cohesion in the UN General Assembly', *Occasional Paper*, no. 49, Paris: European Union Institute for Security Studies, 2003.

Lundestad, G., *'Empire' by Integration: The United States and European Integration, 1945–1997*, Oxford/New York: Oxford University Press, 1998.

Luttwak, E., *Strategy: The Logic of War and Peace* , Cambridge, MA: Harvard University Press, 2002.

Lynch, A.C., 'The Realism of Russia's Foreign Policy', *Europe-Asia Studies*, 2001, vol. 53, no. 1, 7–31.

Lynch, D., 'Russia Faces Europe', *Chaillot Papers*, no. 60, Paris: European Union, Institute for Security Studies, 2003.

—— 'Russia's Strategic Partnership with Europe', *The Washington Quarterly*, 2004, vol. 27, no. 2, 99–118.

Lynch, D. (ed.) 'The South Caucasus: A Challenge for the EU', *Chaillot Paper*, no. 65, Paris: European Union Institute for Security Studies, 2003.

Mace, C., 'Operation Artemis: Mission Impossible?', *ISIS Europe European Security Review*, Brussels, number 18 (July 2003)

McInnes, C., *Spectator-Sport War: The West and Contemporary Conflict*, Boulder, CO: Lynne Rienner, 2000.

Malcolm N., Pravda A., Allison R., Light, M., *Internal Factors in Russian Foreign Policy*, Oxford: Clarendon Press, 1996.

Manners, I., 'Normative Power Europe: A Contradiction in Terms?', *Journal of Common Market Studies,* 2002, vol. 40, 235–58.

March, J. and Olsen, J. P., Rediscovering Institutions. The Organizational Basis of Politics, New York: The Free Press, 1989

—— 'The Institutional Dynamics of International Political Orders, *International Organization,* 1998, Vol. 52, No. 4, 943–969.

Mastanduno, M., 'Preserving the Unipolar Moment: Realist Theories and U.S. Grand Strategy after the Cold War', *International Security*, 1997, vol. 21, no. 4, 49–88.

—— 'Economics and Security in Statecraft and Scholarship', *International Organization*, 1998, vol. 52, no. 4, 825–54

Mastanduno, M. and Kapstein, E.B., 'Realism and State Strategies After the Cold War', in M. Mastanduno and E.B. Kapstein (eds), *Unipolar Politics: Realism and State Strategies After the Cold War*, New York: Columbia University Press, 1999.

Matlary, J.H., 'Human Rights', *ARENA Working Papers*, no. 19, 2003.

Mead, W.R., *Power, Terror, Peace, and War: America's Grand Strategy in a World At Risk*, New York: Knopf, 2004.

Menon, A., 'Why ESDP is Misguided and Dangerous for the Alliance', in J. Howorth and

J.T.S. Keeler (eds), *Defending Europe: The EU, NATO and the Quest for European Autonomy*, New York: Palgrave/Macmillan, 2003.

Meshkov, A., 'Russia and the European Security Architecture', *International Affairs*, 2002, vol. 48, no. 5.

Michta, A. (ed.), *America's New Allies: Poland, Hungary, and the Czech Republic in NATO*, Seattle, WA: University of Washington Press, 1999.

Mihalisko, K., 'Belarus: Retreat to Authoritarianism', in K. Dawisha and B. Parrot (eds), *Democratic Changes and Authoritarian Reactions in Russia, Ukraine, Belarus, and Moldova*, Cambridge: Cambridge University Press, 1997.

Missiroli, A. (ed.), 'Bigger EU, Wider CFSP, Stronger ESDP? The View from Central Europe', *Occasional Paper*, no. 34, Paris: European Union Institute for Security Studies, April 2002.

Mörth, U., *Organizing European Cooperation – The Case of Armaments*, Lanham, MD: Rowman & Littlefield, 2003.

Moscow Times, 8 and 15 September 2003; 27, 29 and 30 October 2003; 20 February 2004.

Moses, J., 'The Politics of Kaliningrad Oblast: A Borderland of the Russian Federation', *Russian Review*, 2004, vol. 63, no. 1, 107–30.

Moshes A., 'The Evolution of Relations within the Slavic Triangle: a view from Russia', in A. Moshes and B. Nygren (eds), *A Slavic Triangle? Present and Future Relations between Russia, Ukraine and Belarus*, Stockholm: Swedish National Defence College, 2002.

'Mr Gross goes to Brussels', *Radio Prague,* 10 June 2004. Online. Available HTTP: www.radio.cz/print/en (accessed 12 November 2004).

Myrdal, S. (ed.), *EU som civil krishanterare*, Stockholm: Utrikespolitiska institutet/ Säkerhetspolitiska rådet, 2002.

Narochnitskaia, N.A., 'Russia in the New Geopolitical Context (Part II)', 18 May 2004. Online. Available HTTP: http://www.narochnitskaia.ru/cgi-bin/main.cgi?item= 1r200r040518142429 (accessed 20 June 2005).

NATO, Washington Summit Communiqué 24 April 1999, press release NAC-S(99)64, 1999.

—— 'Prague Summit Declaration', press release 127, 21 November 2002.

—— Ukraine-NATO Action Plan. Online. Available HTTP: http://www.nato.int/docu/ basictxt/b021122a.htm (accessed 12 May 2005).

Neack, L., Hey, J. and Haney, P., *Foreign Policy Analysis: Continuity and Change in its Second Generation*, Englewood Cliffs, NJ: Prentice Hall, 1995.

Neumann, I.B. and Ulriksen, S. (eds), *Sikkerhetspolitik: Norge i makttrianglet mellom EU, Russland och USA*, Oslo: Tane Aschehoug, 1996.

Nezavisimaya Gazeta, 9 December 1999; 20 May, 11 and 20 June, 14 August 2002; 29 April, 20 June, 8, 22 and 23 October 2003; 28 July 2004.

Nolan, J. E., *An Elusive Consensus: Nuclear Weapons and American Security after the Cold War*, Washington, DC: Brookings Institution Press, 1999.

Norris, P., '*Le Divorce*: Who Is to Blame for the Transatlantic Rift?', *Compass: A Journal of Leadership,* Fall 2003, 22–5. Online. Available HTTP: http://www.ksg.harvard. edu/leadership/Pdf/LeDivorce.pdf (accessed 23 June 2005).

Note pour le Haut Représentant, Stratégie de securité de l'Union européenne. Compte rendu du séminaire sur les menaces – "Identifying and understanding threats", Rome, 19 September 2003, Institute for Security Studies, 23 September 2003.

'Nuclear Posture Review [Excerpts]', 31 December 2001. Online. Available HTTP:

http://www.globalsecurity.org/wmd/library/policy/dod/npr.htm (accessed 3 December 2003).

Nye, J., *Soft Power: The Means to Success in World Politics*, New York: Public Affairs, 2004.

Nygren, B., 'Russia and Europe, or Russia in Europe?, in Y. Fedorov and B. Nygren (eds), *Russia and Europe: Putin's Foreign Policy*, ACTA B23, Stockholm: Swedish National Defence College, Department of Security and Strategic Studies, 2002.

—— 'The History of the "Slavic Union" Idea', in A. Moshes and B. Nygren (eds), *A Slavic Triangle? Present and Future Relations between Russia, Ukraine and Belarus*, Stockholm: Swedish National Defence College, 2002.

—— 'Continuity and Change in Russia's Foreing Policy in Putin's First Presidential Term', in P. Forsström and E. Mikkola (eds), *Russia's Military Policy and Strategy*, series 2, no. 27, Helsinki: National Defence College, Department of Strategic and Defence Studies, 2004.

Odom, W. E. and Dujarric, R., *America's Inadvertent Empire*, New Haven, CN and London: Yale University Press, 2004.

OECD Factbook 2005. Online. Available HTTP: http://ceres.sourceoecd.org/vl=1711156/cl=78/nw=1/rpsv/factbook/03–01–01-t01.xls (accessed 15 April 2005).

OECD, 'International Investment Perspectives: 2004 Edition'. Online Available HTTP: (accessed 26 May 2005). http://www.oecd.org/document/8/0,2340,en_2649_33763_33702536_1_1_1_1,00.html

Official at Department for International Security Affairs, Swedish Ministry of Defence (MoD), Interview17 February 2003.

Official at Secretariat of Strategic Planning, Swedish Ministry of Defence, Interview, 2 April 2004.

Officials at Joint Strategic Plans and Policy, Swedish Armed Forces (SAF), Interviews 22 April 2003, 23 April and 2 June 2004.

OzForex Foreign Exchange. Online. Available HTTP: http://www.chartflow.com/ozforex/averageRate.asp?period=yr&ccy1=EUR&ccy2=USD&days=1095&amount=1000 (accessed 16 April 2005).

Pape, R., 'Coercion and Military Strategy: Why Denial Works and Punishment Doesn't', *Journal of Strategic Studies*, 1992, Vol.15, No.4, 423–75.

—— *Bombing to Win*, Ithaca, NY: Cornell University Press, 1996

Patoka W., 'Victims of Geopolitical Legacy: An Analysis of Security Policy and Army Transformation in Poland 1989–2002', Mimeo, February 2003.

Piening, C., *Global Europe. The European Union in World Affairs*, Boulder, CO: Lynne Rienner, 1997.

Peters, I., 'ESDP as a Transatlantic Issue', *International Studies Review*, 2004, vol. 6, issue 3, 381–401.

Pinder, J. and Shishkov, Y., *The EU and Russia The Promise of Partnership*, London: The Federal Trust, 2002.

Pollack, M. A. and Shaffer, G. C. (eds), *Transatlantic Governance in the Global Economy*, Lanham, MD: Rowman & Littlefield, 2001a.

—— 'Transatlantic Governance in Historical and Theoretical Perspective', in M.A. Pollack and G. C. Shaffer (eds), *Transatlantic Governance in the Global Economy*, Lanham, MD: Rowman & Littlefield, 2001b, 3–42.

Pond, E., *Friendly Fire: The Near-Death of the Transatlantic Alliance*, Pittsburgh, PA: European Union Studies Association/Washington, DC: Brookings, 2004.

Posen, B.R. and Ross, A.L., 'Competing Visions for U.S. Grand Strategy', *International Security*, 1996–7, vol. 21, no. 3, 5–53.

Pozen, R. C., 'Mind the Gap: Can the New Europe Overtake the U.S. Economy?' *Foreign Affairs*, 2005, vol. 84, no. 2, 8–12.

'President Klaus Slams EU Integration on a Visit to Spain', *Radio Prague,* 30 November 2004. Online. Available HTTP: http://www.radio.cz/print/en/58673 (accessed 23 November 2004).

Presidential Election Forum: The Candidates on Arms Control', *Arms Control Today*, 2000, vol. 30, no. 7, 3–7.

'Press Review', *Radio Prague,* 16 March 2004. Online. Available HTTP: http://www. radio.cz/en/article/51732 (accessed 12 November 2004).

Primakov, E.M., *Mir posle 11 sentiabria*, Moscow: Izdatelstvo 'Mysl', 2002.

Prins, G., *The Heart of War*. London: Routledge, 2002.

Preston, C., *Enlargement and Integration in the European Union*, London: Routledge, 1997.

Radaelli, C., 'Policy Transfer in the European Union: Institutional Isomorphism as a Source of Legitimacy', *Governance: An International Journal of Policy and Administration*, 2000, vol. 13, no. 1, 25–43.

—— 'Europeanization of Public Policy', in K. Featherstone and C. Radaelli (eds), *The Politics of Europeanization*, Oxford: Oxford University Press, 2003.

Radio Free Europe/Radio Liberty Newsline, 17, 18, 19 and 25 September, 3 October 2001; 3 January, 9 December 2002; ; 5, 17 and 31 March, 4 and 21 April, 19, 25 and 26 September 2003; 6, 7, 13 and 14 October 2004; 7 February 2005. Online. Available HTTP: http://www.rferl.org/newsline/.

—— 8 February 2001; 17 April, 16, 19, 20, 25 and 27 June, 16 July, 14, 15, 19, 20 and 29 August, 10 and 17 December 2002; 30 and 31 January, 28 February, 12 March, 19 and 25 June, 31 July, 12 and 28 August, 2, 15 and 19 September, 3, 14, 15, 17, 20, 21, 23, 24, 27, 29 and 31 October, 6, 7, 13 and 20 November 2003; 12, 23, 26, 27 and 30 January, 3, 11,13, 17, 18, 19, 20, 23, 24, 25 and 26 February, 3, 11, 24 and 31 March, 18 and 26 May, 9 June 2004. Online. Available HTTP: http://www.rferl.org/ newsline/fulltext.asp (accessed 12 May 2005).

RFE/RL Poland, Belarus and Ukraine Report, 18 June 2002, vol. 4, no. 24. Online. Available HTTP: http://www.rferl.org/reports/pbureport/2002/06/24–180602.asp (accessed 12 May 2005).

—— 20 August 2002, vol. 4, no. 31. Online. Available HTTP: http://www.rferl. org/reports/pbureport/2002/08/31–200802.asp (accessed 12 May 2005).

—— 2 September 2003, vol. 5, no. 32. Online. Available HTTP: http://www.rferl.org/ reports/pbureport/2003/09/32–020903.asp (accessed 12 May 2005).

—— 29 October 2003, vol. 5, no. 4. Online. Available HTTP: http://www.rferl. org/reports/pbureport/2003/10/40–291003.asp (accessed 12 May 2005).

—— 13 January 2004, vol. 6, no. 1. Online. Available HTTP http://www.rferl.org/ reports/pbureport/2004/01/1–130104.asp (accessed 12 May 2005).

—— 20 January 2004, vol. 6, no. 2. Online. Available HTTP: http://www.rferl.org/reports/ pbureport/2004/01/3–270104.asp (accessed 12 May 2005).

—— 27 January 2004, vol. 6, no. 3. Online. Available HTTP: http://www.rferl.org/reports/ pbureport/2004/01/3–270104.asp (accessed 12 May 2005).

RFE/RL Belarus and Ukraine Report 18 February 2004, vol. 6, no. 6. Online. Available HTTP: http://www.rferl.org/reports/pbureport/2004/02/6–180204.asp (accessed 12 May 2005).

—— 2 March 2004, vol. 6, no. 7. Online. Available HTTP: http://www.rferl.org/reports/pbureport/2004/03/7–020304.asp (accessed 12 May 2005).

—— 15 June 2004, vol. 6, no. 22. Online. Available HTTP: http://www.rferl.org/reports/pbureport/2004/06/22–150604.asp (accessed 12 May 2005).

—— 20 July 2004, vol. 6, no. 26. Online. Available HTTP: http://www.rferl.org/reports/pbureport/2004/07/26–200704.asp (accessed 12 May 2005).

—— 23 December 2004, vol. 6, no. 47. Online. Available HTTP: http://www.rferl.org/reports/pbureport/2004/12/47–231204.asp (accessed 12 May 2005).

Radio Free Europe/Radio Liberty Weekday Magazine, 3 October 2003, and 18 November 2003. Online. Available HTTP: http://search.rferl.org/ (accessed 19 December 2003).

'Reforming the Czech Armed Forces', *Radio Prague,* 30 November 2002. Online. Available HTTP: http://www.radio.cz/en/article/35075 (accessed 23 November 2004).

Rengger, N., *International Relations, Political Theory, and the Problem of Order beyond International Relations Theory?*, London: Routledge, 2000.

Report from the Pew Global Attitudes Project, *Views of a Changing World*, Washington, DC: The Pew Research Center for the People and the Press, June 2003.

'Republican Party Platform 2000', 2000. Online. Available HTTP: http://www.cnn.com/ELECTION/2000/conventions/republican/features/platform.00/#52 (accessed 16 July 2004).

Reynolds, C., *The Politics of War: A Study in the Rationality of Violence in Inter-State Relations*, New York: St Martin's Press, 1989.

Rhodes, C. (ed.) *The European Union in the World Community*, London: Lynne Rienner Publishers, 1998.

Rhodes, E., 'Transforming the Alliance: The Bush Administration's Vision of NATO,' *CIAO Working Papers*, November 2003.

Rice, C., 'Promoting the National Interest', *Foreign Affairs*, 2000, vol. 79, no. 1, 45–62.

Rieker, P., *Europeanisation of Nordic Security The EU and Changing Security Identities of the Nordic States*, Oslo: Department of Political Science, Faculty of Social Sciences, University of Oslo, 2003.

Rienstra, D. and Hulm, P., 'New EU Countries Expand Market Horizons', *International Trade Forum*, 2004, issue 1. Online. Available HTTP: http://www.tradeforum.org/news/printpage/.php/aid/649/ (accessed 5 May 2004).

Risse, T., 'Beyond Iraq: The Crisis of the Transatlantic Security Community,' *Die Friedenswarte*, 2003, vol. 78, no. 2–3, 173–94.

Rittberger, V. and Zelli, F., 'Europa in der Weltpolitik: Juniorpartner der USA oder antihegemoniale Alternative?', *Tübinger Arbeitspapiere zur Internationale Politik und Friedensforschung,* 2003, no. 41, Eberhard-Karls-Universität Tübingen.

Rontoyanni, C., 'So Far, So Good? Russia and the ESDP', *International Affairs*, 2002, vol. 78, no. 4, 813–30.

Ruggie, J.G. (ed.) *Multilateralism Matters: The Theory and Praxis of an Institutional Form*, New York: Columbia University Press, 1993.

Russia. '2000 Russian National Security Concept', adopted 17 December 1999. Online. Available HTTP: http://www.russiaeurope.mid.ru/russiastrat2000.html (accessed 21 June 2005).

Russia. 'Russia's Middle Term Strategy Towards the EU (2000–2010)'. Online. Available HTTP: http://www.eur.ru/en/p_245.htm (accessed 20 January 2004).

Russia. Ivanov, I.S., 'Stenogramma press-konferentsii . . .', 10 July 2000, *Informatsionnyi biulleten'*, 11 July 2000. Online. Available HTTP: http://www.ln.mid.ru/bl.nsf/clndr (accessed 8 February 2005).

Russia. Ivanov, I.S., 'Stat'ia ... opublikovana v zhurnale "Internationale Politik" ...', *Informatsionnyi biulleten'*, 24 October 2000. Online. Available HTTP: http://www. ln.mid.ru/bl.nsf/clndr (accessed 18 April 2005).

Russia. Ivanov, I.S., 'Vystuplenie ... v MGIMO(U) ...', 1 September 2003, *Informatsionnyi biulleten'*, 1 September 2003. Online. Available HTTP: http://www. ln.mid.ru/bl.nsf/clndr (accessed 11 January 2005).

Russia. Ivanov, I.S., 'Stat'ia ... opublikovannaia v zhurnale "Mezhdunarodnaia zhizn" ...', *Informatsionnyi biulleten'*, 22 October 2003. Online. Available HTTP: http://www.ln.mid.ru/bl.nsf/clndr (accessed 11 January 2005).

Russia. 'Kontseptsiia natsional'noi bezopasnosti Rossiiskoi Federatsii', 17 December 1997, *Diplomaticheskii vestnik*, 1998, no. 1. Online. Available HTTP: http://www. ln.mid.ru/dip_vest.nsf (accessed 8 June 2004).

Russia. 'Kontseptsiia natsional'noi bezopasnosti Rossiiskoi Federatsii', 10 January 2000. Online. Available HTTP: http://www.scrf.gov.ru/documents/decree/2000_24_1.shtml (accessed 8 July 2005).

Russia. 'Kontseptsiia vneshnei politiki Rossiiskoi Federatsii', 28 June 2000. Online. Available HTTP: http://www.scrf.ru/documents/decree/2000_x.shtml (accessed 8 July 2005).

Russia. Putin, V. V., 'Rossia na rubezhe tysiachetelii', *Nezavisiamaia gazeta*, 30 December 1999. Online. Available HTTP: http://www.ng.ru/politics/1999–12–30/ 4_millenium.html (accessed 8 November 2004).

Russia. Putin, V. V., 'Vystuplenie na zasedanii Soveta Bezopasnosti', 31 December 1999. Online. Available HTTP: http://president.kremlin.ru/text/appears/1999/12/59568.shtml (accessed 8 November 2004).

Russia. Putin, V. V., 'Vystuplenie na zasedanii Gosudarstvennoi Dumy ...', 14 April 2000. Online. Available HTTP: http://president.kremlin.ru/text/appears/2000/04/ 28658.shtml (accessed 21 January 2004).

Russia. Putin, V. V., 'Interv'iu ... gazete "Vel't am Zonntag" (FRG)', *Informatsionnyi biulleten'*, 14 June 2000. Online. Available HTTP: http://www.ln.mid.ru/bl.nsf/clndr (accessed 13 March 2005).

Russia. Putin, V. V., 'Interv'iu kanadskim telekompaniiam ...', 14 December 2000. Online. Available HTTP: http://president.kremlin.ru/text/appears/2000/12/28434.shtml (accessed 21 December 2004).

Russia. Putin, V. V., 'Beseda s rukovoditeliami predstavitel'stv vedushchikh ameri-kanskikh SMI', 18 June 2001. Online. Available HTTP: http://president.kremlin. ru/text/appears/2001/06/28569.shtml (accessed 4 February 2004).

Russia. Putin, V. V., 'Zaiavlenie ...', 13 December 2001. Online. Available HTTP: http://president.kremlin.ru/text/appears/2001/12/28746.shtml (accessed 21 January 2004).

Russia. Putin, V. V., 'Interv'iu frantsuzskoi telekompanii "Frans-3"', 9 February 2003. Online. Available HTTP: http://president.kremlin.ru/text/appears/2003/02/29764.shtml (accessed 11 February 2004)

Russia. Putin, V.V., 'Interv'iu telekanalu "Al'-Dzhazira"', 16 October 2003. Online. Available HTTP: http://president.kremlin.ru/text/appears/2003/10/54204.shtml (accessed 18 May 2004).

Russia. Putin, V. V., 'Otvety na voprosy uchastnikov Delovogo sammita ATES', 19 October 2003. Online. Available HTTP: http://president.kremlin.ru/text/appears/2003/ 10/54264.shtml (accessed 21 December 2004).

Russia. Putin, V. V., 'Interv'iu kitaiskim gazetam . . .', 13 October 2004. Online. Avaiable HTTP: http://president.kremlin.ru/text/appears/2004/10/77852.shtml (accessed 8 November 2004).

Russia. Putin, V. V., 'Interv'iu "Radio Slovensko" i slovatskoi telekompanii STV', 22 February 2005. Online. Available HTTP: http://president.kremlin.ru/text/appears/2005/02/84394.shtml (accessed 26 June 2005).

Russia. Putin, V. V., 'President Putin's Annual State of the Nation Address to the Federal Assembly', 18 April 2002. Online. Available HTTP: http://www.usrbc.org/Transcripts-Summaries-testimonies/2002/PutinApril02.htm (accessed 20 June 2005).

Russia. Putin, V. V., 'Russian President Vladimir Putin Interview with the Italian News Agency ANSA, Newspaper Corriere della Sera and the Television Company RAI', the Kremlin, Moscow, 3 November, 2003a. Online. Available HTTP: http://www.ln.mid.ru/brp_4.nsf/0/76eba5a9835b2b9dc3256ec9001c9338?OpenDocument (accessed 28 January 2004).

Russia. Putin, V. V., 'Russian President Vladimir Putin's State of the Nation Address to the Federal Assembly', the Kremlin, Moscow, 16 May 2003b. Online. Available HTTP: http://www.ln.mid.ru/Bl.nsf/arh/7F2BDEECE0C7A13143256D2B002714BA?OpenDocument (accessed 23 December 2003).

Russia. Putin, V. V., Address to the Federation Council 16 May 2003. Online. Available HTTP: http://president.kremlin.ru/eng/speeches/2003/05/16/0000_type70029_44692.shtml (accessed 12 May 2005).

Russia. Putin, V. V., Address to the Federation Council 26 May 2004. Online. Available HTTP: http://president.kremlin.ru/eng/speeches/2004/05/26/1309_type70029_71650.shtml (accessed 12 May 2005).

Russia. Russia and World Trade Organization, 'Current state of accession negotiations'. Online. Available HTTP: http://www.wto.ru/russia.asp?f=dela&t=11 (accessed 7 June 2005).

Russia. Russia and World Trade Organization, 'Main stages of negotiations'. Online. Available HTTP: http://www.wto.ru/russia.asp?f=etaps&t=10 (accessed 7 June 2005).

Russia. Russia and World Trade Organization, 'Aims and Objectives of Accession'. Online. Available HTTP: http://www.wto.ru/russia.asp?f=target&t=9 (accessed 7 June 2005).

Sanger, D.E. and Tyler, P.E., 'Officials Recount Road to Deadlock Over Missile Talks', The New York Times, 13 December 2001, A1, A18.

Saryusz-Wolski, J., 'Looking to the Future' in Enlargement and European Defence after 11 September, Chaillot Paper, no. 53, Paris: European Union Institute for Security Studies, 2002.

Schelling, T.C., The Strategy of Conflict, Cambridge, MA: Harvard University Press, 1960.

—— Arms and Influence, New Haven, CT: Yale University Press, 1966.

Schimmelfennig, F., The EU, NATO and the Integration of Europe. Cambridge: Cambridge University Press, 2003.

Schön, D. and Rein, M., Frame Reflection Towards the Resolution of Intractable Policy Controversies, New York: Basic Books, 1994.

Schopflin, G., Nations, Identity, Power, London: C. Hurst & Co, 2000.

Schweller, R.L., 'Bandwagoning for Profit. Bringing the Revisionist State Back In,' International Security, 1994, vol. 19, 72–107.

Schwenninger, S.R., 'Revamping American Grand Strategy', World Policy Journal, 2003, vol. 20, no. 3, 25–44.

Sciolino, E., 'French Struggle Now With How to Coexist With Bush', *The New York Times*, 8 February 2005.

Sedivy, J., 'The Constraints and the Opportunities', in 'Enlargement and European Defence after 11 September', *Chaillot Paper*, no. 53, Paris: European Union Institute for Security Studies, 2002.

Sedivy, J., Dunay, P. and Saryusz-Wolski, J., 'Enlargement and European Defense after 11 September', *Chaillot Paper*, no. 53, Paris: European Union Institute for Security Studies, 2002.

Segal, G., *The Great Power Triangle*, New York: St Martin's Press, 1982.

Shambaugh, D., 'The New Strategic Triangle: U.S. and European Reactions to China's Rise', *The Washington Quarterly*, 2005, vol. 28, no. 3, 7–25.

Shoumikhin, A., 'Current Russian Perspectives on Arms Control and Ballistic Missile Defense', *Comparative Strategy*, 1999, vol. 18, no. 1, 49–57.

―――― 'Evolving Russian Perspectives on Missile Defense: The Emerging Accommodation', *Comparative Strategy*, 2002, vol. 21, no. 4, 311–36.

Simon, J., *Czechoslovakia's 'Velvet Divorce', Visegrad Cohesion, and European Fault Lines*. Washington: National Defense University, 1994.

Singer, M. and Wildawsky, A., *The Real World Order: Zones of Peace/Zones of Turmoil*, Chatham: Chatham House, 1993.

Sjöstedt, G., *The External Role of the European Community*, Westmead: Saxon House, 1977.

Skak, M., 'Russian Security Policy After 9/11', paper prepared for the joint International Convention of Central Eastern European International Studies Association & International Studies Association, Budapest, 26–28 June 2003.

Skålnes, L.S., *Politics, Markets, and Grand Strategy: Foreign Economic Policies as Strategic Instruments*, Ann Arbor, MI: The University of Michigan Press, 2000.

Smith, H., *European Union Foreign Policy: What It Is and What It Does*, London: Pluto Press, 2002.

Smith, J., 'Introduction: The Future of the European Union and the Transatlantic Relationship', *International Affairs*, 2003, vol. 79, no. 5, 943–9.

Smith, K.E., 'The European Union: A Distinctive Actor in International Relations', *Brown Journal of World Affairs*, 2003, vol. IX, issue 2, 103–113.

Smith, M.A., *The Russia-USA Relationship*, Russian Series 04/12, Camberley, Surrey: Defence Academy of the United Kingdom, Conflict Studies Research Centre, 2004.

Smith, M. E., *Europe's Foreign and Security Policy: The Institutionalization of Cooperation*, Cambridge: Cambridge University Press, 2004.

Snyder, G. and Diesing, P., *Conflict Among Nations: Bargaining, Decision Making, and System Structure in International Crises*. Princeton, NJ: Princeton University Press, 1977.

Sokolsky, J., 'The Power of Values or the Value of Power? America and Europe in a Post-9/11 World', CIAO Working Papers. Online. Available HTTP: http://www.ciaonet.org/casestudy/soj01/index.html (accessed 17 June 2005).

Solana, J., 'The EU-Russia Strategic Partnership', speech in Stockholm 13 October 1999. Online. Available HTTP: http://ue.eu.int/solana/details.asp?BID=107&DocID=69417 (accessed 2 February 2004).

Stadtmuller, E., *The Issue of NATO Enlargement in Polish – Russian Relations*, NATO Research Fellowship Report, Brussels: NATO-EAPC, 2001.

Steinbruner, J. D., *Principles of Global Security*, Washington, DC: Brookings Institution Press, 2000.

Stratfor, 'Fourth Quarter Forecast: Gaining Traction and Reclaiming the Initiative', 2003. Online. Available HTTP: http://www.stratfor.biz/ (accessed 23 November 2004).

—— Annual Forecast: When Other Things Start to Matter – Part II, 2005. 17 January 2005. Online. Available HTTP: http://www.stratfor.biz/ (accessed 23 March 2005).

Strömvik, M., 'Fifteen Votes and One Voice? The CFSP and Changing Voting Alignments in the UN', in Statsvetenskaplig tidsskrift, 1998, vol. 101, no. 2, 181–197.

—— 'Sverige och EU:s utrikes- och säkerhetspolitik: ett intensivt men hemligt förhållande?', in K.M. Johansson (ed.), Sverige i EU, Stockholm: SNS förlag, 1999.

Sullivan, M. P., Mechanisms for Strategic Coercion: Denial or Second Order Change? Maxwell AFB, AL: Air Force University, 1995.

Sundelius, B., 'Functional Security', in M. Ekengren (ed.), Functional Security – A Forward Looking Approach to European and Nordic Security and Defence Policy, Proceedings of the Conference held at the Swedish National Defence College, 5–6 December 2003, Stockholm: Swedish National Defence College, ACTA B30, 2004.

Suskind, R, 'Without a Doubt', The New York Times Magazine, 17 October 2004, 44–51, 64, 102, 106.

Sweden. Defence Commission, Försvar för en ny tid, Departementsserien, 2004:30.

Sweden. Government Bill 1999/2000:30, Det nya försvaret, 2000.

Sweden. Ministry of Defence, Björklund, Leni, Defence Minister, press release, 17 May 2004.

Syrén, H., 'ÖB föreslår Svenskt försvar för Europa', Insats & Försvar, 2004b, no. 2.

——, Internal Television Broadcast, 29 April 2004a.

Szayna T., 'The Czech Republic', in A. Michta, A. (ed.) America's New Allies: Poland, Hungary, and the Czech Republic in NATO, Seattle, WA: University of Washington Press, 1999.

Tax, V., 'Spidla Supports NATO Mission to Iraq' Radio Prague, 15 February 2004.

'Towards a Wider Europe: The New Agenda', Bratislava document adopted by the prime ministers of Albania, Bulgaria, Croatia, Estonia, Latvia, Lithuania, Macedonia, Romania and Slovakia, 19 March 2004.

Trenin, D., 'A Russia-within-Europe: Working towards a New Security Arrangement', in F. Heisbourg 'Russia's Security Policy and EU-Russian Relations', ESF Working Paper, no. 6, March 2002.

—— The End of Eurasia: Russia on the Border between Geopolitics and Globalization. Washington, DC, and Moscow: Carnegie Endowment for International Peace, 2002.

'Triumph of the Will', The Warsaw Voice, 22 December 2002.

Trofimenko H., Russian National Interests and the Current Crisis in Russia, Aldershot: Ashgate, 1999.

Trzaskowski, R., 'From Candidate to Member State: Poland and the Future of the EU,' Occasional Paper, no. 37, Paris: European Union Institute for Security Studies, 2002.

Tsoukalis, L., The European Economy Revisited, Oxford: Oxford University Press, 1997.

United Nations. Operation Artemis: The Lessons of the Interim Emergency Multinational Force', Peacekeeping Best Practices Unit, Military Division, October 2004.

United Nations. UN General Assembly resolution no. 56/24A, 29 November 2001. Online. Available HTTP: http://www.un.org/Depts/dhl/resguide/r56.htm (accessed 25 January 2004).

United States. Census Bureau. Online. Available HTTP: http://www.census.gov/foreign-trade/balance/c4621.html (accessed 8 March and 10 June 2005).

United States. Congress, Congressional Budget Office Report, Integrating New Allies into NATO, Washington, DC, October 2000.

United States. Department of Commerce, Bureau of Economic Analysis, *Survey of Current Business*, October 2004. Online. Available HTTP: http://www.bea.doc.gov/bea/ARTICLES/2004/10October/1004_IntlServ.pdf (accessed 16 April 2005).

United States. Department of Commerce, 'TradeStats Express Home'. Online. Available HTTP: http://tse.export.gov/ (accessed 18 February 2005).

United States. Department of Defense. Rumsfeld, D. H., *Annual Report to the President and the Congress*, 2002.

United States. Department of State. 'Text of U.S.-Russia Joint Declaration', Moscow, 24 May 2002. Online. Available HTTP: http://www.state.gov/p/eur/rls/or/2002/10469.htm (accessed 28 January 2004).

United States. Department of State. Bush, G.W., 'Radio Address by the President to the Nation', 25 May 2002, U.S.-Russia relations. Online. Available HTTP: http://www.state.gov/p/eur/ci/rs/usrussia/ (accessed 28 January 2004).

United States. Department of State. Bush, G.W., 'Remarks by the President and Russian President Putin in Press Availability Camp David', Maryland, 27 September 2003. Online. Available HTTP: http://www.state.gov/p/eur/rls/rm/2003/24608.htm (accessed 28 January 2004).

United States. Department of State. Bush, G.W., 'Roundtable Interview of the President with European Print Media', 18 February 2005. Online. Available HTTP: http://usinfo.state.gov/eur/Archive/2005/Feb/21–17990.html (accessed 1 April 2005).

United States. Department of State, 'Performance and Accountability Highlights Fiscal Year 2004'. Online. Available HTTP: http://www.state.gov/documents/organization/40183.pdf (accessed 24 May 2005).

United States. Department of State. Powell, C.L., 'Interview on The Charlie Rose Show', 22 September 2003. Online. Available HTTP: http://www.state.gov/secretary/former/powell/remarks/2003/24295.htm (accessed 10 June 2005).

United States. Department of State. Secretary of State Condolezzea Rice, 'Briefing En Route to Moscow', 19 April 2005. Online. Available HTTP: http://www.state.gov/secretary/rm/2005/44868.htm (accessed 7 June 2005).

United States. International Trade Administration. Online. Available HTTP: http://www.ita.doc.gov/td/industry/otea/usfth/aggregate/HT03T09.html (accessed 15 April 2005).

United States. White House. *A National Security Strategy of Engagement and Enlargement*, 1995.

United States. White House. 'Jackson-Vanik and Russia Fact Sheet', 13 November 2001. Online. Available HTTP: http://www.whitehouse.gov/news/releases/2001/11/20011113–16.html (accessed 27 May 2005).

United States. White House. Bush, G.W., 'Remarks . . . to Students and Faculty at National Defense University', 1 May 2001. Online. Available HTTP: http://www.whitehouse.gov/news/releases/2001/05/20010501–10.html (accessed 2 June 2004).

United States. White House. Bush, G.W., 'Press Conference . . .', 15 June 2001. Online. Available HTTP: http://www.whitehouse.gov/news/releases/2001/06/20010615–4.html (accessed 2 June 2004).

United States. White House. Bush, G.W., Remarks . . . in Address to Faculty and Students of Warsaw University', 15 June 2001. Online. Available HTTP: http://www.whitehouse.gov/news/releases/2001/06/20010615–1.html (accessed 2 June 2004).

United States. White House. Bush, G.W., 'President Discusses National Missile Defense', 13 December 2001. Online. Available HTTP: http://www.whitehouse.gov/news/reseases/2001/12/20011213–4.html (accessed 21 January 2004.

United States. White House. Bush, G.W., 'Interview of the President by Trevor Kavanagh of "The Sun"', 14 November 2003. Online. Available HTTP: http://www.whitehouse.gov/news/releases/2003/11/20031117–3.html (accessed 14 April 2004).

United States. White House. Rice, C., 'Press Briefing . . .', 16 June 2001. Online. Available HTTP: http://www.whitehouse.gov/news/releases/2001/06/20010618–1.html (accessed 2 June 2004).

United States. White House. Rice, C., 'Remarks . . .', 26 June 2003. Online. Available HTTP: http://www.whitehouse.gov/news/releases/2003/06/20030626.html (accessed 27 January 2004).

United States. White House. 'Text of Strategic Offensive Reductions Treaty', 24 May 2002. Online. Available HTTP: http://www.whitehouse.gov/news/releases/2002/05/20020524–3.html (accessed 3 February 2004).

United States. White House. *The National Security Strategy of the United States of America,* September 2002.

United States. White House. 'President Meets with E.U. Leaders', 22 February 2005. Online. Available HTTP: http://www.whitehouse.gov/news/releases/2005/02/20050222–8.html (accessed 5 April 2005).

United States. White House. 'Joint Statement by President Bush and President Putin on Russia's Accession to WTO'. Online. Available HTTP: http://www.whitehouse.gov/news/releases/2005/02/print/20050224–5.html (accessed 7 June 2005).

Vaknin, S., 'Commentary: The Euro-Atlantic Divide', *United Press International,* 18 February 2003. Online. Available HTTP: http://www.upi.com/view.cfm?StoryID=20030218–124211–2209r (accessed 12 November 2004).

Van Ham, P., 'Europe Gets Real: The New Security Strategy Shows the EU's Geopolitical Maturity', *AICGS Advisor,* 9 January 2004. Online. Available HTTP: http://www.aicgs.org/c/vanham.shtmll (accessed 23 June 2005).

Van Oudenaren, J., 'Europe as Partner', in D.C. Gompert and F.S. Larrabee (eds), *America and Europe: A Partnership for a New Era,* Cambridge/New York: Cambridge University Press, 1997, 104–42.

Volgy, T. and Bailin, A., *International Politics and State Strength,* Boulder, CO and London: Lynne Rienner, 2003.

von Bogdandy, A., 'The Contours of Integrated Europe', *Futures,* 1993, vol. 25, no. 1, 22–7.

Wæver, O., 'The EU as a Security Actor: Reflections from a Pessimistic Constructivist on Post-sovereign Security Orders', in M. Kelstrup and M.C. Williams (eds), *International Relations Theory and the Politics of European Integration: Power, Security and Community,* London: Routledge, 2000.

Wagnsson, C., *Russian Political Language and Public Opinion on the West, NATO and Chechnya,* Stockholm: Department of Political Science, Stockholm University, 2000.

—— 'Expanding on the "Moral" Arguments: Russian Rhetorical Strategies on Security Post-Kosovo', *Occasional Paper,* no. 28, Paris: The WEU Institute for Security Studies, 2001.

—— 'Russia's Choice: Preserve the Status Quo', in J. Hallenberg and H. Karlsson (eds), *The Iraq War: European Perspectives on Politics, Strategy and Operations,* London and New York: Routledge, 2005.

Walker, R.B.J., 'Europe is Not Where it is Supposed to Be', in M. Kelstrup and M.C.

Williams (eds), *International Relations and the Politics of European Integration: Power, Security and Community*, London: Routledge, 2000, 14–29.

Wallace, W., *The Dynamics of European Integration*, London and New York: Pinter Publishers, 1990.

Wallander, C.A., *The Sources of Russian Foreign Policy After the Cold War*, Boulder, CO: Westview Press, 1998.

—— *Mortal Friends, Best Enemies. German-Russian Cooperation After the Cold War*, Ithaca and London: Cornell University Press, 1999.

—— 'Russia's Strategic Priorities', *Arms Control Today*, 2002, vol. 32, no. 1, 4–6.

Waltz, K.N., *Theory of International Politics*, Reading, MA: Addison Wesley, 1979.

—— 'The Emerging Structure of International Politics', *International Security*, 1993, vol. 18, no. 2, 44–79.

—— 'Structural Realism after the Cold War', in G.J. Ikenberry (ed.) *America Unrivaled: The Future of the Balance of Power*, Ithaca, NY: Cornell University Press, 2002.

Weale, A., et al., *Environmental Governance in Europe*, Oxford: Oxford University Press, 2000.

Webber, M., *The International Politics of Russia and Its Successor States*. Manchester: Manchester University Press, 1996.

—— 'Third-Party Inclusion in European Security and Defence Policy: A Case Study of Russia', *European Foreign Affairs Review*, 2001, vol. 6, 407–26.

Wedin, L., *Reflektioner över ämnet strategi*, Stockholm: Swedish National Defence College, 2002.

—— 'Tre år i EU:s militära stab', in *Kungliga Krigsvetenskapsakademiens Handlingar och Tidskrift*, 2004, no. 1, 119–54.

WEU Council of Ministers, *Western European Union Council of Ministers Petersberg Declaration*, Bonn, 19 June 1992. Online. Available HTTP: http://www.weu.int/eng/comm/92-petersberg.htm (accessed 16 October 2000).

White, B., *Understanding European Foreign Policy*, Basingstoke: Palgrave, 2001.

Whitman, R.G., *From Civilian Power to Superpower? The International Identity of the European Union*, Basingstoke: Macmillan, 1998.

Windsor, P., *Strategic Thinking. An Introduction and Farewell*, London: Lynne Rienner, 2002.

Wohlforth, W.C., 'The Stability of a Unipolar World', *International Security*, 1999, vol. 24, no. 1, 5–41.

—— 'U.S. Strategy in a Unipolar World', in G.J. Ikenberry (ed.) *America Unrivaled: The Future of the Balance of Power*, Ithaca, NY: Cornell University Press, 2002.

Wolfowitz, P., 'Remembering the Future', *The National Interest*, 2000, no. 59, 35–45.

Woodward, B., *Plan of Attack*, New York: Simon & Schuster, 2004.

Woolf, A.F., *National Missile Defense: Russia's Reaction*, CRS Report RL30967, Washington, DC: The Library of Congress, Congressional Research Service, 2002.

—— *Nuclear Arms Control: The U.S.-Russian Agenda*, CRS Issue Brief IB98030, Washington, DC: The Library of Congress, Congressional Research Service, 2002.

—— *U.S. Nuclear Weapons: Changes in Policy and Force Structure*, CRS Report RL31623, Washington, DC: The Library of Congress, Congressional Research Service, 2004.

World Bank, *World Development Indicators 2005*. Online. Available HTTP: http://www.worldbank.org/data/wdi2005/wditext/Table4_2.htm (accessed 27 May 2005).

World Trade Organization. 'European Union', online. http://stat.wto.org/CountryProfiles/ G32_e.htm (accessed 3 March 2005).

World Trade Organization. 'Russian Federation'. Online. Available HTTP: http://stat.wto. org/CountryProfiles/RU_e.htm (accessed 3 March 2005).

Yost, D., 'The NATO Capabilities Gap and the European Union', *Survival*, 2001, vol. 33, no. 4, 327–51.

Zabrowski, M. and Longhurst, K., 'America's Protégé in the East? The Emergence of Poland as a Regional Leader', *International Affairs*, 1993, vol. 79, no. 5, 1009–28.

Zapletnyuk, K., 'Czech Military Reform Could End in "Ruins" Says Ex-Minister', *Transition Online*, 2003. Online. Available HTTP: http://www.ciaonet.org/pbei/ tol/tol_2003/jun3–9/jun3–9_h.html (accessed 12 November 2004).

Zielonka, J., 'Challenges of EU Enlargement', *Journal of Democracy*, 2004, vol. 15, 22–35.

INDEX

ABM Treaty: *see* Anti-Ballistic Missile
  Treaty
actorness: cohesiveness 36–7; EU 3–4, 12,
  17n6, 108–9, 169–70, 180, 205–8;
  international 8–9, 100, 171–2; regional
  cooperation 32–3; Russia 10–11;
  security and defence 6–7; strategic
  coercion 88; trade 180; US 10–12
Afghanistan: Bush 160; control of 113;
  Czech Republic 72; EU 23; Poland 28;
  Russia/US 117; terrorism 71, 116
African continent 49
Albright, M. 154
Allied Force Operation 92, 97–8
Allison, G. 94
Althea Operation 49
Americanization 158–9
Amsterdam Treaty 19, 52, 59n3, 119
Andrews, D.M. 11
Annan, K. 85
Anti-Ballistic Missile Treaty 188, 189–91,
  193, 194, 213
APEC 25
appropriateness, logic of 120–1n1
Art, R.J. 152
Artemis Operation 49, 54, 85–6, 100
Asia-Pacific Economic Cooperation
  (APEC) 25
Atlanticism 13, 85, 147
Austria 75
Azovsk, Sea of 131, 132

Balkans 5, 23, 49, 79, 88, 98; *see also*
  specific countries
Balkenende, J.P. 142
Baltic countries 27–8, 31, 73; *see also*
  specific countries
Barcelona process 88
Battle Group concept 50–1, 52, 54–5, 58

Belarus 14–15, 71, 125, 126, 128, 132,
  194; *see also* Russia–Belarus
Belka government 71
Beltranshaz 138–9
Benes decrees 74
Berlin Plus 56
Beslan hostages 116
bipolarity 146, 184
Black Sea co-operation group 27
Black Sea Fleet issue 127–8, 131
Blair, T. 8–9, 75
Bosnia 48, 101, 107, 112
Bretton Woods 168
Britain: *see* United Kingdom
Brooks, S.G. 184
Bulgaria 31
Bush, G.H.W. 170
Bush, G.W.: Afghanistan 160; Chechnya
  161; EU visit 214; foreign policy 192;
  imperialist tendencies 159; Middle East
  148; mission 164; Poland 71; primacy
  210–11; and Putin 10, 117, 161–2, 175;
  Russia 161–2, 192–3; START II 194;
  strategic triangle 159–61, 164;
  unilateralism 4, 159–60, 195–6, 213;
  see also Iraq War
Byman, D. 92, 94–5
Bynander, F. 13, 57, 206–7

Canada 102, 173
Carter, A.B. 155
Caucasus 117, 125
Central and Eastern European states (CEE)
  30, 34; investment/security 28;
  multilateralism 27; security 73, 78
Central European Initiative 27, 79
Chechnya: Bush 161; cooperation 107; EU
  110, 115–16, 119; Putin 162; strategic
  coercion 102; terrorism 149, 161

242